AMAZED BY GRACE

Some Stories
Defy Explanation

BY: DR. BILL SHADE

AMAZED BY GRACE
Some Stories Defy Explanation
by Dr. Bill Shade

Printed in the United States of America

ISBN 9781626977273

Unless otherwise indicated, Bible quotations are taken from the King James Version of the Bible.

www.xulonpress.com

Dedicated to my faithful wife
Ruby
Whose price is truly

Far above rubies

TABLE OF CONTENTS

ACKNOWLEDGMENTS

No man is an island and I owe an infinite debt of gratitude to the scores of people God has brought into my life who have had a profound effect upon me. Those who have contributed to making me who I am are legion and it is inevitable that when I begin to name them, I will miss some. For that I am profoundly sorry. Nevertheless, I must at least try.

Without a doubt both my mother and my father had a most indelible effect on my life. Mother, because she made God so real to me as a little child and Dad because he modeled for me what a living faith in God should look like.

There were, of course relatives, teachers, and neighbors who influenced me. But some of my greatest impressions were of those Pastors who visited our home and not only preached to me from the pulpit, but took a personal interest in me as well. I think especially of Pastor G. R. Strayer, who prayed for me, encouraged me and took me hunting with him as I was growing up.

During the turbulent teen years, the man who left the greatest impression on me was Pastor Ralph H. Stoll. Both his Spirit-filled life and his messages were used of God to give me assurance, direction and a desire for a life of service. I thank God for Rev. W. W. Breckbill who hired me as a counselor at Camp Manahath when I don't think anyone else would have.

My professors at PBI left an indelible mark on my life. Men like Dr. William A. Mierop, Dr. Clarence E. Mason, Dr. William Allen Dean, Dr. Andrew Telford, and Dr. Dwight Pentecost, and others.

Dr. Larry Lufburrow our Dean of men greatly encouraged me. What a heritage God gave me.

When Ruby and I answered the call of God to Southeastern Kentucky, we had to raise our support as missionaries. Two churches got behind us then, and God has used other churches and individuals to meet our needs every month for all these years. Our supporters, both churches and individuals are the ones who enabled us to accomplish whatever we have. We owe them immeasurable gratitude.

The dear people of McRoberts Baptist Church not only allowed me to be their pastor when I was much too young, but loved me, encouraged me, rebuked me at times, and responded to God and His Word as I preached it. I thank God for them and love them dearly.

God blessed me with wonderful in-laws. Ruby's mother and dad, and dear, dear Granny Asher loved me and treated me like their own. Her brothers and sisters became my own and I am deeply grateful.

The missionaries at Camp Nathanael were a constant inspiration to me and Raymond Haddix, my leader in the High School ministry, traveled together with me many hours every week for over eight years.

When coming to York, my first helpers were Herb Lippy and Harold Dubs, the "Soup Twins", owners of Aunt Kitty's Soup. Then God brought other wonderful men on the Board – men that invested not just in the work but in me. I can't name them all, but many stayed on for years and helped me through many formidable projects.

Captain Charles McCaffery of York Police's Juvenile Division made himself my friend as did Mayor Eli Eichelberger. These men enabled much that we did that could not have been done without their blessing.

Pastors like Dr. Ralph Boyer, Pastor Roy Smith, Dr. Earl Johnson, Pastor Donald Hurlbert, Pastor Ron Schmuck, and Pastor Richard Kidd were a great blessing and encouragement to me.

God placed a wonderful and supportive staff around me. What a debt I owe to Larry and Ethel Hodgson, Bruce and Pat Dick, Dean and Patty Bult, Russ Aults, and my business manager, Bob Bracilano. Then there was the publishing staff of World Wide Bible Institutes,

Dr. Leonard Smith, Dr. Gerald Stover, Norm Gordon, Emerson & Rosina Brandon, Ray & Jean Acker and many more.

Some of these stayed with me as we put together the ministry of Camp of the Nations, and the Wayside Maternity Home. Howard Clinger was our first cook and dear friend for many years. The Camp staff, some of whom came when we opened and stayed until we left, made every accomplishment we had possible.

Men like Dr. Al Smith, Dr. Bill Rice, Dr. Dave Virkler, Dr. Glenn Dix, Dr. Andy Telford, Tom Maharis, Ding Teuling and a veritable panoply of others came across the stage at CN, and each of them left their mark upon me.

It is impossible for me to express the gratitude I owe to my faithful secretary of twenty one years, Bernice Petticoffer. She is the one who encouraged me to write it down and patiently took the first dictated stories off tape. Along with her I owe an immense debt of gratitude to Dr. Peter Teague, Rev. Don Lowry and Eula Keener who reviewed and critiqued the manuscript. If you find my story readable, it is largely due to their investment of time and expertise.

In the final analysis however, my greatest human help has come from my wife Ruby, whose "price is far above rubies." She has loved me, walked with me, gently counseled me, and supported me above and beyond anything I could have ever hoped for. She has been my inspiration and help and I owe a debt of immeasurable gratitude to her.

It has all been of Grace. God did as He as ever promised to do, *exceedingly abundantly, above all that we could ask or think.* And His strength, His power and His faithfulness did not end with my generation. He is ready and able to do the same for you if you will put yourself completely in His hands. As soon as you do, you will be Amazed by His Grace. That is the message of this book, and that is the driving conviction that produced it.

FOREWORD

AMAZED BY GRACE

Those words appear at the closing of my letters, but they also describe my life. It was Grace that answered my parent's prayers when they were told they could not have children. It was Grace that made me conscious of His presence long before I knew Him. It was Grace that turned my eyes upon Jesus, when they were full of the world.

Grace overshadowed me during the years of rebellion and bitterness. Grace delivered me from the grasp of death, not once, but again and again. Grace called me to the high and holy calling of a servant of the Lamb. Grace gave me the most perfect helpmeet a man could ever have and the absolute compliment to all I am – and all I am not.

Grace enabled me, provided for me, protected me, directed me, and was pleased to use me despite all the failures and inadequacy that have been ever a part of my life.

If ever a single thing has been accomplished through our ministry together it has all been because of Grace. And that Grace has amazed me over and over again. It is more than the ending words to my letters, it is the prevailing theme of my life – I am still and always, amazed by His Grace.

I REMEMBER, I REMEMBER

It was one of those hot summer evenings in June on a date I could hardly forget, for it was our 14th wedding anniversary. Ruby and I had seen little of each other all day in the midst of an immense pile of office work and driving to a state park with a bus load of inner-city teens. I was wishing for a quiet moment when I could at least sit down over a cup of coffee with my wife, but we agreed to let that wait just a little longer.

I really couldn't blame our three children for coaxing me to take them for a ride on the newly inspected red Honda motorcycle sitting in the driveway. The cycle was one of two loaned to us by an interested serviceman and used for shuttling our staff workers between our three Urban Youth Centers. It was the third summer we had used them, and that particular bike and I had covered many miles of road together.

The first trip went off without a hitch, and the second was almost over, with only one more to go. My 12-year-old son, Phil, hung around my waist as I sat waiting for traffic to pass so we could make the left turn into our lane. Suddenly the night air was pierced by the shrill squeal of brakes and one sudden crash and then . . . darkness and nothing.

It was much later that I gradually came around in the emergency room at York Hospital and realized that we had been hit and that I was about to lose my left leg. The strangest thing was that there was no sense of panic—just a settled calm seemed to possess my whole being.

Phil, I learned, had suffered multiple fractures of the left leg, but would come through it alive even though he would have a leg-length problem that would take years to overcome. Even so, I lay there on the hospital table and rationally discussed the amputation of my leg with a doctor I had never seen until then.

Such calm is just not my nature. I should have been pushing all kind of panic buttons and been desperately sick to my stomach, but I wasn't. Only one factor could have made me calm at a time like that. That one factor was a verse from the greatest Book in all the world — the Bible — that kept coursing through my mind like a cool brook would course through a hot, barren desert and turn it into an oasis.

That verse was Paul's promise to the Roman Christians that those who yield their whole life and body to God would experience nothing less than His *good, and acceptable, and perfect will* (Romans 12:2). As I went under anesthesia that night, Ruby and I agreed that we can't get anything better than perfection, and so we would accept His will and rejoice in it. That agreement was the one stable thing that would see us through the many months of pain and trials and sleepless nights that would follow.

How certain could I be that God's hand was really in this, permitting and yet controlling it all for our ultimate good and His glory? The very facts that surrounded the accident helped indicate as much.

Why did there just happen to be a neighbor walking past that place at that moment who would immediately step out onto the road and stop on-coming traffic from running over us? Why were a nurse and her husband on hand to put a tourniquet on my leg that had already pumped three pints of blood onto the ground? How ironic that two different cars that stopped had in them Christians who had drifted away from their walk with God, but who, watching the calm efforts of my wife and my son's confidence in prayer in such a moment, returned to their separate churches that same week with a new commitment to Christian living.

Such facts, and many others, helped demonstrate God's care in the matter. In the final analysis, however, it was His promise alone that was enough. We had committed our bodies to Him, and He promised nothing less than His "good, and acceptable, and perfect will," and we could simply rest in that.

It had not always been like that in my life. The wild and rebellious teens with whom we worked each day were only replicas of my own rebellious past. The years of Bible school and missionary work in the southern Appalachians had not erased the vivid recollections of my checkered teenage career. That career had finally landed me on another hospital bed some 19 years earlier at the point of death with a body broken by sin.

It was there on that bed that I first rested in another Bible promise, *"The blood of Jesus Christ his (God's) Son, cleanseth us from all sin."* There I had placed my whole case in the hands of the Son of God who loved me and died in my place on the cross. That night, at my personal invitation, He who rose again the third day, took control of my life, and the greatest change I have ever experienced took place. I can never explain it, but that night the struggle ceased, and old habits and vices I could never break just passed away. Suddenly everything was new – I was new (2 Corinthians 5:17). I began that night the most exciting and wonderful adventure of all—just living with and loving the Son of God. As the Hymn writer so aptly expressed it:

> *"I need no other argument:*
> *I need no other plea.*
> *It is enough that Jesus died,*
> *And that He died for ME!"*

Because He did, because that is true, I have put my life in His capable hands, and I am over and over again amazed by His Grace – Not only the Grace that saved me, but the Grace that continues to lead me, enable me, provide for me and empower me.

Today I have been an amputee for more years than I enjoyed having two good legs. Yet God has sustained me and allowed me to do unbelievable things. I have tried to record a few of those things in this book. I trust they will inspire and bless you as you too become amazed by His Grace.

CHAPTER ONE

Who Am I?

O God, thou hast taught me from my youth: and hitherto have I declared thy wondrous works. Now also when I am old and greyheaded, O God, forsake me not; until I have showed thy strength unto this generation, and thy power to every one that is to come. (Psalm 71:15 –18)

Roots: My Mother's Side

Until very recently I knew little of my Grandmother Singer's background and nothing of my grandfather (John Singer) who died before I was born. However, my cousin Don Singer contacted me recently as I was writing this account and passed along some very interesting information on the background of the Singer family.

My great-great-grandfather Franciscus (Frank) Xavier Seninger was born on December 25, 1817 in London, Bavaria, Germany. He was married in 1843 in Germany to Annie Fischer who was a little more than two years younger; Annie was born in 1820 in Germany.

Sometime around 1845 Frank moved his family to America where he first settled in Hollidaysburg, Pennsylvania. On his arrival in America his name was anglicized from Seninger to Singer. At the time he moved he apparently had two children (Theodore and Frances). About 1850, the family moved from Hollidaysburg to Altoona, Pennsylvania.

Eight additional children were born between 1849 and 1860. They were Sally and Mary Jane, twins (1849), Barbara and Anna, the second set of twins (1850), Rachel (1852), John F. (1855), Joseph (1857), and William (1860).

Franciscus Xavier Singer died on July 17, 1896 at the age of 78 in Altoona, Blair County, Pennsylvania. He was buried in St. Mary's Cemetery. St. Mary's was a Roman Catholic Cemetery and all the Singers at that time appear to have been Catholic. Annie died two years later on February 6, 1898 at the age of 78 in Altoona. She was also buried in St. Mary's.

I have only to look at my great-great-grandfather's name to know that this must have been a very, very staunch Roman Catholic family. He was obviously named for Francis Xavier, the most famous Jesuit missionary ever known, who spread Catholicism widely across Asia and India during the 1500s. Xavier's first name was actually Francisco. I can only conclude that this family took their Roman Catholicism very seriously.

Joseph was my great-gandfather. He married Catherine "Katie" Harkins. The couple had seven children: Anna (date unknown), Frank J. (date unknown), John Thomas (1883), Clarence W. (1888), Thomas James (1895), Edward S. (date unknown), and Barbara (date unknown). John Thomas Singer was my grandfather.

My Grandmother

Martha West was born December 1, 1882 in Springfield, Kentucky. She was the daughter of Thomas and Patty West. Martha was orphaned as a result of a house fire and was placed in a Shaker Home in Union Village, Ohio. She had a surviving brother named Hundley West who remained in Kentucky. At the age of fourteen she professed faith in Christ as Savior at the Shaker Orphanage and was given a Bible which I still have in my possession. She seemed to have a genuine love for and trust in the Lord, though she was very private about it.

From Ohio she migrated to Altoona Pennsylvania. I have no idea when, or how, or why. She met my grandfather there and they were married. He was a fireman for the Pennsylvania Railroad Company

(PRR), by trade, and worked out of a firehouse on 12th Street in Altoona. I remember visiting the firehouse as a very little boy, but my grandfather died before I was born so I never knew him.

I do know that Grandpa John was formerly a Roman Catholic and came to faith alone in Christ alone for salvation through the ministry of the United Brethren Church sometime after marrying my grandmother. It appears that my grandfather was the first in his family to break from a Catholic tradition to an evangelical faith. He was apparently very musical (which my grandmother was not), and loved to sing the old hymns of redemption and play them on his violin.

John T. Singer (my grandfather) married Martha West on September 16, 1903. Their first child was Esther (my mother) born on May 10, 1904. Robert was the second child. He was born in 1906. Harry was next, born in 1908. Finally, John (Jack) was born in 1917.

When Esther was only five years old she (or a proxy) wrote a letter to Santa. She had quite a Christmas list, but was mindful of her brothers as well. It apparently was published in the local newspaper (Altoona Mirror) and survives in the archives as follows:

Dec. 12, 1910
Dear Santa Claus:
I am a little girl 5 years old.
Will you please bring me a big doll a black board a box of paints and a sled.
Robert wants a doll a train a big drum and a horse and wagon.
Bring my baby brother something too.
Don't forget my Aunt Anna — she lives with us.
Bring lots of candy and nuts.

By your little friend,
Esther Singer

"Robert" obviously referred to my Uncle Bob, "baby brother" was my Uncle Harry, and Uncle Jack had not yet been born. It is interesting to me that "Aunt Anna" lived with them. Anna was Grandpa John's sister and the only member of the original family ever mentioned.

There was apparently a complete disconnect between my grandfather and the remainder of the Singer/Seninger family for I never knew of them at all growing up. I can only imagine that it was most likely caused by my grandfather's conversion. With Anna coming to live with them, I am left wondering if she too had experienced salvation through faith in Christ alone? It is a question I will have to wait for eternity to answer, but one worth contemplating.

I never meet Grandpa, and after his death in 1925, Grandma not only supported herself, but her three younger children as well. My mother was the oldest of the four children. Esther (mother) got married before Grandpa died. But Grandma was left with Bob, Harry and Jack to care for after his death.

So from the time I could remember anything, Grandma worked at Gables Department Store in Altoona, which was the largest department store in that area. She was a waitress in the business section of the famous Vipond restaurant in Gables basement and was such a jolly soul that all the business men loved it when she served their tables.

My uncle Bob was already married before I was born, but Harry was not. Uncle Bob had a son two years my junior named Donnie. He (and later his sister), were my only cousins on that side of the family. We loved to get together and we always had a great (translate "boisterous") time much to the disapproval of my two uncles who were still unmarried.

One early recollection was of Grandma's reaction when Harry joined the Navy in the early days of World War II. Grandma was devastated and cried and cried, but for no reason – Harry was assigned to the Caribbean and never saw action during the war.

The Navy experience was enough however to give him a taste for the night life and when he returned he frequented the Bars and the Nightclubs. He eventually married a Catholic lady who was a barkeeper and a widow much to Grandma's dismay. Years later I made a very earnest attempt to bring my uncle to Christ during his stay in the hospital for a bleeding ulcer. I was in the area holding evangelistic meetings and visited him every day.

The first day I visited him he listened carefully as I explained his need to receive Christ in a personal act of faith. On that day he was,

I believe, very near to trusting Christ. The second day he was some better and was not as open to what I had to say. The third day he virtually told me that he was not ready to receive Christ at that time. He was scheduled to go home that day, but an hour after I left the hospital the ulcer hemorrhaged and he died on the operating table.

As far as the extended family goes I never met any of the Singers (probably because they were still Catholic and we were not), but I met Grandma's brother Hundley West once on a train trip to Louisville with my grandmother. Actually I made two trips to Louisville with Grandmother. The first when I was about eight years old. Since my dad, and my grandfather had worked for the Pennsylvania Railroad Company (the old PRR), we were all eligible for free passes, so when we traveled in those days it was always by train. We went down to see my grandmother's nephew married. His name was Denny West and his bride's name was Ethel. It was a Catholic wedding, but all I remember was the bride. She was the first bride I had ever seen and dressed in her white lace gown I thought she was the most beautiful lady in the world.

Later, when I was about twelve we went again. This time we spent most of our time with Hundley, Grandma's brother. All I remember was that he and his wife Lena were very kind to me while I was there. They kept a goat and some chickens in their back yard to which I became very much attached and wrote a childhood poem about their place on an old envelope on the way home by train – a poem I named, "You Say Goodbye." My mother kept it for years, among other things she treasured and I found it recently while going through some old papers. I obviously built a very strong attachment to my relatives and their menagerie of animals.

Roots: My Father's Side

On my father's side of the family I know little of certainty beyond my grandfather's generation. Some research was done by one of my grandson's which suggested that the Shade family had also orig-inated in Germany along the Rhine valley. His study took him to the 1700s when a Johann Shade (actually the name may have been Scheidt originally), married a girl named Elizabeth and eventually migrated to America where it seems they may have settled in the area of Lancaster, Pa. There they apparently prospered in farming. As far as I can tell the Shades were all Lutheran by tradition. There is some evidence that at least one of them was a Lutheran pastor.

There is an intriguing story of one of them loading his several Conestoga wagons with farm produce and other supplies and delivering them to General George Washington who was at the time encamped at Valley Forge during the long winter that became the turning point in the Revolutionary war. But all of that is somewhat vague and I would not be able to affirm it as a certainty.

What I do know is that eventually the Shade clan seemed to have migrated further up into the area of central Pennsylvania to what became Blair County and settled around Duncansville. There is where my grandfather was raised.

From what we learned from others who have written, the Shades were known for being builders, carpenters, farmers, and blacksmiths; and they had the distinction of being expert riflemen.

Of my grandfather's youth I know very little. He was slight of build but strong and wiry and they named him William Augustus Shade or "Will" for short, a nick-name he kept for the remainder of his life. Although slight of build, or perhaps because of it, he was extremely competitive. He could outrun any boy his age and kept on running up into his seventies.

In fact one of the keenest memories I have is of our walks back to the farthest field of his farm to where the creek finally terminated his property. When it was time to return, he would always challenge us boys by saying, "Come on boys, let's have a foot race to the barn." He always beat me – all but once. When I finally grew old enough to be competitive, I was able to overtake him by about one step. He never raced me again – his pride would not allow it.

As a boy, he was a very bright student in a little one-room schoolhouse where he attended. The only thing I know about those early years was a story he used to tell of a spelling bee in which he participated. It was a story my grandfather was fond of telling and he told it to me one Sunday afternoon after our walk in the fields. Sitting in his rocker next to the radio, he related it with some pleasure.

He had become the best speller in his school and he and a number of other children were taken to another one-room schoolhouse, where they had a spelling bee with several other schools from that area.

The day of the event all of the spellers had missed a word and had to take their seats except Will, and a pretty little girl named Mary Ruth Delozier. The two stayed up word after word until at last Will faltered. "She spelled me down," he would say. And then, with a gleam in his eye, "It made me so mad, I married her."

I remember that story well because it isn't all he said. In his late seventies at the time, he looked away very wistfully, and said, "Billy, it seems like just yesterday – in fact, all my life seems like just a dream." I couldn't understand that at the time, but I certainly understand it now.

So my grandmother on Dad's side was Mary Ruth. I never knew her; she died when my father was only seven years of age. Grandpa was a truck farmer and worked as a boss for the Pennsylvania Railroad Company. The farm was small. He had approximately seven acres of ground just outside Hollidaysburg on the road to Duncansville.

Will Shade was not only wiry, he was a natural leader and scrappy as a bantam rooster. My father had a very young and innocent face far into his adult manhood (a fact that served him quite well when he got older). He looked so much like a boy that back in that day when laws that were meant to protect children were not only on the books, but actually enforced, he found he often had great difficulty buying a pack of cigarettes, long after he had passed the legal age of twenty one.

He had the same difficulty when he drove a car. Although holding a license and quite legal, he was stopped on several occasions by zealous policemen who deemed him obviously too young to be driving. One such officer, a very large and bombastic man who was overwhelmed with his own importance, used to stop him repeatedly each time he would venture into the central square in the town of Hollidaysburg, the county seat. My father complained at home about the harassment, but, as usual, got no sympathy from Grandpa Will. No sympathy that is, until one day when Will himself parked the vehicle at the square to care for some business. They had just applied parallel parking lines and the same officer was present to see that everyone parked well within them – apparently Will had not.

As soon as the car stopped the officer approached my grandfather with a loud, "Now see here, you are not within the lines and you will have to try again." Will did not try again. Instead, he turned off the motor and got out of the car approaching the surprised officer. It must have been a hilarious sight. Will, barely five feet seven inches tall must have looked hardly a match for the huge hulk of a man that towered over him – however, that never seemed to deter Will. Taking his forefinger he pushed it into the policeman's chest and gave him such a tongue lashing that the poor fellow backed away from him until he stood with his back against the Bank Building. There little "David" continued to berate large "Goliath", and after telling him all that was on his mind, though I know little of that, he finished with, "And the next time my son comes up here and you stop him and ask for his license, I will personally come after you and bloody your big fat nose." I'm told that my father was never stopped again.

Grandpa Will was both a farmer and a foreman working in the Altoona shops of the Pennsylvania Railroad Company. The PRR had built what was reputed to have been the largest railroad production center in the world in Altoona. Grandpa considered the PRR the securest bet in town and saw that both of his boys got employment there. "If you work for the company (PRR), you have nothing to worry about," he would say. "The PRR will be here long after all of us have gone."

He might have been right had things continued as they were in his day. But they did not. Railroad men unionized as did some of the shops. One of the benefits was a retirement fund. But the unions insisted that it be paid retroactively to former workers. I still remember the day my grandfather got his first retirement check. He sat at the table looking at it and shaking his head. "They can't do this," he said. "I haven't worked a single hour for this money. If they do this they will go broke," – and as it turned out, he was right.

The unions got some much deserved benefits for the men, but like all things human, men by their fallen nature, have a way of ruining even that which is intended for good. When the PRR went to diesel instead of steam, the unions demanded that the company continue to pay firemen who were absolutely essential to stoke the boiler on a steam engine, but totally useless in the diesel revolution. Yet the company was forced to continue their employment creating a senseless waste of funds.

Another story I heard my father tell was about a young man that was hired to sweep the shop. The day he came on the job, the union man directed him on the way to do his work. The man was equipped with a broom, a shovel and a large drum on wheels. He immediately put the tools in the drum and began to make his way to the other end of the shop (which was about a city block long). The union man stopped him. "You won't have enough to keep you busy if you do it that way," he said. "Come on, I'll show you how to do it." Whereupon he instructed him to pick up one tool at a time and carry it the length of the shop. Then return for the second tool, and so on, thus making at least three round trips before beginning his real work of sweeping. I have no way of verifying that story, but those who observed similar situations recognized that such totally inefficient behavior would eventually ruin the company and indeed it did.

There were many other factors involved in the demise of the PRR, but I grew up believing that certain institutions were forever. I learned through my rather long lifetime they are not. Nothing in this world is lasting. How wise the man who sets his sights on eternal riches.

There were seven children in Will Shade's family. There was Zuala, then Chalmer, Martha, Mildred, Kenneth (my dad), Nellie and finally Helen. My grandmother Mary Ruth died during, or shortly after the birth of Helen so I never knew her except by a large portrait that Grandpa hung over the piano in the living room. The older girls looked after the house, Grandpa Will, and the younger children, until several got married and moved away, and finally grandpa remarried a single neighbor woman, Clara Smith. The children were all either grown or already married, so no one ever called Clara *mother*. She was simply Clara to all the children and grandchildren, but she was a wonderful, quiet helpmeet to grandpa and took care of him until the end.

My father was an attractive child from the beginning. Adored by his sisters, bullied by his older brother, he developed a sweet disposition that never left him over the years. He was so cute one of the neighbors – a maiden school teacher named Nellie Berg nick-named him *Teddy Boy* and the name stuck. As I was growing up, all the old friends called my dad "Ted". It wasn't until we left Central Pennsylvania that he finally became known as Ken.

I am told that little Teddy was always into something and con-stantly curious. One story my grandfather used to tell about Dad made the point. Grandpa had spanked him for getting into something and told him to sit up at the table. Grandpa left the room just long enough to put the paddle back in its place and when he returned, little Teddy Boy was sitting obediently at the table, still crying from the whipping and mixing together the pepper and salt in the shakers.

Dad's older brother had a much different disposition. He was obviously jealous of the attention and favor shown his younger sibling and was often mean and caustic. So he took it out on Teddy Boy by beating him with his fists whenever he pleased. I'm not quite sure how old Teddy was but the day came when the worm turned and he appar-ently gave Chalmer such a beating that he never touched him again.

Teddy was full of life and fun and made friends easily. Simple pleasures entertained boys back then and one day, Teddy harnessed the horse to the spring wagon and went off to visit a friend named Chuck – I never met him but I've heard the story so often I feel as if I actually was there. Chuck was a rather plump boy who had the distinction of owning a BB gun. Teddy went over to see his friend with the purpose of getting Chuck to allow him to shoot it.

Well, Chuck was more than anxious to show off his gun so the boys went out to the back road where Teddy had tied up the horse and wagon. There they set an old bell up on a fence post. Then they stepped back and shot at the bell. Each time they hit the bell it would ring, but after frequent hits, the bell finally toppled off the post. Chuck went to pick it up leaving the BB gun in Teddy's hands. Now I'm told that Chuck was wearing a pair of shinny blue surge trousers that were a bit tight and stretched to their limit. When he arrived at the fallen bell he bent over and jokingly called back, "Hey Ted, shot at this," which was all the encouragement Teddy Boy needed. He took aim and landed a BB directly on the shinning seat of Chuck's britches.

Chuck left out an awful war hoop and turned to attack his assailant. Teddy realized the jig was up, Chuck was no longer joking, so he dropped the offending rifle on the ground and headed full steam for the wagon. As he tells it, "I started talking to the horse before I even reached the wagon and by the time I got there she was already on the move." Teddy was on his way back home.

I mentioned that a spinster by the name of Nellie Berg had given Dad his nickname. Actually, there were two Berg sisters – Annie and Nellie. Both were unmarried and both were teachers. They lived only a short distance from the Shade homestead and apparently took a great interest in all the Shade children, especially after the death of their mother Mary Ruth.

I remember rather vaguely (because I was probably not more than seven or eight years old), going over to the Berg place and playing board games, of which they had a seemingly endless supply. My older cousins seemed to love to retreat there every time we all got together and Nellie always welcomed them.

Apparently Annie had already died and I have only the vaguest of memories of Nellie as a very kind and generous old lady dressed in long skirts and lace, but I do remember that when Nellie died she willed all of her possessions to the Shade clan and so we grew up playing some of those old board games. I believe that may have been where we got our set of Chinese checkers.

Grandpa Will used to tend a stall at the Farmer's Market in Altoona on Saturday nights, and it was one of those occasions when Dad was tending market that he met my mother, and they talked and got to know one another. Dad would ride the street trolley, which ran all the way from Hollidaysburg, in to get to see her. Esther was also working at Gables Department Store where my grandmother worked. Later he came to see her at her home, to meet her parents. After a couple of years of courtship, they determined to get married.

My grandfather John Singer liked my dad and was happy about the marriage, but my grandmother was very strong willed and opposed the marriage and made no secret of her disapproval, and so Mother and Dad ran off, to Cumberland, Maryland, and were married there. They went down by train, got married, stayed the first night in a hotel there and came back and started their married life in

Altoona. An interesting side light here – they were married, I was told, by an old United Brethren preacher who had lost his leg – a fact Dad recalled after I lost mine.

All of the family faithfully attended the Lutheran Church each Sunday and each child in turn was sprinkled at birth, went through the catechism and took their first communion at age twelve. Whatever else all that accomplished, it seemed to place in each one a strong sense of morality and respect for God and the Bible, though I do not think there were any of them that actually achieved a personal relationship with Christ until much later.

Dad had never really been exposed to the Gospel. He was raised in that high Lutheran tradition, and he would attend church with Mother occasionally, but he particularly made fun of the revival meetings the United Brethren used to have. One night he went to revival meeting and an old preacher, took his Testament out of his pocket, and leaning across the pulpit read just a couple of verses, *"What shall it profit a man if he gain the whole world and lose his own soul? And what shall a man give in exchange for his soul?"* He put the Testament back into his pocket and preached. And Dad came to faith in Christ that night. He never moved out of his seat, but in his heart cried out to God, asking for forgiveness and salvation and knew in his heart that he had been saved.

Mom and Dad wanted children very badly, but because of some physical restrictions in her pelvic area, doctors had told her that she would never be able to have children. However, after ten years of marriage, and many prayers, my mother began to detect signs that perhaps she was pregnant.

She went to the doctor and though he examined her he told her, "Esther, I am not sure what the problem is right now, but as I told you, you just can't get pregnant, so there is no use getting your hopes up." When they left the doctor's office that night, Mother said to Dad, "Well, now what do you think?" And Dad responded, "I think you are pregnant! That is what we asked God for isn't it?" From the very beginning Dad had an almost child-like faith.

Well, it became quite apparent that Mother was pregnant, and so the time came for me to be born, she was in the hospital, and her labor had been long and difficult. The doctor decided to go out and play a game of golf while they waited. I do not know what Dad said, but Dad can be pretty forceful when necessary and he insisted the doctor stay with Mother because she had been in labor pains for some time and Dad was beginning to fear for both her life and mine. Finally the doctor put away his golf plans.

When I came he had to deliver me with forceps. They named me William, after my grandfather and Kenneth, after my dad. After the delivery, the doctor told Dad, "well, you sure did shoot the 'h_ _ _' out of my golf game, but it's a good thing you did – the baby probably would have died if we would have hesitated." It seemed from the very first that God had a plan for little William. Born of prayer, preserved through a difficult birth, Mother and Dad both believed this child, like Samuel of Biblical fame, was destined for something special.

John & Martha with Baby Esther (age 2)

Esther with Bob & Harry

4TH GRADE AT WASHINGTON SCHOOL

Esther with her Father

Back Row: Ken Shade, Dorcas, Esther, Martha, Haddie Miller, Marian,Geraldine
Center Row: Harry, Bob, Jack, and me
Front Row: Donnie, Robbie, and dog "Boots"

W.A. & MARY RUTH SHADE

TEDDY BOY WITH SIBLINGS
ZUALA, MARTHA, MILDRED, CHALMER

TEDDY BOY IN GERMAN SOLDIER UNIFORM 1908

TEDDY BOY ON HORSE WITH CHALMER LEADING

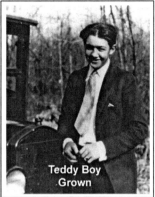

Teddy Boy Grown

SHADE HOMESTEAD HOLLIDAYSBURG, PA

W. A. & CLARA THE LATER YEARS

Pappy Bill ~ As I Remember Him

CHAPTER TWO

From My Birth to Conversion

God never did that miracle for my mother the second time, and so I was an only child. Dad was absolutely determined that I would not be spoiled, and so he put forth his best efforts to see to it that didn't happen. On one occasion when my grandmother was rocking me and I was crying, Dad came in and said, "Mother, you are planning to stay with us?" She said, "No, I am going to go home in a little while." He said, "Then put the baby down, because I am not going to rock him when he cries and there won't be anyone here to do it when you go." Well, perhaps he was a little harsh, but he was trying to be sure that this only child didn't become a spoiled only child!

I was brought up in church; in fact, my earliest recollections are those of pastors visiting us. I remember Pastor Boyer, one of our first pastors. I was probably only about 5 or 6 years old when I remember his being there. And I was always very excited to see him. I remember one evening when he taught me how to shuffle my feet across the living room carpet, creating static electricity and then touch a metal object and produce a large spark. I was really fascinated by that.

Mother was always telling or reading Bible stories to me; I was very conscious of God. I remember one night I had a terrible dream and I woke up screaming. Dad came over to the room and carried me out – I couldn't stop sobbing. When he finally got me calmed down and asked what was wrong, I told him I dreamed that I was in a great circus tent, and all of a sudden, I saw them bringing Jesus into the tent down to the arena. There was a pole there and they tied His hands around that pole and they began to beat Him, and I began to cry and weep hysterically. I believe that these were just early evidences that God was at work in my life, and wanted to do something in my heart.

When I was 10 or 11 years old, I had an emergency appendectomy – they had to rush me to the hospital, and they put me in Mercy Hospital which was full, it seemed, of black robed nuns who scared me to death. I thought they were witches and made the mistake of saying so. I remember our pastor G. R. Strayer (but everyone just called him G. R.), coming to visit me before the operation. After praying for me he said, "Bill, God will take care of you!" And I never forgot that. From that time on, the old hymn, *God Will Take Care of You*, was very, very precious to me.

My church used to send the young people to camp each summer, and so from the time I was about nine I started to go to camp. I went to that camp four years. I was supposed to be ten before starting but the camp was always held in August and every year it fell on my Birthday. It was conducted at a place called Camp Harmony that was very near the Quemahoning Dam, out towards Johnstown. We used to walk to a hill overlooking the Dam for evening vesper services that I found meaningful and moving.

Camp always left a tremendous impression on me. I remember the first national Indian pastor/evangelist, (I am talking about someone from India) that I ever met or heard. He spoke at camp and they took an offering for him. I was so moved that I, literally took my wallet out and dumped everything that was in it into the offering plate. That was one of the first meetings in the week and I didn't have anything for the offering or to spend at the camp store for the rest of that week, but it was also an early indication that I would have a love for India for the rest of my life.

I remember the last year best of all. They had built a new auditorium, the old sawdust tabernacle was gone, and we were meeting there that night. The preaching was over and I was under deep conviction. I knew I needed to be saved, and they were singing,

Turn your eyes upon Jesus,
Look full in His wonderful face...
And the things of earth will grow strangely dim,
In the light of His glory and grace.

There was a tremendous battle going on inside me and an equally tremendous storm going on outside. There was lightning, thunder, and about fifteen feet from were I was standing, there was an iron vent pipe that went all the way from the basement where the kitchen was and out through the roof.

I had been holding onto the seat ahead of me because I didn't want to go forward. Suddenly there was a tremendous crash. I don't remember moving — I don't remember going forward. All I remember was that I was at the front of that auditorium asking God to save me. They told us later that lightning had actually struck that vent pipe. If that was my wake up call, it certainly got my attention. At any rate, I remember calling out and asking the Lord to save me.

When I talked to my counselors they showed me the verse, Romans 1:16, *"For I am not ashamed of the Gospel of Christ, for it is the power of God unto salvation to everyone that believeth, to the Jew first and also to the Greek."* They encouraged me to memorize it and live by it. I did memorize it, and I was determined to live by it as well. I had a verse, but I had no real idea how to sustain my spiritual strength and I was an easy target for the devil.

When I got home, I immediately told the guys that I ran around with, that I was a Christian. I told them what I had done, and as I should have expected, I began to get a lot of teasing and mocking. All of my insecurities began to come into play and I began to feel isolated, and alone. Then, somewhere within those next several months, the pressure got too much for me. One day one of these guys said, "Bill can't do that with us cause he's a Christian." And without thinking, I denied the Lord, I said, "No, I'm not; I'm not a Christian!" And from that moment everything began to fall as far as my spiritual life was concerned.

What I know now, but didn't know then, was how to be restored – how to confess my sin, be forgiven and start again. Coming from a United Brethren Church with an Armenian background, I assumed that having denied the Lord, I was doomed and I began to live like a doomed person lives.

I never was a particularly great student in school; I just couldn't get motivated, and never did have very good study habits. I got into the seventh grade in school and for those of us on the east side of the railroad tracks (that cut directly through the center of Altoona), that meant Roosevelt Junior High School. Students on the west side attended Keith Junior High, our permanent rivals. Junior High meant a much larger school, and a completely new environment. It was also the autumn after my camp experience and I had already failed the Lord and was in a miserable spiritual state so it became one of the worst years of my young life.

My performance was so poor, both academically and socially, that I was under discipline for the second half of the year. I had to go to the Guidance office every single morning. Miss Gephardt was the Guidance counselor, and she was a large and fearsome woman. I would pick up a form at her office and take it to every class I had. I would give it to the teacher and each teacher would write on it whether I had turned in my homework and, whether my conduct was good that day. Then I had to take it home for my father to sign. I think Mother actually signed it most of the time – Dad was not happy that I had gotten myself into such a situation and it was easier to avoid going to him. Then I had to turn the signed slip into the guidance counselor the next morning and pick up another slip! It was one of the most embarrassing times of my life. I was absolutely humiliated; because underneath a brave exterior, I had always been a very sensitive and insecure kid.

I got through the seventh grade, not triumphantly, but somehow. The eighth grade I did much better. I settled down a bit. They put me in Oliver Dreese's home room. He was a science teacher and I liked science so I did well in his class. Dreese was very strict, and I needed that, so I got along pretty well. Eighth grade was a much better year and ninth was better still.

I always loved drama, and I joined the stage crew, because the stage crew guys were always the first to get a chance to try out for any of the plays. I don't remember ever really getting in any of the plays in a serious way. I don't think they thought that I would really learn my part, and they were probably right. But I was in the stage crew nevertheless, and it put me into the upper echelon socially, and I enjoyed the prestige of being part of that.

It was through that particular group of friends that I was introduced to DeMolay. DeMolay, is a high school fraternal organization and although it denies any official connection with the Masonic Order, is basically a junior branch of it – at least the stepping stone into Free Masonry. You had to have some prestige to be a member because the other members voted you in (or out) and one black ball in the box was all it took to keep you from membership. Eventually I joined. Dad at that time was a Mason and mother was then in Eastern Star (the woman's branch of the Masonic order) and since they were concerned about my social skills they were trying to get me involved in what they considered "good activities."

Part of those "good activities" was seeing that I learned to dance. They began to go to a square dance every Saturday night, and indeed I learned to dance. I learned to square dance and then waltz. I also learned what it meant to be around girls and I started to smoke, and developed a passionate attachment to both.

When I got into DeMolay, it was quite a prestigious thing, so we were looked up to by the other students. The City of Altoona actually turned over its City management to the DeMolay officers one day each year and since I eventually became an officer, I helped run the city (well, sort of) for that day. I also took up drinking, swearing, dancing about three nights a week, and just generally living a wild life. My academics began to go down badly, and I did not do real well in tenth grade.

By the time I was in eleventh grade I was ready to hit bottom. By the middle of the year, I was failing a number of subjects, and I had come to the place where my vices, my drinking, smoking, and swearing had made me undesirable even to the socially elite group that I was with. I was falling from grace socially, and I knew it.

In the meantime God was at work in my father's life. Dad had met a man in the shop where he worked as a machinist operating a lumber planer for the PRR. Every lunch time, Bert McCaulley would get his lunch box and his Scofield Reference Bible and climb up on a pile of lumber and read as he ate his lunch. Dad was fascinated and began to ask Bert questions – and Bert seemed to have the answers. Soon Dad began to express concern over things that were taking place in our denomination. The very conservative United Brethren had now merged with the less conservative Evangelical Denomination to form the Evangelical United Brethren Denomination. They would later go on and merge again with the United Methodists, but this predated that action.

Dad taught Sunday School, and was Superintendent of the Young People's Department. In addition he was on the Board of Trustees and served as Delegate to Annual Conference. He was increasingly disturbed by what he heard coming out of the conference. Then our pastor was caught in immorality. When the men of the Board tried to deal with it, he strongly denied it. Within a few months, he was dead of a sudden heart attack.

Then there was the case of the four young men who had been saved some years before and wanted to serve God. All of them went to our denominational schools; two of them to Otterbein College in Westerville, Ohio and two went to Bonebreak Seminary (now called United Seminary), in Dayton, Ohio. When they returned at Christmas, it was evident that their zeal was gone and their faith had been substantially weakened if not destroyed. Within a year one died in an auto accident, one contracted polio, another suffered a nervous breakdown and the final one dropped out of Theology and went into business. Dad was heartsick.

Bert gave Dad a lot of information about Liberalism and the unbelief that had overtaken the mainline churches and seminaries and Dad was seeing it first hand. The final straw came when at annual conference, they voted to receive a minister that openly denied the virgin birth of Jesus Christ. I was not there, but was told what happened. When none of the pastors would raise strong objections, Dad rose and said, "I am only a layman, not a theologian, but I am smart enough to know that if my Lord was not born of the virgin then he was a bastard, and I do not want a Lord like that." Dad walked out of the conference and out of the denomination and never returned.

On a Wednesday evening Dad decided to quietly attend a prayer meeting at Calvary Baptist Church in Altoona. He had heard that

Calvary had a strong Biblical position and a great pastor, but Dad had never been in a Baptist Church. He had no idea what he might find, so he went alone.

Unknown to him they were not having a prayer meeting. They were, rather, in the midst of a week of Revival meetings with evangelist John Carrara, a converted former Roman Catholic who had been destined to the priesthood. Dad had never heard the Word of God preached with such power and when the invitation was given he was the first to go forward. Dad knew he was saved, but he also knew he had a lot of things in his life that were inconsistent with a strong testimony. Bert had pointed out much of that to him before and now it was time to deal with it.

Dad went into the counseling room and talked with Pastor Ralph H. Stoll, one of the godliest men that ever stood behind the sacred desk. After asking forgiveness of God for himself and dedicating himself completely to Christ, Dad said, "Pastor Stoll, I have a son, and he is far from God." Pastor Stoll looked at him with compassion, but replied, "And brother Shade, he will never be closer to God than you are." Dad said those words stung like a knife and he determined right then to separate himself fully to God. He came home that night and threw all of his pipes into the furnace. He was done with the dance hall and anything that bespoke the world. And he wanted me to change as well.

I certainly had no intention of changing. I was completely involved with the world and I had drunk of the cup of the world and found it bitter and toxic. In my folly I had come to the place where I was bitter, I was sick, and I was tired of living and scared of dying. I really had lost my desire to live. Yet I could not imagine the kind of "change" Dad desired.

Suddenly, in the midst of my despair, I found myself being dragged to a new Church where I was under the sound of Bible teaching that made me very uncomfortable. I didn't like it – no, I hated it, and I hated Dad for making me be there.

Pastor Stoll would preach and then go to the back, as was his custom, to greet the congregation as they went out. I would walk past him with my hands stuffed down in my trouser pockets and not even look his way. My Dad was embarrassed and mumbled something to the Pastor one day and Pastor Stoll replied, "That's alright brother Shade – I'm praying for him and God will get him."

I was not only spiritually sick however, I was physically sick as well. I had gone to the doctor on several occasions complaining of shortness of breath and pain in my chest, and he told me I had to quit smoking. I was smoking by then about three packs of cigarettes a day. I knew he was right but no matter how hard I tried, I could not quit.

Altoona High School was a large school. There were over six hundred students in the senior class. The school covered an entire city block. Many times I had classes in the basement at one end of the school, and the next class would be on the third floor at the other end of the school. And you had to move to get to class on time! I began to realize I couldn't run up the stairs as I once had. I'd go up two or three stairs and then I'd get pains in my chest, and I had to stop. Of course I didn't want to admit that to anyone, so I would try to joke around while I got my breath and then go for a few more stairs.

I remember one Sunday afternoon. I went out without Dad realizing that in one pocket of my coat there was a bag of poker chips and in the other pocket there was a deck of cards. I was off for my friend Dick's house where we intended to spend the afternoon playing poker.

The night before I had been dancing and a girl make a pass at me and I had been very receptive. I danced with her most of the evening, and that Sunday afternoon while we were engaged in that poker game, the boyfriend of the girl found me there at Dick's house. He happened to be the wrestling champion of the State of Pennsylvania!

He challenged me to come out onto the porch. I knew this wouldn't be much of a match because at that point I was physically hardly able to get myself around. He swung a couple of times, landed a good blow on my chin and put me down on the porch. They carried me in with blood in my mouth, and I knew that I was about at the end.

A week later we experienced a very severe "ice storm" in that area. Trees and power lines were down and flood waters were rising. I was working at the time for Blatchford Furniture Company in

Altoona, and I got a call to go down to Tyrone where Blatchford had a second store and help move furniture that was in the flood area. I worked all day and into the night wading in cold icy water.

Next day I came down with a very high fever. For four days I carried a fever of about 104 to 106 degrees. The doctor was called in on several occasions, but nothing they did seemed to do any good. Then one evening I had a strange experience.

Mother had begun to hold a Child Evangelism Class in our home. She needed a certain scene painted on a flannel background for her next lessons. My fever was down a bit that evening and she asked if I would to it. I complied and worked on the project for several hours. Finally finished, I returned to bed. But something had happened. I was weeping, and I remember saying to God, "Lord, I am sixteen years old and that is the first thing I have ever done for you. Lord I have wasted my entire life." My hard heart had broken and I wanted so much to be forgiven and cleansed.

Finally the doctor realized that my heart was weakening and he ordered me to the hospital. When I got there and was examined, they discovered I had a heart swollen three times its normal size. I had a very, very severe case of rheumatic fever.

They called in two heart specialists to examine me, Dr. English and Dr. Maniglea. They told my father that my condition was very critical. They told him that if I made it through the night, it was possible I might survive, but I probably would be an invalid for the rest of my life because of the heart damage.

That night, not realizing how sick I was, but feeling very, very ashamed of the life I had lived, and under tremendous conviction, I cried out to God and turned my life over to Him. I told Him I was ashamed of what I had done and that I knew this was His chastening, and I told Him that if there was anything left, it all belonged to Him.

Suddenly there was a wonderful peace that flooded my soul and I knew I was forgiven. I told God I knew I didn't really deserve to live, but if He would let me live just long enough to win one soul to Him, I would be eternally grateful. I knew God had cleansed me; and I went to sleep with a deep peace in my soul.

The next morning, when the doctors came in to do examinations, I was in an oxygen tent; they zipped down the side of the tent and put the stethoscope to my chest and listened, doing it again and again. Then they went to the foot of the bed and talked for awhile, and came back, and tried again.

Finally I learned that they were surprised, first, that I was alive, and secondly, that they could not even detect a heart murmur. They asked the nurse what drugs they had been giving me because they said it must be miracle drug because the swelling in the heart had gone down.

As I lay there later that day I looked down at my hands. You can imagine what my hands looked like after the amount of smoking I had done for a number of years and my index finger and the next finger were dark, yellow brown from the residue that the tobacco had left on my fingers. I looked down at my hands and they looked pure white. That high fever had sweated all of the poisons out of my system, and tears came down my cheeks because I saw that my hands were clean, and I knew that my heart was clean as well, and God had done a miracle in my life. I had promised Him that if He would just let me live long enough to lead one soul to Him, I would be thankful, and God had done the miracle.

CHAPTER THREE

I take a New Direction

The next few months I had to be confined to bed. Since I could not negotiate stairs, they set up a bed for me on what we called the "sun porch." It was a glassed in area off the living room that we seldom used except at Christmas time when we set up the train platform and the Christmas tree. I was confined in that room for the next several months.

I had to be tutored to keep from falling a year behind in school. It was still in the middle of the year, and I was tutored for four classes. The fellow the School District sent to be my tutor was a social studies teacher, and a political liberal of the first order. Up until then I never even thought about the difference between a conservative and a liberal. When I started that class I was a political non-entity, but as he tried to propel me toward his liberal views, I found myself disagreeing with him about almost everything.

It was at the time of the Korean conflict; and General Douglas MacArthur was under fire from Washington. I was on MacArthur's side! I kept a scrap book of newspaper articles on the war and followed it very carefully. I came out of that tutoring experience understanding the difference between liberalism and conservatism and found I was a dyed-in-the-wool conservative!

However that was not all I learned in those days. For the last several years I had little interest in the Bible. Dad had bought me a new Scofield Reference Bible for Christmas, and I had carried it obediently to church and left it lying on my dresser the rest of the time.

Now, suddenly I couldn't get enough of the Bible. Each evening, after my parents went to bed, I would begin to read the Scripture and sometimes continued far past midnight. I wanted to understand what I was reading and Dad had been collecting some of Dr. M. R. DeHaan's booklets. I devoured them! I read the book of Revelation over and over again. The Scripture so spoke to my heart that I often wet the pages with my tears as I read and turned my heart in thanksgiving to God for all He had saved me from and forgiven me for.

I remember one day when I was finally strong enough to wander out into the living room and sit down for the first time at the piano. A few months before, I had been studying with Mr. Bohn, a music teacher that loved the classics and especially Bach. But when I sat down that day I began to leaf through the pages of the hymnbook. I played several hymns and then I stumbled upon *The Ninety and Nine*. I read the words as my fingers played the notes and the tears streamed down my cheeks. I can hardly remember ever crying with such gratitude and joy as I did that day. I, indeed, was that poor lost sheep for whom the Shepherd had suffered so much and for whom He cared so deeply. At that moment His love for me simply overwhelmed me and I wanted to serve Him for the rest of my life.

That spring, I was getting around some, and physically getting stronger. I was getting stronger in the Word as well. Dad had broken ties with the Masonic Lodge, having seen it as a contradiction to all that Scripture taught about salvation through faith alone. As usual, he did not go out quietly. He wrote a letter, expressing his faith in the saving work of Jesus Christ alone and telling them why he could no longer be part of such an organization. A few months later I took the same action with my membership in DeMolay.

I had to take summer school to make up for some courses I missed, but after school I had the opportunity of going to Camp – this time as staff. That spring, Vince Porte told me that he was going to work at Camp Manahath under its director, Dr. William Breckbill.

I asked if I could work, too, and so Vince took me to meet Dr. Breckbill. "Dr. Bill", as he was called, was a fundamental Free Methodist preacher and he welcomed me without knowing very much about me other than that I testified to being a Christian. He took me on the staff, and it was one of the greatest summers I had ever had.

It was while I was there at Manahath, that I had the opportunity to lead a young man to Christ one night. He came to me in great need; I didn't know very much, but I shared with him John 1:12, *As many as receive him, to them He gives the power to become the sons of God, even to those who believe on His name;* and he accepted Christ.

I asked him if he understood what he had done and he said, "yes." "Do you have any questions?" I asked. Thankfully he didn't because I'm not sure I could have answered them. He went away rejoicing, and I walked out into the star-lit night, overwhelmed by the joy of being used of God.

Then, as I looked up on that starry night sky, it suddenly dawned on me that I had asked God to give me just one soul – I had asked that He'd let me live just long enough to win one soul, and now it had happened. I'm not sure exactly what I thought, except that I assumed that God would certainly now take me home. Well the following day He certainly had the opportunity to do so.

I drove into Williamsport for the camp every day to get groceries – and I drove in a little model A Ford coupe that had the rumble seat taken out and a big box built in its place which made a truck out of the coupe. That next day I was going to get groceries, and Frank Ostenich, who was also working at the camp, asked if he could drive. He had a learner's permit, and he wanted a chance to practice. When I wouldn't do that, he went to Dr. Bill and asked Dr. Bill whether he could drive. Dr. Bill, without ever questioning him, said, "Oh, sure." So Frank drove into Williamsport.

To complicate things, several of the other staff boys had asked to ride into town that morning, so I had Vince Porte, Carl Ross and Henry McNight sitting in the box in the back of the coupe.

Frank had never driven much and certainly not a model A, and he pressed the pedal to the floor almost the whole way into town, taking us around blind curves on the left side of the road. I kept quietly trying to tell him that if anyone was coming the other way we would hit head on, but it didn't seem to register. Finally, when we got to the top of Williamsburg hill, he took his foot off of the accelerator, and put it on the brake.

But we were going down hill very fast, Model A Fords had mechanical brakes and it was quickly obvious that Frank didn't know how to use them. Soon we were going at over 60 miles an hour (that's as far as the speedometer went on those cars). We barely missed a truck coming up, and when we hit the curve, we were on two wheels. Those three boys were sitting in the box in the back and Frank and I in the car, and when we hit that curve, at such a speed I knew we were going to crash. I covered my face with my hands and that is all I remember. We jumped a high curb, hit a tree and plowing it completely down, went over top of that tree and hit a second tree going part way up in it, before we finally came to a standstill.

The first thing I remember was someone saying, "Get Shade out – I think he's dead." I was lying on the running board on the passenger side of the car. I had been knocked out and there was blood all over my clothes, but I wasn't bleeding by the time I woke up. All three of the guys in the box had been catapulted out when we hit the curb. One had landed in a newly plowed field. The second landed in the branches of the second tree. The third was thrown into the air and managed somehow to land on his feet. He actually saw the car hit the second tree. All three walked away with minor injuries. Frank was bleeding from a cut over his eye, but was apparently alright.

It fell to my lot to find a phone and call Dr. Bill. He came in and saw what had happened and turning to Frank he snorted, "Why didn't you tell me you were trying to get your pilot's license?"

No one knew just what to do with the car. I suggested we try pushing it down out of the tree, which we finally did. After examining it, I saw that while the radiator was leaking, it would still hold water. I decided to try to start the engine, and to the surprise of all of us, it started.

All the glass was broken in the windshield and shards were lying all over the hood. I brushed them away as well as I could, tied a handkerchief that I could see through over my eyes and drove the battered Model A Ford back to the camp at about 5 to 7 miles per hour. It never ran again, but I managed to get it back on home turf.

When it was all over I went to bed nursing my battered head. I had a bump on every side and there was no way I could lay comfortably. But I had a profound feeling that if God had wanted to take me home, He certainly had a great opportunity to do so. Apparently He had something else for me to do.

49

ESTHER ON CHIMNEY ROCKS

TED ON CHIMNEY ROCKS

BILLY
3 MO. 3 WKS.

JUST MARRIED 1924

BILLY
AT
18 MONTHS

BILLY
AGE
2

MY FIRST RABBIT

ALWAYS A COWBOY

PAPPY BILL & ME ON THE NEW TRACTOR & JIMMY

GRADUATION FROM AHS

CAMP MANNAHATH 1951

Back Row 4th From Left Next To Vince (Bud) Porte

The Years at PBI and a Bride

I graduated from Altoona High School in the upper one third of the class which, considering my student record until then was pretty remarkable. Furthermore, after the experience at camp that summer, I was determined to be used of God. My senior year I was vocal about my Christian faith. I joined the Bible club at the high school, was elected President of the youth group at church and attempted to start another Bible study group with some friends from Hollidaysburg.

Everything had changed in my life. I wanted more than anything to learn the Scripture and I admit I sometimes sat in class and daydreamed about getting to Bible School. I didn't know anything about evangelical schools at the time, but as I met college kids home for holidays I listened to them talk about the colleges where they were going.

There were twin boys who attended Wheaton College in Illinois. They were members of a group called, The Navigators. They earnestly tried to disciple me in the days after my sickness and I was inclined to think about Wheaton as a possible choice.

Eventually I was accepted at Wheaton and then Bert Schultz, enlisted several of us to go down and visit the newly formed Philadelphia Bible Institute in center city Philadelphia. The school had come about as a result of a merger between the former Philadelphia School of the Bible and The Bible Institute of Pennsylvania. I went because I could still get a free pass on the train and the girl I was dating wanted to go since she was interested in taking nurse's training at Hahnemann University Hospital just a short distance away.

There were certainly nothing about the school's location, or the building (the old YWCA) that attracted me, but still, I questioned if perhaps God wanted me to go there. I decided to ask counsel of Pastor Stoll. His response was simple. "What do you want for your schooling?" he asked, "Credentials, or the ability to expound the Word of God?" I assured him I wanted to know the Scriptures and be able to preach them. He said, "Then go to Philadelphia – you will get that there. You can go after your degree when you've finished." Following Pastor Stoll's advice I applied to Philadelphia Bible Institute and set my course to go there.

As things began to wind down at AHS, Dad and Mom drove to Florida and later York (Pennsylvania), looking for an opportunity to begin a construction business. Dad had taken an early retirement from the PRR after a light heart attack. Dad's attacks were always related to one thing – frustration. If he got into a situation where there seemed no way to go, he invariably suffered a heart attack and started in a new direction. That's what happened in 1950 so he retired from the PRR and began exploring opportunities.

While they were gone, Grandpa Will became ill, sunk into pneumonia and died. His death occurred the evening before my "senior day" at high school. Mom and Dad were down in York looking at business possibilities. I got permission to leave school and went to the homestead in Hollidaysburg where I tried to help all I could. I mowed lawns and got things ready for the viewing which would be held at the homestead. I have always found that the way to get through a really difficult and painful experience is to get busy, and I was hurting deeply, so I stayed as busy as I could.

The day of graduation I marched across the platform with 625 classmates, reported back to the school, turned in my academic robe, picked up my real diploma and started for York. We gathered at Grandma Singer's just before leaving. Somehow in the conversation, Mother raised the question of thirty six cents which she thought I had spent wastefully. I very foolishly responded, "Well, Mother, it was my money. I guess I can spend it as I please." I was seated at the table and Dad took two steps in my direction. One second later

I was lying on the floor and Dad was standing over me. He pulled me to my feet, held me against the wall and said, "Now apologize to your mother." I did.

I drove to York, and went to work for Dad. He had purchased twenty five acres of land on the East Prospect Road and planned to develop it. He named it Panorama Hills from the excellent view it had.

We moved to Yoe, Pennsylvania not far from where our development was located. Just imagine trying to tell someone you are from "Yoe." I took a lot of ribbing in Bible school over that one. We rented a second floor apartment and did everything to economize, throwing all our resources into the business.

Dad and I usually left each morning long before daylight, carried our lunches with us to cut down on time loss and returned home after dark. There were only two of us and we had a house to build. Understandably, we became tired and, at times, irritable.

One afternoon Dad told me to pick up the cutoffs from the Celotex sheeting and try to use them up. I did. I picked up scraps of different colors and used them to fill a section around a window which faced the road. It was late in the afternoon when Dad saw it and he said something like, "Well, that looks like the deal (translation 'the devil')." I tried to defend it and he became more irritated. Finally he said, "Just take it off." I did – with one swipe of my hatchet.

We went home that evening without a word. The next morning we stopped at the Lumber Company and picked up one additional piece of sheeting. I was almost certain we needed more than one, but was still angry, so I didn't say anything. Once we got to the job and put on the sheeting we had purchased it became apparent we needed one more. I made the mistake of saying, "I could have told you that." Dad said, "Really? You mean you knew I was making a mistake and didn't tell me?" When I answered in the affirmative he simply said, "You're fired."

Now, there was only one problem with getting fired out there. We had only one vehicle, we were a long way from anywhere I would have wanted to go, and so I had no alternative but to finish out the day. We stopped for lunch and sat down to eat. Since we always stopped to pray before we ate, we discovered we had a dilemma – neither of us was in any condition to pray. We looked at each other, began to laugh, apologized, wept a little, prayed over our food and learned to love each other more than ever. I finished the summer working for Dad.

Arriving at PBI was a new experience for me. After working construction all summer, I found it a bit difficult to actually sit quietly and observe study hours. As a result, I tended to get into trouble for things like doing chin-ups on the door transoms or fencing in the gym without proper protective gear. I loved the Bible classes and did fairly well, but I had not developed my study habits to fit the demands of a college regimen.

I had been dating the same girl from the Altoona area when I went to PBI, and she was in nurses training at Hahnemann University Hospital just a few blocks away. We took every opportunity to spend an hour together and it became apparent to me that the relationship was not helping either of us grow spiritually or achieve academically, so about mid year I broke it off. The emotional pain that caused both of us made me determine to forget dating altogether and focus on my studies.

When the first year ended I had applied to work at a Christian camp for the summer. But as I waited the several weeks for the camp to open, I began to think about needing more money than I could earn working at a camp. I went back to York intending to work for Dad, but business was very slow and he recommended I find another contractor to work for.

I was able to hire on with a larger company and worked that summer for a better rate than I ever had made before. I convinced myself that I could be a witness on the job and accomplish as much as I would working at camp. I was soon to learn that was a very naive hope – this was a typical rough and tough construction crew, and although I maintained my own reputation and testimony, I seemed to have little impact on the others.

In order to work, I had to have transportation and my old '42 Plymouth (which turned out to have been a retired taxi cab) was just worn out. As the summer wound down, I had to trade cars. When it was all over, I had exactly the same amount of money to enter school with that I would have had if I had worked at camp. It was a lesson I needed to learn and one I would never repeat.

About two weeks before returning to school I began to have some serious thoughts about the first year at PBI. I had done fairly well academically, and had stayed out of any serious trouble, but I had also fallen into some very bad habits. I spent non-study hours in those great "bull-sessions" with guys in the dorm. I frequently stayed up much later than I needed to and I was not spending the time necessary to really master the material I was studying. Although I had learned, I knew I had failed to really give myself to my studies. As the time became closer to return to school, I determined that I dare not repeat the patterns of my first year.

I became serious enough about my failures that I started getting on my knees and talking to God about it. I cried out, confessing my weakness and my tendency to fritter away my time. I asked for some genuinely spiritually minded companions. I pleaded with God not to allow me to waste the precious opportunity He was giving me.

As I got up off my knees to get into bed I realized that I had spent more than an hour on my knees. The next night it was the same and the third night. For a full two weeks I prayed for at lest an hour every evening asking God to keep me and help me.

As I arrived at PBI that year, I had a suitcase in each hand and was pushing my way backwards through the glass doors to the main entrance when I heard someone call my name. I turned to see Bob Anthony at the top of the stairs. He called out, "Bill Shade, praise the Lord." Then he came down and offered me a hand.

We went up the elevator to my assigned room on the seventh floor and Bob stayed while I got things put away. Then, just before leaving, Bob said, "Let's pray together before I leave." We did, and I knew that God had answered my prayer for a solid friend who was seeking to know God better, as I also was. Once school got underway, I realized that a large number of the guys I had hung with the year before never returned. I am so thankful I did, and that God was pleased to put His hand on me for that year.

I had to work each year to get my bills paid and I arrived early to try for a good job. My first year I had worked for an architect, filing plans and doing various jobs. But though I got my tasks accomplished, I never fully understood what I was doing or why. When I returned the second year I learned that there was an opening for a carryall driver. The school had two (later three) Chevrolet carryalls in their fleet and the driver was responsible to both drive them and keep them in good shape.

It was both an important and prestigious job and I applied for it. The driver not only did all the pick ups and deliveries for the school, but also transported faculty and staff when necessary. It was a great way to get to know your professors.

When I went in for the interview Miss Roebuck, a very large and formidable lady, asked me, "Bill, do you know your way around Philadelphia?" I assured her that I did, and in fact, I did know my way around – within about four blocks of the school in any direction. She accepted my assurances and gave me the job, but my salvation lay in the employment office just next to Miss Roebuck's. There was a large city map on the wall and I could find about anything I needed to do my job by studying the map.

Beside that, I had another reason to study the map. There was a very pretty little lassie who served as secretary to the employment director who sat just across from the map. Having to study that map gave me an occasion to attempt to get a conversation with her. I frequently failed because I learned that this was one very conscientious young lady who didn't believe in carrying on conversations during work hours. Nevertheless, I visited the map frequently. One day, after a particularly long session of looking at the map, my boss suddenly appeared in the office door. "I think you have studied the map long enough," she said knowingly.

By Thanksgiving time I had visited the map often enough to know that there was more in that office that I wanted than directions. Bob Anthony and I were still meeting for prayer every week and sometime around that time I simply said, "Bob, I am going to marry Ruby Sizemore." Obviously Bob was totally surprised. "But you hardly know her," he said. "You've never even dated her." "I know," I responded, "but I have a deep conviction that she is the girl for me."

Ruby was vice president of the class, and a recognized spiritual leader. It was her quiet commitment to Christ and her irreproachable life that drew people to her. The school made her an RA because she was a stickler for rules – not just for others, but for herself. She was totally admired and neither Bob nor I could imagine how or why she might take an interest in me. Most everything she was, I was not. Yet I was convinced – God will do it – Ruby will be my wife.

At Thanksgiving the school held a special dinner and service. I invited Ruby to sit with me and she accepted. I can tell you to this day what she was wearing. Then as we approached the Christmas vacation I told her that I was planning to attend a Word of Life rally at Madison Square Garden the last day of the vacation and invited her to come back early from her home in Kentucky and go with me. I knew she traveled to Kentucky each time she could by bus and I offered to pick her up in Baltimore. Again she accepted.

I really worked on getting the car looking good for that day. I drove to Baltimore starting long before sun up, and picked up Ruby from the bus depot about 8am. We drove the old Susquehanna Trail back to York (no throughways in those days), and I took her to my home to meet my parents.

I've always considered my dad an excellent judge of people and I had never brought home a single girl he had ever really approved of, but this time it was different. "You'd better take good care of this one," he said. "Don't lose her."

I drove to NYC to the rally. I was on the Pulaski Skyway and I was going too fast and whizzed past my intended turn off. The proper thing to do would have been to get off at the next exit and try to get back, but I was afraid of getting lost. I told Ruby, "Close your eyes, I'm going to make a U turn." With traffic coming in all directions and horns blowing, I made a U turn and got off at my proper exit. Ruby was learning a lot about me already.

Sunday of that weekend I asked her to go to church with me. When School was in session we both had Christian Service assignments and couldn't ever go to Church together and there was not real "dating" permitted at the college. We went to Church and I took her to a Howard Johnson's for dinner (that was big stuff for two Bible school kids). Monday passed normally, but I had something burning in my soul.

Tuesday after lunch I announced, "Ruby, I need to see you in the student lounge." She complied and I got right to the point. "Ruby,"

I said, "I want you to know that I am in love with you and I am very serious." Her response was typical Kentucky hillbilly. "What do you expect?" she asked. What she meant (I later learned) was, "what do you expect me to say?" But that isn't what she said. She said, "What do you expect?" and I told her. "I expect you to marry me," I said. She cried and it was obvious I had completely taken her by surprise. "Look," I said, "I don't expect you to know how to answer me now, but I want you to know that I want to marry you and I will wait as long as I need to for your answer." I didn't realize how long that would be.

By the end of our second year Ruby was still undecided. For the summer she was going west to work on a Navajo reservation and I was going to Deerfoot Lodge in the Adirondacks to work as a camp counselor. We agreed that we would focus on our assignments and determine what God was saying in the fall.

Deerfoot was a game changer for me. Even though I had made an exemplary record in school the second year, most of the faculty still remembered some of my shenanigans from the first year and I had little credibility with them. At Deerfoot they asked me not only to counsel, but to be the head counselor of a "section" meaning that I had three cabins, two other counselors and three junior counselors under my supervision.

I was also responsible to plan and execute the overnight hikes each week for the entire group. I was responsible to see that we had enough food, that it got cooked, that we planned our route properly, that we didn't get lost, that the boys had a great time and got back in one piece. It was a large assignment and a first experience for me at exercising leadership and I thrived on the challenge.

In addition Chief Pat (all the staff at Deerfoot were addressed as "Chief"), asked me to teach riflery. I had been in the riflery club in Junior High and had shot under the NRA regulations so I accepted the task. The first thing I learned was that there was no true rifle range – there was only a sand pit where they had done their shooting in the past. I asked permission to gather boards, posts, etc. from where ever I could and build a true range. Chief Pat agreed. I put together a range with a shooting platform and a target wall at the regulation fifty feet.

I also learned that in previous years, instructors had spent a good bit of time explaining how to clean a rifle, or break one down. I figured the guys wanted to shoot. Once the class got started we really began to win medals. I kept ordering quantities of ammunition and the camp office wouldn't believe we needed what I asked for. I had two scheduled classes each day, and as the guys got more interested I offered to take my free time in the afternoon and go to the range and help them finish for awards.

That year we shot more than 15,000 rounds of ammunition and the boys earned so many medals the camp had to mail them out after the season was over. I loved what I was doing and I worked hard at it. What I didn't know was the effect it would have on my future.

When we returned to school I must confess I was a little depressed. I felt like having done my best last year and achieving much better grades, I was still viewed by much of the faculty as a goof-off. I returned not expecting anything to change, but I was in for a surprise.

Almost as soon as I got to the school, faculty members began to come up to me and tell me they heard what a great job I had done at Deerfoot. One of the faculty was a director at the camp and had told all about my exploits during the summer. Suddenly I knew I had at last earned the respect I needed to become recognized as a leader.

The Christian Service department broke the student body into four segments and place students in charge of each segment. I found myself in charge of issuing Christian Service assignments for one fourth of the student body. The arrangement made it possible for me to take many assignments myself and I did some serious preaching that year.

We were in the last year now. Thanksgiving was past and we were nearing Christmas vacation. Ruby had planned to go into medical training and become a doctor and she had appointments at both Women's Medical College and University of Pennsylvania for interviews. I took her to both appointments and she was accepted at both schools. Now we had to decide. What did God want?

We set a go/no-go date on our marriage plans on a Saturday and took a walk up to one of Philadelphia's many beautiful parks. We prayed and we talked and Ruby still did not know for sure. She said she loved me, but wanted to be sure of the will of God. We returned to the dorm and I asked God what to do. I decided, "OK, if she can't make a decision I will make it for her. She will go to medical school and I will go on to Wheaton and then Seminary at Dallas. If, after all of that (about seven years), we still love each other and feel we should be together, we'll get married then."

Once I have made a decision it is very difficult for me to change. We were to meet for lunch and I would simply tell Ruby my decision. Suddenly there was a knock on my dorm door. One of the guys informed me I had a call on the dorm phone. I walked down the hall and picked up the phone to hear Ruby's voice. This was totally uncharacteristic of her. She had never called me in the three years we were at college. Beside that, in about an hour we were to meet for lunch. She most certainly would wait till then to say anything she wanted to say. But she didn't. She said, "Bill, I've made up my mind, I believe God wants us to get married." Her timing was perfect. I said no more.

The final year was our best. Ruby had been on the Dean's list from the very first, but it took me a little longer. Once she had convinced me that the way to excel was not to take a break after study hours and go to the snack shop, but to stay at the books until I was sure I had done everything I could, I finally made the Dean's list too and once, I even made it a fraction of point ahead of her. But I owe her for that. She taught me the discipline of study.

Our Wedding

After graduating from PBI Ruby and I were married two weeks later (as soon as Bob and Caroline Anthony got back from their honeymoon). I had been Bob's best man, now Bob was our soloist for our wedding and Caroline played the organ.

We sure didn't have much money in those days. As soon as school was over I went to work for Dad and Ruby stayed at the school and worked for two weeks. By the time she paid for her gown, she was about broke and I think I had something like $30 in my pocket as I drove up to Altoona for our wedding. Going through one of the little towns along the way I managed to get a speeding ticket, which took half of the money I had.

But God was completely faithful to supply for our wedding. First, Pastor Stoll refused any honorarium for the service (an example I have followed ever since). Calvary Baptist Church invited us to use their auditorium free of charge. My best man, Bob Kantner, housed all of my party (Bob Anthony, Don Shirey, Jack Crawford, and myself) at their large stone mansion up Riggles Gap while Grandma Singer housed Ruby and her party (Bobbie Sizemore, Lois Snyder, and Ruth Kohler).

Ruby and I had talked and prayed about what we were going to do for a honeymoon. We didn't have many options. I told her about the cottage my Aunt and Uncle owned at Spruce Creek (about 45 minutes drive from Altoona), but I didn't want to ask them if we could use it. So we prayed and about a month before the wedding I got a card from Aunt Mid, telling me that she and Uncle Melvin had decided to give us the cottage for our honeymoon as their wedding present if we wanted it. We were ecstatic.

Then there was the matter of pictures. I wasn't sure how we were going to manage that, but my former Youth Director at Calvary was a professional photographer, and he contacted us to tell us he would do the pictures as his wedding present to us.

Of course there was the matter of flowers – they were "necessary" but we had no resources. Aunt Mid came through again. There was a yard full of flowers of many varieties at the cottage. We could go down and cut all we needed and arrange the flower baskets ourselves.

As if that were not enough, Bob Kantner contacted one of the guys from our old Calvary youth group who happened to own a very nice Buick convertible. Bob convinced him to let us use it for the get away car and return it after the reception.

Mom and Dad financed the private reception for us at a little spot on the way toward Bellwood. After the reception we all returned to Grandma Singer's place to open gifts. Wow, I can't tell you how tired I was of smiling and trying to show gratitude for one more pan, or pot. Of course we needed about everything we got, but right then, I was ready for some time alone with my bride and really didn't care much about gifts.

We finally left and began our drive to the cottage, but I was so emotionally exhausted it took me over an hour to arrive. After we changed into our nightwear, we sat on the screened porch and read together the Song of Songs which is Solomon's.

With typical youthful forethought, we had very little with us to eat and as we woke early the next morning I heard a noise and ran to the door just in time to see Dad's car going up the hill out of the lane. When I opened the door there set a box of food and the leftovers from the reception. Thankfully they were thinking ahead even if we were not.

We had a delightful time that week. We went swimming each day in the very cold waters of Spruce Creek which flow directly from mountain springs. We found the road from a park down the way which led up the mountain and traveled to the top looking down on our cottage.

Ruby was wearing my favorite dress with a black peasant top and white pleated skirt (hardly hiking attire). When I stopped at the top and wanted to take her over to the edge of the cliff looking over the cottage (and several counties) I had to go through some soft mountain paths and some fairly heavy woods. She willingly started down the trail, but with high spike dress shoes it was impossible. Determined to make it happen, I simply scooped her up and carried her to the cliff. Then I climbed down the face of the cliff and took some pictures of my lovely bride settled on a rock at the top. We did manage to spend three dollars to visit the Indian Caverns before returning to York.

Many of our York friends had not been able to be at the wedding in Altoona so Dad and Mom threw a second reception just for them. It took place in the basement garage of the home they were living in located at Dad's development, Panorama Hills. This reception was open to all our friends and there were quite a few who attended. We had a second wedding cake, with punch and Ruby and I got dressed up in our wedding attire for the occasion. Like our wedding, it wasn't costly but it was a lot of fun and everyone seemed to have a great time including Ruby who got a second chance to wear her wedding dress.

Looking back over our days at PBI and our wedding we could see God's guiding and directing hand all the way. There were times

I doubted that Ruby would ever marry me, but I held onto a verse of Scripture which read, *"He shall not be afraid of evil tidings – his heart is fixed, trusting in the Lord."* What a wonderful place that is to be.

CHAPTER FIVE

We Go To Wheaton

After completing three years of work at PBI, and getting a bride, I decided to look at Wheaton once again. I had been accepted just out of High School and choose the Bible Institute instead. Now we were thinking about the next step. So I reapplied to Wheaton, was accepted again and Ruby and I headed for Illinois.

I had seen Wheaton briefly the previous spring when over our Spring break Ruby and I drove to Kentucky to meet her parents. It was my first opportunity to see the Kentucky Mountain area and meet some of the missionary ladies who had been instrumental in Ruby's life as a young girl. On our way we stopped by Camp Nathaniel in Emmalena, Kentucky, and visited for about an hour with the Franklins. Garland Franklin was Director of Scripture Memory Mountain Mission which operated Camp Nathaniel where Ruby had spent so many summers. It had been simply a "social visit" and was seemingly nothing more, but would play a large part in giving direction to our lives in less than a year.

From Kentucky we drove to Wheaton, where I got the bright idea I wanted to purchase a house trailer to live in – a motivation that would take me eventually to Montrose, Pennsylvania in the coming months to meet the man who traded in trailers, Douglas Roe. We never got a trailer, but little could we have realized the effect Doug Roe would eventually have on our lives in the years ahead. We stopped to meet Marshall Swoverland, Ruby's former pastor, on the way back through Illinois and began planning to go to Wheaton in the fall.

When we arrived at Wheaton we were without a trailer or any means to get one so I had to humble myself and look for a rental unit. We found one just one block off campus in a house owned by Dr. Eugene Harrison, the head of the Missions Department at the Graduate School.

The house sat on the corner and was a large and very old frame structure. I remember one would open the front door, which opened into a large hallway. Ours was the first door on the right after entering. You opened our door and stepped (or slid) into our two room apartment. I say "slid" because the floor sank drastically from the hallway as you entered our living room.

We had a pull out couch which served as our bed, and one or two other chairs, and a good sized kitchen with a table and four chairs which set beside a double window that allowed us to look out to the small walkway beside the house overhung by forsythia.

Our bath was a shared one at the end of the hallway. There were a couple male students who shared a room across the hall and used the same bath (which kept us on our toes to get in and out as quickly as possible).

Indeed we did have some additional space. The apartment had a large three car garage in the back and I got one of the stalls. Before the year was out I had built a work bench against the rear wall of the garage and installed an old pot bellied wood stove I had scrounged up from somewhere, so I could work out there when the weather was cold – which it frequently was. During the winter the icy air would freeze the moisture in your nostrils every time you drew a breath.

Finally, we shared a glassed-in porch with Edna – a maiden lady who served as secretary to one of the departments at the school. Edna's kitchen door and our kitchen door both opened onto the porch, so Edna came knocking shortly after we arrived to inform us that there was an invisible line that ran cattycornered across that porch. On the one side we could place whatever we wished, but the other side was strictly Edna's. I tried to obey religiously, because Edna had a very sharp tongue and a difficult disposition, and for the sake of peace it was much better to stay on her good side (if indeed she had a good side).

Our first Sunday at Wheaton we attended Wheaton Bible Church where Malcolm Cronk was the pastor. Hardly had we arrived to our Sunday School class when we bumped into Art and Colleen Coleburn, a couple I had met about three years before when I attended a New Years party at Roger Schultz's house in Hampstead, Maryland. As we talked I learned that Art had a home remodeling and repair business. I hadn't found any regular work and was doing just some odd jobs for my landlord. Art offered to take me on and so we worked together until I got so busy with jobs that came my way that I eventually went on my own.

Although we lived off campus we had quite a few friends. There were about thirty students that had transferred from PBI and so we actually were often visited by former classmates. I remember when Isabel Rogato had asked if she could bake a cake at our apartment for Russ Bishop's birthday. We of course welcomed her and Ruby got out all the necessary equipment for the operation. At some point, Izzie decided to look at the batter by raising the beaters out of the pan before turning them off. The cake batter landed on ceiling, walls and floor and we had a bit of a mess to clean up.

Ruby found a job at DuPage Title and Trust Company which was located about eight to ten blocks away from our apartment in downtown Wheaton. To get there she had to cross the railroad tracks which ran through the center of the town connecting it and all other small towns along the way to the city of Chicago. It was a great job and paid well and helped meet our needs during that year.

Academically Wheaton College was challenging but I had learned to study during my Bible School days so I found I could keep up by working hard. However, my real challenge was not the studies but the philosophy that I soon encountered in nearly every class. Ruby and I, at the time, were still set on going to India as missionaries. So I took a course load that I hoped would prepare me for that – Anthropology, Sociology and Geology (the later being my science requirement).

In Anthropology Wheaton used a completely secular text book and we were assigned to read such classics as Ruth Benedict's,

Patterns of Culture — a book that knew no absolutes but considered the concepts of right and wrong, the mere out workings of any given culture. Then we got a dose of Margaret Meade's cultural anthropology. Meade was a disciple of Benedict and the most avid proponent of relativism of her time.

It was evident in each of the disciplines that Wheaton had accepted the general presuppositions of the "millions of years" framework to tell their story of man's development from primitive to modern and the story they told was entirely different from the story of Scripture.

In Sociology we got a similar diet. We learned things about social structures and how to discern real power from apparent power. Some of that I found useful as I later tried to analyze cultures in which I worked. But all of it was totally humanistic and relativistic.

In Geology I faced my greatest challenge. We were presented with Charles Lyell's famous dictum, *The present is the key to the past,* and taught that all that is found in the geology of the earth can be explained in terms of present processes working through almost limitless ages of time.

Lyell's Theory of Uniformitarianism was sacrosanct to Wheaton's Science department and while it is not evolution, it is the necessary precursor to evolution and creates an interpretational grid that insures an evolutionary supposition as the logical outcome of any investigation. My professor was unswerving committed to a Uniformitarian approach to the subject of Geology in spite of the contradiction it held to a biblical approach.

All of this had a rather profound effect on me. I became deeply disturbed as I wrestled with the naturalistic world view I was confronting in the classroom every day. In fact, the wrestling continued even after I left Wheaton, until one day (about two years into my first pastorate), I simply determined that I would rest in the fact that *"Thy Word is Truth"* (John 17:17), and wait for God to make clear to me the things I could not explain.

In addition to all of that, Wheaton was moving away from the Dispensational understanding of Scripture that I had fully embraced during my years at PBI. After all, I had been trained under men like Clarence Mason, William Allen Dean and Dwight Pentecost. I was

Dispensational, Premillennial and Pre-Tribulation Rapture to the core. I began to develop a dislike for Wheaton and a distrust of what they were teaching me – not a very productive attitude for a student.

I remember one day as I sat drinking coffee in the Student Union Building (affectionately referred to as "the STUP"). I was just ready to leave for my next class when one of the Professors asked if he could join us at the table. We of course were glad to comply, but the first words out of his mouth were, "Well, I just read The Blessed Hope: by George Eldon Ladd and I've become a post-tribulation rapturist."

Now I know you should show respect to professors, but by this time I was thoroughly disgusted with the academic snobbery and what appeared to me to be a willingness to reject a strong Biblical position for the sake of getting approval from an elitist intelligentsia. I responded to the surprised professor, "That was a stupid thing to do, but tell me, why you did it." That opened a two hour discussion during which I cut two classes to debate this gentleman. In the end I remember him saying, "Well young man, you haven't convinced me, but I must admit you do know the subject very well."

As we moved toward the end of the semester I became more and more depressed and troubled. I hated going to class and hated studying – little realizing at the time how what I was learning would help give me discernment toward error in the future. One evening as I sat in our living room/bedroom studying, I picked up the third book filled with the same naturalistic garbage and suddenly I broke. I tossed the book across the room shouting something like, "I don't have to wallow in the mud to know that it is dirty!" Then I broke into sobs and began to cry uncontrollably. Suddenly, I blacked out and fainted on the floor.

My poor little bride working in the kitchen was frightened I'm sure. In a few minutes I revived and we talked for a long time. We decided that I needed to see a doctor and so the next day I went to a doctor related to the college. After telling him what had happened, he inquired, "What kind of student load are you taking? How many hours?" I replied that I was taking the maximum allowed by the college (18 hours) and that in addition I had gotten permission to audit a course in Greek." He immediately told me to drop the audit hours and consider cutting back my load even further. I dropped Greek, but continued with the rest of the courses and seemed to begin to fair a little better.

Christmas came and we decided to stay around Wheaton so I went out and bought our first Christmas tree. We proudly displayed it decorated with a string of lights and what few balls we had. Underneath Ruby placed "Skipper," the little black stuffed dog I had given her in Bible school the day she agreed to marry me – it was the best I could do until I could afford a ring. Somewhere we still have pictures of that tree and our first Christmas.

During the break we made a second trip to see Marshal and Dorothy Swoverland. It was winter and lots of snow and ice on the roads. On the way back the car engine threw a rod. I knew from the sound of the engine what had happened but we were in the middle of a three or four hour drive and could hardly afford to be stranded. We prayed for help and wisdom and I decided to try to limp on home.

I found that if I kept my foot on the accelerator, and the engine revolutions (rpms) at one steady speed it would keep running. So the engine ran one speed whether we were stopped or moving and I used the hand break and all the skill I had to coax the car home. Many hours later we drove into the driveway of our apartment and I shut it down. The engine never ran again.

As the second semester got underway it seemed we were busier than ever. I was working as much as I could and the work kept me from thinking too much about my studies. I found I could pass the courses with a decent grade, but determined that I didn't have to believe what I was being taught.

Our plan was for Ruby to start the next year so we were trying to get ahead a bit financially as well. One day I learned that Dr. Ralph Keiper, one of my professors from PBI, and a very brilliant man, was to speak at the graduate school. I determined to attend the session and afterward invited him to have lunch with Ruby and me. Of course Ruby was still at work and knew nothing of all this, but we had learned to be pretty flexible with people dropping in unexpectedly.

Dr. Keiper asked if "Sister Ruby would be there?" Ruby was one of his favorite students and while he might have turned me down,

I was sure he would not pass up a chance to see Ruby. He did not and so we began making our way down the campus walk toward our apartment. Dr. Keiper was legally blind and so he held on to my elbow as we walked.

"Is sister Ruby going to school?" he asked. "No, Dr. Keiper, Ruby is working to try to help me get through this year, but she intends to begin in the fall." He never hesitated a moment. He stopped me dead and looking up into my face he said, "See to it that you do not give her any biological difficulties." Enough said; Dr. Keiper wanted his best student in school.

One of the reasons I persevered at Wheaton was my desire and intention to prepare for missions. Ruby and I had both committed ourselves to go to India in the future. I had come to that persuasion after a long and difficult battle and having made the decision I was not about to be moved from it. But something happened I never expected.

I had been working for Dr. Harrison in a number of his rental units and finally persuaded him to allow me to redo our little place. I widened the doorway between the kitchen and the living rooms and repainted everything. The job had dragged on longer than I wanted and although Ruby was wonderfully patient, I knew it was bothering her so I told her that morning that I would have it complete by the time she got home for lunch.

I got down to business as soon as she left. But I was troubled because I had gotten up late that morning and had failed to have my devotions. I had a compulsion that I needed to stop and just take a few minutes for reading and prayer.

But as I prayed, God showed me some attitudes and things in my life that desperately needed correction. I cried out for forgiveness and knew the sweet sense of His presence and His pleasure. But then it happened.

I had been burdened for southeastern Kentucky ever since we had visited there a year ago. In fact I had talked about the need down there to numerous people trying always to awaken in them a desire to do something about it.

However, while I wanted someone to go, I had no thought of going myself. I had already settled that and I was going to India.

But that morning God began speaking to me about the mountains of Kentucky. Every verse I read seemed to be about mountains. I resisted, but the verses and the strong impression became only stronger.

Finally, sensing that indeed God was redirecting my steps, I said, "but Lord I am not ready. I just can't do it." And then I opened the Scripture and read these words, *"But He is of one mind and who can turn Him? And what His soul desireth, even that He doeth. For He performeth the thing that is appointed for me, and many such things are with Him"* (Job 23:13, 14). There was no answer for that and I surrendered.

Suddenly I realized that I had been on my knees nearly three hours and that Ruby would soon be getting home, and the place looked just the way it had when she left. I hurriedly tried to get a few things accomplished but she arrived to find me pretty much in the same mess I had been in that morning.

I knew I owed an explanation so I asked her to sit down and I recited the entire struggle to her. "I believe God is calling me to southeastern Kentucky," I said. "I hope not," she replied. I'm afraid everyone would still think of me as a little girl and I think it would be hard to minister effectively in the place you grew up." Little could either of us have known how very wrong she was.

"Well, honey," I said, "I promise you that I will not do anything rashly. If God really wants us there He can show us that somehow. But right now, I just have such a persuasion that God is directing us there." We prayed and I went back to work and finished the apartment so by supper time it was all back in place.

But we didn't have long to wait for God to act. When the mail came the next day there was a letter from Garland Franklin, Director of the mission asking us to consider coming to Kentucky to work that summer. When we read it we could hardly doubt that God had prepared my heart in advance. Apart from the experience I had the day before, I would have said, "Thank you, but God is taking me to India." Instead, I wrote and said we would plan to come to Kentucky.

Life is made up of choices and sometimes they require an extra degree of commitment. My intention was to answer the call of Mr. Franklin and go to Kentucky for the summer, then return to Wheaton to finish my work there and let Ruby begin hers. That is not what God had in mind.

I was lacking a couple of credits to graduate the next spring from Wheaton and I had planned to make them up with summer school. Obviously I could not attend summer school and still fulfill my calling to come to Kentucky for the summer so I went to see Dr. Durness, the College Registrar and let him know of my intended change.

Dr. Durness was not happy. "You will not be able to finish next spring unless you make up these courses," he told me. "I know," I replied, "but my wife is enrolled for the next two years and I will have to be here anyway. I will just plan to stretch out my studies and graduate when she does."

"Not possible," he replied. "I am turning away twenty five hundred applicants every semester, you need to get through as soon as possible. Unless you finish next spring you will have to drop out completely" he told me. "Alright then," I replied, "you have made my decision for me. I know what God wants me to do this summer and if I can't do that and finish Wheaton, I will simply not finish." I walked away, not sure what the future now held but content that I had made the choice God wanted and the rest would be in His hands.

Monroe & Marie ~ Ruby's Parents

GRANNY ASHER

MORRIS & SPORT

BOBBIE & RUBY WITH BABY DON

RUBY 1941

1950

1952

PBI CLASS
VICE PRESIDENT

1955

Fairmount Park Philadelphia
1953

FIRST DATE
(Thanksgiving '53)

STREET MEETING

LOOKING
FORWARD
TOGETHER

JUNE 19, 1955

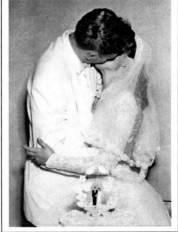

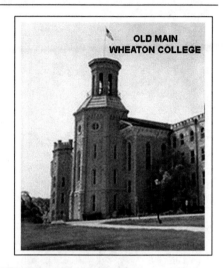

From Wheaton to Kentucky

When the time came to leave Wheaton I was driving a 1954 Nash Ambassador that had belonged to my landlord Dr. Eugene Harrison. It had been all the way to Alaska and back over the Al-Can Highway, but was the newest and biggest car I had ever owned.

Some school buddies and I had pushed our 49 Nash with blown engine to the local dealer. Dr. Harrison had just turned in this car for a new one, and I was able to make the trade for $1,000. Of course I didn't have money like that but Dad offered to loan me what I needed and I would pay him back at the rate of $100 per month. That went well until I met a dear friend from PBI days checking out of school. When I asked why, he told me that he had simply run out of money and could not continue. I asked if $100 would help and he said that it would make the difference in his being able to continue. I'm glad I made that difference because Russ went on to become a professor in another Christian College and influenced hundreds of young lives.

When I realized I was going to be late with my payment to Dad, I wrote and explained what I had done and assured him I would get the payment to him as soon as possible. He responded telling me he thought I had done the right thing and then cancelled the entire debt.

We had accumulated a few things of our own in Wheaton and I needed a way to move them to Kentucky. I purchased a home-made trailer constructed from the steel bed of an International truck and a Plymouth front axel. The truck bed was super – boy did they ever put the metal into those things — but the axel was too narrow for the bed so if the trailer swayed even the slightest, the tires rubbed against the wheel wells. Nevertheless it worked for our purposes.

It made the trip to Kentucky without incident and I had just unloaded it in Emmalena when going down a hill near Mayking, I suddenly felt a bump and saw one of my trailer wheels careening past me down an embankment. I managed to retrieve it but decided to change springs and axels before going to Pennsylvania for another load.

When Ruby and I got moved we went to work immediately at Camp Nathanael. Since we were counseling and working in various other capacities (I did kitchen duty at least one week during the summer), we took all our meals at the camp and slept there, even on weekends when we didn't drive over to McRoberts to stay with Ruby's parents.

I had apparently not given much heed to the words of Dr. Keiper that day in Wheaton, because by mid summer, Ruby realized she was pregnant. We were a number of miles from the little Homeplace Hospital at Airy, Kentucky but that was the closest place we could go and many of the staff were believers. Dr. Martin was himself a graduate of Wheaton College, and Dr. Cameron had been a missionary with China Inland Mission before the communists drove all missionaries out of China. One of the nurses there not only helped deliver several of our children, but became a friend and a supporter and has continued to this day to support us.

About the end of the summer Garland Franklin, our Director, asked me to consider staying on and working with the High School team. He told me that I could meet Raymond Haddix, the director of the team when he came to the camp and indeed I did. It was a memorable meeting.

Raymond was a soft spoken man of the Hills, but in the way of the Hills he let me know that he would call all the shots if we worked together. He told me that I was new and really didn't know a thing and he was native to the area so he would not need any ideas or suggestions. I would just need to do as he directed.

Somehow I managed to retain my composure during the conversation – I drove quietly off the camp ground, but when I hit the highway I was livid. I had never met anyone so arrogant. When I arrived home I told Ruby I could do anything but work with this guy. I later went to the Director and told him the same thing. I said, "Mr Franklin, I love the Mission and I love the work here and I will do anything you ask. I will scrub latrines, and dig ditches, but please do not ask me to work with Raymond."

Mr. Franklin was sympathetic telling me that I was not the first who found Raymond difficult, but he asked me to reconsider and pray about the matter – a fatal exercise. I accepted the assignment.

True to his word Raymond called all the shots even down to telling me how to wind a cord or shift gears on a car, but I soon learned he did understand the Hill people and I came to love our times of working together. I learned a great deal from Raymond and I believe having to follow his kind of leadership was great preparation for what God had ahead for me.

We were able to rent an empty house right across the highway from the camp road at a reasonable rate, but it had not been lived in for several years and was grown up all around. Some of the weeds were actually over my head, but we got them cut down and were able to buy our first push lawn mower. Before we finished the place really looked great.

It was a frame house with a partial second floor. None of the walls were plastered. They had simply used one by six inch boards and created walls and ceilings. Lighting was sparse as well, but we liked the house and its setting. But there was no heating system, and only cold running water in the kitchen sink. There was an old shed out back where I set up my shop and there was an outhouse – necessary because there was no inside toilet. Those small inconveniences were minor until winter came and then they were a bit more of a challenge.

I had preached several times at Ruby's home church and was asked to consider becoming pastor there. I had questioned whether they would want me, since I was an independent. They agreed to consult with someone from the SBC. A week later I met two men from the Convention. They simply wanted my assurance that I would not try to take the church out of the Convention. I was cordial, but said that I didn't know enough about the Convention to make that kind of commitment. In the final analysis, they left the matter with the local church and the church voted to accept me as pastor.

I felt I needed to be ordained and I knew that if we stayed we would have to make a trip to Pennsylvania to get some of the things we left there. So in late August we headed north with the trailer in tow.

Before I left, Raymond had offered to help me, and we welded a different frame under the trailer and attached an International front end axel and springs to it which was a perfect fit and made it a very safe and sturdy unit. I had not done much welding up until that time and we only had one mask which Raymond used. I did manage to find a pair of goggles for acetylene welding, so I wore them not realizing that I had more to protect from the radiation than my eyes. I woke up in the middle of the night with sever burns all over my face. One more lesson learned.

Once we arrived in York, I requested Pastor Ralph E. Boyer at the York Gospel Center to arrange for my ordination. Boyer was an IFCA member and so the examining committee were all IFCA men as well.

I prepared diligently for my examination but the one thing I could not resolve was the timing of the Rapture. Although I had argued fiercely for a Pre-Trib position while at Wheaton, when it came down to honestly examining my heart, there had been enough doubts planted that I could not say with absolute confidence that was my position. I spent half of the night wrestling with it and finally just drew up a very strong Premillennial statement and tried to avoid dealing with it – a very foolish thing given the make up of the ordination committee.

They were satisfied with every answer I gave, but when they confronted me for a clear statement about the timing of the Rapture I had to say, "Gentlemen, if you wish I can give you all of Dr. Pentecost's fifty four reasons why the Church will not go through the Tribulation, but if you want to know what Bill Shade believes on this matter, I can't give you an answer."

The response from the committee was predictable. There was an immediate call to delay my ordination until a later time. Pastor

Boyer saved the day however when he quietly reminded them, "Brethren, we are not examining our brother for membership in the IFCA, but for his eligibility to preach the gospel." On that ground they unanimously voted for approval.

I was always glad they did because I do not know what effect a negative response might have had on my being able to later resolve the question in a completely unbiased manner. What I do know is that within three months after ordination, while teaching through the prophetic significance of the seven Feasts of Jehovah from Leviticus chapter twenty three, the clear distinction between God's program for Israel and His program for the Church became so clear that I resolved the Rapture issue once and for all and have never wavered since.

After ordination I approached the Gospel Center about supporting us as missionaries. They almost at once agreed to give us $100 a month (half of what we were told we would need). Then we traveled to Altoona and approached Dr. Stoll about whether Calvary would do the same. He told me he would meet with the Deacons and let us know and we shortly got the answer that they too would support us for a like amount.

One interesting sidelight to this – Gospel Center did not begin their support until October. Calvary did not begin until November. We arrived back on the Field in September. The next couple months were growing times as we watched God provide. We frequently had no funds, even for food, but we would find a bag of garden produce on our front porch, or perhaps something one of the missionaries had made.

With what we could bring from York in our trailer we now had a new refrigerator, a table and four chairs and an electric stove. We also had a trunk and a couple of Indian blankets Ruby had gotten while working with the Navajo Indians that summer before we were married. We had no bed and for a while we slept on the floor, eased by the packing material from the refrigerator. Later we borrowed two bunk mattresses from the camp.

By fall we were traveling back and forth to and from McRoberts twice a week, about sixty miles one way. It usually took us a couple of hours on Kentucky roads. The Church was struggling – or perhaps that is not the right word – it was dying. On two occasions I made the trip to minister to one person. I began to feel that I needed to spend more time in the community, but then there was the school ministry and I was fairly central to where the other members of the team lived. For the time being we decided to stay in Emmalena.

There were three of us on the high school team and each of us was expected to drive our car one month. We traveled to seven different counties every month – a lot of driving. Then the following month another one of us would drive his car. My turn came in October and we had no money for gas. It was a time before credit cards and we didn't know anything to do but pray. Shortly after prayer that morning, Ruby was going through the pockets on my suit jacket and discovered a twenty dollar bill that someone had slipped into my pocket as a gift. I had forgotten all about it, but God knew exactly when we would need it. I could fill the tank for about five dollars back then, so the money got us through the entire month.

But winter does come to Kentucky and it was getting increasingly cold. Most of the people in the hills heated with coal stoves, but we had no stove and no money to buy one. There was a fireplace in the living room that had been bricked up and a pipe inserted in the flue to accommodate a stove if you had one – but we did not. Further we did not have money to buy coal, but there was an old chicken coop collapsed in the back yard and I reasoned that if I tore the brick out of the fireplace and used the wood from the chicken coop I could keep us warm. One Saturday I removed the brick.

I had to go over to the camp later that day, and although I had washed, the soot was still evident on my hands and the old maintenance man, Mr. Leib looked at them and ask, "Bill what have you been into?" "I tore the brick out of that fireplace," I told him. "Why in the world would you do that?" he asked. "I don't have a heating stove," I said, "and I plan to heat with the fireplace." Leib looked at me and smiled knowingly, "You can't heat that house with a fireplace," he said. "Well, I took those brick out in faith," I replied. Leib chuckled and said, "And you will put them back in sweat." He was right.

Each day as I would leave I would cut enough wood to last through the day, but it was a loosing battle. I remember the evening

I came home and there sat my little wife in front of the fireplace on her Indian rug (which was all we had in the living room at that time). She was wrapped in my Woolrich jacket and feeding the last pieces of wood on the fire. The sight was a reality check for me.

Honey, I said, "I do not think God wants us to freeze. We've prayed about this but it is time we get serious." We got on our knees and cried out to God in our helplessness and need. When we got up we realized it was time to go to prayer meeting, so without supper we headed up the road.

Prayer meeting was held in different homes and this one was at Jerry Pierce's cabin, about a mile up the road. We arrived a little late and there were only two seats left in the circle. I took one and Ruby took the other across the room from me. Before I hardly sat down, the man next to me leaned over and asked, "How are you heating that house?" "I'm not heating it," I replied. "Oh, I'm so sorry," he said. "I have an extra heating stove at home and the Lord laid it on my heart weeks ago to talk to you about it, but I just kept forgetting." "I know why you forgot," I said. "*We have not because we ask not*, and it took Ruby and me until about twenty minutes ago to get really serious and ask God to do something for us. You just responded as soon as we prayed." "When can I get it?" I asked. "I'll be home all day tomorrow," he said. "Are you going to be home tonight?" I asked. "Yes," he said. "I'll be down to get it," I told him, "we are cold."

The stove was not the only thing God provided for us. We had absolutely no furniture except the four chairs that went with the kitchen table. Over the next several months some of the older missionaries would contact us from time to time and offer us a chair, or a sofa. These were always in very poor condition, but I enjoyed the challenge of repairing them and making them look as new as possible. In the next months I glued and refinished a variety of chairs, tied up collapsed springs on a couch and did a little re-upholstering – things I had never done before, but having worked with Dad on so many building projects it all came pretty naturally to me.

At Thanksgiving time Dad and Mother made the trip to Kentucky to be with us. It is impossible to tell how much they helped us. All through our ministry they were ever mindful of our needs and tried to meet them as they could. This time, they not only brought the Thanksgiving meal, but they brought us their former bed with mattress and springs as well. At last we were sleeping in a real bed again. They also brought another large coal stove so we could move our little one into the unheated hallway.

As the winter progressed the outhouse was a real challenge. I had thoroughly cleaned it and painted it inside, but it sat just by a creek that ran very close behind it out of the hollow. On those freezing mornings the steam would rise from the creek and form picturesque webs of ice inside the outhouse. We always had to brush away the icy cobwebs before using the facility. We finally learned to keep an old toilet seat close by the back door and take it with us when we needed to visit the "ice house."

Doing laundry was another challenge. The cold water that flowed from our faucet was not just cold, it was full of iron as well. When it was heated the iron would form as a scum on the top of the water. Anything washed in that water would come out with iron stains the color of rust and they could not be gotten out.

Furthermore we had no machine to do the laundry. Bob and Caroline Anthony had joined us to work in the High schools and they had a washing machine with a power ringer, but no indoor water nor any place to keep the machine. So they brought it down and I fixed up a place in our shed to do the laundry.

I wired the shed to provide electricity, then I installed the little stove I had purchased in Wheaton and found a ten gallon copper tub to heat the water in. Then I purchased a milk filter from a local hardware store. It was in the shape of the very large funnel and was used by farmers to transfer and filter their milk from buckets to milk cans during milking. There were paper filter pads that laid on the seven inch metal screen in the funnel that collected the rust scum from the water.

Once I got a tub of water rolling on a hard boil, I would dip the water out with a bucket, and put it through the strainer into a second tub. The filter would catch the scum. After emptying the first tub I would rinse it and put the strained water back in to reheat it. From there we bucketed it out into the washing machine to do the wash. I had drilled a large hole in the wood floor to drain the washer and the water ran under the shed into the creek (the acceptable way in that culture of disposing with almost anything unwanted).

It was undeniably an arduous process and understandably one that was almost too much for Bob and Caroline who were both city dwellers. It was one of the many challenges that would eventually make them decide to leave the Field after the first year.

The high school ministry was a tremendous blessing and an opportunity. We sang, usually as a trio, although Bob sometimes did a solo with his rich tenor voice. Raymond played his guitar and we took turns preaching. Each of us would bring a particular message for one month and then another program would be put together for the next month. We traveled several days each week, often leaving before daylight and driving for an hour or more before arriving at out first chapel.

Our schedule took us over seven counties to such notable places as Kingdom Come, Leatherwood, Pippa Passes, (named after Browning's famous poem, "Song from Pippa Passes), and Dilce Combs Memorial High School (just south of Hazard). We visited the schools in Harlan County (then known as "Bloody Harlan") and were warmly received in all of them.

These were still the days when schools (and everything else) were segregated in the south, so we covered both the "Black" schools and the "White" ones. Our objective was the same. We wanted to bring a strong God-consciousness to the schools, both to students and faculty where possible. We always made the gospel as clear as possible, and while we could not give an overt invitation, we found ways to invite people to trust Christ and come talk to us later. Our goal was also to challenge students to start memorizing Scripture to earn a free week at Camp Nathanael.

Many of them did and once at camp many of them would come to a clear understanding, of the gospel, receive Christ and have their lives transformed. Those who had been campers during the summer were always our best supporters when we visited them at their high schools during the seven months when we held the chapels.

The one high school that we consistently requested permission to visit and were refused was Prestonsburg High School in Floyd County. It was a large city school, a lot of kids, and the principal had no real interest in anything religious so he consistently said "No," to our offers. But we continued to stop and offer our program each year and interestingly enough, in the fall of 1957, we visited him again, and he said "Yes." Actually what he said was, "You can't come every month, but I have an opening for an assembly in January – you can come and do that one." So he scheduled us to come in January.

It turned out that it was my turn to preach in January. Raymond and I took turns, and I had forgotten all about Prestonsburg. When I planned my message for January the Lord laid on my heart the most straightforward, strong message about heaven and hell, grace, the cross, sin and salvation that I ever preached during those years in the schools.

About halfway through the month, I suddenly remembered that we were going to be in Prestonsburg, and I wondered whether that would be an appropriate message for our very first break-in with these students. Where students were familiar with us, I felt I could be that straightforward, but these students had never heard us before. Furthermore, I reasoned, if I would do something a little softer, maybe the principal would allow us to come back again.

But no matter how I rationalized God impressed on me that He wanted me to go ahead and so the day came, and I preached that strong message. I gave an invitation of sorts at the end for them to at least bow their heads and talk to God and do business with God.

When I was finished, the principal very publicly said, "This is not the kind of message that I expected, not what I wanted, and we assure you that we are not going to have these gentlemen back." Nothing like that had ever happened to us in any other school and you may know that we left that day somewhat disheartened.

One month went by, it was February 28, 1958, and it rained and rained in Kentucky, and the Big Sandy River was full and overflowing. On that fatal morning, a busload of children, on their way to that very high school, were swept into the river. Their bus had come suddenly upon a tow truck on a curve and struck it, causing the bus to go out of control, and careen a short way down the bank into the Big Sandy. There were forty nine people on the bus – twenty seven of them drowned that morning in the Big Sandy in the worst school bus accident that had ever occurred.

I first got word of it as I was returning to McRoberts from a retreat where I had been speaking at Camp Nathanael. I heard the news report and suddenly I realized that most of those children had been in chapel that day, just one month previously. They had heard a clear presentation of the gospel, they had been warned to flee from the wrath to come, and perhaps some of them, on that very day had called upon the Lord for salvation.

I will never know this side of eternity the results of that one meeting, but I will never doubt the importance of the school ministry which God gave me for those eight years, or the necessity of obeying the impulses of the Spirit. We never know, when an opportunity is given us to share the good news of forgiveness and eternal life, whether the one hearing the message that day, may be closer to eternity than we, or they, ever imagined.

CHAPTER SIX

We Begin a Family

The high school ministry lasted all winter and it was a winter to remember. Ruby went one month with Miss Sproul to help minister in the grade schools. Marg Sproul was an elderly missionary who had a great influence on Ruby's life and had both visited her while she was at PBI and attended our wedding. Ruby stayed with Miss Sproul during that time which left me "batching it."

Of course I had my own assignments and I recall one particular morning when I woke late and had to rush to get ready on time. I put the bacon on the stove to fry (over the highest setting on the burner – if a little is good, more is better) and went to the bathroom to shave. That, of course was the first mistake. In the midst of shaving I became aware of smoke coming down the hallway. I rushed to the kitchen in my pajamas, shaving cream still covering part of my face to see smoke billowing from the skillet.

The second mistake was when I lifted the lid from the skillet. That allowed sufficient oxygen to reach the super heated grease and the pan burst into flames. I followed that with the next blunder – I plunge the skillet into the sink and turned on the water. The cold water caused the flaming grease to explode into the air igniting the curtains over the sink. I then tried to remove the still flaming pan from the sink and get it out of the house but found the back door still bolted and only one hand free to move it. After considerable struggle, I got the door open and flung the still flaming pan into the snow in the back yard. I then pulled down the curtains and put out the fire in them, but smoke had cover the kitchen ceiling and walls with a black and greasy scum.

I managed to get myself together and leave for school ministry on time, minus my breakfast or the lunch I would need at noon. That evening I came home to my mess and spent the evening scrubbing the kitchen ceiling and walls and laundering the curtains. Fortunately I discovered that only the small valance between the curtains had been burned. I replaced everything just as it had been thinking I might get away with the whole episode without letting my wife know what had happened, but when she returned and walked into the kitchen, her first words were, "What happened to the valance between the curtains?" I was busted!

Ruby was gone several times that winter, and while I managed to keep from burning any more bacon, the experiences were not uneventful. One time she had taken our car and I was riding with Raymond. She was to come back to Raymond's house after her doctor's appointment and I would wait there for her to arrive – well, at least that was the plan.

When Raymond and I finished our chapels that morning and started back toward his house it was raining. Then it began freezing. I was duly concerned. Ruby had not driven much on ice and snow and she was six or seven months pregnant.

When Raymond got to the town of Bulan which was at the mouth of the hollow, I begged him to let me off there. I could wait for Ruby at the Post Office and flag her down, keeping her from having to drive up the mountain road to Raymond's place. But short of bailing out I could not convince Raymond to stop and we ended up in his driveway.

When we tried to get out and go into the house we both ended up on our tush. We literally crawled up the bank on our hands and knees to his back door. Now I was both worried and angry, but there was nothing I could do but pray.

About an hour later there came a knock at the door. I had not heard a car drive in so we were completely surprised to see Ruby standing there in her high heels. "What happened?" I asked. She told us she had been coming up the ice covered dirt road to the house when suddenly her wheels were going forward but the car was going backward. It had skidded back down the grade and gone over the edge of the road (there were never any such things as guard rails on those back roads), and was suspended on the frame of the car teetering over the edge of a twenty foot drop.

"How did you ever get out" I asked. She told me she had opened the door and realized she was hanging out over the precipice. She managed to swing herself, baby and all, onto a ledge and then, without even turning off the engine she had climbed onto the road and walked in from there. Ruby said the car was so precarious that she was afraid to turn the engine off for fear that even that small change might put it over the edge.

Raymond called for a wrecker and we made our way carefully down to the site. The car was still there and I managed to climb down and reach in and turn off the key. When the wrecker arrived they decided that it was too dangerous to try to pull the car from a position on the road. Instead they anchored a pulley from a tree on the upper side of the road and ran their cable through the pulley to bring the car back up onto solid ground.

I forget now what the bill was for all of that, but I was too overjoyed to have my wife and unborn baby back to stay angry at Raymond. In retrospect, neither of us could understand how Ruby managed getting out and walking all that way, but it was evident that God was watching over her.

As the winter wore on snow turned to rain and the creeks began to swell. It was late February and Ruby was due any time now. I remember it was raining so hard that I moved the car from the usual place just passed the little bridge into our front yard to higher ground. We lost power that evening and so we prepared supper by roasting a small chicken wrapped in tin foil on the coals of our fireplace in the bedroom. We sat there on the hearth and enjoyed our food and then cracked some walnuts and ate them before turning in.

In the middle of the night I heard a noise and turned on my flashlight to see a mouse trying to drag one of the left over walnuts up under the fireplace mantle where he apparently lived. There was enough room for him to pass between the mantle and the stone but not enough for the walnut to get through and so each time he would try he would loose it just as he tried to get it though the space, the walnut would fall to the floor with a clunk and then roll across the hearth making a terrible racket. After sitting there watching the hilarious procedure several times by the light of our flashlight, I finally threw a shoe at the offending mouse and that ended the ruckus for the evening.

The next morning we awoke to find water from the bottom step of our front porch stretching as far as we could see across the valley to the opposite mountain. It covered the bridge, the road – everything. Only the concrete camp bridge over Troublesome Creek could still be seen above the water.

Now we began to wonder what we would do if Ruby went into labor. How would we ever get out? Well, the truth was, there was no way for us to get anywhere. With mountains on either side of us, the long hollow leading upward behind us and nothing but water in front of us, we would have needed a Red Sea kind of miracle had the baby decided to come.

After about a week the water subsided and we saw the roads again. Thankfully the baby waited until March seventh, and after twenty four hours of intense labor, Ruby brought forth our firstborn son whom we named Phillip Joel – Phillip for the evangelist in the book of Acts and Joel for the dynamic prophet of the Old Testament.

Ruby had lost a lot of blood and was pretty anemic after her ordeal and I began buying steaks for the first time in my life to try to build up her blood. The baby was doing well and we took him that very first week to McRoberts for the Sunday service and then for his Grandparents to see.

Baby Phillip loved his grandmother and his mother and any woman that would hold him, but he had some kind of an unexplainable aversion for men. Every time I tried to hold him he screamed. I checked his diaper pins, everything I knew but he would have none of me or any other male.

One night as I tried to hold him he began to cry and to scream. I just sat down with him on my lap with him looking straight at me and said, "Tell you how it is little fellow, I am your father, and whether you like it or not you might as well get used to me. So as long as you cry you are going to lay here and I am going to hold you." He set up a squall for about twenty minutes and finally cried himself to sleep. I continued to hold him until he woke and when he saw me it all started again. I rocked my legs and tried to comfort him but he cried till he wore himself out and went to sleep the second time. I still held him and after about a half hour he opened one eye, saw I had him and resigned himself to his fate. After that we got along pretty well.

Phillip was only about three months old when Ruby discovered that she was pregnant again. Steve was born three days less than one year from Phillip's entrance into this world. His birth was not a "planned pregnancy," but neither was it an unwanted one. We were delighted when God gave Phillip a little brother so close his own age, even though it soon became apparent that the boys were natured very differently. Phillip was always serious and more sensitive than I realized at the time. In looking back I realize I over disciplined him – a fact I have since deeply regretted.

Steve, on the other hand, was natured a great deal like my father. He was always pleasant, and always into something he shouldn't be. He was a constant challenge to his older brother and I'm not sure they either ever really learned to fully appreciate each other.

Both boys were born at Homeplace Hospital and we were becoming well acquainted with the staff there. I remember Steve got a bit jaundiced a day or two after he was born but the hospital staff didn't tell us why and we were too naive to ask.

It wasn't until after Rachel was born three years later, we learned we had a problem. Rachel was a planned pregnancy. I had visited some folks with a small baby and decided that it was far too long since we had a child so this one was intentional. However, she acted differently from the boys and was much less aggressive in the womb. We began to suspect we were going to have a girl and also began worrying about her when she was over due.

I was preaching a week at Kentucky Mountain Mission's camp in Beattyville and Ruby was still in Emmalena. There were very few phones in that area in those days and I had no way of knowing what was happening. I did considerable praying and finally, on a Wednesday night, after preaching at the camp, I jumped in the car and drove the long trip to Emmalena, arriving sometime in the wee hours of the morning. Ruby was still waiting so after about an hour of sleep I jumped back in the car and drove back to do a session at about nine that morning.

When I got back from camp Ruby was still waiting and I took her to Homeplace to see the doctor. Dr. Cameron was on duty and after examination he said we would probably just have to wait. I said, "Doc, she is already almost two weeks overdue. Don't you think you ought to give her something to induce labor?" Well, I had never seen a Brit get angry before, but the red came up in his face in a flash and he turned on his heals and sharply commanded a nurse to "get her ready!"

Within a couple of hours labor began and lasted during the night. I was actually in the delivery room for this one and because they were short handed I helped administer anesthesia. When Rachel was born she was a beautiful little girl but was already showing signs of jaundice. That is when they told us that we had a blood conflict and would probably never have any more normal children.

Within a day the jaundice grew worse and Ruby and baby had to stay in the hospital. There were no such things as Billie Lights back then to deal with a Billy Rubin Blood conflict and the only approach was a transfusion. They told us that Rachel's BR factor had already risen to 14 points and if it got above 18 they would have to transfuse.

Now the problem became really complex. There was no known donor in the area. The hospital was not equipped to do a transfusion – we would have to take the baby to Hazard – and the only donor we could find was a former camper who was in Harlan. Trying to put those pieces all together at the right time with limited phone connections would be a miracle in itself.

Beside those problems there were more. The boys had stayed with their grandparents in Pennsylvania for a few weeks before the baby was due and now Mom and Dad Shade were on their way to Kentucky to bring the boys back and see the new baby. The problem was, we had no way to reach them and no way to tell them we were not at McRoberts but at a Hospital nearly one hundred miles away.

And the situation was further complicated by the fact that I had engaged Carlo Pietropaulo as our evangelist and learned that he and his family were on the way to McRoberts for the meetings that were to begin that weekend, with no way of knowing our situation. They too were to arrive the next day.

We got everything lined up at the hospitals as best we could for possible intervention, then I went to Ruby's room. We sat there holding our precious baby in our arms and prayed for her. But the Lord allowed us to agree on a very specific prayer; "Dear Lord, we thank you for this child and you know we already love her very much. But Lord, you know the future and you know what is best. If this little girl will grow up to love you and serve you, then Lord please heal her and give her back to us. But if she will be rebellious and turn from you, then dear Lord we pray that you will take her now." God certainly heard our prayer.

After we prayed I went into another room to lie down and rest. "Don't go to sleep," the nurse had warned me. "The baby is already at 17 points and she could reach 18 at any time. You need to be ready to move her to Hazard at a moment's notice."

I knelled down beside the bed and cried out to God. "You are not the God of confusion, Lord, but confusion is all I see. Please show me what you are going to do in this situation." I picked up my Bible and it fell open to Isaiah chapter sixty one. I read, *The Spirit of the Lord GOD is upon me; because the LORD hath anointed me to preach good tidings unto the meek; . . . to comfort all that mourn;* *To appoint unto them that mourn in Zion, to give unto them beauty for ashes, the oil of joy for mourning, the garment of praise for the spirit of heaviness*.

It was especially those last words that spoke to me. I was indeed mourning, but I would see God bring beauty, not ashes, and joy not weeping! I wept with joy and gratitude and then lay back on the bed and fell fast asleep.

At 6 am the next morning a nurse came in to wake me. "You can go now," she said. "The baby stabilized at about three o'clock this morning and she will be alright now. She will be a little yellow for a few days, but she will gradually lose that, so you are free to take her home." Later, Dr. Cameron told me that he was glad I had insisted on inducing labor. "The longer she was in her mother's womb the worse her condition would become. If we hadn't done something we would probably have lost her."

Ruby and I were weary but overjoyed. We took the baby home arriving late morning. An hour or two later Grandpa and Grandma Shade arrived with the boys and late in the afternoon Carlo arrived with his family and we prepared for a very intense week of evangelistic meetings. As always, God had kept His word to us and had orchestrated the entire situation so that just on time every piece fell into place. What a God we serve!

CHAPTER SEVEN

From Emmalena to McRoberts

When I came to McRoberts Baptist Church in 1956 I became aware of several things. First we had few people who were really faithful. While I was commuting from Emmalena some eighty miles away, I had, on two occasions only one person attend the mid-week prayer service. Sunday School had been given considerable emphasis, but most people, especially younger people, went home after Sunday School and did not stay for the morning service. Our dear people desperately needed teaching, but as I looked over what had been left behind by my predecessor, I found several thousand leaflets of various kinds almost all on the subject of tithing. It was a legalistic approach and like all such efforts, it produced very little in the way of positive response.

I also learned that Missionary Baptists do not elect their deacons – they ordained them for life. The church had two deacons (theoretically). One ran the Sunday School program and exercised considerable control on everything else. The other had dropped out of church altogether and refused to attend, in spite of the fact that I visited him on several occasions. I was deeply concerned about the spiritual condition of both men, but had no real alternative but to live with the situation as my predecessors had done before me.

One night, about three months into my time there, we held a business meeting and true to pattern both deacons were present and active. I don't recall exactly the question that was before the church but before we could even get it to the floor for discussion the deacon that had not attended a single service since I had been there interrupted me and said, "Preacher, that's always been a matter for the board of deacons to decide."

I could hardly believe my ears. Here is this guy who refuses to even attend church having the audacity to declare himself, and his equally backslidden buddy, the decision makers for the whole assembly. I hesitated a moment and then I said, "Thank you brother J. but this church does not have a board of deacons."

Once it was out of my mouth there was no going back. I really believe the first time I said it, I was simply making an observation. But J. was not content to let it rest there. He stood and said, "Preacher, I don't think you understood me. I said, this has always been a matter for the Board of Deacons."

Now it was past time for mere observations. I looked at him and said, "I'm sorry brother J. but apparently you did not understand me. I said this church does not have a board of deacons." I referred the matter we had been discussing to the church, the church voted and we closed the meeting.

I went home and literally threw myself on my face before the Lord. I said something like, "Lord, I told you I couldn't do this. Now look what I've done. I've drawn a line in the sand and they are going to step over it." I couldn't have been more correct.

By the time I got to the post office on Monday morning the matter was all over town. The new preacher had stood up against the two men that had run the church for as long as anyone could remember and now his days were numbered.

One of those deacons had been a mine boss and was powerful even from his position in the mines. B. was not only a strong willed man, he was as strong and healthy as any man who ever worked the mines. No one could remember when B. had been sick for even a day.

Both of them began to visit former church members and call for a move to replace me. I learned that information from the general gossip around town on Monday. Tuesday, I heard the movement was gathering momentum. Then it happened. Suddenly, and without warning B. was stricken with a heart attack. He was rushed to the hospital in critical condition.

I said nothing, I even tried to avoid the rather obvious implications, but the community did not. There was an immediate reaction of "Don't mess with that preacher, God's on his side."

I visited B. in the hospital, we prayed for him. He later returned to church and at one point I publicly recognized him for the work he had done for the Sunday School, but the influence and power of both of the men was broken. The church simply assumed that "this church does not have a board of deacons."

While we were traveling back and forth from Emmalena twice each week, the church gave us a room in the basement of the church and set it up as a bedroom. We could do our meals on the stove in the church kitchen and use the church bathrooms as needed. There were, of course, no showers, or means of washing so we went up to Ruby's home when we needed to bathe.

We next moved into an apartment in the Union Building. It was a three roomed apartment with a very narrow kitchen in between the front room and our very small bedroom. The only appliance was a small electric hot plate and a bathroom size sink that hung at a 20 degree angle precariously from the wall. There was no refrigeration, so keeping formula for the baby fresh was a problem.

The bathroom was down the hall from the apartment and we shared it with the restaurant. Upstairs was the dance hall and every Saturday night crowds of young people would gather to dance until about midnight. Trying to prepare for Sunday service was a bit difficult, especially when the music changed to the earliest form of what we began to call Rock-N-Roll. Suddenly things seemed to come unglued.

On several occasions chairs went through windows on the upper level and crowds of teens became unruly. Our apartment was on the first floor next to the gravel parking lot. The old building had ten foot ceilings and the windows were about six feet high, covered only with old green window blinds.

The building was heated with steam and sometime got very uncomfortable so we would open the windows to let some cool air in. That's when the kids from upstairs learned a new trick. They would leap up from the ground outside, reach through the window and grab the blind for one instant, then let it go. The blind would fly to the top of the six foot high window making an awful clatter. The noise would terrify baby Phillip sleeping in his bassinet, and he would begin to scream in fright. Several times I ran out to catch the culprits but they were nowhere to be seen.

One evening it got so bad we turned off the lights and got down beside the couch and just wept. It was a difficult time and as I think back over it I wonder how many wives would have stuck it out? Later we were able to rent and finally buy a house in the community. That action allowed us to make our final move from Emmalena.

Of course all of the houses were "coal camp houses", and were constructed as cheaply as possible to house the families of men who were brought in to work in the mines. Each house was exactly like the others. Each had four rooms, each room leading to another so there was no lost space. Every house set on poles and had no basement. Behind each house was a coal house and the very essential outhouse. When the original coal company moved out, the houses were sold to the people for a standard price of $1,400. We bought our house for $1,500 from a man who had moved out of state to work.

Many of the people, after they owned the houses began to put in bathrooms. Often the effluent simply discharged into the creek. Ours was one of those where the former back porch area had been turned into a bathroom and two bedrooms. That was the good news. The bad news was that the house was in deplorable condition. When I first moved there I dragged three pickup loads of garbage from under it.

After we purchased the house I began in earnest to transform it. We had very little cash but when a large home was gutted by fire at the lower end of our camp, I paid the owner $300 for the right to salvage it. We salvaged such goodies as a real furnace with a stoker, real aluminum crank out windows (though I had to replace most of the glass). We even sided our entire house with asbestos siding which we took from that house, and I successfully tore up a hardwood floor and reinstalled it in our living room.

Dad came down with one of the men on his construction crew and helped me enlarge the living room. I re-roofed our house with shingles from the other. Finally, I began to dig under the house and was able to create an entire basement where we had a second bath room, our laundry, the furnace with stoker, a workshop for me and a large recreation room complete with fireplace. We had one of the finest houses in the camp and had done it using used materials.

When we began our work with the church I wanted to start ministering to the young people. They had not had anyone working with them for some years and the spiritual condition I found them in made that evident.

I can't forget the first time I gathered them in our living room. We were still in the apartment at the Union Hall. As I recall there were four or five and they were all girls and all in High School. They came in and one of them sat down, threw her legs up over the arm of the chair and kicked her shoes across the room. I decided I had my work cut out for me.

We tried to work with that first group and I believe we got as far as knowing that they were trusting Christ for their salvation. If any of them had not been baptized, I eventually baptized them. But as far as long term commitment, a life lived out for Christ – it was just not there.

I had my highest hopes for Ruby's sister Shirley. She had been to camp Nathanael, had learned Bible verses, and even went through the Leaders in Training Program. But Shirley had other interests as well. She was an extremely attractive girl and a cheer leader for the High School football team. I knew she had been dating a top football player from Whitesburg, but that's all I knew – all I knew until I tried to counsel another parent at the church about her son's behavior and she shot back at me with, "Well you can't even care for your own family. Your sister-in-law ran off and got married and you didn't even know it." She was right – I didn't. I came home and confronted Shirley, who was our chief baby sitter at that time, and she denied it . . . "Nothing but gossip and rumors."

I accepted that until the second person told me the same tale, then I decided to find out for myself. I knew that kids who wanted to get married before they were of age often ran away to Clintwood, Virginia, just across the Kentucky line. They wrote marriage licenses over there without any proof of age and performed the ceremonies right on the spot for a fee. I called the Clintwood Courthouse.

"Can you tell me if you have on record a marriage license for a Shirley Sizemore and a Ronnie Frazier," I asked. A few moments later the clerk affirmed that they did. "Make me a copy," I told them. "It will cost you a dollar," the clerk replied. "I don't care what it will cost, just make it and I'll pick it up this afternoon," I responded.

That evening I confronted Shirley again. "I'm asking you one more time, did you and Ronnie run away and get married?" She assured me they had not, showing a little irritation that I had asked again. "Then can you explain this to me?" I asked, reaching into my pocket and producing her marriage license.

Thankfully, Mother Sizemore knew what had happened and insisted that Shirley stay at home and finish High School. Ronnie was allowed to visit her on the weekends but that was the extent of things until she graduated. I learned to dearly love them both, but any hopes I had for Shirley to devote her life to Christian service were dashed.

As the first group of teens moved beyond High School we found ourselves working with a younger group. We had already been pretty active with this bunch during their formative years in Junior High and even younger. We had sponsored events like Halloween Parties, Vacation Bible Schools, Day-Trips. I had a stake-bed International truck and I used to put hay bales in the back and transport the kids all over several counties – it was legal back then. We did everything we could think of to reach the kids. We had treasure hunts that ran us and them from one end of the little town to the other. We followed with regular Bible study times with games afterward. This new group began to show some genuine spiritual response.

We put on special Christmas programs and one very impactful drama on the life of Lottie Moon, early missionary for the Southern Baptists. The lead part was played by Eileen Williams who had made a strong commitment to Christ. I really thought perhaps she would follow in Lottie's steps.

But Eileen's father was unsaved. One of the most pleasant men you could meet, James Williams had served overseas in England during the war and brought an English war bride home with him. He and Doris had a whole raft of girls, and Doris and the girls had all come to know and trust Christ. But James was a holdout.

One day James stopped by the church on his way from work in the mines to watch as I and several of the men swung a large steel baptistery through the opening we had made by removing a double set of windows from the church. The baptistery had been welded by Creight Hall, who was another friend I dearly longed to see come to Christ.

The project of getting that twelve foot long steel tank into place was notable enough that we had attracted considerable attention and James stopped to see the action. When we explained what we were doing, I commented, "And you are the first person I want to see use this baptistery." James had laughed, but I reminded him that all his family were going to heaven, he needed to come to Christ so he could go as well.

He didn't dispute me, but gave me an answer as he walked away that went something like, "Well, you never know preacher, you might baptize me one of these days." I did not. That very night James died of a sudden heart attack. Ruby and I took some of the girls home with us the next day and tried to be as helpful as we could through the funeral and in the days after.

But I was young, and really had no idea how very devastating the loss of a father could be to a girl like Eileen. Neither did I realize the natural tendency of every one of us to blame God for the things in our lives that we don't understand and seem to us so wrong.

I stood by helpless in the days that followed and watched Eileen's whole demeanor change. Her deep devotion to the Lord had cooled and even her appearance began to reveal that there was a battle going on inside. Ruby and I loved Eileen and I only wish we had been older and wiser – perhaps we could have helped her through her heartache. Eileen's interest turned to boys and she married not long after that and although I never doubted her salvation, I had so wanted to see her yield her entire life to God.

But God was working and with all that was happening among the youth the work in McRoberts was growing and we were encouraged and energized. It was about this time that another door opened very unexpectedly.

CHAPTER EIGHT

Radio – the Beginnings

The local radio station had a fifteen minute morning devotional program as part of their public service commitment that was shared by various pastors. I did not get in the rotation since I did not belong to the ministerium. But then the holidays would come when pastors got very busy and they did not want the extra burden of doing a broadcast, and so the station manager began calling on me to do those weeks.

He had gotten to know me because I was interested in the lack of available Christian broadcasts over our local stations. The Church of Christ was there several times a day with their doctrine of essential baptism, and the rest was pretty much a wilderness. I had convinced the local station to carry the Old Fashioned Revival Hour broadcast each Sunday afternoon. I had to actually make the contact and see that the large hour-long recorded disks arrived. Those discs were about 18" in diameter and would only fit on a professional studio turn table. I had also gotten a syndicated daily broadcast to air but it was more "conservative" than Christian. But apart from getting some good programming on, I had no further ambitions as far as radio was concerned.

Then one day in November of 1958, as I completed a devotional program over the Thanksgiving season, the station owner approached me. His name was Hillard Kincer and he not only owned the largest hardware business in the area but was our state representative as well. Hillard said, "Preacher, I've been listening to your devotional broadcasts and I think you need to be on radio. Tell you what I'll do. You can have any time slot you want and it won't cost you a dime." I thanked him kindly for his offer but assured him that with pastoring a church, conducting a high school ministry in seven counties and filling in at Camp Nathanael, I was sufficiently busy and didn't really need another challenge.

But Hillard was not a man to be easily put off. He approached me several more times – one time in which I had the liberty to talk to him about his own relationship to Christ. Assured that he was saved, I finally relented. "Alright," I said, "I will give it a try. I'll come on the first Monday in January (1959) and I want the 4:45 time slot right before the afternoon news." Hillard agreed and I went back to plan for a daily broadcast.

I was still ill at ease about the matter, because I knew it would be tremendously demanding and confining. So I set my self to prayer and ask God, "If you really want me to do this, please give me someone who will be saved on the very first broadcast."

I began that first Monday of 1959 and did each day through Wednesday, still questioning whether God would show me if this was indeed what He wanted. Wednesday at prayer meeting a new lady came whom I had never met before. After the meeting she told me, "I listened to your broadcast this Monday and God spoke to my heart. Can you tell me how I can be saved?" God had done His part and now I had nothing to do but follow and obey.

I produced a fifteen minute broadcast every day Monday through Friday for the year. During that time the Lord provided me with a piece of professional recording equipment and I rigged up a studio table with a turn table to play records. The broadcast produced an unbelievable response. I was invited to preach evangelistic meet-ings. I was recognized by local people wherever I went. Many doors of opportunity were opened to me as a result.

I usually used the three point outline of the message I had preached on Sunday to do Monday through Wednesday, covering about one point each day. Then Thursday I did a news program that covered events that were significant and that touched upon religious issues. That became the most controversial broadcast I made. Then on Friday, I would teach the International Sunday School lesson. I disliked these because they skipped around all over the Bible and never really covered anything well – and I used to say so while I was teaching them. But I also knew that scores of Sunday School teachers would be using that lesson the next Sunday, and if they listened to me, I knew they would present it in a little different fashion. It became the most popular broadcast I did.

Suddenly, one year into broadcasting my patron died. Hillard suffered a sudden heart attack and went to be with the Lord. He was a member of a fairly liberal church and his wife Alma wanted a clear proclamation of the gospel at his funeral so I was asked to preach. Alma had become one of my most faithful listeners and some years later she went with us to the Holy Land with a tour I put together (but that is another story).

Of course, Hillard's death meant change in ownership for the station and it didn't take long for me to find out the direction things would go. The new station manager told me he was planning to change all the current broadcasts so I would be finished as of that moment. I pled that I had only one day left to finish a full year and to complete the current week, so I asked if he would allow me one more broadcast so "I can say goodbye and sing my swan song." He agreed, so I came down to the studio to do the broadcast live. However, I forgot to say goodbye and I forgot my swan song, and just went ahead and did my regular broadcast.

As I stepped out of the studio the new owner was there to meet me. "I've changed my mind," he said. "I want you on every day, and that includes Saturday." I was both thankful and fearful. I was having all I could do to keep up with five days and to add a sixth? I thought for a moment and asked, "Wouldn't Saturday be a good day for a children's broadcast?" "Yes it would," he said. "Can you do that?" "No," I answered, "but my wife can." "Good," he replied. "I want her to start tomorrow." "You know I don't pay for radio time," I said. "Yes, I know," he replied – "but I want you on anyway."

I went home and gave Ruby the good news. "He wants me to continue just like before and there will be no charge." "That's wonderful," Ruby responded. "Yes," I said and one more thing – he wants you to do a children's program every Saturday beginning tomorrow." Sweet submissive wife that Ruby is, she accepted the challenge and we began to put together the program that for the next twenty years would be known as *Aunt Ruby's Story Time for the Boys and Girls*.

In retrospect, we know of more children who came to Christ through that program than anything we ever did. We had over 3,000 who joined the "Birthday Club" and received a gospel booklet every year on their birthday. Each week, our little "Christian Chipmunks" would announce their names and sing happy birthday to them. Years later I met one of them when I was speaking at Liberty University. She told me she was from the Virgin islands and had heard the broadcast on WIVV out of Puerto Rica. She had come to Christ through Aunt Ruby's program.

The Effects of Radio in Kentucky

Radio has a profound effect on a ministry. Especially was that so when there was little else available. It was not long before I found myself being a household name. It seemed everyone was listening. The men would get out of the mines about four thirty, and start home. They typically set their dial to get the five o'clock news and I preceded it, so many of the men listened to me every day either by accident or by choice.

One of the more interesting stories was that the local Catholic priest listened as well. Of course the broadcast was the very time he was in transient driving the school bus full of children from the Parochial school. In order to listen to me, he had to listen on a radio he had installed in the bus. Of course, all the children who were on the bus listened as well.

I did some pretty controversial programs on my Thursday broadcast which covered current religious news and events in the light of Scripture. It seemed there was no end of news that touched in one way or the other the Roman Catholic Church and its doctrine of salvation by sacraments and works. I took full advantage of every opportunity to expose those situations and present a biblical perspective.

Obviously that angered the priest and on several occasions I was notified that he had written letters to the FCC in Washington, DC to try to have me put off the air. Each time I answered the charges with a full disclosure of the facts I had covered and what I had said. In each case the matter was simply dropped.

Finally, the priest could take it no longer. I'm not sure why I was actually at the broadcast studio on that particular day but as I completed my broadcast a bus load of school children arrived outside the studio. The enraged priest got off the bus and confronted me as I left the sound booth. "The bigger the lie, the more people believe it," he exploded.

Now usually I am very slow to think of a proper response, but somehow that day I had an immediate reply. "I can accept that," I said. "How many Catholics are there in the world?" Well that got his attention.

After about fifteen minutes of back and forth, I made this observation, "Have you noticed that in this discussion you and I are coming from two completely different perspectives? I reply to you by quoting what the Scriptures say and you respond by saying, "Yes, but it is reasonable." I rely on Scripture and you rely on reason. St. Paul said, "*For in the wisdom of God, man by reason knew not God.*" The priest immediately responded that "Aristotle came to know God by reason" (which was, of course, not true – he merely reasoned to the likelihood of there being a God).

It was time for the clincher and I responded, "Are you contradicting what God said? *To the law and to the testimony, if they speak not according to this word, it is because they have no light in them*" (Isaiah 8:20). That ended the matter. My priest friend puffed three times as if he wanted to say something, then suddenly turned and went back to his bus.

After my first two years with WNKY in Neon, the station decided that it was time for us to begin paying for our radio time. It also became increasingly evident that the Whitesburg station WTCW was gaining the ear of many of the people in the area. They had increased their AM output and then added FM placing their transmission tower on the very top of Pine Mountain. I approached Don Crosswaite, the owner about broadcasting with him.

Don actually wanted our broadcast because he knew we had many listeners and while he too made us pay for radio time, the cost was not much different and so we moved to WTCW AM and FM. That dramatically increased our coverage. How important was that?

I remember doing meetings in the Millstone area. When I did evangelistic meetings anywhere, I made it my goal to visit every house in the area, inviting people to the meetings and leaving some gospel literature behind. That particular morning I had climbed to the very top of the hollow when I spotted one last house far up through the trees.

As I approached the house it became evident that it was a very poor family. The house was in very run down condition with cardboard covering missing windows and sections of the outside. It was a typical mountain setting with the front of the house up on high posts and the back setting on the ground. The first thing I noticed was an abundance of very young children running around outside – some of them with only a shirt and several who were stark naked.

I climbed up onto the porch and knocked at the door. A young woman came to the door, her head wrapped in a bandana wearing a well worn dress and in her bare feet. I greeted her and when I told her who I was she began to cry. "What's wrong?" I asked. "Oh, preacher, you are the only church I have. I never get out of this hollow – I can't leave the children and the only way I get to hear preaching is by listening to you." I had prayer with her and tried to be as encouraging as I could, but as I turned to go back down the mountain, I determined I would keep broadcasting as long as I could for people like her.

By visiting schools, preaching in various places and broadcasting daily over the radio, we became well known to the area and there was hardly a business or a home I could go into that didn't know who I was. I was also known to the preachers and not popular with many. I confronted the Catholics with their sacrament based system of works, the Campbellites (Churches of Christ) with their version of Galatianism called "essential baptism", the Pentecostals with their "signs, wonders and miracles" that were neither signs or miracles and the Masons with their secret system that comes right out of pagan Babylon. I preached a strong message of grace and faith and assurance and a life separated unto God, and the large outreach of our broadcast made life a bit uncomfortable for those whose teaching or lifestyle was contrary to those things.

The time came when the ministers of the area decided to form a county-wide ministerium. They had their first meeting and though I knew about it I had no plans to go. Shortly after the meeting however I receive a phone call from the man who had been appointed clerk, asking if I would consider coming to the next meeting and bringing a message on the basis of fellowship and union. I had already been thinking about that just knowing what was happening, and I immediately told him that I would.

When I brought that brief message I told them that while we could and would doubtless disagree on many issues, there were certain non-negotiables that were so essential we could not have real fellowship or unity without agreeing on them. I listed them as three: First, we must agree that the Bible is the inspired Word of God authoritative for doctrine and practice, for without that we would be hopelessly without direction. Secondly, I said that we must agree on both who Jesus Christ was and is, and on what He accomplished on the cross. We must agree that He is the virgin-born Son of the living God and that His substitutionary death on the cross and His subsequent resurrection paid the sin debt of the whole world.

Finally, I declared, we must agree that Salvation comes to man by grace through faith alone apart from any work or sacrament. "If we can agree on those very basic and essential things, we have a basis for fellowship and cooperation," I said. Of course I knew I had cut across the grain of liberals, sacramentalists, essential baptism proponents, the *Jesus Only* (Anti-Trinitarians) crowd and more – but I had been able to declare the truth and I was thankful for that. I didn't have long to wait for a reaction.

Before I got to my seat a liberal Methodist pastor was on his feet shouting, "That's Baptist doctrine. I believe in Jesus but I don't believe the Bible is inspired." I responded only once during the debate and it was to him. I said, "If you don't believe in the Bible and the Jesus it sets forth, what Jesus do you believe in?" After that it got loud and it was quite evident I had touched the sore spots. However, one dear Pentecostal brother, stood up and said, "You said that he was preaching Baptist doctrine, but I believe all those things and I'm not Baptist."

Well, it was obvious by my conditions we had little in common and no real ground for union. They decided my standards were too controversial, but they went ahead and eventually formed some kind of organization, all without me or my Pentecostal friend who had stood with me.

About a week later I was speaking at Whitesburg High School and the American Legion was there to present a student award. I watched as those old war veterans marched in – some on canes, one without an arm, another without an eye. As they stood proudly to pledge allegiance to the flag of the United States of America, I wondered how many of them would have thought it too controversial to do so – yet my preacher friends thought it too controversial to declare their allegiance to the Word of God, the Son of God and the Gospel of the Grace of God. What kind of soldiers of the cross are we anyway?

It was through situations like that I earned a reputation for being an outspoken fundamentalist. So one evening Don Crosswaite called me. He said, "I want to introduce you to my Brother Ken – he's a radical just like you and he has two radio stations. I'll bet he would love to have your broadcasts on his stations." He was right, Ken and I saw eye to eye on just about everything and my station coverage now went from one to three stations. I was now heard in Kentucky, Tennessee and West Virginia.

CHAPTER NINE

The Through the Bible Correspondence Course

We began ministry in Kentucky in 1956. As I worked among the Hill people one of my concerns was the lack of sound teaching. We had some good SBC churches that had a clear presentation of the gospel, but even there, some of the men who were coming out of the seminaries in those days held liberal views of Scripture, and carried a social gospel. On the other side of the spectrum were the Old Regulars. Those were referred to as the "wind suckers" a rather descriptive, but unflattering term, that characterized their preaching style. They would often cup their hand to their ear as they preached so they could better hear what God was saying, and then, they reputedly repeated what God had said – and God said some very strange things.

At McRoberts Church I had begun trying to teach doctrine by using Dr. Donald G. Barnhouse's book, *Teaching the Word of Truth*. I would adapt the lesson for Sunday school by mimeographing an outline and some questions along with any illustration I thought might be helpful. The adult class loved the studies and the class began to grow in attendance as well.

I had found a very old mimeograph machine in the basement of the church and tried to resurrect it. The drum was clogged by ink that had hardened years before and the entire machine was dirty. I was able after much cleaning and lubricating to get it going, but I never could get the hardened ink out of the drum. Without ink, what good is a mimeograph?

I learned that some of the newer machines were using a paste ink in a tube. I reasoned that I could take that ink, spread it on the drum cover with my finger and then place the stencil over it and print. It worked – after a fashion. I would get about five sheets that were too heavy, about ten that were about right, and then five more that were getting very light, so it was time to apply another layer of ink. It was tedious, but I was excited about the response I was getting.

After working my way through *Teaching the Word of Truth*, I decided to teach the Dispensations – a study that had helped me so very much in my early days and which forms the basic hermeneutic for our Premillennial interpretation of Scripture.

I created a large visual chart for the project and purchased a piece of oil cloth (commonly used over tables at that time), that was about four feet wide and ten feet long. Since I wanted to get started at once, I only painted the first two or three dispensations on the chart for the first week's study. As I gave myself to earnest study, I saw that each of the Dispensations could be analyzed by using six words, all beginning with the letter "R". They were, Responsibility (what God gave man to do during this period), Restriction (what man was forbidden to do during that period), Relationship (how man could approach God during this period), Ruination (how man failed the test), Reckoning (how God judged man's failure), and Remedy (how God exercised grace to meet man's failure). Each week I spend hours on my knees painting the words and figures that illustrated the truth for that Dispensation.

The class really responded wonderfully to the study and continued to grow – some even coming from surrounding communities to get in on the study. But what burdened me was how to reach the wider audience. How to do something that would not affect only my small community of McRoberts, but all of Letcher County and beyond. God made that desire very clear to me one day while I was returning from ministry in the High Schools.

I had about a three hour drive to get home over those old Kentucky roads, and as I drove I thought of beginning a correspondence course that would teach those Dispensational lessons that had impacted my Sunday School class so much. As I thought about it, I reasoned, that there was much more I wanted to teach as well, and the entire spectrum of truth began to form in my mind.

By the time I reached home I was ready to burst. I came in the door, greeted my wife and began to tell her what I believed God was challenging me to do. "I will write five correspondence courses," I announced. "Each course will have twenty lessons – there will be one hundred lessons in all. I will name it *Through the Bible Correspondence Course* (this was before I had ever heard of J. Vernon McGee). The first course will be Through the Bible Dispensationally, the second will be Through the Bible Historically – Old Testament. The third course will be Through the Bible Historically – New Testament. The fourth course will be Through the Bible Doctrinally, and the final course will be Through the Bible Prophetically."

I think I left Ruby a bit overwhelmed and she expressed some doubt as to whether I could actually complete such a project. But I was so sure that the whole thing had come from the Lord, I immediately began to outline and get prepared.

Suffice to say, I did, by the grace of God complete those courses, but doing it demanded about three days of study and writing each week for the next seven years. It became obvious that I could not do the job of producing them on my old mimeograph machine so I began to look for another method. It was that search which eventually led me to the A.B. Dick office in York, Pennsylvania. I was visiting with Dad and Mom and shared my need with them. I was talking about an offset press but didn't have a real clue about the process. I found a slightly used A.B. Dick desk top offset, with basic friction feed for under a thousand dollars at a local office supply.

It was more money than I had so I would have to buy the machine on a payment plan, but when the owner learned that I was from out of state and would take the machine to Kentucky, he balked. "I can't let you have it unless your father co-signs for you," he told me. "Well, I'll tell you," I replied, "I'm sure he would be glad to do that, but I will not allow him to. If you cannot trust me, then the deal is off." I think he was so shocked at my reply that he agreed to let me have it on my terms. And I can say to the glory of God that I was never late with a payment.

I took that machine back to Kentucky with me. I remember asking the dealer what I needed to know about offset printing. His response was, "oil doesn't mix with water." That was it. It is a two part process in which the one element cancels out the other allowing just the parts of the printing medium (or plate) that have been prepared to accept the ink, while the remainder stays wet repelling the ink. Unbelievably I learned to use it and began producing courses and many other things on this rather remarkable piece of equipment.

As I offered the courses over the air the response was far greater than I had expected. It was not long before we had more students than we could comfortably service. I used to refer to the Courses as, "The best kept secret around."

One of the first graduates from the Dispensational Course was a lady who was a retired school teacher. She had earned her Masters Degree in teaching but had never had the opportunity of studying the Word of God. I still have a picture of her somewhere in my archives showing her proudly displaying her diploma. She had other degrees that were far more prestigious from the world's perspective, but for her, it was the most important diploma she had ever received. It was responses like hers that kept me going and motivated to complete the entire five courses.

CHAPTER TEN

The Challenges of a Segregated South

I hadn't been in Kentucky long until I realized that race relations between whites and the black community were much different than I had experienced in the north. I went to school with black students and we socialized freely. Pearl McGee was a lovely black girl with a beautiful voice and an equally beautiful personality. We were friends in high school and occasionally, at school functions, we danced together. I soon learned that was not the case in the south.

All the schools were segregated. "Separate but equal," was the slogan, but the reality was the "colored schools" were far from equal to white schools. I know because from the beginning Scripture Memory Mountain Mission had endeavored to minister to both black and white and so we visited every black school that would have us. We brought the same messages, sang the same songs and attempted to get the kids to memorize enough Scripture to earn a free week at camp during the summer.

Of course camp had to be segregated too – that was just "how it was." Camp Nathanael held a week of "Colored Camp" toward the end of the camping season and a hundred or more young people attended each year.

In our own community it was the same. Actually, practical integration occurred in the mines and both black and white worked together taking out the coal. Many of them became friends and socialized freely on the job, but once home from work intercourse between them was usually restricted to some business transaction.

In our community there was an unwritten law that blacks lived up a hollow named "Tom Biggs." There was a branch of that same hollow named "Little Tom Biggs" and that is where we lived. So we were geographically close but had little real contact.

At camp one year they invited Ruth and Eddie Carter from New England to minister to the "Colored Camp." I was so blessed by their music and message I determined to bring them to my church in McRoberts. So without any approval from deacons or congregation I simply engaged them and announced that they would be with us the following Sunday.

There were a few noticeable absences, but for the most part our people came out to at least give them a hearing. I believe they trusted their pastor enough that they were willing to experience a black couple ministering in a southern, lily-white church.

Things were a little "stiff" for a few moments at the very beginning, but as soon as Ruth and Eddie began to sing and minister our people were delighted. They immediately fell in love with them and wanted them to stay for the evening service as well. However they had an appointment in Virginia and had to leave after lunch.

It was late in the afternoon and I remember begging them to stay for supper. In those days places to eat in the Mountains were few and far between and not always very desirable. After assuring me they had to go, I said, "Well Eddie, you are going to have to eat somewhere and I don't know a restaurant this side of Abington, Virginia I could recommend. There is a place just as you are leaving Abington driving north that is nice and reasonable," I said, "and cleaner than most." "Will they serve me?" Eddie asked, with obvious sincere concern. It was a question I had never considered, because I never had to and just the thought of it made me angry! To imagine my friend and dear brother in Christ being denied access to a restaurant cut me to the heart – but I simply didn't know how or what to answer. "I don't know," I admitted. "Well, we'll just keep going," he said in a friendly tone, "we'd rather not be embarrassed." It was a situation I would never forget and one which helped frame my desire to do more for the black community.

The next summer I realized that, while all the churches held Vacation Bible Schools for the white children, no one held a VBS for blacks. The Lord convicted me that it was a situation that had to change, so, after conducting a week long VBS for our usual white kids, Ruby and I planned a week long VBS at the church and decided to invite the children from Tom Biggs.

Looking back I am amazed that I was able to get away with it. I'm not sure whether it was boldness, or a simplicity that just didn't understand how deeply some ideas were ingrained, but God certainly allowed me a liberty not every pastor enjoyed. I announced on a Sunday that we were going to hold a VBS for the colored children in two weeks and would like to have some help. I could tell by the silence no one was very enthusiastic, so I said, "We would really appreciate some help, but whether we get help or not, we are going to have the school." We did have the school and we didn't get any help.

The first challenge I faced was when it finally dawned on me that the idea was just as radical to the black community as it was to the whites. I suddenly realized that even for a white man to go up into Tom Biggs usually meant either he was serving a warrant or trying to collect an unpaid bill. In either case he was an unwelcome intruder and his very presence could be a bit intimidating. I tried to decide how to change that. I think the Lord gave me the perfect solution.

My two boys were about four and five years old. I decided to take them with me as I went door to door trying to convince parents to trust me with their children. A man with two small boys is not much of a threat to anyone, and their presence seemed to help give parents assurance that I knew how to care for children. In any case, I was courteously treated and got to meet people I lived close to but never had any connection with. VBS was to start on Monday.

Nine o'clock Monday morning and I was ringing the church bell and playing some lively music over the PA system mounted in the bell tower. No one came. About nine thirty, several children braved the entirely new idea and showed up. Ruby and I had planned to split the groups – she would take the younger ones outside for games, while I taught a Bible lesson to the older ones in the church. Then I would take the older ones downstairs for crafts while Ruby taught the younger ones upstairs. At least that is what we planned, but the

119

first day we had all of eleven students – so everyone followed the same schedule.

One of the things we planned was to make some little "sailor caps" out of some white poster paper. We just cut the paper in strips and stapled it to fit each child. It was such an insignificant thing – who could ever have predicted it would accomplish what it did.

Those eleven children had a wonderful time, but the best thing was the hats. They wore them shining brightly on their little black heads and went up through town singing some of the songs they had learned. We were a little discouraged but thanked the Lord for those who came and prepared for the next day.

The next day came and with it exactly twenty two kids. We were able to divide them up for the classes. But one thing they all required. They all wanted a paper hat – so we did it again.

The following day there were forty four. I know that sounds like I'm stretching it but honestly we counted. It doubled every day till the last day and we had over eighty, but not quite eighty eight. We had kids from very young to teenagers but everyone required a hat and most wore them faithfully every day.

One day Ruby was teaching the younger kids and I was downstairs with the older ones doing crafts. The girls were lacing some Tom Thumb leather purses we had cut out from leather scraps left over from Camp Nathanael. One of the older girls was having difficulty with her stitching and I took the purse and demonstrated a couple of stitches for her so she could see how it was done. She thanked me and went back into the next room.

Those Sunday School rooms were divided by very thin walls and you could hear anything that was said even in a whisper. And here is what I heard. She whispered to her friend, "I touched his skin." "You did!" her friend responded. "What did it feel like?" she asked? "It felt just like ours," said the girl whose purse I had helped with.

The full significance of that story illustrates so well the almost total lack of understanding between the two races and suddenly a black youngster knew that while I was a different skin tone, I was a person just like she was.

But it wasn't improved race relations that motivated us. It was the spiritual condition and needs of those children and I'm happy to say that a sizable number of them understood the gospel and made life changing decisions to receive Christ that week.

At the closing program Friday evening a handful of the parents actually ventured out. The children all were wonderful. They recited their Bible verses, showed off their handcraft and several of the older ones actually gave testimonies of their new found faith in Christ.

Interestingly, several of the ladies from our congregation ventured to the closing program as well, and were so overwhelmed by what they saw and heard that afterward they told us, "We are so sorry that we didn't help you. This was a truly wonderful idea and if you ever do it again, you can count on us."

The VBS also built some lasting relationships with those youngsters. Two of them used to stop at our home and Ruby would help them with their homework. They were from the same household up the hollow, but had no resident father (in fact had different biological fathers), and there was no one to take interest in them. They also became friends with our boys, who were a little younger, and they played together from time to time.

Then one day the following summer I noticed that they weren't coming by any more – and I also noticed that the wagon my boys owned, and parked in the carport was missing. Several weeks went by and I was on my way down to Neon one day in the car when I glanced out the window and saw the same two boys walking up the hollow – pulling a wagon that look strangely familiar. They had changed the wheels for some different ones to disguise their theft, but I easily recognized the wagon as belonging to my boys.

"Hi boys," I greeted them as I pulled the car to a stop. "I haven't seen you for a while, where've you been keeping yourselves?" They stammered and stuttered to get out an answer, but it was obvious they were as guilty as sin and very uncomfortable. "Nice wagon you got there," I continued. "Where'd you get it?"

One of them began something about his brother finding it. I listened for a moment while they squirmed, then I looked them square in the eye and softly said, "Let me tell you where you got it. You got it in my carport and then you changed the wheels so I wouldn't be able to recognize it. But I do recognize it, and I'll tell you what I want you to do. You take it back home and get the right wheels back on it and then bring it up to the house and put it back in the carport where you got it. Do you understand?" They assured me they did and I finished, "Boys, I'm on my way to Neon. I will not be gone long. When I get back the wagon had better be back in the carport with the right wheels on it. OK?" They nodded affirmatively and hurried up the road. An hour later, when I returned from Neon, there sat the wagon in all its glory, proper wheels and all. Later, during the days of racial tension that began before I left the mountains, I always got the deepest respect from the black youngsters in the community.

There are lasting results sometimes to such God ordained ventures. A few years later when I was working in the inner city of York, Pennsylvania, and had a particularly difficult weekend retreat where we saw little results and a lot of conflict, I knew I needed to somehow encourage my staff on Monday morning and I wasn't just sure how to do it.

As I left the house that morning on my way to the staff meeting I glanced at the newspaper on my desk. We continued to get the Kentucky paper delivered to us long after we had left the mountains, just to keep track on happenings there. On the front page of that paper was a picture of a face I recognized and remembered. It was the face of Jackie Cook, one of that group of eleven youngsters who had the courage to attend the first day of the white man's VBS. Jackie had been one of the first to receive Christ that week. Later, after the school, Jackie used to come to our house and Ruby would help him with his homework because there were no electric lights at Jackie's house and no one to show that interest in him.

Under Jackie's picture was this caption; "Jackie Cook Drowns in Jenkins Lake." I was glad that morning that Ruby and I had made the effort to have that VBS for black children. It had been a hard and strenuous week back then, but I was more than rewarded to know that one dear child was in heaven and that I would see him some day because we did what we did.

That was the message my weary and discouraged staff needed on that bleak Monday morning as well. It is worth it all, no matter how hard it is, if one soul finds Christ and is given a home in heaven.

From time to time Ruby and I still get back to McRoberts and have an opportunity to preach, and it is always a special joy when some dear black family attends and a mother or father tells us that they were in our VBS years ago. If I had my life to live over again, there is nothing I would rather do, than just what God has allowed me to do by His grace.

CHAPTER ELEVEN

McRoberts For Christ Crusade

By 1959 things had begun to turn around at McRoberts Baptist Church. I had taught my way through the book *Teaching the Word of Truth* by D. G. Barnhouse, in Sunday School and had begun a Dispensational Study. Interest had grown and I had a class of twenty or more people every Sunday morning.

One of my early projects was to build a library at the church. I had a Colportage relationship with several book companies and could get up to forty percent off the cost of books. When the High School burned at Fleming, I had offered to help them rebuild their library with donated Christian books.

I approached Miss Ruth Huston, missionary and one of the heirs to the Lukens Steel fortune. I requested a grant of three hundred dollars to stock two school libraries and our church library and Miss Huston responded positively. So our people began to read books like Ironsides *Commentaries*, Owen's *Abraham to the Middle East Crisis* and other books that got them into the Word of God in a new and fresh manner. As a result, spiritual growth began to be evident. The people became excited about the Word.

I talked to the people about communion. The church had been observing it once or twice a year depending on who was pastor at the time. I challenged them to consider observing it every Lord's Day as I believe the churches did in Apostolic days and as I had learned to do at Calvary Baptist in Altoona as well as at the York Gospel Center. The church agreed and soon they would not think of coming together without the Lord's Table as part of the worship service.

Then I suggested something else that was totally radical – no offerings! We would place a box and a plate at the back of the church and people could give freely as the Lord led them. Certain that we would soon have to shut the doors for lack of funds the people nevertheless agreed to try the experiment. The offerings began to grow almost at once and we used the "Deacon's Box" to support widows and the needy.

We established for the first time a Constitution for the church that could define what we believed and how we conducted our business. This was a new idea for them and we formed a committee of our best leaders and met with them on a frequent basis. We ratified the document section by section before bringing it to the church. It was accepted unanimously. The new Constitution set up the standard for a board of deacons and determined how deacons would be chosen and the length of term they would serve.

As the year 1959 began, I was ministering to a different church. They were excited, growing, witnessing, organized and I felt it was time to try to reach the area for Christ. Some of the biggest growth was in the work with the young people. Ruby and I took every opportunity to try to reach the kids starting from the very young to the high school crowd.

From the first year that I came to McRoberts, some of the older members would ask me, "When are we going to have revival" (their word for evangelistic services). I remember once saying, "We will have revival services when we have something to offer people. Right now this is not a church, it's more of a social club. When I see this church growing and getting serious about eternal things, then I will think about having meetings to win the lost." It had taken more than three years to get there, but now I believed we were ready and I didn't want to do something that was just usual.

As I prayed about it I began to visualize holding a tent crusade. The previous summer Camp Nathanael had invited Evangelist Chick Kiloski to preach the Family Bible Conference over the forth of July. Chick was solid doctrinally and effective evangelistically and I talked to him about the possibility of doing a two-week tent Crusade in McRoberts.

Chick confirmed and suggested he could contract for a tent from Highland Lake Bible Conference in New York. Chick was from Scranton, Pennsylvania and was very familiar with Dick Kruger and Merle Dense who owned a 40 X 60 foot tent they would rent to others for meetings. Of course had I known, I probably could have rented one within a few counties of where I lived, but in my simplicity I accepted the offer for the one from New York.

Merle Dense asked us one hundred dollars per week for the tent and threw in all the seating frames and a truck to transport it. With our other expenses I estimated the entire venture would cost about $500. Now as modest as that figure may sound in today's economy, it was about $400 more than the church had ever put out for meetings. When I laid the plan before our men, they liked the idea, but flinched at the price. "Maybe if we get really good crowds and take offerings every night we might be able to pay for it," was the general consensus.

I then revealed the next part of my strategy. "There is a general perception," I said, "among the Hill people, that churches have meetings to make money. They take offerings every night and plead for money. I do not want to do that. In fact," I continued, "I do not want to take any offerings at all expect perhaps a final love offering for the team." "OK preacher," they responded, "so how do you propose we pay for these meetings?" "I propose the church pay the entire bill," I replied. "That way the unsaved cannot charge us with just being after their money and maybe we can remove that barrier to their coming."

About that time one thoughtful soul suggested, "Well, I guess we could take pledges and see if enough comes in." "I don't want to do that either," I said. "I want this to be so evidently of God that no one can explain it any other way." "OK," they said, "but how are we going to do that?"

I suggested we do the following. First commit ourselves to this effort by earnest prayer. Pray that God will awaken the community and souls will be saved. Then let each of us, ask God what He wants us personally to give. Then when we have the answer, let's obey

Him. "If we do," I said, "I believe God will provide all we need." The men reluctantly agreed, but I can't help but think they thought this preacher a little strange and were not at all sure this experiment would work.

The following week I explained the plan to our people and we set a date about a month in advance to take the offering. One thing I emphasized over and over, "Don't tell anyone else what God is saying to you. Let your gift be completely between you and God." That way I knew they could not get their heads together and try to help God out. In the weeks that followed I thought I could perceive a new excitement and anticipation. Many wanted to see if we could really do this and if God would really come through.

The day came and the offering was taken. I had not preached any special message, the only difference in the service was that a special plate was made available to put monies in for the Crusade. I remember it as if it were yesterday. I was standing at the door greeting the final people as they filed out after the service when I heard the distinctive sound of high heels clicking rapidly against the tile floor.

Minnie Flint, the wife of our treasurer rounded the corner from the sanctuary to where I was standing and the tears were coming down her cheeks. "Preacher," she cried, "You aren't going to believe this, but the offering was $500.05." I smiled and replied, "I wonder who put in that extra nickel?" God is a great accountant isn't He? It was things like that which God was using to transform a doubting people into a people of faith.

I went to the School Board and requested the use of the McRoberts Ball Park for the meetings. After some hesitation, they granted my request. It was right in the middle of the community and an ideal place to reach the maximum number of people.

Ruby and I drove to Highland Lake to get the tent. I would drive the truck back with the tent and equipment and Ruby would follow in our car. Since I had never erected a tent of that size before in my life, I asked Merle Dense to give me the instructions I needed. Merle pulled out a three by five card, took a pencil and made two dots. Drawing a line between them he wrote the number twenty on it and said, "Here is what you need to know. Set the two poles twenty feet apart. Then attach the ropes and the pulleys. Lay the tent out on the ground around the poles and lace it together. Attach the hooks on the pulley ropes to the ring in the center of the pole holes and get two people on each rope under the tent to pull it up the pole. When you get it to the very top, secure the ropes and start to stretch the tent and stake it – that's all you have to do." Well, yea, sort of? I could have used a lot more instruction but with that he handed me the keys to the truck and we were off for Kentucky.

Today's four lane highways had not been built back then so we drove the arduous old route eleven that wondered through every city and village from New York to southern Virginia. At Abington we turned west and went over the mountains through Wise and Pound Virginia, finally entering Kentucky through Payne Gap into Jenkins and on up to McRoberts. I think as best I can remember the trip took about eighteen hours.

Ruby followed the truck all the way so if I hit a bump and the tent stakes began to bounce out, she could blow the horn and I would know I must pull over and go back and pick up what I lost. To this day ask Ruby what it said on the back of the truck and she can tell you instantly. She stared at it for eighteen hours and it read, *"America for Christ Crusade, Kruger and Dense Evangelistic Association."*

We arrived with the tent and began to make preparations. Our men had hauled in truckloads of sawdust for the floor. We waited for a Saturday to erect the tent to get as many people to help as possible. It was a beautiful day and no one, including the guy in charge (me) had ever put one of these things up before.

Well, everyone pitched in. Even the curious lent a hand when we got the steel bench frames out and began to clamp the 2x12 planks into them. As the men began to stretch the tent and drive the stakes things began to take shape. True, there were a couple small swags that were not completely stretched as they should be, but they didn't seem very important at the moment. I would learn later how important they really were. After a few hours of enthusiastic work, I stepped back to look at the result and it looked good to me. We finished off by erecting a large banner at the site, **"McRoberts for Christ Crusade."** The small community had never had anything like this before.

When Chick had consented to come we needed to get someone to do the music. Bob and Caroline Anthony had worked with us in the first year of the High School ministry and the people liked Bob. He had a great voice and communicated a message when he sang. I contacted them and they agreed to come. Caroline had just recently had their second child but seemed to think she could come with no problem.

As it turned out, Bob came down with their first son David and Caroline was supposed to follow – she never did. So in addition to hosting Chick and Pat Koloski, Ruby was feeding Bob and little two year old David and then looking after him while Bob worked with us during the days and evenings. That was, of course in addition to caring for our two boys who were of similar age. Looking back I wonder how she ever kept it together.

Our days began with united prayer. Then we did the daily devotional radio program at WNKY. That was at eight o'clock. Then we did some visitation and preparation for the meeting in the evening. We did another live program on radio at 4:45 each afternoon on my regular slot.

The services began at seven and went until about eight thirty. Bob led the singing and directed the choir while I played the organ. Chick preached and gave the invitation. The crowds were light at first but began to grow until toward the end of the first week we were filling about two thirds of the tent which would seat four hundred people – not a bad record for a community whose population was only twelve hundred.

Saturday night came and the tent was filled to capacity. John Henry, missionary pastor from Pound Virginia brought a large number of people over and there were people from several counties. There was only one problem. The skies had been threatening rain all day and as we got the service started the clouds became darker and more ominous. Off in the distance we heard the rumbling of thunder.

As a young pastor, I could not think of God allowing this meeting to get rained out with the greatest number of people gathered to hear the gospel I had ever seen in that small town. As the rain commenced I stepped to the podium and prayed that God would stop the rain.

It became very quickly evident that God had not heard me, nor did anyone else past the third row. The thunder roared and the rain pelted us with a deafening sound of pounding drops on canvas. And that is when I learned the significance of those few swags we had left in the tent. Each swag began to fill with water. The weight of the water gradually stretched the canvas creating a pool of water. As the water increased so did the size of those swags and as I watched they became huge and dangerous.

I motioned to one of the teenage boys sitting close the front to push the water out of one of the swags before the tent gave way. He picked up a board and placing it against the largest of the swollen tent sections, he gave a mighty heave and the seam tore on the tent allowing about seventy gallons of water to come crashing down on him and leaving a huge hole in the tent. At that point everything became a matter of survival.

The water came flooding out of the hollow behind us and broke easily through the small ditch we had made around the tent to prevent that very thing. Ladies tucked their feet up on the benches and men began to push the water out of those other swags before they too burst.

One of those who helped was John Henry. John was an old seasoned missionary who had lived through many a crisis and seemed almost to enjoy the present calamity. He pushed water out of one swag after another and as he did he would laugh out loud and say, "Well Praise the Lord." I was not so mature and I did not share his enthusiasm. I felt like God had abandoned me and while I was working at crowd control and water control I was not really in a rejoicing mood.

Suddenly, in the midst of everything, I felt the entire tent shake as if it was going to take off. I looked to see the problem and it was not hard to find. One of the ladies, Gerry Champion, had run through the rain and gotten into her car. Now it wasn't just any car – it was one of those 1959 Buick Roadmasters that weighed a ton and was the size of a battleship. She had backed it up to the tent to load her children and unwittingly had backed over a tent stake. When she tried to go forward the car caught the stake and was pulling the entire tent.

I ran out into the rain to the side of the car. Gerry had the windows up tight and hadn't any idea that what was holding her back was a tent stake and by trying to go forward she was in danger of causing the entire tent to collapse.

I knocked on the window and hollered as loudly as I could. "Gerry! Stop! You're over a tent stake and you're going to pull the whole tent down." She cracked the window a little so she could hear. I said, "Look Gerry, just back up a tiny bit. Then we will lift the back of the car up off the stake and when I say go, you go – OK?" She agreed and I went to the back of the car.

Gerry obediently backed up very slightly, but enough to get the bumper loose from the stake. I got several other men and together we lifted the car. I yelled, "Go! – Go! – Go!" But nothing moved. How long can you hold one of those Buicks in the air?

We tried again. I yelled "Go!" several times but again, nothing happened. I ran up to the side of the car to see what was wrong. Gerry didn't want to get wet so she had rolled her window up tightly once again and could not hear me over the sound of the rain. By now I was soaking wet and not a little unhappy and I said, "Gerry, you roll down your window so you can hear me, and when I say go – you go!"

I returned to my place at the rear of the car and once again gave the command, "Heave!" The men obediently raised the car once more and I yelled, "Go!" and Gerry went – in reverse. If the stake had not had a chain which attached it to the tent we would all have been run over. When we finally gained composure and made sure Gerry had it in drive instead of reverse we tried once more and Gerry pulled away.

It was evident there would be no meeting that night. When the rain subsided the people went home. Several tried to encourage me and John promised he would bring his gang back the following Saturday night but all I could do was just stand there and survey the situation.

There were song books lying in the water here and there. Streams of water had washed the sawdust into little gullies and large mountains and we would have to remove all the benches and rake out the floor. The platform was a mess. Thankfully, the organ had survived and so had the sound system. I went home discouraged and threw my soaking wet suit into the dryer – it was not wash and wear.

It took me some time before I could get a grasp on just what had happened. In my heart I was complaining, "God, aren't you all about bringing people to yourself. Here we are, we have worked day and night to fill the tent so people could hear your gospel, and you let it rain on the biggest night we have had."

What I later realized was that as much as God was concerned about the lost people that night, He was even more concerned about a preacher who was working in the strength of the flesh and needed desperately to be humbled. I later had to thank Him that He loved me so much that He used that night to deal with me.

As the second week got under way the crowds began to return. Dramatic conversions took place. I remember Jimmie Zidaroff coming forward. He was so deeply under conviction that he held onto the tent pole and trembled. Young people came. Nadine Mann, a young lady who was a deep thinker and a good student came as God convinced her that He was real.

Gerry Champion's husband was a Kentucky State Trooper. Before the meetings had begun he had tried to give me a gift to help finance them. As he tried to press a five dollar bill into my hand I looked him in the eye and asked, "Elwood, are you a Christian?" He answered me that he was not. "Then God doesn't want what you have," I said, "He wants you," and I returned the bill to him. He later testified that I was the first Preacher who had ever refused his money and it made him realize he needed to come to God.

The final week found the three preachers beginning to wear out. Two broadcasts a day, visitations, and an evening service were taking a toll. One morning as we did the broadcast I played the piano, Bob sang and Chick stepped up to the mike to speak. Just as he did, I got up from the piano and the hymnbook from which I had been playing began to slide off the rack. Bob leaped into action to keep it from crashing down on the piano keys. He dove through the air catching it in his hand just before it reached the keyboard. The effort however left Bob himself in mid air and he landed on the floor hymnbook in hand.

It was all too much for me. I doubled over in a subdued laughter and poor Chick had to try to keep preaching. I thought he did a superb job and that no one would have noticed anything, but his wife Pat was listening to the broadcast. When we got home we got an earful. "Chick Kiloski," she began, "don't you know you were dealing with eternal souls this morning and you were laughing." Well, it took some explaining before Pat cooled down.

The final Saturday night we filled the tent once again. John Henry was back just as he promised and the meetings ended victoriously. We paid all our bills and gave Chick a love offering. I'm not sure exactly how many we baptized from those meetings but it was enough that being a small church, when we turned in our numbers to the Association, we were later told that we had topped all Kentucky Baptists in per capita baptisms for that year. The McRoberts for Christ Crusade changed things for the church and we began to see numerical growth take place. But just as important, it changed things for a young preacher who was beginning to learn that God wants our full dependence and trust no matter what storms come our way.

CHAPTER TWELVE

Some Kids from McRoberts

As I sat down to reminisce about McRoberts kids, I was reminded of what God did for our two boys. Of course both of them were in service every time the church was open so they were well exposed to preaching. Ask either of them and they will tell you they attended church faithfully for nine months before they were ever born.

Ruby, mindful of the distraction very young children can be and wanting to be as unobtrusive as possible, always took her place on the back row. From there she managed the children very effectively, giving them just enough liberty to squirm a bit as children will do, but no more. If one of them got out of hand I seldom knew it until I would see her quietly exit the sanctuary with someone in tow and return a short time later with a chastened and obedient child.

Of course the penalty for the worse offences was, "I'm going to tell your father when we get home." The boys insisted that was the "death penalty" and to hear them tell it, every Sunday the first order of business when we arrived home was, "Boys, drop your britches and grab your ankles." I'm sure I have a much more accurate view of it, but there were times when it did happen.

I had only to remember that Biblically, the children derived their fallen, sinful nature from their father (me) at conception, to know that each of them needed to be born again. But I never talked to either of them directly about it – after all, how young can a child be and really understand his need for Jesus Christ? Well, I was to learn – pretty young.

Whatever Scripture I preached on, I usually tired to clearly present the gospel and the need of every person to receive Christ by a personal act of faith before closing the service. I would ask that those who sensed their need indicate it by raising their hand while we bowed our heads in prayer.

When Phillip was about four and a half years old, he responded in a service one morning by raising his hand. I did not acknowledge it assuming that he could not have really understood and was only trying to please his father.

The next Sunday however, the hand appeared again, and this time, Phillip was in tears. While I still hesitated to acknowledge it publicly, when he continued to cry the whole way home I suggested Ruby delay dinner and talk to him.

When she asked him why he was crying he immediately told her, "Because I need Jesus to come into my heart." Ruby followed with, "Why do you think you need Jesus?" Phillip responded, "Because I've sinned, and I want Him to forgive me." It could hardly have been clearer. Ruby told him that if he was ready to ask Jesus to forgive him and come into his heart she would pray with him. They knelt beside the couch and helped by his mother, Phillip prayed that Jesus would forgive his sin and come into his heart.

Because he was so young we thought it best to never mention what he had done to him again, but there was an evident new interest in Phillip for the things of God. When he was about seven years old, he asked me to baptize him. I insisted that the deacons examine him before I would do so, and they came to our home and talked with him.

When asked about when he received Christ, Phillip related the entire experience right down to kneeling by the couch with his mother and praying. One small detail, he said, "we knelt down right by this couch and I prayed."

Now we had two couches in our living room and I as I listened I was distinctly remembering he was at the other side of the room (a small detail), but then Phillip suddenly added, "Only this couch was over there back then." We decided he was certain enough about his decision and His hope was built on nothing less than Jesus. Yes, . . . I did baptize him.

Our son Steve was an early responder as well. Because Ruby and I frequently had to teach classes of youth at the church by ourselves, it simply meant that our boys had to be there with us even when the ones we were teaching were older. That's what happened one day when Ruby was teaching a group of junior boys. Stephen was in the class because he had to be and Ruby told the story of *Snowflake, The Naughty Lamb*, (a illustrated child's version of the parable of the lost sheep).

As Ruby ended the lesson, Stephen was crying. As soon as she had prayer and could dismiss the others, Ruby took Stephen on her lap and asked, "Why are you crying?" Stephen immediately replied, "Because I am just like that naughty lamb." Ruby agreed, but asked, "What do you want to do about it Stephen?" "I want the Shepherd to save me," he responded. So Ruby led him in prayer right there, and Stephen asked the Good Shepherd to be His Savior as well.

Once again, we never mentioned the incident to him but two years later something very strange happened. Stephen came home from first grade talking about a story the "Bible Lady" had told. Missionaries were able to go into the schools back then and God blessed that ministry to the salvation of many hundreds of children. But on this particular day, as Ruby tried to get supper, Stephen would not be silent. He kept talking about this story of a little lost lamb called *Snowflake*.

Ruby wisely recognized that God was doing something in Stephen's heart, so she turned off the stove and said, "You know Stephen, I have that same story." "You do?" he responded with wide eyed amazement. "Yes," said Ruby, "I do," and she went to the filing cabinet and drew out the illustrated story of *Snowflake*.

Once again she rehearsed the story and as she turned the pages, Stephen began to sob. "What's wrong?" Ruby asked him, and then there followed the exact same response that had happened several years before.

Stephen had completely forgotten his earlier commitment, but when confronted with the same story, the Holy Spirit used it to again awaken his heart to his need of forgiveness and a Savior, and Stephen made a decision that day he has never forgotten.

As I share the children's stories I must say a word about Rachel. Of course she was the youngest of our children, but she remained unconscious of her need for the Savior for several years beyond the age when the boys had first responded. In fact we had left Kentucky and were already in ministry in the north, when we attended an evangelistic meeting where a very clear presentation of the gospel was given.

Rachel was standing beside me during the invitation and I noticed that she seemed oblivious of her own need. I had been concerned over this seeming lack of awareness for some time, so I leaned over and quietly whispered, "Rachel honey, don't you think it's about time that you let Jesus come into your heart?"

I will never forget her answer, "Why Daddy?" she asked. "Well," I continued to whisper, "aren't you a sinner?" "I don't know," she replied. Now I began to understand why Rachel's response was so different than the boys. Rachel had always been a very obedient child. I used to characterize her as one of those, *I will guide thee with mine eye* children. If she did anything out of line, all I had to do was glance disapprovingly toward her and she immediately stopped whatever it was she was doing.

I had a characterization for the boys as well. They were more like, *I need thee every hour* – they were always in trouble, and so it was no problem for them to know clearly that they were sinners and needed a Savior. I needed to help Rachel understand that, so I asked, "Well, honey have you ever told a lie?" Instantly the tears began to stream down her young cheeks and without a moment's hesitation she stepped out and started for the front to receive the forgiveness and redemption she needed.

Some may ask, but can children really understand what they are doing at such and early age? They may not understand the theology of the atonement, but then neither do we understand it completely, but they know they are sinners, they know they need forgiveness and a brand new heart, and they know that no one can do that for them except Jesus.

Our children are, of course, all grown now. Phillip has been an organist and choir director for years, Stephen and his wife operate the *Charis House* in Philadelphia where they minister to international students and try to introduce them to Jesus, and Rachel and her husband have been missionaries for over twenty years in Austria where Dan pastors a Baptist church and Rachel works with the youth and conducts a ministry to street women caught in the slavery of prostitution. I think their young decisions were real enough.

But there were other kids as well. While my radio broadcast did not have a huge effect on church attendance, occasionally there were those who came because of it. One was Ted Hall. Ted (her name was Tessabell – she understandably preferred Ted), came to prayer meeting one evening. She came with Goldie Dorton, a neighbor who was a faithful believer, but she had been motivated by listening to my radio program.

Ted indicated that she had been saved and that she genuinely knew the Lord, but she had gotten out of fellowship with God and had not been attending church. She hadn't been doing anything for the Lord for years. Ted's heart was fully prepared to respond to God. She covenanted with me that day that she would start coming back to church, and she did – she was very, very faithful to all the services.

Ted had a husband who was unsaved, and three daughters and a son – all of them unsaved. The son's name was John. All of them were more or less brilliant kids – they were excellent at whatever they did. They were all good students.

John was only sixteen or seventeen at that time, but his voice had changed and he had a very deep full voice. He was not a large fellow at all – he was, in fact, of rather slight build. But John had this deep voice, and so he had gotten a job at a radio station as an announcer, while he was still going to high school. Personable and good looking he was one of the most popular radio announcers in the area. John also played the guitar and sang, and he and his sister Margaret had appeared in competition at the Grand Ole Opry in Nashville, Tennessee.

I began to try to influence John and Margaret but it was not an easy matter. There seemed to be little interest from them in spiritual things. John, because he was in radio broadcasting, had some interest in anything that had to do with radio, and so one day I invited him to come up to my house and look at my radio equipment. I had a professional recorder and a turn table that I had set up to make my broadcasts.

John came and looked over the equipment, and then as we sat there and talked, I began to talk to him about the Lord. He indicated he felt a need for the Lord, but could not find any assurance or certainty of how to be saved. I went over the Gospel with him several times, and finally, I dwelt on the verse, *Whosoever shall call upon the name of the Lord shall be saved.* Finally, John got down on his knees and prayed and asked the Lord to save him. When he got up, I said, "Can you thank the Lord for saving you, John?" He said, "Well, I'm still not sure."

I didn't know what to do at that point, so I said, to him, John, let's just take the Word of God and I want to share some verses with you. I had him read John 1:12, *As many as received him to them he gave the power to become the sons of God, even to them which believe on His name.* I said, "Did you do that?" He said, "Yes." I said, "Well, are you a child of God?" John said, "I'm just not sure." I said, "What did God say He would do for those who received Him?" John, said, "Give them power to be the sons of God, but I'm not sure what that means."

So I went to John 3:16 and we went through a similar exercise. Finally, we got over to John 5:24, *He that heareth my words and believeth on him that sent me hath everlasting life and shall not come into condemnation, but is passed from death onto life.* I had him read each verse aloud and as He was reading that verse I said, "Have you heard his words?" "Yes," he replied. "Do you believe on Him?" Again the answer was, "Yes." "What does it say you have?" I asked. When I asked that question John came right up out of the chair and he said, "I've got it! I have eternal life!" Well, he did indeed, and John became a very faithful, wonderful Christian and began to play his guitar and sing for the Lord and testify where ever he went.

Later on, Margaret, his younger sister got saved during the Jack Orr meetings. I had invited Jack and his team down from York, PA for a week of evangelistic effort. Jack had visited in their home and went out into the kitchen where Margaret was doing the dishes and lead her to Christ. Then Carol, another one of the sisters got saved during Vacation Bible School. I had the privilege of leading her to the Lord.

John went on to college and I believe that it was while he was away at college that he wrote a song, based on John 5:24, the verse that God used to give him assurance of eternal life. John then went on to West Point, and later joined the FBI and majored in law. He finally became the Chief Legal Council for the FBI. John was also a firearms expert, and helped design the ten millimeter handgun that the FBI had produced to replace their nine millimeter guns after loosing a famous fire fight in Florida.

Years later, after we built the camp, I invited John to Camp of the Nations as a speaker. He came to Camp of the Nations as a Bible teacher that year, and we recorded him singing that song, *I Have Eternal Life* and the words of that are on the Camp recording we produced that first year.

Nadine had a different story. She grew up in McRoberts, Kentucky, the oldest of three sisters. Her father was dead, and her mother had a succession of boyfriends. The girls were a handful, to say the least. Gerri, the youngest, appeared to be the liveliest, and then there was Darlene and finally, Nadine. Nadine was somewhat of a thinker, and an excellent student, responsible, and level-headed, but she didn't want to have anything to do with God.

Nadine came to Christ as a result of the tent crusade with Chick Kiloski in 1959. That Crusade was in the spring, and through the summer she began meeting with the young people and immediately trying to get into the Word of God. It was obvious that God had done a real work in her life.

I brought a message from the twelfth chapter of Romans about presenting our bodies to Christ, and she responded to that. I counseled her afterwards, and in tears she presented her body to the Lord and almost immediately said, I want to go to a Bible College.

It was already late in the summer. She had just graduated from high school that year and I knew she had a good academic record, but I also knew it would take a miracle to get her in at this late date. I think it was in August, but I told her I would work on it.

I went home and called Appalachian Bible Institute. I explained all the circumstances, and they finally responded that they would make a place for Nadine. Well, I went back and told her that, and everybody was all excited, and rejoicing. Then all of a sudden on the next Sunday, Nadine didn't show up at church.

One of my deacons told me that Nadine's mother had confronted her. Nadine had said she was going to go to a Bible College. Nadine's mother said, "No, you are not!" Nadine set her face and said, "This is what God wants me to do."

Back then, the miners wore what was known as a miner's belt – it was a big, thick leather belt that went around them and all of their tools and equipment hung on that belt. Nadine's father's old belt hung there in the kitchen, and her mother took that miner's belt and beat Nadine black and blue and told her that she dare not go back to church, dare not see me, and that she was not going to a Bible College; she would go to a secular college.

I remember how very, very disheartened I was when I heard that. I could hardly believe it, and as a young, zealous pastor it shook my faith. It had me asking, "Where is God?" "Lord, here this girl has yielded herself to you and she wants to follow you and serve you and look what has happened? Why don't you intervene?" Obviously my faith was very immature and I needed to do a lot of growing. At any rate, I was not allowed to see Nadine nor even allowed to talk to her.

Sure enough, fall came and Nadine was placed in a junior college over in Jackson, Kentucky which was one of the University of Kentucky campuses. About mid-year, the high school team on which I served from Scripture Memory Mountain Mission, was scheduled to have a chapel in Jackson High School, so I arranged while I was there to go down to the campus and try to see Nadine. I expected, to find a girl despondent and with her faith badly shaken.

Instead, I found a girl who had been able to accept what had taken place as something from the Lord. She had begun a Bible study in her dormitory, and she had a number of other girls studying the Bible with her. There was, at that very time, a revival service going on in the community, and she had convinced one of her professors to attend the revival service that evening. I went back tremendously elated and buoyed up at what God was doing, and chagrinned that my own faith had been so weak.

Nadine went two years to that school, and by that time she was 21. She came back to McRoberts and said to her mother, "Now, Mother, I have obeyed you and gone to college, but now I am twenty one and I am going to Bible College." At that particular point, her mother just simply yielded.

This time Nadine got interested in Philadelphia College of Bible. That was a little bigger step, and a little more money and a bigger hurdle. But that is what she said she wanted to do, so I began to work on trying to get an opening for her. Now while Nadine's mother was somewhat passive about her going, she still was highly resentful toward me as being the reason that Nadine was going to do this "foolish thing," so I was persona-non-gratis at their house, and I got to see Nadine very seldom that summer. I never got an opportunity to sit down and really plan her next step with her.

I went ahead and got the papers for her from PCB and she filled them out, sent them in and was accepted. So we let the folks know on a given day that we were going to take her to Philadelphia and help her get situated, since of course we had gone to the same College and knew our way around. In fact, that was the one thing Nadine was a little concerned about; she was somewhat timid and being from southeastern Kentucky was not too sure about going to the big city of Philadelphia.

We loaded Nadine and her few possessions into the car, and Ruby and I headed north with her. After we had been on the road probably an hour or so, I said to Nadine, "Nadine, how are you off financially – I mean, I know you'll have to try to work to go to school, but what do you have right now? What have you been able to save?"

Her response was that she had something like forty nine cents. Well, we all laughed – Nadine tended to like to tease, and I assumed that she was joking, and a few minutes later, I said to her, "Now, Nadine, we need to talk about finances a little bit, so seriously, how much money do you have?" And she looked at me dead serious and she said, "Forty nine cents."

I remember my reaction. Everything inside of me said, "Oh, my goodness, Bill, what have you done? Why didn't you tell this girl she had to have money to go to college?" All I could think of was that I had made a mistake, that I had failed, that I should have counseled her further.

God had done enough miracles for me that I could certainly believe God could work, but this was ridiculous. How do you go to college on forty nine cents? However, I kept all of this bottled up inside of myself, and gulped and sputtered and decided, well, we are on the way, and whatever comes, comes at this point, but I knew that I couldn't help her much.

We stopped to see some friends on the way, and I think we may have stayed overnight. We told them that Nadine was going to school, but we didn't tell them anything about her financial situation, and as we left, they handed her an envelope. When we got in the car, Nadine said to us, "Now I have $100.49." Well, it began to become apparent to me that God intended to care for Nadine.

We stopped at my home on the way up, and before she left there, Dad had given her $200. Now she had $300.49. Before we got to school, she had $400 and her famous 49 cents!

We arrived early because we planned to help Nadine get a job. The best jobs always went to those who arrived before school actually got underway. If you waited until school started, most of the good jobs were taken, and you had to take whatever was left. I knew she needed the extra work anyway, so we arrived at the school two weeks in advance of opening.

I went in to see Miss Helen Coe who was the Assistant to the Counselor of Women at the time I was a student and I knew her well. I said, "Helen, I have a girl here all the way from Kentucky and I need to get her settled. I need a place for Nadine." Helen said, "Oh Bill, you haven't heard?" And I said, "Heard what?" And she said, "Dr. Mason has made a rule this year that no one comes early to school. We are not taking any students until school actually opens."

I replied, "Whoa, I am here with Nadine – It's two weeks until school opens – what am I going to do?" I asked again, "who made that rule?" She said, "Dr. Mason." I said, "Well, I guess I'd better try to see Dr. Mason."

I had Dr. Mason for many classes during my time at PBI. I loved his teaching, but Dr. Mason is a large man and he was the Dean in every sense of the word. He was pretty fearsome as far as most of his students were concerned. You just didn't want to cross Dean Mason. But I was desperate so I went into his office, sat down, and explained the situation. When I was done explaining, he said to me, "Well, Bill, I understand, but the rule is. . ." and he explained the rule. The bottom line was no student could come to school early.

When he was done, I said to him, "Okay, Dr. Mason, I understand, but what am I going to do with Nadine? If I take her back to Kentucky, she's not going to come to school because she has no way of getting up here, and I've got to return to Kentucky; I have no other place that I can put her, what am I going to do with Nadine?" Dr. Mason sat there thoughtfully for a moment and then he reiterated the rule and why he had made the rule. When he was done, I said to him again, "Okay, Dr. Mason, I understand, but what am I going to do with Nadine?" Finally he looked at me with just a bit of frustration and without saying another word, he pressed his intercom button and said to his secretary, "Please tell Miss Coe that Nadine is staying." I thanked him with all the sincerity I had and left his office.

We had just seen God do another miracle. We moved her into a room, and decided to go job hunting. Ruby and I were able to get another room and we stayed overnight. The next day we went down to the employment office where Ruby used to work as a secretary, and we inquired about various openings.

There were a few jobs open, but the one that we chose was down at Lit Brothers Department Store. They were advertising for a clerk, and I remember Nadine saying to us, "Oh, my, I am not sure about that. I have a really thick Hill-Billy accent, and the first time I try to talk to someone and they ask, 'What did you say?', I'll be so intimidated I won't even be able to answer. I just don't know how I can do that!" We decided to go anyway, because she definitely needed a job and she wanted to go to school.

When we arrived at the store we learned that job was no longer available. But they asked Nadine, "Do you type?" She said, "Oh, yes, I worked in an office for a couple of years in college." "Well," they said, "There is an opening in the office – would you like to apply?" And to make a long story short, within about an hour and a half, she was interviewed, she got the job, at much better pay rate than she would have gotten as a clerk, and we went back to the school.

There she was, secured in her new room, with a good job within walking distance of the school, fully enrolled in school and accepted . . . I walked out and got into the car and put my head down on the steering wheel and began to cry. My wife said, "Honey, what's wrong?" And I said, "Ruby, do you realize that we just watched God turn the world upside down, change the rules, change everything for the sake of a little girl from Kentucky, who nobody knew but God, but who was willing to trust Him completely?" Oh, why can't we trust Him to do the exceeding abundant things we desire – to do above all we could ask or think? Is it because we haven't ventured everything on His provision and grace?

CHAPTER THIRTEEN

My Attempt to Move the Church

W hen God called us to the Hills of Kentucky, we went and never questioned that we would spend the rest of our lives there. That was certainly my plan. But I had a vision for more than just McRoberts. I knew that as long as we were located up a hollow, we would never be able to draw people from other areas into the church.

There was an empty area of several acres right next to the road at Neon junction just below us. Everything that traveled from Whitesburg to Jenkins had to cross that junction. Furthermore, everything that moved from Deane across the mountain, down through Hemp Hill and Neon had to cross that junction as well. Every time our people from McRoberts or Fleming wanted to go anywhere, they had to cross that junction.

I had a vision for planting a church at that location. Then I dreamed of getting two busses (by the way, that was years before the Lynchburg bus phenomena). I planned on sending one west and the other east and looping both back to the junction. It seemed a perfect plan for building a church that could reach the entire area of Letcher County.

In 1963 I got my chance. I had been offered a practically new gospel tent with all the equipment for $2,000. I had even gotten an extension on the payment so that I could wait until after we used it a month to pay for it. All I had to do was pick it up in northern Kentucky.

I had arranged to use the lot at the junction. The owner had at first said no – he could make more money letting the carnival that was coming in that next summer use it. Then the carnival decided to move its operation to Payne Gap, and he approached me again and said we could have the lot.

I had once again contacted my favorite evangelist, Carlo Peitropaulo, and we had planned to begin meetings and keep going until we had a church. I had laid the whole plan before my deacons and they had agreed. That Sunday, all that was left was to decide who would drive the truck to pick up the tent and equipment.

I preached in the morning, but left the deacons to conduct their own meeting that afternoon as I preached a Baccalaureate service at the new high school at Blacky Kentucky. I even took the opportunity to announce the upcoming meetings to the large crowd gathered there that afternoon.

When I returned I went to my head Deacon. "O.K.," I said, "tell me how this is going to happen." Curt began shuffling dirt around with his foot, and finally he said, "Preacher, it's not going to happen. We decided we are not going to do it." Obviously, as a leader, I had been way out front and failed to bring the troops along, but it was too late now. They had decided that any grandiose dreams of moving the church to Neon Junction were not going to happen and McRoberts Church would stay in McRoberts. They also informed me that they had chosen another evangelist and the meetings would be at the church.

All I had dreamed since I came to Kentucky of tent crusades and of reaching the area was put to death in that one moment. They did get an evangelist. A man who did not share the doctrinal orientation I had worked to give them for eight years. Ruby and I were obliged to house him in our home and the experience was not a pleasant one. When he left, not a single soul had trusted Christ and it was the driest meetings we had ever experienced.

But after the meetings, all of my energy, all of my vision was gone. I could not read, I could not study – finally I told my wife I would go down and work in my shop which I had set up in the basement. I did, and in the process of sharpening a rotary blade for a tubing cutter, I slipped and cut my finger through the nail right to the bone. I stopped the machine, wrapped my handkerchief around the now bleeding wound and headed upstairs back to the office.

When I arrived Ruby asked, "What wrong?" "Oh, I cut my finger," I replied. "I can't even do a common task today." "You don't look very well," Ruby said. "You know, I don't feel very well," I replied. "I feel faint. Maybe you should get me the smelling salts". . . and that is all I remember.

The next moment I was sky diving and when I regained consciousness I was lying behind my desk on the floor and I could not move – I mean, really – I could not move anything. I became intensely cold and Ruby covered me with blankets. At last she called for our deacon, who was also a neighbor, and somehow, I got to Jenkins hospital. I believe I traveled by ambulance, but I can't really remember.

There I stayed for three days. In the end the doctor told me they had put me through all kinds of tests and concluded that it was simply extreme exhaustion. I know myself well enough to know that the exhaustion did not come from the intensity of my work. I thrive on work – as long as I am moving toward whatever goal it is I have. But if I hit a brick wall, the emotional let down leads to such a state of extreme weakness I can hardly move.

Interestingly the only other person I have ever known who reacted like that was my father. Dad had a series of heart attacks in his lifetime. None of them killed him although one nearly did, but each was brought on by a situation of extreme frustration and inability to reach a goal. I think I've learned something of the pattern, and perhaps it isn't as severe now as in the past, but I'm sure it was depression and a loss of everything I had set my sights upon that put me in the hospital. But the Lord is always faithful. He knew the earnestness of my heart and He also knew the therapy I needed to get beyond my circumstances.

The doctor who had examined me was also a flight examiner and I had begun about a year earlier learning to fly. I had stopped just short of soloing when I ran out of money from a gift of $100 my Dad had given me. When I went to the hospital, I was worried that since I had passed out, the Doctor would pull my flight permit. Instead he sat down on my bed the final day and said, "Preacher, what have you been doing except working?" "I guess not much," I replied. "I thought you liked to fly," he said. "I love to fly," I replied. "Then why don't you take some time off and fly? It would do you good."

Sometimes my honesty can be a bit caustic and I replied, "Because I'm not a doctor, and I can't afford to fly." "Touché", he said and left my room. But an hour later he returned. "Look," he said, "I've written you a prescription and I want you to take it." I waited a moment, mentally picturing myself going into the drug store. Then he continued. "I have controlling interest in Beechcraft Aviation over at Tri-City airport in Bristol. I've made arrangements for you to get the rest of your flight training from them. It won't cost you a thing. Anytime you want to fly just call them, they will fly over to Wise Airport and pick you up. And when you're finished, if you ever want to buy a plane, I'll see that you get one at my price."

Talk about exceeding abundant and more than you could ask or think. I accepted his generosity and I'm sure it was one of the things that brought me though my very discouraged state and helped me to begin to dream again. It is amazing how God can use the most unlikely people to bless us. My doctor was not a Christian, even though I had witnessed to him on several occasions. Yet God used him to meet my need at a very crucial time in my life. I may be without resources, but God never is.

CHAPTER FOURTEEN

Flying High

I did start flying again and had the opportunity to fly many of the various planes Beechcraft built as the instructors ferried me back and forth to Tri-City. I will never forget the day I soloed.

It was a dreary day and the clouds were hanging a bit low, but I decided to try to get in an hour of flying anyway. My instructor obliged me and we practiced a couple of landings. They were well done, but with him sitting beside me, and me following through on the second control wheel, I was never quite sure whether I made the landing, or he did.

The clouds were continuing to get lower and so it did not surprise me when after only about a half hour we landed and instead of a "touch and go" he instructed me to taxi over to the hanger. I assumed we were through for the day.

When I got to the hanger he turned to me and said, "Now don't take off again until we have established radio contact – then you are on your own." I just hadn't expected it to happen that day and I stammered something about, "Are you sure you know what your doing?" He replied, "Yes, I'm sure! This is my plane isn't it? If I wasn't sure you could fly it I wouldn't be getting out." And with that he dropped to the ground and shut the door. I had a few moments of panic attack, but I decide that if he thought I could fly it, then why should I question it, so I established contact and taxied back out to the runway.

My takeoff run was the first thing that surprised me. With only one person in the plane it was shorter than I had ever experienced and my climb out was faster as well. I hadn't realized how one additional body could affect a small plane.

I made my left turn after climbing out and started down wind. When the plane neared the place where I had been taught to turn onto the base leg I pulled back the throttle to about 1,700 rpms and pulled engine heat to the half way mark. Base leg looked good as I descended and I turned onto final approach.

Clearing the engine I pulled full carburetor heat and pulled the throttle back all the way. I began floating quietly toward the end of the runway. Lined up with the center mark I forced my eyes to glance back and forth over the entire runway to avoid fixing them on a single spot, then I crossed the end of the runway and began to pull back into my flare to lose the remainder of my speed. When my wheels touch the ground I could hardly feel it and I could have shouted with joy, except I was too busy getting the engine heat off and throttling up to take off and go around again.

Three times I went around and every landing was nearly perfect. The third time I had to go below the thousand foot landing pattern because the clouds were continuing to lower. My radio cracked and my instructor said, "OK, that's enough, you'd better bring it in this time – Good job!"

When I got to the hanger and had tied down the plane, chocked the wheels and made sure everything was locked up, I walked into the hanger to the sound of hurrahs and two guys started pulling out my shirt tail with another ready with the scissors. It's an old pilot's tradition that you lose your shirt tail the day you solo and so mine was cut, my name and the date carefully written on it and it joined the other patches of shirt tails on the wall recording other victorious solo flights. After a couple of cold drinks I started home, happy and proud of my accomplishment.

I had waited a long time for this and it really felt good. I was in such a good mood that I didn't think twice when I saw a guy hitch-hiking as I drove out of Wise toward Pound, Virginia. I immediately picked him up planning to bore him with the details of my triumph. However, it became very quickly apparent that he would not hear my grand tale that day. He could not hear because he was deaf, and he was also dumb. The only way he could tell me where he wanted to go was by making gestures. He smiled and tried to show me he was thankful for the lift as I let him out just before I got to Pound.

A moment later it hit me and brought me to tears. I said something like, "Dear Lord, you have been so good to me. Lord you have saved me, you have called me into your service, you have provided for me and today you even allowed me to fly. Lord, you allowed me to fly, and you haven't even allowed that man to hear or to speak. Lord forgive me, when I fail to give you the thanks and gratitude I owe."

When I got home, I told Ruby and the kids about the flight – about the solo – but I told them too about the God who had been so good to me that He allowed me to fly and of the man He had not even allowed to speak.

My next solo flight was a little more dramatic. I decided to fly over to McRoberts, buzz over the house and let the kids see Daddy flying. Now understand that we lived in a hollow between two very steep mountains. However, I had planned ahead. I planned to fly over the mountain, drop down into our hollow (Little Tom Biggs) at the upper end, buzz the house, then follow Tom Biggs Hollow down to where Band Mill Bottom (the main hollow) intersected it, and simply fly out the lower end of Band Mill Bottom, which would give me plenty of room to climb to altitude. Well, that's what I planned.

Everything went well until I got over the house. I had told the family what I was going to do and expected them to be out in the yard. However, they had not heard the plane until I was in the hollow and did not get out of the house till I had passed.

There was not enough room in that hollow for a novice like me to turn around so I flew down to Band Mill Bottom rather disappointed. I was climbing out to proper altitude when I happened to think – if I turn up Chopping Branch (a side hollow) I could come over the mountain again and back down over the house. Maybe they would be out this time. So without any further thinking, I turned up the side hollow (Chopping Branch).

Now there was a bend in Chopping Branch, so when I turned into it I could not see the upper end where the hollow ended and the mountain began, but as soon as I rounded the bend I saw it – and it was right upon me. It was too high to go over, I didn't have enough air speed or distance left to climb out, and too narrow between the mountains to turn back. I felt the sweat begin to come down my face rather profusely.

I prayed and pushed the power throttle tight against the dash and began looking for any way out of this. I was climbing and gaining, but it was obvious I could not get over the mountain that was coming up faster than I wanted it to come. At the last moment I saw it – a cut made in the mountain by a strip miner just off to my left. I banked left and flew through the cut barely skimming the ground.

My heart pounding I dropped down again over Little Tom Biggs and the house, but not as low as the first time. Yes, they were all out on the lawn to see me. I waved and headed down to Band Mill Bottom. This time I followed my plan and flew out from between the mountains and back to the airport. There had been a little more excitement on that flight than I cared for and I was ready to hang it up for that day.

I made a number of flights after that around the Kentucky mountain area. I flew over to Prestonsburg and landed at the air strip along the river. I flew to Hazard and landed there. At that time the airstrip was actually on a bend of the river. Across the river from the strip was a high hill.

If wind conditions demanded that you land from that direction, you had to come in high, over the hill, side slip across the river and level out at the end of the strip. It was probably more fun because it was rather challenging. Despite down drafts and thermals over the river, the landing went very well and I was pleased.

Eventually, every student pilot must make a solo cross county flight of at least 100 miles that includes at least two landings at airports other than where the plane is based. The conventional way of doing that is to choose a location that would be 30 or more miles from the home airport, fly there and land. Then fly to a second location an equal or greater distance and at a 90 degree angle to the first and fly the last leg of the triangle back to your home airport. The exercise tests both your skill as a pilot and your ability to navigate.

But I didn't want to do that. If I was going to do a solo cross country, I wanted to go somewhere where I actually wanted to go.

So I choose York, Pennsylvania a distance of about 500 air miles one way. Furthermore, it meant flying across mountain country where I would have little by way of check points to determine that I was on my correct heading. It was long enough that I would have to refuel somewhere along the way – I choose Beckley, West Virginia, because Appalachian Bible Institute was there and I thought I might want to fly over there in the future. Amazingly, my flight instructor agreed to let me go.

I left Wise early in the morning on an absolutely beautiful day. My flight to Beckley was uneventful since I was able to lock onto the Omni beacon at Bluefield, West Virginia and had easy navigation all the way. Nevertheless, while exhilarating, I must confess there was some stress. After refueling at Beckley I was climbing out to altitude when I made the mistake of deciding I was hungry. I had brought along a bologna sandwich and a thermos of coffee.

As I checked my gages for heading, altitude and airspeed, I took a large bite out of that sandwich. No sooner had that bite hit my stomach when suddenly I felt dizzy. My stomach began to churn. I was light headed and quickly loosing the ability to fly. I trimmed the plane to continue a steady climb and took my hands and feet off the controls. Planes are built to fly and sometimes they do better on their own. I grabbed my thermos and poured a cup of coffee. Several swallows and things began to settle down. I laid the uneaten sandwich on the seat beside me and began flying the plane.

The most difficult area for navigation was the mountainous area between Beckley and Morgantown. I ran out of contact with an Omni signal along the way and the terrain is just mountain after mountain all looking a good bit the same. I decided I would not take this route on the way back.

Once I got out of the mountains something happened that I hadn't expected either. When you are flying mountains, especially like the ones in the southern Appalachians, there are always thermal drafts rising at different speeds due to the extreme terrain below. A small plane flies normally at an altitude that is effected by this phenomena and so the plane sort of bounces through the air. Having never flown anywhere other than the mountains I had always just accepted that as the norm.

Now I was cruising over vast areas of level valley and it felt like I was flying a completely different plane. I went from a go-cart to a Cadillac and I loved it. I decided I could really get used to this kind of flying. Now I could understand better that flight instructor that flew into Wise from Florida some months before. He got out of his plane white as a sheet and scared. He said the plane was bouncing through the air and it had never acted like that before. Now I understood. He had flown the low country all his flying experience and had just gotten a taste of real mountain flying.

I landed at a small airstrip in East York not far from Hellam. The strip was unattended so I tied down the plane, locked it up and walked to the nearest telephone. From there I called Dad and he came over to pick me up. I couldn't offer him a ride, since I still had only a student license, but I think he was as excited as I at what I had accomplished.

On my return flight I choose to fly the Shenandoah Valley through Virginia. Navigation is much easier and the flight a lot smoother as long as the weather holds. I decided to refuel in Dublin, Virginia and check weather there. They were predicting clouds and rain, but not for a couple of hours. I decided maybe I had time to get in under the weather since it was Wednesday and I wanted to get to prayer meeting.

I left Dublin and flew over the first range of Mountains going southwest toward my destination. As I few down the valley I was looking at the map for checkpoints and noticed an airstrip marked on the map at Tazewell. It was only a grass strip but usually such features are easy to spot from the air. I just couldn't find it as I passed over.

The further I flew down the valley between the mountains the lower the clouds were becoming. I decided I had better find a place to put it down before I got into real trouble. I started to look at the map again. There was a paved airstrip up to my west just beyond Richlands, Virginia, but when I turned to go up between the mountains, I saw a wall of clouds reaching to the ground ahead of me. I did a one-eighty turn and started back toward Dublin, but looking to the east I saw that the clouds had now covered the tops of the mountains there as well. I was going to have to put her down somewhere in the valley.

It had now begun to rain and it was getting dusk. I knew I had to find that strip because it would likely be my last chance at getting the plane back on the ground. As I strained my eyes suddenly I saw it – a rather tattered windsock hanging limply on a pole in what looked like nothing but a farmer's field. I decided I didn't have a choice; I would have to try to land.

Next question was which way to approach for a landing? The windsock told me nothing so it was optional. There was a large barn at the one end of the strip and a hill and a fence at the other. There is an old rule in flying which says, if you are going to crash, hit the softest thing possible and the cheapest thing possible as slow as possible. I put that rule to work. I decided that replacing a fence would be cheaper that replacing a barn so I elected to come in over the barn and land toward the fence and the hill beyond.

What you can't see from the air is the tilt of the land. I came in over the barn in a side slip that slowed me down and pulled back into a flare for landing, but nothing happened. The plane was settling, but so was the ground. It fell away from the barn, something I could not have known from the air and I was drifting further and further down the field toward the fence. Finally my wheels touched the earth and I began to apply brakes. However, the field had not been mowed, and the grass was really low hay and wet. I skidded and slid and came to a stop only feet away from the fence.

It is times like these that make you thankful you have a guardian angel. I prayed and thanked God profusely for keeping both me and the plane safe and began to taxi back up the grade toward the barn. As I approached an old farmer came out of the house with a large chew of tobacco in his jaw smiling and shaking his head. "Well, ya did pretty good sonny," he said, "I've seen a lot of them crack up getting in and out of here." That was only mildly comforting. I was thankful I had gotten in, but I realized I still had the challenge of getting out, but that would have to wait for another day.

The old man let me tie down the plane in a shed and walked me back to the house where I called a cab. The cabbie took me to a nearby motel where I rented a room for the night and called my wife to let her know I was ok. I did ask for prayer for my flight in the morning without telling her how iffy it really looked that I could get out of there. I took a very hot bath, prayed earnestly and went to sleep asking for wisdom to face the next day.

Next morning I got breakfast and caught another taxi to the airstrip. Looking over everything there was no question about the direction to take off. I would go down the grade toward the fence and the rather high hill just beyond it. But could I make it? Did I have enough room to gather enough speed to get off and get altitude? I just wasn't sure.

I had just fueled up back at Dublin and had only flown for about an hour. That meant I had more gas in one tank than in the other and more gas on board than I needed. I also knew that I did not have that far to fly to get back to my base at Wise, maybe another hour so I decided to lighten up. I dumped several gallons of gas on the ground to even the weight in the two wing tanks.

Then the grass was a challenge. It would definitely slow me down. I decided to taxi back and forth several times to open up a path in the meadow. Finally, convinced I had done everything I could, I taxied as close to the barn as I could get, said my last prayer, pushed the throttle full in and held onto the brakes as long as I could. The plane literally trembled and I popped the brakes and shot down the path I had made.

It all worked just as it should and I was airborne almost before I knew it. I had sufficient speed and climb to get beyond the hill and was taking off into a beautiful, sunlit sky – that was directly over me. As soon as I got aloft where I could see a broader area, I realized there were heavy clouds all over and I had just been sitting in a spot where there was a large break in an other wise very heavy sky.

I decided to go VFR on top, meaning I would still be flying by visual reference, but I would be above the clouds and would have no ground reference checkpoints to go by. I set my omni and did an ETA.

Flying above the clouds is a great experience. I was rejoicing in all that had taken place and singing at the top of my lungs, "How Great Thou Art." Then after my time of rejoicing, I started to think about how I was going to get back down. A VFR pilot and especially a student must maintain at least a one thousand foot distance from any cloud. It was both illegal and dangerous for me to just fly down through the clouds.

I was just coming up on my ETA when I spotted a large opening in the clouds up ahead. I aimed the plane directly for it and began decent. As I looked down, I realized I was actually looking at the Wise airport. God had opened the clouds for me to get up and He had now opened them again for me to get down and I was home safe at last.

I taxied into the hanger and did all the post flight stuff including filling the tanks. As I did my instructor came out of the hanger office. "Well, good to see your back." He greeted me. "Have any trouble?" "Not really" I replied, "everything went great." "Really?" He said. "Then how did that hay get wrapped around the wheels?" Busted again!

I cleaned the wheels and told my story – at least most of it. I had accomplished more than enough to care for my cross country requirements and I would now need to prepare for the written exam.

While I was actively flying I decided to use it to open some doors as well. I gathered the Junior High boys and told them we were going to be building airplanes at the next Vacation Bible School. I got a better than usual attendance. Each boy built a model Cessna 172. I told them at the beginning of the week that on Saturday, I would take them all over to the Wise airport. Each boy would bring his plane and we would fly them from a hill that ran along side the runway down onto the airport surface. The boy whose plane flew the longest and the furthest would get a free ride in a real airplane.

I was still not licensed to carry passengers so I asked Fred Dodson, my instructor to do the honors. Fred was a great guy. Although unsaved at the time, he had given me flight lessons free. All I had to do was pay for the plane. While flying together I had many opportunities to talk to him about his need for Christ. Several years later Fred did trust Christ and became an outstanding Christian.

On this special day he took one of the boys up for a ride. I don't even remember who it was. But I still have some of the pictures from that day at the airport. I have often thought that as much as I wanted to fly I never made flying my goal in life. When I dedicated my life completely to Christ, His service has been what my life had been about. But God knows each of us – He made us like we are and when we make our passion to please Him, He brings into our lives

158

in unexpected ways many of the desires of our hearts. After all, that is what He promised, ***Delight thyself in the Lord and He shall give thee the desires of thine heart.***

I still had to take my written exam and then my final flight test. Exams were given at Bluefield, Virginia so I made arrangements to go there for my test. I had only a few sessions of formal ground school. We lived about forty five minutes from Wise and it just wasn't feasible for Fred to come all the way to train us. I read everything I could get my hands on and took a mock test out of a book I had gotten, and watched film strips (yes that is what we had back then) over and over. But I felt the lack of formal training.

I realized my greatest hurdle would likely be the challenge of navigation which entailed reading the weather bulletins and computing weights, distance, temperature and such – math had never been my strong suit. I had to arrive early at Bluefield so I slept in the hanger at Wise that night (well, sleep I did not, but I was on a cot in the office). I flew out at daylight and arrived on time for the test.

There were about four of us that day and the test is at least four hours long. It is based on an actual flight plan but the tests given in the eastern US are always based on a flight that is to take place in the west and the tests out west are based on supposed flights in the east. The logic is to force you to plan a flight over unfamiliar territory so that you are completely dependent upon reading the maps correctly. The way the test is constructed, you have to figure your weight, altitude, distance, temperature, right up front. If you happen to make a mistake on one of those figures, the next ten or more questions will be wrong. I must admit that the only time I ever questioned my desire to fly was about two hours into that test, when I seriously asked the question, "Are you sure you want to do this?"

In the end I made a score of 89 which was the best score that day. The other guys had gone through formal training and I had not, but I passed my written. Maybe they didn't have anyone praying for them.

Finally it came time for my flight test. I scheduled it but when I arrived to take it Beechcraft had just landed a new turboprop King Air and was planning to demonstrate it to one of the pilots that flew for a large coal operator. Fred was invited to go along so he asked if we could delay the flight test. I responded, "Certainly, as long as I can go too." In the end they agreed and I got one of the thrills of my life.

I had never been in a plane with that much power before (never mind the sleek leather appointments). We took off and assumed an almost vertical climb at over 260 knots. Then with out warning the pilot suddenly feathered the left engine leaving us climbing on a single engine. The plane hardly noticed. This was one beautiful and powerful bird.

I made one mistake, I sat along a side seat and looked out the porthole on the other side while we went through several rather extreme maneuvers. Suddenly I felt my head go light. Determined to overcome the problem without letting anyone know I was in difficulty, I climbed to a position where I could kneel between the two pilot seats and with my hands on the back of the seats looked out of the front of the plane. The change in perspective was enough to relieve the problem and no one knew I had nearly gotten airsick but me.

When we got back, Fred put me through my paces doing multiple landings and take offs, stalls, even a stint under the hood having only the gauges to fly by. In the end I passed with flying colors. At last, I was a full fledged Private Pilot and could carry passengers. And I did. I wanted to take everyone up I knew.

I loved flying so much I couldn't imagine anyone who would not. I learned there were such people, among them Ruby's dad. Monroe crunched down in his seat on takeoff and refused to look at anything until I got him back on the ground. He could go deep into the coal mines every day without a care, but was frightened to death in the air.

Shortly after I got my license, my good friend Harold Dubs had decided to fly and wanted to buy a plane. I knew I would probably never be able to afford a plane so I told him about the offer of Dr. Musgrave to let me buy one at cost. I suggested we ask him to give Harold that deal on the condition that I be allowed to fly it occasionally.

Well, as it worked out Harold did buy a Beech Musketeer at Bristol and not having a license as yet I flew it home to Hanover, Pennsylvania for him. A few weeks later it was due to go for servicing to the dealer and still Harold had not gotten his license. I got the job again. This time we loaded up with four men, all of us good size guys and made the trip.

A Beech Musketeer is a four place plane, but marginally so. I mean that under normal circumstances it has enough power to handle that kind of weight. But you don't want to get into situations where the air is too thin or it can get a little hairy. I remember once taking off in that very plane on a hot day with a similar load and on a dirt strip. About halfway down the field I suddenly realized that this field was beginning to rise as you approached the half way point. I knew if I was going to get airborne I would have to do it before we started going up hill or it would not happen. I gave it all she had and pulled it off the ground just before reaching the rise. Then I flew straight and level about three feet above the ground to gain speed while the stall warning sounded incessantly. I remember someone asking, "What is that buzzer?" I think I said, "Oh, that's just to alert me to conditions" (a rather obvious observation). When we came to the end of that field I was still struggling to maintain speed and cleared the high corn by about a foot.

On the trip back from getting the plane serviced we got a bit of a late start. The service was performed in Bristol, Virginia and we needed to get back to Hanover, Pennsylvania before dark. I was not checked out for night flying and had never landed a plane at night.

We refueled at a small field in Winchester, Virginia and then headed for Hanover. But I soon realized we could not make it before dark. I explained that I was not licensed for night flying, but it was Saturday and several of my passengers were Sunday School Teachers. So their question was, "OK, you're not legal – but do you think you can do it?" I told them I thought I probably could, and they decided they wanted to chance it.

Flying after dark was no problem as long as I was at a good altitude. In fact it was rather fun and very beautiful. Learning to read the gauges by infrared light was also interesting. The real challenge would come when we approached the York Airport. The runway was lit so I could easily pick it out, but I knew there was a hill just southwest of the airport and there was no light on it and I was not sure how high it was. Beside that it was a very dark night with no moonlight at all. I made my first approach higher than I wanted worrying about the hill and found I had used up more runway than I should have so decided to go around.

The second approach was better, but I still was using a lot of runway and had more speed than I wanted. We went around again. The third time was about the same, but it suddenly dawned on me what I was doing. I was coming down the middle of the runway by keeping my eyes on the runway lighting. In order to lose enough speed to land I had to pull the nose up and flare and doing that meant loosing sight of the only thing I could see, those runway lights. Nevertheless, I realized I would have to do it.

I think there was probably more sweat on the faces of my passengers that on mine. I simply said, "Guys, we are going to get this done, but I will not put it down until I'm sure I can do it safely." That time I pulled up the nose, the plane flared, the lights disappeared, and the plane gently settled onto the runway – a perfect landing.

I flew quite a bit the first year Harold had his plane. Ruby and I flew to Kentucky to explore becoming president of a college. I flew to Altoona and took my parents up to see the famous Horseshoe curve. I flew my boys several times and let them take the controls. But in the end Harold not only got his private ticket, he went on to get instrument, commercial and finally instructor ratings. He also got a more advanced aircraft than I was qualified for and my pilot days were about over.

God who made me knows my desires and my ambitions. As long as I keep my focus on serving Him, He will give me more than I could ever have dreamed possible. He already has. I needed the diversion of flying at that time in my life and God provided it. I sometimes miss it, but I learned that there are "seasons" to life, and what is so important in one, may be unimportant in another. I have always thanked God for allowing me the privilege of flight.

CHAPTER FIFTEEN

We Leave Kentucky

With the refusal of the church to move to a more promising location, I began to question whether I had taken this congregation as far as they were willing to go. While I was considering that question there was the second thing that occurred which increased my suspicion that it was moving time.

That year Madelyn Murray had taken her case against the Bible and prayer in the public schools all the way to the Supreme Court and the Court had ruled in her favor. At the same time, my partner in the school work, Raymond Haddix, had been asked to assume the Directorship of SMMM. That meant the formation of a new High School team – If there were to be any High Schools left for a team to visit.

As it turned out, I stepped out of the situation to allow the new High School team director, Dennis Cline, to choose his own team and start fresh. We learned that there were about five schools (mostly small country ones) that would test the new ruling and let a team come in, at least occasionally. But gone forever were the days when we had open access to twenty seven high schools every month in seven counties reaching over 10,000 high school students with the gospel. For me, the High School work there in Kentucky was over.

The final part of the decision occurred when it became time for the State Baptist Convention. All that was coming out of the Convention at that time was troubling to me. Southern Seminary in Louisville had become known as a hot bed of liberal teaching.

Professors openly asserted that they believed nothing of the Scriptures. The radio and television commission were producing broadcasts void of the gospel of Jesus Christ. The State Convention publication consistently took positions on issues that were at odds with what I believed and what I taught. I believed it was time for McRoberts Church to declare itself independent.

While I never made my fight with the Convention prominent in my ministry, I felt I had been there long enough and pointed out their faults often enough that there should be no real opposition. We never gave to the Cooperative Program because of what it supported that we could not support, and we never attended many of the regional meetings. I alerted the Church that we would take a vote on the issue and that since this was such an important matter, I wanted a unanimous vote.

The day came, the vote was cast. I don't remember the exact tally, but it failed of being unanimous and I took that as the final indicator that the church was not ready to go any further along the road I wanted to go. The following Sunday I tendered my resignation effective at the end of the year.

Well, the effect was electrifying. There were many tears and the Deacons called for a meeting. I obediently complied and they told me none of them wanted me to leave. I responded, "if I stayed, what difference would it make in your lives?" Finally, knowing each of them and really loving each of them, I went down the line one by one. "Junior, as long as I have been here, for eight years, I have told you that smoking hurts your testimony and your health. If I stayed eight more years, would you give up smoking?" "No," he responded. "Then why should I stay eight more years to achieve nothing?"

"George, I have told you often that membership in the Masonic Lodge is a contradiction of the gospel of grace you profess to believe. If I stayed eight more years, would you get out of the Lodge?" Again the answer was "No." "So you see," I told them, "I have taken you as far as you are willing to go. If I thought I could stay and effect a genuine change in your lives I would do it, but you won't allow me to do any more."

About that time Jr. Flint (whom I loved dearly), said, "Preacher, you're just stubborn and bullheaded." I answered, "You are no doubt right and I need to change, so I will tell you what I will do. I own my home so in order to leave, I will have to sell it. I want more for it than any home has sold for in this community in my memory. I will not advertise it, I will not put a sign on it, I will not even talk to anyone about it unless they ask, and if I do not sell it for the full amount by October 31st I will stay."

The reaction was instantaneous! "Meeting's over," Jr. announced. "He's stayen." Perhaps it was a bit presumptuous, but houses were almost impossible to sell in McRoberts and no one had paid what I was asking for a house the size of mine up to that time.

I did a lot of praying during those days because I did not want to miss the will of God. Dr. Pipkin, President of Appalachian Bible College asked me to candidate at another church in the Mountains so I would not leave the area, and I complied, but I was not a fit for that ministry and I was glad when both the church and I agreed on that.

On October 29, John Monhollan knocked on our front door. "Preacher," he said, "I hope you won't mind my asking, but someone told me that maybe you would be willing to sell this house." I told him he was right. John asked if he could see it and I invited him in. When I named the price, he flinched, and asked, "What's the best you can do Preacher." "Exactly what I asked and not a penny less John," was my reply. "Give me a couple hours," he said as he left. The same day he returned with the full purchase price and the house was sold. I had till the end of the year to vacate.

I announced Sunday to the Church what God had done. I told them I thought it was evident that God was orchestrating what was happening and we would obey. I preached my last sermon on the Sunday before New Years and my replacement preached the following Wednesday at the Prayer meeting. When God orchestrates things He does it very smoothly.

Our good friends Harold Dubs and Herb Lippy arrived the day before New Years. They loaded all our earthly possessions in their Aunt Kitty's Soup truck and started us on our way to Pennsylvania and a whole new adventure. Things we could never have dreamed of, were just ahead.

Packed up to go to Kentucky

House in Emmalena

Mother & me

McRoberts Baptist Sunday School Teachers
circa 1959

Circa 1960

MY OLD KENTUCKY HOME

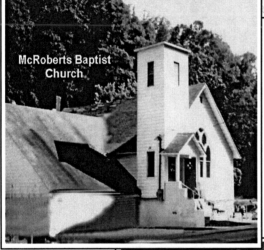

McRoberts Baptist Church

LEARNING ABOUT JESUS AT MOTHER'S KNEE

YOUTH REVIVAL AT JENKINS HS
BILL SHADE & JERRY BRUBAKER

McROBERTS FOR CHRIST
CRUSADE

VBS "FLY YOUR PLANE" COMPETITION

FIRST VBS FOR BLACK CHILDREN AT McROBERTS BAPTIST CHURCH

FIRST VBS FOR BLACK CHILDREN AT McROBERTS BAPTIST CHURCH

CHAPTER SIXTEEN

Early Ministry in York – Pinebrook

After coming to York in 1964, we settled in Dad's development at Panorama Hills. He had graciously offered us a lot there and we began to build a house. The monies from the sale of our home in McRoberts provided about one third of the cost to build. Then we cashed in our savings of eight years and Dad carried the balance for us. For the first three months we lived with Mother and Dad. They were very gracious but Mother was obviously not used to three children running in and out of the house and being everywhere at once, and while they were, for the most part well behaved, they were, well, frankly, children.

We built a very small house (the smallest that the restrictions would allow). But it was a very efficient house designed so that the drawers and cupboards all recessed into wall space eliminating the need for anything but a bed and perhaps a bed stand for furniture. To expand its appearance we added a two car garage, but shortly turned the one bay into a radio studio and the other into an office.

Since we already had a radio ministry and intended to do evangelistic work I wondered about forming a formal organization. With no background for such matters I decided I needed counsel and made a call to Dr. Jack Murray, former pastor of Church of the Open Door in Philadelphia.

Dr. Murray had come to PBI one evening at the invitation of a group of us students who wanted to know more about the subject of revival. He had graciously met with us in a dorm room and talked and prayed with us about how real revival happens. Although I was sure he would not remember me I asked if he would give me an hour of his time to talk about my new venture.

Jack not only gave me an hour, he invited me to live with he and his wife Eleanor for an entire week and to travel with him to meetings he was holding in New Jersey for Dr. William A. Mierop, former President of PBI. I cannot recount what that time with Dr. Murray meant to me and in addition to everything else, Mrs. Murray wrote the Chorus; *Grace & Truth Came by Jesus Christ,* as a theme song for my Broadcast, Moments of Grace and Truth.

Following the advice and counsel I received from Dr. Murray, I began putting together the plan to create the Grace & Truth Evangelistic Association to give direction to our ministries. We formed our first Board of Directors from our new home in York and my dad, our dear friends Harold Dubs and Herb Lippy and another newer friend, Len Deichman, along with Ruby and me were the first Board members. Our total treasury consisted of less than one hundred dollars.

I began almost at once doing some evangelistic meetings. I remember the morning I was invited to preach at a United Methodist Church. Having come out of a part of that denomination years before and aware of the apostasy within the denominational colleges, I began to have second thoughts even as I was on my way to the church. Was I compromising to even go there? Would I have the courage to preach the Word of God without fear or favor in such an environment. As I drove, the sweat literally began to break out on my forehead.

The pre-service was typically formal with the liturgies borrowed from their former Anglican past, from which they had separated a century before. But I sensed a freedom as I began to preach and when I gave the invitation the altar was full of those who wanted to receive Christ. I determined that if God would grant me the grace to preach an unadulterated gospel, I would preach it where ever he opened the door.

Soon I was asked to preach a week of meetings in Maryland at a Church of God. The evangelist who asked me to take the meetings was a sound fundamentalist and I could hardly understand his taking meetings in a Church of God. The Church of God people I had known in Kentucky, not far from where I lived, were snake handlers. He assured me that was not the case and that this Church of God was aligned with the Winebrenner Denomination out of Finley, Ohio, a much more conservative group.

I decided to go, and to my surprise and delight, found the pastor to be a graduate of Washington Bible College and a kindred spirit in every sense of the word. We had a wonderful week of meetings and saw many come to Christ. I believe the one I best remember resulted from a visit we made.

We were visiting people on a Sunday afternoon and almost drove by a driveway that led up into the woods when the pastor suddenly stopped and backed up. "I have been meaning to visit these people for some time," he said, "but just haven't gotten around to it. I understand they are Catholic and both of them work as nurses in the Catholic hospital." We arrived and knocked on the door and a man, I would judge in his late thirties, opened the door. When he recognized the pastor he responded at once and said, "Please come in", we have been waiting more than ten years for this visit."

Of course we were surprised and asked what he meant. He called his wife into the living room and when we were all seated he said, "Ten years ago I watched one of our priests die, and I decided, that if that is how a priest dies, I am in trouble – it was a terrible sight."

I asked him if he had any hope of heaven at all. He said that he hoped he would go to heaven after he spent enough time in purgatory. "Why do you think you need to go to purgatory," I asked. "To have my sins purged," he responded. I replied, "I'm glad you realize that you are a sinner and that you need to have your sins purged. That's a good start. I'm afraid many Protestants no longer realize that."

"There aren't too many verses in the Scripture that talk about the purging of sins," I continued, "but if you have your Bible I would like to show one of them to you." He quickly handed me his edition and I turned to Hebrews chapter one. There I began to read, *God, who, at sundry times and in divers manners, spoke in times past to the fathers by the prophets, last of all, In these days, hath spoken to us by his Son, whom he hath appointed heir of all things, by whom also he made the world. Who being the brightness of his glory and the figure of his substance and upholding all things by the word of his power, making purgation of sins, sitteth on the right hand of the majesty on high:* (Douay Version 1899) Then I continued from my KJV, listen to what it says, *when he had by himself purged our sins, sat down on the right hand of the Majesty on high.*"

"You see," I said, "the purging of sins is not some future event but one that has already taken place. It is because our sins are purged that Christ is seated at God's right hand. He is seated because His work of purging our sins is complete, or as He Himself said, *"It is finished."*

When Christ died on the cross for your sins, He purged them with His own blood, and if you will believe Him and trust his work to save you, He will forgive you and give you eternal life right now, so that you can know beyond a shadow of a doubt that when you die, you will go to heaven." Both of them immediately got on their knees and called upon Christ to save them. They were at all the meetings that week and testified of knowing they had eternal life.

I spent the first months in the York area, doing meetings as they came in and working for Dad to earn enough to pay the bills. The thing that most dramatically changed my life and ministry was the morning I attended a Pastor's Breakfast.

The invited speaker that morning was Lieutenant Charles McCaffery of the York Juvenile Police Department. York was a very clean city. Having grown up in Altoona during the days of steam engines and heavy industry with lots of smoke and cinders, it was never clean, and the black soot fell all the time. York on the other hand was a very clean, pleasant place with a Dutch heritage. I used to say it was a place where you could wear white buckskin shoes all summer and they didn't get dirty.

Little did I expect what I heard that morning when McCaffery told us that over 2300 young people were in trouble with the law that preceding year. McCaffery went on to relate several specific cases of very troubled teens, and when he was finished, I was compelled to go and speak with him directly. He invited me, if I was interested, to go out with him in the patrol car that Friday evening, and I accepted.

I don't remember a lot of what happened that night, but I arrived about 7 o'clock, and we got in the car and began to drive around. He took me down Princess Street to what he referred to as the three-ring circus. There were three bars on that street, one on one side of the road; two on the other, and most of their complaints were about the fights and the stabbings that took place within that particular area. I do remember that as we later talked in his office, he took me through the files and showed me a number of cases, particularly involving juveniles.

One that stuck very vividly in my mind was a young man who had been brought in on some kind of a charge; he was a motorcyclist, wearing a black leather jacket and with all of the regalia of a biker. According to McCaffery, someone in the course of things, had told him that Christ was the answer to his problems. He rejected that, and about a week after his release, driving very fast down a road, struck something on the highway, and was propelled off of his cycle and skidding about 100 feet face down on the road he landed against a concrete curb. His helmet had flown off and he was dead on the scene. He showed me the picture of that young man, and I still have a copy of it in my files. On his shirt were emblazoned the words, "Cool Man – Death". I wondered if he still thought that death was "cool?"

We went back out in the patrol car and made several calls. Eventually they brought in a couple of juveniles. I was on hand when they did some initial questioning; long enough to see something of the plight of those teens. I know that I didn't get home until about six in the morning, but I had seen enough to have a deep burden for the youth of the city.

I began to go into Freys Avenue, which at that time was a very depressed place. The York Rescue Mission had their first building on Freys Avenue, a racially tense place where a year before racial riots had occurred, so a white man was not particularly welcome in the area. I went in with my pocket Bible and some Gospel literature and tried to meet some of the guys and talk to them. I obviously didn't speak their language, but I was determined it was the only way I would ever make any progress. I did that for several weeks, on certain afternoons. I would just go in and hang around and try to get a conversation started.

One morning, Bill Drury came to North York Bible Church, where I was attending at the time, and Bill told about his organization called Teen Haven and the work they were doing in Philadelphia and Washington DC. In fact, they had established Teen Haven Centers in both those places.

We invited Bill to our home for dinner. As we ate, I talked to him about what I was trying to do and how we were trying to get this work started. I invited Bill to go into the city with me that afternoon and meet some of the fellows I was talking to, and he did.

I shall never forget the experience. Bill just began talking to them about a retreat that Teen Haven was going to have at Pinebrook in the Pocono Mountains. Pinebrook was Percy Crawford's old camp in Stroudsburg, Pennsylvania. He told them about this place where "The world is your little oyster." You can go indoor swimming/ outdoor swimming, horseback riding, tobogganing with or without snow, and ice skating – all the works!" And then he told them, "And if you guys would like to go, it will just cost you $3.00."

Now I knew that I had heard him tell this story that morning in church, and he said very clearly that it was going to cost $6.00 for every one of the kids he would take, but he told these guys, "It will just cost you $3.00." Then when he had pumped them up about going he told them, "If you want to go, just contact the Reverend here" – that meant me.

A lot of them indicated they were interested. We walked away from the group and about halfway across the street. I said to him, "Bill, you know what you said was great, but what can I do? I know you said this morning it would cost $6.00 for each one." "Well," he said, "I figured you could make up the difference." At that point I was really feeling desperate. I said, "Bill, I have no way to get anyone there; I don't have a bus; I have an old dilapidated car . . ." and he looked at me and simply said, "Look, you wanted to get started? You are started!" And that was it!

I went home and got on my face before the Lord, and cried out, "Lord, this mad man has put me in a terrible position. I'll lose all my credibility with these kids. He's told them that I can do something that I can never do." And as I was praying, or maybe really fussing, about all of this, the Lord reminded me of Ron Schmuck.

Now I had worked with Ron on several occasions. Ron had started the Youth for Christ meetings in an old store front just south of York in the town of Red Lion; and out of that work had grown the Red Lion Bible Church. They had just built a large building and Ron had begun to establish several bus routes to reach the kids in the area. He was running maybe three or four buses at the time, bussing kids in for their church services.

The Lord brought Ron to my mind as I was praying, and so without even thinking it through, I got on the phone, and I told him what had happened, and I said, "Ron, is there any possibility that you could loan us a bus for this project?" And he said, "When did you want it?" And I said, "Well, we need it Friday, Saturday and Sunday such and such a date."

Ron said, "Bill, if a preacher has a bus, why do you suppose he has it and when do you suppose he uses it?" Well, obviously I was embarrassed. I said to him, "Ron, I am terribly sorry, I just didn't think it through." But Ron replied, "No, that's all right. I am not saying you can't have it, but that is the time we use it." He said, "I have one bus route that is fairly small right now. I think we could use a van to pick up on that particular weekend, so yes, I will loan you the bus."

That was the first hurdle. I remember drawing a deep breath and saying to him, "Ron, I never drove a bus, and I'm not sure I could handle that." He paused for a long moment, and said to me, "Well, I tell you, the guy who drives that particular bus is a really dedicated fellow who loves the Lord. If I talk to him, I think maybe he would drive the bus for you."

Boy, I was really getting excited now! I said to him, "Great Ron, okay, what is this going to cost me" (knowing of course, that I had no money at all)? And Ron said, "Well, it's not going to cost you anything except the, ah, . . . , Oh well, let's face it; it's not going to cost you anything!"

By this time I was literally in tears. And I remember thanking him and then getting on my knees and confessing to God that it was my own unbelief that had stood in the way of laying hold of the answer – and how wonderfully God had supplied!

Before it was over, there were more kids who wanted to go than I could take on a single bus, so I talked to Dick Burd of the Church of the Open Door. As a result Church of the Open Door loaned us their bus, and Dick drove it, so two complete busloads of teens went up to camp. Yes, it cost me $6 for each kid who went, but God wonderfully supplied that need as well.

Two things occurred just as we were about to leave. First, I still needed about one hundred dollars as I drove into town to meet the busses. I stopped to get gas and a voice called my name from the other side of the gas pumps. When I looked it was a dear brother in the Lord who was a contractor. He asked what I was doing and where I was going and I told him how God had put together this remarkable retreat with two bus loads of inner city teens. As we finished he asked if there was anything I needed. I responded that I still needed about one hundred dollars to pay for the kids. I remember he said, "Bill that's great. I have a hundred dollars of the Lord's money and was just asking God what I should do with it. It will be in your secretary's hand within the hour."

The second thing that occurred just as we were about to leave, was designed by the Devil to derail us before we could even get started. We had about seventy plus teens signed up and paid to go. Just as I arrived several of the older guys, who I judged to be leaders, told me they had changed their minds and wanted their money back. It was a tense moment because these guys were big and none too friendly, but the Lord helped me realize that if I gave them their money back, every teen who had signed up would follow their lead and the entire project would fall through.

I stared them down and said, "Look, it's too late now for that. The busses have been engaged and the number turned in. You don't have to go, but I'm not returning anyone's money." Well, these guys did everything but threaten my life, but I held my ground by the grace of God, and finally, they relented and in a not-very-good frame of mind or humor, loaded on the buses to go.

Bill Drury had also told me that I had to have a counselor for every three kids. That seemed a little much for me at the time, but looking back on it now, I think it was a mistake – we should have had a kid for every three counselors – It was really that difficult.

Nevertheless, God supplied even the counselors. He laid the burden on hearts, and it seemed where ever I spoke to people, immediately they would respond and volunteer. So we took a large number of counselors and two full busloads of kids up to the camp.

Besides committing themselves to a difficult task, the counselors had to pay fifteen dollars each for their meals and lodging. But they did it without a word of complaint.

When we got to Pinebrook, Bill Drury had brought about a hundred gang teens out of Philadelphia and another hundred or so out of Washington DC. Besides that, of course, our kids were there, every one of which had a police record. So there were somewhere around 300 kids at that one place that weekend.

The Philadelphia Bulletin had sent a reporter to cover the story when they heard what Drury had planned to do. He was a Roman Catholic fellow and I got to talk with him the second night. He told me, "You know why I am here?" And I said, "Well, I guess you are here to get a story." "No," he said, "I am here to measure the blood, because there is no way that you guys can do what you are trying to do here, with all of these warring gangs, and not have a major riot." I discovered he was right.

The first night Bill had planned to have a Christian comedian and a music team with a lot of pretty upbeat songs to try to set the tempo and get the gangs in a receptive mood – It didn't work. They didn't laugh at the comedian; they didn't enjoy the music; they got up and walked around, and just laughed, talked, fooled around, and did whatever they wanted to do. Nothing really got through that first night.

During the second day, in the middle of the afternoon, they decided to play Capture the Flag – a really bad idea! In the middle of that very competitive and combative game the teams broke up along gang lines, and in the middle of the event, tempers suddenly flared, and these guys who had no idea of how to just play a game, started picking up rocks the size of grapefruit and throwing them at each other, and suddenly it became major warfare! Shouting orders didn't accomplish anything, and soon I was standing, frozen to the spot, just watching to see what would happen.

Philadelphia Police officer Mel Floyd, who was on Bill's staff at that time, was not frozen. It was obvious he had seen this sort of behavior before and he was in full action mode. I saw him coming down the hill past me, holding an arm lock on a gang leader by the name of Caesar. He was leader of one of Philadelphia's fiercest warring gangs. As they passed by me going down that hill, I could see that Caesar was really angry, and I heard Mel saying, "Caesar, you are going to get killed or you are going to kill somebody, and I'm not going to let you do that out here." As they passed I could see Mel was just about in tears. It was obvious that Mel loved this guy he was marching him down the hill in that arm lock.

By God's grace the rumble finally broke up without major incident. Then as I was feeling numb and wondering who in the world could do anything with this bunch of kids, Bill came to me and said, "You are going to speak tonight." Well, I certainly didn't expect that, and furthermore I had no idea what to say.

I said, "Bill, I can't. I have laryngitis," and I did. I had been up all the night before – we had disturbances of one kind or another all night long. I learned that these gang guys didn't sleep so we had to stay up all night to see that nothing happened. I had literally been awake all night long, and now I had been awake all day long, and I really had a terrible case of laryngitis. But Bill would not be deterred, he said, "Well, you are going to speak anyway."

I went back to the dorm and found an empty room. I walked in, closed the door, and fell on my face before the Lord, and I said, "Lord, what can I do? These guys will not listen to a comedian; they won't laugh at his jokes. We can't get their attention with music, what possible chance do I have to say anything that they would listen to?" As I prayed and as I poured out my heart to the Lord, the Lord laid on my heart the verse from John 6:35, where Jesus said, *I am the Bread of Life, he that cometh to me shall never hunger and he that believeth on me shall never thirst.* I didn't know if I could communicate or not, but I determined that this was what God wanted me to say.

And so when the time came, they came in their usual rowdy and sullen fashion. Bill's staff tried to do some singing with them, but it didn't work, and then Bill put me on. I remember I stepped up to the microphone and as I looked out at this huge group of young people that were so completely disorderly and without any respect at all, my heart simply broke and the thing that I didn't expect happened. I just literally went into tears, and for a few moments I could not get control of myself.

I felt extremely foolish and embarrassed as I just stood there crying. Then suddenly I realized that as I was crying and trying to

179

get composure, everything was getting very quiet. When I finally got control, I looked and there wasn't anybody moving, there wasn't a sound, and I opened the Scripture and I began, not to preach, but simply to talk to them.

I talked about a gnawing hunger and a burning thirst deep down inside of them that they had been trying to fill with sex and drugs and thrills and everything else, and nothing had worked – all they had achieved was to clutter it up. They hadn't filled it; they hadn't satisfied it, and then I told them that the empty space within can only be filled by Jesus Christ.

I spoke for about 20 minutes, and then I said to them, "We are not going to sing any songs, we are not going to bow our heads and pray, we're not going to do anything like that. If you are here tonight and God has spoken to your heart and you are ready to repent and come to Christ and let Him fill the emptiness in your life, I want you to get out of your seat and come right now."

I waited a long time. At first nothing happened. I began to sense there was restlessness on the periphery of the group and particularly the girls in the back were beginning to get noisy again. And then, all of a sudden, one of the gang leaders got up and he was actually sobbing as he came.

These guys never cry – as part of the gang, they must never cry, it's one of the rules of the gang. This guy was a leader and he was sobbing. He came to the front and got down on his knees. I got down on my knees with him for a moment, someone else came and knelt down with him, and when I stood up again, it looked as though everybody was going to come, and I found myself standing there saying, "Look, if you don't mean business, don't even come. We don't even want to talk with you, unless you really mean business with God."

Forty-three gang members came forward that night. I am talking about teens generally anywhere from 17 to 20 years of age, and we dealt with them for an hour or more after that. God literally broke in upon that particularly situation, and showed His power and strength in spite of my weakness. Paul had said, *"When I am weak, then am I strong,"* and I began to understand how very true that can be. It was the most fruitful Pinebrook retreat we ever had.

CHAPTER SEVENTEEN

First Teen Encounter Center – The Work Begins

After the retreat at Pinebrook I wanted to know more about what Bill Drury was doing so I went to Philadelphia and visited one of Drury's Teen Haven centers. Doug Rogers was in charge. That afternoon as the kids gathered after school, Doug asked me to speak. As I spoke various kids got up and moved around. One walked to the window and stood gazing out. I shared some Scripture and a bit of my own testimony. Afterward Doug remarked, "Don't let their seeming inattention bother you. They were listening, even if it didn't look like it."

After seeing what Teen Haven was doing, I decided we needed to do something like that in York, and I went back and began praying and walking the streets, looking for what God might have for us. When I say walking the streets, I literally walked the streets, praying and looking for a place that would lend itself to the kind of ministry we wanted to have in one of the neighborhoods where it would be needed. Interestingly enough, I couldn't find anything around the Frey's Avenue area.

Across Market Street, on the north side, there was a large neighborhood where there had been trouble, more among white kids than black, but still a very troubled area. It was right around Franklin Street, and as I was walking there one day, I came upon an empty corner house, at 37 N. Franklin St. I saw it had a 3-car garage out back, that would make a recreational place where we could set up games and put in a modified gym, so I contacted the realtor and he took me through it. They wanted $10,000 for the property.

When I walked in, I saw the large living room that was perfect for a chapel, and the more that I looked, the more I became convinced that it was perfectly situated, and perfectly laid out, with four or five large bedrooms, and a kitchen on both floors. It was a place we could definitely house kids.

I knew I did not have $10,000, in fact, I didn't have any money, but I felt that if the Lord wanted me to have it, He would indicate that by giving it to me at a very reduced price, and the price that came to my mind was $6,000. I didn't say anything to the realtor at the time, but I told him I would like for several others to see it and he offered to let me have the key. "Just bring it back to the office when you are finished," he told me.

The realtor left, and I was still standing on the porch just contemplating our next move when all of a sudden I heard someone call my name. When I turned around, I saw a car and the driver who recognized me was Dick Reynolds. Dick had an auto parts dealership just about a block away. I had met Dick at a CBMC meeting in York where Dad served as Chairman and he recognized me from that single contact.

Dick had come down Franklin Street that day on his way to work and when he saw me standing there he stopped and called, "Bill, what are you doing in this neighborhood?" I began to explain to him what I was doing and our desire for a building for a Center. He pulled the car over to the side and said, "Do you mind if I look at the place with you?" I said, "No, I'd love to take you through."

As we went through I explain to him everything as I saw it, what we would do with each room, where we would have the chapel, where we would feed the kids, and painted my vision for the place. When I was finished, I said to him, "The Lord's laid it on my heart that if He wants us to have it, we should offer $6,000."

Dick said, "How are you going to get the money?" I said, "Dick, I haven't any idea." I had never borrowed money in my life. I had no idea how to go about anything like that. Dick said, "Well, I can't buy it for you, but if you decide to go ahead with it, I'll sign your note." I'll never forget, I looked at him like a kid, and said, "Dick, I'm sorry, but I don't know what you just said. I heard the words, but I don't know what you mean."

You see, to me a note was something you got in trouble for passing in school. I had no idea what a financial note was, what it was to sign a note and become obligated for someone else's debt – that's just how very naïve I was. So Dick actually had to explain it to me. After considerable prayer I made the offer of $6,000 to the Realtor and waited.

After several days I got my answer. The owner was willing to sell at the price I had offered. Dick and I went to the bank and Dick told the banker what we were planning to do with the building. After listening, the banker looked at me and said, "How do you plan to pay for this?" I said, "I don't plan to pay for it. I believe that what God orders He pays for and I believe this is of the Lord, and He pays all His bills on time."

I could see right away that was not a satisfactory answer to him because the banker laid his pen down. Dick said, "Don't worry, he is sane and if they can't take care of it, I will. I believe that God is in this thing too." And so, Dick signed my note, and we set out to pay for our first building in the next six months.

We purchased 37 N. Franklin Street toward the end of the summer, and I was having meetings at Keyport in New Jersey. At that time, Dave Boyer was singing for my broadcast so Dave came down the last weekend of those meetings and sang. We had great meetings there with Pastor Gene Gregory. On the closing night, one of the men told me that he had a gift he felt burdened to give toward the building we had purchased, and he handed me a check for $1,000.

That was the first $1,000 check I had ever seen in my life, and it was a tremendous amount of money to me. I was so excited and thrilled that I drove home from the meetings that night and almost got lost coming home on the turnpike! Actually, I really did. I got off at the wrong exit and found myself driving though some pretty desolate county. I was afraid everyone in the world knew I had $1,000 in the glove compartment and I would get robbed before I got home! It was really an amazing thing to me to be given that amount of money.

As it always does, the day came when we needed to finish paying for the property, and we still owed about $2,000, and frankly did not have the money. I remember we fasted that day and we got down on our knees and told the Lord about it. I told the Lord that He had directed us, and we had told that banker that what God orders He pays for on time, and now, for His own name's sake, we asked Him to meet the need that very day.

As the morning wore on, several of our volunteer office staff gave some gifts. Actually they were small gifts, but sizable for kids living on nothing but faith. Ruby and I made as large a commitment as we could, but still we lacked over a thousand dollars of having what we needed.

Early in the afternoon, the phone rang. The voice on the other end said, "I am secretary to Burnell Paules. My boss heard you speak about a month ago. Right now he's out in Colorado on a hunting trip. He came down out of the mountains to a telephone and called me and told me he couldn't keep his mind on hunting because God had laid a burden on his heart to get some money to you today." So the secretary promised him she would get the money to me that day. She didn't know what it was for or why I needed it, but ask me if I would please come down and get it. She assured me she would have a check ready for me.

I didn't have any idea how much the check might be; I didn't really know Burnell at that time, but I thanked her, hung up the phone and got in the car and drove down to his plant in Glen Rock. When I arrived she handed me a check for a thousand dollars. When I got back to our office, several other gifts had been given and before the Bank closed at 4:30 that afternoon, I was able to go and make the complete final payment on time, just as I had told the Banker we would.

Once having obtained the building the first thing I did in my naivety was to hang a sign on it that said "Youth Haven." No one had moved in yet and we had not gotten anything going but I got an immediate call from the City Hall Zoning Commission. "You are in a R-2 zoning area and you cannot operate a group home in that zone." Frankly, I didn't know cities had zones. I had just come from eight years of ministry in the coal fields of Kentucky and we certainly didn't have anything like "zones" down there.

I have often found that the best way to keep out of trouble with the law is to know the law, so I made a trip downtown and secured a copy of the Zoning Laws. I poured over them, especially the ones which concerned the R-2 zone where Franklin Street Center was located. What I found was, while indeed a "group home" was not permitted, a "recreational center" was. I took down my sign.

The new sign read, "Teen Encounter Center." I defined it as a "recreational center" ministering to teens in that area. But what about any resident teens we might take in. I defined them as "house guests" of the resident staff. The Zoning Commissioner was not impressed. He immediately saw through my play on words but I had one more recourse.

I had come to know the City Controller so I called him about the matter. After listening he told me he thought he could help us and just as we were about to end our conversation the hapless Zoning Commissioner apparently wandered into his office. He immediately put me on hold, but not before I overheard some heated discussion. In a few moments the Zoning Commissioner was on the phone with me explaining that he fully understood our situation and would not give us any further difficulty.

We operated 37 N. Franklin Street for the entire time of our ministry in York. During that first year we had a variety of staff. Several were college kids who had to return to school at the end of the summer such as Carolyn Debusk from Blacksburg Virginia, and Nadine Mann (whose story I have already told).

Our first permanent staff consisted of Larry Hodgson, who came from the Pittsburg area and was attending Appalachian Bible Institute. He volunteered for the summer, but became so involved with the kids and burdened for the work that he asked to stay on. I agreed on the condition that he would enroll in Lancaster Bible College and finish his work there. I told him that in a few years he would not thank me if I simply let him drop out to work with Teen Encounter.

Then there were two young ladies, Ethel Kreeger and Edwinna Roper that also joined us. Ethel did most of the letters and the secretarial work and Edwinna picked up on things like mailings. They both came to live at the Franklin Street Center.

One man who joined the staff that first summer was Alfredo Fernandez, known either as "Al," or "Freddie." He was from California and had grown up in a family of drug users. He had started on drugs at the age of nine and by twelve he was main-lining heroin. He told me of standing at the casket of his brother who died of an overdose and saying to himself, "I'll get shot or I'll die of an O.D. just like my brother." He was completely without hope. At sixteen he was arrested and thrown into Federal Penitentiary, where even on the inside he continued to use drugs as he could get them.

Released at nineteen on a technicality, he returned to his house and as soon as he entered the door his brother offered him a gram of heroin and a needle. But before Freddie could get his "fix," a loud knock at the door startled him and he flushed everything down the toilet. When he answered the door, one of his former buddies stood there with a large Bible in his hand and stepped into Freddie's house and without any hesitation he told Freddie what Christ had done for him and confronted him with his desperate need for Salvation. Freddie then and there received Christ and never used drugs again.

Freddie had come to one of Bill Drury's Centers and when he heard that I needed help he came back to York with me. Freddie lacked many things – he lacked personal discipline, especially regarding time, he lacked a solid work ethic (he was so relational that given any task he would soon be talking to people rather than working) and he lacked a structured theological training – but I learned many practical things from Freddie as we worked and traveled together. I used to call him the "Pied Piper" because where ever he would go kids would follow him. He would come into the Saturday Night Rallies fifteen minutes late, but have twenty street kids trailing behind him. I learned from Freddie how to really fast and pray.

As the first summer ended we reached a crisis. The staff couple who were serving as coordinators at Franklin Street decided that the pressure of the work and the continuous interaction with the kids was more than they had expected – they had decided to resign. The national average of tenure for those who worked in this kind of ministry is about eighteen months. We hadn't quite made it, but the ministry was going and kids were being reached and helped. Suddenly we were left with a Center to operate and no adult supervision to operate it.

Dad and Mother were great prayer warriors for our work. They had helped again and again. Now they took the greatest step of faith ever – Even though they were in their late sixties at the time they actually left their comfortable home in Dad's Development and moved into the center. Dad ran his construction business during the day and came back to the Center to work with the kids at night. Mother cooked the meals and kept the house. They served there for over three months.

It was right about that time that I was having evangelistic meetings down in Maryland with Pastor Bruce Dick. Bruce was unmarried at the time. The Lord was giving us some wonderful meetings and Dave Boyer joined us again to minister in music. In fact, Mrs. Anna Boyer, Dave's mother, came down to play the piano.

As I talked to Bruce about what we were doing his interest increased. Bruce was pastoring a Church of God in Westminster Maryland. I had previously had meetings with his brother, Argyl, at another Church of God a few miles away, and after meetings with Bruce, I had the third series of meetings with Ernie Baker at Westminster Church of God.

All of these churches were Winebrenner Churches of God, a more conservative denomination by far than the Churches of God I had experienced in Kentucky. Their denominational seminary was in Finley, Ohio. However, none of the men I had meetings with had attended there. They had all graduated from Washington Bible College.

All that came about because Ernie Baker had attended Washington Bible College. He came to the pastorate with a solid grasp on the Word of God, a strong conviction of the eternal security of the believer, and a Dispensational and Premillennial understanding of Eschatology (Prophecy). None of those things were typical of the Theological orientation of the Churches of God. God used him in the salvation of literally scores of young men and a number of them ended up going to WBC and coming back to pastor additional churches in that denomination.

Just before I arrived, Ernie Baker had gone out to the seminary in Finley, and after seeing and hearing what was being taught, he wrote a letter to them and asked them to respond to him on ten different issues of doctrine and practice. Instead of responding, the denominational leadership sent a letter demanding that all of the pastors in the Maryland Eldership censure Ernie Baker.

Now, quite of number of those pastors had been won to the Lord by Ernie Baker and if he hadn't won them to the Lord, they had been taught by him in Bible classes he held for pastors, since many of them had never had formal education. The reaction to the Seminary's letter was electrifying. Almost the entire Maryland eldership responded by saying, "Censure him? We support him."

Just as that was happening I was having meetings at another Winebrenner Church of God in Pennsylvania with Pastor Russ Aults. As I was telling Russ about what was taking place there in the Maryland situation, Russ said, "Don't you know that the denominational leadership is planning to split the Maryland eldership? They are going to force half of it to go with the West Penn Eldership and half of it with East Penn and that way they'll gain back control by weakening the voting block of the men in Maryland." When I heard that I knew we had to take action.

I was still flying a good bit at that time, so I borrowed Harold Dubs airplane and I got Russ to go with me, and we flew down to Westminster, Maryland. I met with Ernie, Bruce and Argyl and I had Russ explain to them what was about to happen. These men in turn got the word to the other churches and a resistance movement took place against this attempt to politically control the churches.

Before long the Denomination made their move. They first tried to take over Bruce's church by sending a man in one Sunday morning who announced to the congregation that he was now their pastor. When he did, all but about 15 people walked out the door with Bruce and over 100 people founded what became Clearfield Bible Church. They simply left behind the property and everything they had and began a new work in order to remain true to the Word of God.

Bruce at that time became its initial pastor, but about the same time, started working with me. Ultimately he became the coordinator for our center there at 37 N. Franklin Street and the Lord used him to bring stability, both to the work and to the lives of many of the kids who came to the center. He and the staff ran an after school program for the kids and took in resident teens placed by the police or Children's Services.

And Now Youth for Christ?

We had barely gotten the inter city work going when I was approached by a number of the pastors of the area and asked to assume the directorship of the local Youth for Christ Rally and club ministry. Having begun Teen Encounter, I felt I could not run a separate organization, but offered to take the Rally and the clubs under the umbrella of the Teen Encounter Ministry. The men on the YFC board agreed and we now had a full orbed ministry not only to the inter city but to the suburbs as well.

I began by renting the facilities at the YWCA on Market Street (the main thoroughfare in York from east to west), to hold our Saturday night rallies. We met there during the spring and summer and for sometime in the fall. During that time Bob Neff, former YFC Director and well known announcer on WDAC radio, was over as a speaker one night. After the service Bob observed, "You've just about outgrown this YWCA thing, and if they put you out, (which we had heard there was some talk of because of our strong evangelistic style), where are you going to go?" I told him I really didn't know, and he said, "Well, you know, the old Christian and Missionary Alliance Tabernacle building is empty on South and Duke Streets." Then he surprised me by saying, "If I had the opportunity, I wouldn't even pray about it, I would just buy that building. It would be ideal for what you need and it's in the right neighborhood."

Well, I didn't exactly take his advice – I did pray about it, and then we went down and looked at the building. I approached the folks at C&MA, and they offered me the building and the adjacent house for $35,000. I made a counter offer of $25,000 and they accepted it. We went ahead on faith and purchased the properties. That was during the second year of our operation.

Then in the third year, a man contacted me from York Federal Savings and Loan and told me that they had a building that he thought I ought to consider opening as a center on King Street. After much urging, I went and looked at it. It had been a former tavern that had closed in something of a fight and there were buckshot holes in the wall where there had been a shoot out, but it was a good solid building and located right on an important corner.

The man from York Federal kept saying, "Just make an offer," and I said, "Look, I really don't have any money to offer." He countered, "Well, I think the bank would accept almost anything." As I went through the building I began to understand why. Finally I said to him, "Look, I told you I couldn't make an offer and you are insisting, so I will make an offer. I'll give you $500 for the building."

Of course he laughed, and I said to him, "If you have enough gall to even tell them what the offer is, you tell them that is all I can offer for it." So I went back to work, thinking that was certainly over.

A couple of days later, Stan Gladfelter, who was president of the York Federal, called me and said, "Bill, we got your offer on that building. I took it to the Board and they rejected it." I laughed and said, "Well, that doesn't surprise me, Stan, but I'm in no shape to buy another building right now." Stan continued, "Well, that's not all. They rejected it; but they are going to deed the building to you and then give you $1,000 to get it into operation." And they did exactly that. It seemed that God was always surprising us with things we could never have dreamed of.

More Open Doors

There was another thing God did about this time. Because of our activity in the city we were gaining a reputation. It wasn't something we tried to do, it was simply the result of all we were doing and it opened doors of testimony and witness to all kinds of people from every echelon of life.

I was in my office one day when my secretary came back with a business card in her hand. She handed it to me and told me that a man was in the front office and that he wanted to see me. I asked what he wanted and she said "He wouldn't say." I decided to invite him back and listen.

When Joe came in he hardly got seated when he said, "Reverend, they tell me that you still believe the Bible, is that true?" I leaned back in my chair and gave a hearty laugh. "You've come to the right place," I said, "Yes I absolutely believe the Bible." "Whew," he sighed, "I wasn't sure anyone believed the Bible any more since this Ecumenical Movement came along." I immediately assumed he was from a liberal denominational church. "What can I do for you Joe?" I asked.

Joe told me that the men in his church had gotten permission to hold a men's meeting and invite outside speakers to come and he would like for me to speak to them. "I'd be happy to come," I said, "As long as I can find time in my schedule." He told me I could choose any Sunday night I wanted and I found one in April and suggested that date. He immediately confirmed and as I wrote it down I asked, "OK, Joe, what is the name of this church?" And Joe replied, "St. Leo's Roman Catholic Church." I laid my pencil down and looked Joe in the eye. "Joe," I said, "I'm not sure you want me to come. You see, I believe your problems began a long time before the Ecumenical Movement. I believe they go back to even before the Council of Trent. Let me tell you what I will say if I come."

I opened my Bible to Romans chapter five and read the first verses, *"Being justified by faith we have peace with God through our Lord Jesus Christ. By whom also we have access by faith* (not by the church, not by the sacraments, not by the virgin, by faith*), into this grace wherein we stand and rejoice in the hope* (the steadfast expectation) *of the glory of God."* I explained the verses as carefully as I could, and when I was finished Joe said, "That's what I want you to say." "OK, Joe," I responded, "I'll do it."

I remembered reading Dr. Harry Ironside's book which told the stories of his ministry. One story was about his visit to an Indian village. In the early days of his ministry, Dr. Ironside had been a missionary to the Native Americans. In this particular village there was a Roman Catholic Church, but there had not been a priest visit that village for years. The Tribal Elders asked Dr. Ironside if he would hold a service for them in the church. Although he had to wear a robe and vestments, he agreed and told of the blessing of telling the simple gospel to this people who had been in darkness. I remember reading that story and saying, "Lord, I wish you would do something like that for me." Now it appeared He had.

As the date grew closer I began to have several concerns. One was that St. Leo's was almost in the shadow of the church Dr. Ralph Stoll was pastoring at that time near Lancaster. Pastor Stoll had been my pastor in Altoona years ago and I respected him and did not want to do anything that would embarrass him, so I called and told him what had happened. He responded that he knew Joe and in fact, Joe had invited him to come, but because he was a pastor in the same city it would look like a pulpit exchange and would cause confusion among the saints. But he told me, "I think you are in the perfect position to take the assignment, so go, and I will pray for you."

The day of the event it dawned on me, "You are going to be preaching in a Roman Catholic Church and no one is going to be there with you. Even if you clearly preach the gospel, who will believe you? Even St. Peter, as dumb as he sometimes was, was smart enough to take some others with him when he went into the house of Cornelius the Gentile to be witnesses of what he said and what would happen." I got on the phone and called my good friend Don Hamme, who had worked with Roman Catholics in Haiti for years. When I told him where I was going he immediately wanted to go with me.

We met in the basement of the church and there were about thirty or more men. They were seated comfortably before me and before I knew it pipes and cigars were lit – obviously no one was expecting much. Before I began the priest came in and joined us. Don went over and sat with the Priest. I began by telling the men about our work with the teens and about an answer to prayer. When I mentioned God answering prayer, they began to laugh – they actually thought I was joking. Then I got down to the Word of God. Before it was over I went carefully over the Romans passage. Slowly and quietly the pipes were put aside and the cigars were put out. These men saw I was serious.

I had been given twenty minutes to speak – I spoke for forty five and when I was done after giving a clear invitation to receive Christ and His finished work by faith, they began to ask questions and for another forty five minutes I tried to answer them. Before we left I laid out John R. Rice's tract, *What Must I Do to be Saved?* and Arthur Cutting's *Safety, Certainty and Enjoyment.*

Many of the men took the tracts and as they left the room I overheard one of them say, "I guess Father learned a thing or two tonight." I could only pray that the Word would do its work, but God had indeed given me my desire – to preach the blessed gospel of grace to Catholics in a Catholic Church.

I Dance with the Teamsters

We felt we needed office space. I was up on the second floor at the corner of Market and King Street, and they were going to tear down that building, so we started praying. My volunteer bookkeeper at that time was Mrs. Gertrude Senft and she was living on Poplar Street. She told me about the Teamsters Union office building on Poplar Street which they were vacating and had up for sale. I said, "How much do they want for it?" She said, "$48,000." I said, "Oh, my, that's more money than we would ever spend on an office building." She continued to insist I look at it.

I went down one day and went through the building, and indeed, it was a fantastic building and more space than I could imagine. In fact, they told me it had 5,000 square feet in it and I ended up saying, "Okay, this building has 5,000 square feet. I will make an offer – one dollar a square foot. I'll give you five thousand dollars for the building!"

As you might imagine, they were not happy. I remember they took me by the arms and led me out the door. I thought that was another closed door, but that was in April. In October, I went back to visit the Teamsters once again. By this time they were located in their new office quarters, a very plush and beautiful building. Once again I offered them five thousand dollars, and they agreed. I ended up getting the building for one dollar a square foot.

That building had not only the office space, but in the back they had a large freezer area and a cold storage area, two rooms, with eight inches of cork lining the walls and the ceilings. We were doing radio and having a difficult time finding a quiet area where we could produce a broadcast, and this was absolutely ideal. Art

Colburn came up and designed a beautiful radio studio with perfect acoustic control and everything necessary for a perfect broadcast environment. We could never have afforded to build anything like it. We went in there, renovated the surface, gave it some surface acoustical treatment, and made the most beautiful and efficient radio production and control studio I had even seen. In addition, the building had a large shipping area that we set up for printing.

It was that same summer of 1969, that things really exploded in York. Early in the spring of that year, I went into the city on one very, very hot day in early June. You could sense the tension as you entered the core of the city and the word was out on the street that there was going to be a riot that evening.

I gathered the staff and the kids together at Franklin Street, and we went into the chapel for prayer. We got down on our knees and prayed that God would intervene, that somehow, God would bring calm. After we had prayed for awhile, I left and went down to City Hall.

As I walked in, I sensed immediately the tense atmosphere – It was all over the city. When I went upstairs looking for Captain McCaffery, I found them getting out the riot gear. They had opened the big safety storage room, and they were hauling out the tear gas guns and the face shields and the clubs. I stood and watched for a while and then I said to him, "Mac, I don't want to get in the way here, but since I am here, would you let me have a word of prayer with everybody?" He said, "Sure," and he hollered at the guys and said, "Hey, Reverend's gonna pray—let's be quiet for a minute."

I prayed, and God laid a special burden on my heart to just pray that everything would be all right that night, that God would get us through it, and that the forces that were trying to create the problems would be subdued. While I was praying, I suddenly felt a cool breeze coming across the room. It was a remarkable thing, and you could have heard a pin drop in there.

I finally said, "Amen," and nobody moved. After maybe a full minute, suddenly, Captain McCaffery said, "Guys, let's put this junk away; I don't think we are going to need it." They put the riot gear away and sure enough, it was quiet that night – nothing occurred.

Is there any way to measure the impact of that kind of thing in the lives of those who were involved? Those kids at Franklin Street

– they had prayed so earnestly and it was a big prayer. It was not a prayer about some personal thing or even about the ministry. It was a city-wide prayer, a prayer that concerned forces they could never have influenced much less controlled, and it was answered. Not a single incident took place in the city that night.

And think about the police. They were pumped up and ready for violence. A preacher comes by and says a prayer and everything reverses. As long as the people involved live, I believe they will never forget the night God answered prayer and brought calm to a troubled city. That is what I had prayed York might see. That is what drove my actions. Not that they might see me, or the organization, but that they might experience the actual power of God. God demonstrated His power on that occasion and it would not be the last.

CHAPTER EIGHTEEN

The Gothard Connection

W hile I was still in Kentucky I had met a young man from Illinois who had come down to work at Camp Nathanael on a program called SPAM (Summer Program for the Assistance of Missions). He was with a number of others, but I had observed him because he had a deformed hand and some other physical difficulties, but seemed to overcome them with a vibrant attitude.

One day I mentioned how much I admired him for his positive attitude and he replied, "I don't take the credit for that – I have a great youth director at our church and he has really helped me. In fact," he continued, "he writes letters to encourage me and I have saved them in a notebook. Would you like to see it?" I assured him that I would very much like to see it and he took me to his room and showed me a large notebook filled with letters. As I read the content of several of these, I came to the conclusion that this youth director, in a little Methodist church in Illinois knew some things I did not know. As I read the signature, I learned that his name was Bill Gothard.

I copied down Bill's address and phone number and sometime after arriving in York I contacted him telling him that I wanted to meet and talk with him. Bill said he would be glad to meet me, but it would take at least six weeks for him to share with me what I needed to know. I knew I did not have six weeks to spend so the conversation ended without resolution.

However, I was confronted with dealing with an ever greater number of teens with severe problems, I contacted Bill again a few months later and went through much of the same conversation. Then one day in 1966, Bill called me. He told me that Wheaton College had asked him to do a two week inter-session seminar that spring and there were still some openings. The call came too late for me since my spring and summer were already scheduled, but I urged Bill that if ever he did a two week seminar again to please let me know.

In November Bill called again to tell me Trinity Seminary had invited him to do a one week seminar between Christmas and New Years. It was the first one week seminar he had done and he planned to conduct it from eight in the morning and do both morning, afternoon and evening sessions. I immediately enrolled and enrolled Bruce Dick, our Franklin Street Coordinator, at the same time.

There were thirty five of us in the seminar and for the entire week we often continued late into the evening talking about the various areas of youth conflict Bill had identified. At the end I was convinced I needed to train my entire staff in this material so I asked Bill to come to York. He responded by saying that he did not intend to travel but would plan to hold all his seminars in the Illinois area. I persisted until at last he consented to send his associate, Larry Coy. However, he told me I could enroll no more than thirty five people in the Seminar. I agreed and we set it up for the coming spring (1967).

I began to talk about it and invite registrations over my radio broadcasts. At that time I had about twenty stations some as far away as California. Soon we received a raft of registrations – about sixty five in all. I called Bill and told him what had happened. His response was, "Just take the first thirty five and eliminate the rest." "I can't do that," I told him. "Some of these people have arranged their vacations to come and they have already booked flights and made their travel arrangements. They have overcome some pretty big obstacles to get here and we have to accommodate them."

I remember there was a long pause. Finally Bill replied, "Well, I can't send Larry to do this Seminar. I will have to do it myself." And so he did. Bill held his first one week Seminar away from the Illinois area at the York College under the auspices of Teen Encounter.

The results of that seminar were wide reaching. Captain McCaffery attended from the York Juvenile office. During the seminar he invited Bill to visit city hall. He introduced him to the Mayor and later recommended Bill to the Chicago Police. That open door really put Bill's work on the map. There were many others whose lives were profoundly influenced by that seminar and it was the beginning of Bill doing one-week seminars with larger crowds – eventually into the thousands.

As Teen Encounter became known we were asked to help with a greater and greater number of kids and we found that the training we had received helped us to understand their deepest needs and show them how God could meet them. As I have been writing, I visited an old friend who had attended that first seminar. He was a pastor at the time, now retired and in an assisted living facility. As we visited he rehearsed to me again the blessings of that seminar in his life, his ministry and his family.

CHAPTER NINETEEN

Youth We Met Along the Way

I can't tell all the stories of the kids who came to live at the Centers, and some you would not want to hear – they were certainly not all "success stories," far from it. But lives were impacted and I expect to see many of them in heaven when we meet around the throne, because in the midst of their lost and devastated lives, Jesus Christ made His entrance and began His wonderful work of transformation. As with all of us, they are a work in progress. They were not what they ought to be, and not what they want to be, but they are also not what they used to be.

In all we took in 142 separate cases during our twelve years of operating the Center ministry. I recently dug out the case file and read through the play by play reports. There were victories and there were defeats but even when we seemed to have failed, I knew we had exposed that young person to a loving environment and a clear presentation of the Lord Jesus who could change and transform their lives. Overall it was a costly and exhausting endeavor, but one which God used, and which I will never regret.

Nancy N. was the first teen with which I tried to work. She was in perpetual trouble and Captain McCaffery had asked me to see if I would get anywhere with her. I made an appointment to see her but knew that she could walk out on me at any moment so I arranged to talk to her during a trip to WDAC radio station in Lancaster. I figured that as long as she was in my car, she would either have to talk or listen.

Nancy was not a particularly attractive girl. She was overweight and cut her hair short. She was also domineering and seemed to try to act tough like a boy. I had a very long talk with Nancy and tried to make her my friend, but there was something Nancy was hiding and I wasn't sure just what it was. I went over the gospel story several times but while Nancy listened, she was not ready to yield to Christ.

In subsequent contacts it became evident that Nancy was a lesbian and held a very strong domineering control over several younger and smaller girls. Although several of our workers continued to try to reach Nancy over a period of time, she was a girl who resisted our efforts and the love she could have known from the One who is the Lover of our souls.

King V.

Our first resident case was a boy from the White Hill State Correction Agency whose first name was King. At the intervention of Pastor Evan Schaffer the State decided to make Teen Encounter a sort of "half way house" in this case. King came with us in the spring and stayed throughout the summer. He was employed during that time so was not a usual profile of the kids we worked with. We were just beginning the work and kept skimpy records, but as I recall King did make a profession of faith while with us. Eventually he was returned to his parent's custody.

Shirley H.

Shirley H. was the ninth case we handled at the Center. When Shirley came to the Franklin Street Center, she was the most subdued and withdrawn child I had ever seen. Shirley was Caucasian and she seemed to want nothing more than to be off by herself and in her own world. It was immediately evident that she was a very troubled girl.

Not long after she came, our Coordinator, Bruce Dick, observed that Shirley had a series of scars which ran from her wrists to her elbow on both arms. He wisely tried to ignore them to give this girl time to trust us and adjust to things at the Center. Shirley had a particularly hard time believing that God loved her and Bruce counseled with her at length. At last the mystery of the scars began to emerge.

Shirley's father had been arrested and was in prison for incest. We will probably never know all that he did to Shirley, but we do know this. He was sadomasochistic and got aroused by holding Shirley's arm while he cut it with a razor blade as Shirley would scream. It is little wonder that this girl was emotionally unstable lapsing at times into a trance-like state from which, when she revived she could remember nothing.

Eventually, God worked in Shirley's heart and she trusted herself to Him and became a very sweet person. But only eternity can completely erase the horrors she endured. She spent a stint in the State Mental hospital, and we really felt we had lost her several times. But even after finally leaving the Center, she wrote some of the sweetest notes of thanks and gratitude to me and to the staff.

Every time I think of Shirley, I am thankful that God allowed us to have the ministry of Teen Encounter that could, at least for a time, offer these children the security of a genuinely loving environment and introduce them to a God who cared about them even in their darkest times.

Kathy R.

Kathy R. was case number 31. The night that Kathy came to the center, I got a rather desperate call from our Franklin Street Coordinator. I was told that a young black girl had been placed with us and she was emotionally ballistic. I learned she had been in eleven foster homes before being placed with us. The Coordinator asked for my help.

I remember getting into my car and driving in the snow on a very cold dark night to the Center. I parked along the side of the house by the alley entrance and was just about to step out of the car when I saw the back door of the center suddenly burst open and a very distraught black girl in her bare feet wearing only a dress, went running from the house. I didn't have to wonder who that was.

I slammed the door to the car and took off after her in about four inches of snow. In about a city block I caught up and simply picked her up in my arms and carried her sobbing back to the center. I took her inside and laid her on the couch as the girls gathered around her. I suggested we call Dr. Elmer Hamme who not only served on our Board but gave free medical care to all our staff and resident teens. After describing what was happening Dr. Hamme decided to come to the center and administer a light sedative, which shortly put Kathy to sleep.

It was not an easy start and the road ahead was almost as rocky as the beginning. Kathy had tremendous mood swings and did not get along well with anyone. She was manipulative, lied incessantly and disrupted whatever she could. I asked the agency for a case report so we could better understand what we were dealing with.

I learned that Kathy, like so many of our kids, came from a home without a father. Her father had left shortly after Kathy was born. The new man (her mother did not remarry) sired twelve children. Kathy had lived a tumultuous life from the very start and at thirteen, her mother, who had just been released from the state mental hospital, became overcome by despair, emptied a can of gasoline on herself and then lit a match. Kathy watched helplessly as her mother burned to death. When I read her school report the evaluation of the school counselor troubled me. It read, "Dull / Normal – incapable of average achievement." I refused to believe that.

One day Kathy came into the office and I called her in to see me. She had been doing very poorly in school, was frequently in trouble and was failing several subjects. However, the more I had watched Kathy, the more I was convinced that she was a bright child that just had shut down through the trauma she had experienced.

Finally I said to her, "Kathy, I received a report from the school counselor which I am not supposed to let you see, but I am going to read it to you. Are you ready?" She nodded a yes, and I read, "Dull / Normal – incapable of average achievement." She never flinched. I said, "Kathy would you like my evaluation of that report?" She nodded again and I said, "Bunk! There is nothing wrong with you. You are bright, you have ability, but you put on this act so that no one will expect anything from you. You have your wheelbarrow turned

202

upside down so no one will put anything in it. You know I'm right don't you?" She smiled and shook her head again. I said, "Kathy, I want to see a change. I want you to show them what you can do."

Kathy's change was gradual but real. She had not been at the center long when she received Christ as her Savior. She almost immediately began bearing witness to Christ in school. Her grades improved, she stayed out of trouble and Kathy became a beautiful young lady. I had the privilege of baptizing her with a group of teens from the center.

During the week of Operation Penetration, when Teen Encounter tried to reach the entire city of York with the gospel, Kathy many evenings climbed to the platform of the sound van and declared her faith in Christ in the very neighborhoods where she was well known.

Now it would be nice if I could say that Kathy kept it all together and lived an exemplary life, but as with many of these kids, their baggage shows when they get in any kind of pressured situation. I learned that Kathy had been going to a "girl friend's" house to study during her senior year. Unfortunately, the "girl friend" turned out to be a boy friend and Kathy got pregnant.

I had already published my book on Abortion called, "Murder, and How to Make It Legal; a Study of Abortion." Kathy had developed a tender conscience and convictions about what God says about the value of life and she asked for help. I was able to get her into a home for unwed mothers in Philadelphia and drove her there myself.

There she had her baby letting him out for adoption. Kathy later finished her high school and several years later sent for her baptismal certificate so she could join a church. We truly came to love this girl and I am confident I will see her in heaven.

Marcellus D.

When Marcellus D. was placed with us he had been living in a home where his mother seemed to resent him and his father beat him when his mother complained. When Marcellus did anything that displeased his mother he was beaten and often humiliated. His mother used such unique techniques as forcing Marcellus to eat his food off the floor, or literally sleep in an actual doghouse in the back yard. Do I have to say that Marcellus was a resentful, angry and deeply disturbed teen?

As a result his parents placed him in the County Children's Home, a facility that could have been run by Fagan, of Oliver Twist fame for the reputation it had. Shortly after we opened our Centers that facility closed in scandal with both staff and children infected with STDs.

Marcellus longed for someone who would care for him as he relates in this testimony he wrote for our Teen Encounter publication. I will let Marcellus tell his story since he can do it best.

My name is Marcellus D. and I'm 13 years old. It all started up at Children's Home where the kids are not Christians and they live in sin. I learned about many things that I should not have known at my age but anyway, I did. I smoked, cussed and drank. We had physical fights with the house parents. This kept going on and on and finally one day they kicked me out and sent me to the Detention Home.

At Detention Home you get locked behind bars if you don't behave. The first time I was locked up for two days. I had three meals a day and then when those two days were up, I got to go to the recreation room.

We had ping-pong tables, pool tables and a black and white TV there. I was so much for fighting that I got in a fight and had to go back behind bars for a week. When I got out, I did the same thing again and back up again for another week. Then I prayed that if I got another chance, I would make it good and I did till I left.

Then my mother came and I didn't want to go back with her because she had put me in the Children's Home. Before she put me in Children's Home, she beat me and threw me out in the cold winter. I slept out with my dog in the dog house and went without food. All these things kept going through my mind but I decided to give it another chance.

I did but the same thing happened again. I was always blamed. My sister and boy friend always nagged me and at the time I didn't know how to avoid them. This kept going on and on and my mother and I had arguments and fights, and my father broke them up and I would get all the blame.

One night I got in a fight with her and she went down to the Police Station. While she was gone, I crawled through the window and drank all her whiskey and ran away. I was picked up and taken to court from the Detention Home. They got my mother for child abuse.

At that point I didn't have a home until I came to Teen Encounter. I met Patty and Dean at Teen Encounter and they showed love for me. Before I come to Teen Encounter I said, "God, if you give me a place to live where the people care for me, I will stay straight."

He did and when I came here, I met a lot of people and they were all saved and going to heaven and I knew I wasn't. One day we went to Pinchot Park and I decided I'd get saved, but I wasn't sure how so I talked to Dean. I became saved and I stopped smoking and other things. My life is completely different now.

Rick R.

Rick R. was case number 52. Rick came to us after his release from the York Detention home. I have looked over his files and can't tell exactly why he was placed there, but Rick was a willful stubborn youth and had acquired many vices by the time he came to us including smoking, drinking, a bad temper and foul language.

I think I wanted to include Rick's story, not only because we worked on and off with Rick over a period of several years, but I later provided counseling when he went back to prison as an adult.

But the thing that makes Rick's story so troubling to me is that Rick's grandfather Jake W. was a godly man, a great prayer warrior an excellent song leader and a dear friend. I had invited Jake to lead singing during one of our Crusades in Kentucky and he had taken off work and come all the way down from York to help with that Crusade. He was also a top mechanic and was always ready to help us boys when we wanted to buy a car to choose a good one. How did Rick turn out so badly two generations removed from such an influence?

First, Jake W. was older when he came to Christ. Although extremely talented in mechanics (the Navy flew him all over the world to analyze problems and system breakdowns), Jake had been a hard drinker up until his conversion. While his children all made professions of faith, his older daughter married an unsaved man. She soon realized that she would go through a repeat of the life her mother had lived before Jake came to Christ. Rick was the offspring of that home.

During his stay with us we were able to get Rick a job at Sheltered Workshop, a local effort to assist kids who were slow learners to do something productive. I have a picture of him proudly showing off an office chair he had refurbished.

As already intimated, Rick was not a glowing success story. He seemed to respond at times, but when he wanted to do something, he simply disobeyed all the rules and did it anyway. In 1972 we sent Rick to Harold Witmer's Center in Clarksville, Tennessee, hoping that a new start away from former companions would be the change Rick needed. I received a letter from Harold a short time later indicating Rick was doing much better.

As the years went by we lost track of Rick. Eventually I got a letter telling me that he was married and had several children. At the time both he and his wife were reading the Scriptures together. Still Rick suffered relapses into depression and irresponsible behavior.

At last Rich was arrested and sent to Prison on charges of incest with his oldest daughter filed by his wife. I talked to them by phone and tried to counsel toward reconciliation, but Rick's wife would have none of it. The last I know Rick is still in prison.

Esther K.

Esther came to Teen Encounter when she was recommended to us by her school counselor. She had gone to her counselor to try to escape a situation in which she found herself. As with Kathy (who was a cousin to Esther), Esther had no father, that is, her mother lived with a variety of men and it was never clear exactly whose child she was.

As with almost all these cases, there was turmoil in the home, and Esther's only protection, such as it was, was her mother. One day, when she was about eleven, an angry lover quarreled with the mother and then, right in front of Esther, shot and killed her. Needless to say Esther was traumatized. Naturally Children's Services stepped in to intervene and decided to place her first with an aunt. Not only did the aunt not want Esther, but she was also deeply involved in witchcraft and Esther lived in constant fear.

Next she was placed with her older brother. The only problem was that the agency didn't bother to find out that her older brother was running a house of prostitution. Esther was in constant danger and was exposed to all that happens in such a place every day.

Thankfully, Esther was a stronger personality than Kathy and had sought out help. We placed her at Duke Street Center with Dean and Patty Bult. Patty had grown up in somewhat of a similar situation and could identify readily with girls like Esther. Patty was also a passionate soul winner and Esther had not been at the Center more than a few days before she made a faith commitment to Jesus Christ.

The change was very real with Esther and she vocalized her decision among her peers. Esther had been a fair student in spite of her situation and now began to do even better academically. She was athletic and participated in school activities as well.

Esther developed spiritually very quickly and was actually showing some leadership at the Center among the girls when Dean, who had served with us for several years, felt called into the pastorate. Esther was crushed. For the first time since her mother's death Esther had begun to develop close relationships and now, the person she was closest to was leaving her.

Ruby and I began to observe the change and we did not like what we saw. We decided that this girl was worth investing in and so we offered her a home with us. We had taken a number of the kids to our home for brief periods of time, usually several weeks, when they were experiencing difficulty. But now we were committing to actually take Esther on a permanent basis. After a few days she consented and Esther moved in with us, sharing a room with our daughter Rachel.

Now there were many adjustments to make, for both of us. Esther had always gone to an inner-city school where the preponderance of students were black. Now she found herself at a High School where almost none of the students were black. My heart ached when she came home one day and told me that a student had spit on her. I tried to encourage her to overcome and do well and she did. She carried herself with dignity and earned the respect of students and teachers alike. One of my favorite pictures is of Esther in her RHS majorette uniform.

I remember getting used to the smell of straightening combs heating on the stove and hair gel and a few of those cultural things we had never experienced before having a black daughter. I was glad for both myself and our children that they could experience the richness of cultural differences.

When we traveled as a family, eyes would raise when I would introduce my children, so I decided to get ahead of the audience by introducing her as "My only daughter with a year-round sun tan." That usually got a laugh and relieved any tension.

One year Esther worked as a waitress in the dinning room at Word of Life Inn. I was scheduled to speak that summer and Esther would tell folks that her Daddy was going to be the speaker in a couple of weeks. Harry Bollback's wife Millie, responded by telling her husband, "I didn't know we were having a black preacher this summer." "We're not." Harry replied. "Yes we are," Millie insisted. "Esther says her daddy is on the schedule." Jack and Harry broke up into laughter and neither of them would let Millie forget that one.

There is much more I want to tell about Esther, but that must wait for another time. However, I will say, that in spite of challenges both for her and for us, we never regretted the move. We genuinely learned to love Esther as our own daughter and have always thought of her in that way.

Liz W.

Liz was a handful. She was from Hanover but had somehow gotten shifted to York Children's Services. Looking at her record she was pleasant, usually liked by everyone, and made good grades in school. If it had not been for an unsettled home situation Liz would probably never have been with us.

Her greatest weakness seemed to be that she would attach her-self to one of the other girls at the Center and then just act out in any way the other girl did. I have a very long file of Liz's ups and downs because she was with us for almost a year. In the end she got herself moved to another agency where there was less structure, then ran away to do her own thing.

Several years ago I was standing at our Missions Display Table at Grace Fellowship Church in York. A couple of very sharp looking young people came by and showed an interest in things that were on the table. I learned they were siblings, and they seemed to have a keen interest in missions. They were very pleasant and it was a joy talking with them.

While they were still talking to Ruby and me their mother came by. She chatted with us for a few minutes as if she knew us, but so many people in that area knew us because of our years of ministry there that it was not unusual. Then she said, "You don't recognize me do you?" I responded that she looked very familiar and apologized that I probably should, but had to admit I did not. She said, "I'm Liz – remember me? I'm the one who gave you so much trouble when I lived at the Center." I told her I didn't remember much about the trouble, but I was certainly glad to see her. "You know, you were always one of my favorites," I told her.

"So tell me about yourself and what you are doing now," I said. "Well, I'm divorced, and raising the children alone, but I accepted Christ while I was at the Center and I am determined to raise them for the Lord. I was so rebellious that I had to do things my way and now I'm paying for it," she said. And then she looked at us and said something we will never forget. "I was so foolish," She said, "I didn't realize what I had. That year at the Center was the only year of my life where I really had peace and security." I wonder how many stories we will hear in heaven just like Liz's.

One of the tragedies of our present society is the number of women who are unmarried and who live for a time with a man, bear a child (or several children), then have that man leave and begin the cycle all over again. One of the side effects of such relationships is that children, especially those who belong to some former boyfriend, get abused by the present live-in lover. When the child, or children are girls they are frequently assaulted sexually and simply used at the pleasure of the boyfriend. If the mother cares at all, she is afraid to intervene for fear of loosing her lover. If the child is a boy – well anything can happen.

In a day when less that 50% of those who are living together are actually married we are paying the terrible price for our sin and it is the children who suffer the most. So many kids came through the Centers, sometimes just for the recreation and Bible studies, sometimes just for the Rallies, but many came to live with us and observe for the first time in their lives the dynamics of a genuine Christian life and a Christ-centered home and they will never forget. It is their stories that make all that we put into it worth while.

Cheryl

One final story – as I sifted through some old files I found this testimony written by Cheryl who stayed at our Duke Street Center. She wrote:

I came from a home starved of love; instead of loving, we hated. My father was an alcoholic and my mother seemed so uncompassionate. My mother was married twice; therefore I had two stepbrothers and one stepsister. I distrusted everyone. I tried committing suicide once and was sincerely thinking of it again. I was under extreme mental pressure–But I was a church member of a large denomination and a religious person.

I'll never forget the time my family tried to prove me mentally ill. I went to the hospital, escorted by police. I was praying prayers I'd learned since I was a young child, but they didn't help me in the slightest. After undergoing isolation and some tests, I was proven normal; so I was released and went home to the same environment. I only stayed there for about three weeks and after a series of physical and verbal battles, I contacted some-one with authority with whom I could confide. I left the house the next morning not knowing what I was walking into, but sure it couldn't be any worse than what I'd just left.

When I walked into the Teen Encounter Center on January 30, 1970, I saw a picture of Jesus hanging in the parlor. "What kind of crack pots are these?" I asked myself. "They must be really religious." I was greeted by two smiling faced people who were to be my "mom and dad". They had something, but I was sure it was fake. When they began talking about God and Jesus, I let them know they could have their religion and I had my own.

About a week after I came, I heard a sermon preached on Heaven and Hell. Boy, it brought me around and really shocked me. I wanted to rebel. I wanted their happiness, but I didn't want to pay the price. I wanted to go my own way.

Two weeks later, I went to a Teen Encounter Rally held in a High School auditorium. On that night, February 14, 1970, I accepted the Lord Jesus Christ into my heart to be my personal Savior and things haven't been the same since. Some things disappeared immediately from my old sin life and some others require a little work. I found real love, contentment, satisfaction, happiness, peace of mind, a joy to live and a reason to live. I found real peace–deep down in my heart. I found the Life–it's in Jesus. Believe me, I've given the Lord my life since I have accepted Him.

I believe it is truly of His will that I am here at Teen Encounter with people to love and people to love you back. He has given me everything ANYONE could ever need. I want to thank and praise the Lord for a place called Teen Encounter and I thank Him for the many people who keep it going.

Now I want to tell others of Jesus and the love He has for us. I want to tell them they can be <u>happy</u> *like me and have Christ forever and ever. He has sent me into the world as a Christian to tell people of Him, no matter what their color or creed. He has given me a position on a varsity cheer leading squad and put me in a Bible Club for me to grow spiritually. So I thank and praise the Lord for everything He has done and everything He will do in the future.*

C.W.

CHAPTER TWENTY

The Airport Limousine & A Trip to Texas

Once three Centers got into full operation, transporting the teens to any kind of an event became a major challenge.

We had two Center operations going at that time and when we went anywhere there were about seventeen of us to provide transportation for. That's just how many there were the Saturday night Earl Schultz, Director of Hampstead Youth for Christ, asked me to speak at the Rally. We loaded everyone in an old station wagon, a sedan and a Volkswagen Bug. Those were the days before seatbelt laws and kids were sitting (or scrunching) everywhere. There were even two teenage girls behind the rear seat of the Bug.

I spoke and God did some unusual things. The young assistant director that Earl had left in charge that evening was convicted by the Word of rebellion toward his parents and I had a wonderful time of prayer with him afterward as he repented and promised God to make things right.

After the service I went out in the audience to meet a close friend I had not seen for a very long time. Roger Schultz, Earl's younger brother, had been my roommate during our freshman year at PBI. We had actually roomed together by choice because we had a great deal in common.

Both of our fathers were building contractors and so both of us were familiar with and had worked in construction. We found other commonalities as well, like driving convertibles – although mine was a '47 Chevy and his a '50 Mercury (there was a very big difference in price, power and prestige).

I hadn't seen Roger or his wife Ruth since those PBI days. They had left after the freshman year to get married and had finished their schooling at King's College under Dr. Bob Cook.

Although we each had a real fondness for each other we were always quick to jab and so as I approached, without ever looking at Roger, I ask Ruth, "Do his feet still stink?" While I was talking to Ruth however Roger had done the exact same thing and asked Ruby, "Does he still snore?" We were off to a great start.

After a few minutes of very enjoyable jabs and counter jabs, Roger said, "Look, let us take you out for some ice cream." "That would be great, if it were possible, but you don't really want to do that – there are seventeen of us," I replied. "Absolutely no problem," he responded, I'll be happy to take all seventeen of you – just let me get my car and you can follow me." "OK," I said, "but what are you driving? I will need to recognize you in this crowd." Roger flung back, "You'll know it when you see it," and turned on his heel and walked out of the building.

"Now that was the dumbest statement I have ever heard," I said. "There are a hundred cars out there and I have no idea what he is driving – how am I going to know it when I see it?" I didn't have long to find out.

Suddenly amidst all the traffic there appeared a bright orange airport limousine with a white roof and a lot of lights. I knew it when I saw it. I packed all seventeen of us into the three small vehicles and followed Roger to his favorite ice cream shop.

We talked for well over an hour as I shared what God had been doing in the lives of the kids at the Teen Encounter Centers. I introduced Roger to each of them and let a few tell their story. It was a wonderful time of fellowship and praising God for His great goodness. Finally, we thanked Roger and Ruth, packed our gang into the cars and drove back to York. That was Saturday evening.

Tuesday my secretary came back to my office to tell me that Roger had come to see me in York. I welcomed him and in his typical, matter-of-fact manner he said, "I brought you something," and he laid an envelope on my desk. I opened it to find the title to the

Orange Pontiac Airport Limousine. Roger's comment, "Ruth and I decided you needed it more than we did."

The kids from Teen Encounter became famous for arriving at meetings in their very noticeable and identifiable limousine and while it still had only fifteen seats, it sure made traveling with the kids from the Centers a lot easier.

A Trip to Texas

Among the kids in the city who needed Christ, was an emerging group of almost exclusively white youth who were becoming addicted to various drugs, marijuana being the primary starting point, but progressing to harder substances. I wanted to minister to them, but they had adapted a very hippie type life style and were a much different breed than the multiracial kids we were primarily dealing with at the Centers.

About this time one of the young college students who volunteered with us from time to time, came to me with a burden to work directly with this group of kids and a short time later we took Bob Brenneman on board as Director of Teen Encounter Coffee House Ministry which we opened in the basement of one of the houses near by.

Bob seemed to be suited to the ministry and there were about twenty kids that frequented the coffee house. But there was such a cultural difference between this group and those we normally had worked with that many of the efforts we made that were successful with the others, did not seem to attract them at all.

One day Bob came in with the news that a huge "Jesus Rally" was to be held in Texas and he believed it could be the experience God might use to break through to some of our kids from the Coffee House ministry. Bob wanted to organize and execute a trip to Texas. He reminded me that most of the kids he worked with were a little more affluent than the average and if they could put together a trip that didn't cost too much the kids could probably afford to pay their way. It would just be a matter of getting the transportation.

I asked how many he expected and when he told me about fifteen, I suggested the Teen Encounter Airport Limousine. He could pile the luggage on the roof since it had a built-in full length luggage rack, and we could probably do it fairly economically. Bob agreed and as he left, I reminded him that fifteen was his absolute limit. With driver and chaperon that would be thirteen.

About two weeks later Bob told me at our weekly staff meeting he thought he had a problem. "What is it," I asked? "We have over fifty kids who want to go," he replied. "Impossible," was my first response. But after arguing for the possible benefits of such a trip in terms of changed lives, I told him I would try to work on the problem.

The first thing I did was approach a local bus company and inquire whether we could hire one of their drivers and coaches. Of course it would mean tying up both a driver and a coach as well, and the cost of that, plus the distance made the idea totally prohibitive. Bob had already given the kids a cost based on our original plans and there was no way it could cover the expense of a bus.

Sometime before all of this Harold Witmer had returned to York for some family matters and while he was there, he told me that he needed a coach for his teen ministry in Clarkesville. I don't remember all the details, but we both made some contacts and in a few days, Harold had purchased an older model GMC coach and was on his way back to Tennessee. I began to wonder if that is what I needed to do.

Somewhere along the way I heard about a bus company in Lancaster that was selling their entire fleet of ACF Brill coaches. These were at one time the "Cadillac" of the tour bus industry. They were powered by a twelve cylinder gasoline "pancake" engine that was positioned at the center of gravity under the passenger floor. They had a special seat for a tour-guide up front opposite the driver where that person could talk over a loud speaking system explaining what they were seeing as they traveled. The entrance door was just behind that tour-guide's seat and the luggage compartment was in the rear (where the engine normally is). They were a very comfortable coach and the company that owned them had used them to ferry passengers to the New York World's Fair in 1964. After that they had pretty much been retired. They were asking $1,800 per unit, and there were three of them for sale.

I called, made an appointment, and set forth my case before the owner. The man was not a Christian, although he had many opportunities to hear and respond to the gospel. He told me that he had traveled with a team that set up tents for the Billy Sunday campaigns and that he had known Billy personally.

I explained my need and then said, "Let me make you a proposal. I will purchase all three buses, if you will give me all of the spare parts you have on hand for these units, all of the manuals, and anything else that would be pertinent to their operation. However, I want them for a single figure of $1,800 (meaning I would be paying $600 for each bus)." I'm not sure exactly what motivated him, but after some hesitation he agreed and I moved buses, wheels, parts, manuals and everything to York.

Fred Jones was on my Board at the time and was owner of Jones & Sipe Auto Repairs. I had the buses delivered to him. Fred had his mechanics go over them thoroughly and we determined which two buses were most road worthy. We then called a friend that had a junk yard and ask if we could park the third bus on his property and store in it, all the parts and things we had gotten with the buses. He consented, and we had the first step of our task of finding transportation complete. Now it was a matter of getting drivers and making final plans. In the end, we sent two bus loads of kids on their way to Texas. I do not remember the exact number but there were over sixty.

I had two drivers. One was my very capable and affable maintenance man Dunie Ness. His real name was Clarold, but everyone called him Dunie. Dunie was capable at anything. He could repair almost anything and he had so much of the winsome joy of the Lord in his life that all of the staff and the kids loved him. I had full confidence as they set off with our prayers that God would do great things.

A day into the trip Dunie called me. "We have a problem boss," he said. "Our air compressor went out and I lost my brakes." "Dunie," I said, "are you alright? Was anyone hurt? Did you hit anything?" "No," he replied, "I was able to coast up a grade and get stopped. We're all alright, we didn't hit anything, but we can't go any further. What are we going to do?"

"Where are you?" I asked as the desperate thoughts of their plight rushed through my brain. "Nashville," he replied. Nashville is the reputed music capitol of the world, and that was music to my ears. "Give me the number of the payphone where you are and I'll get back to you within the hour," I told him.

I called my secretary and said, "Get Harold Witmer on the line please." In just a few minutes I was talking to Witmer. He was in Clarksville, Tennessee just thirty miles north of Nashville. I explained what had happened.

"No problem," said Harold. "We will drive our bus down to where they are and we can swap buses. Your driver can take our bus to Texas and we will have yours towed up here to Clarksville. Then if you will send me the part that is broken, I will have one of our mechanics replace it, and on your return trip, we will just exchange buses once again." And that is exactly what we did.

Within less than three hours our convoy was back on the road to Texas with two buses – one of ours and one of Harold's. I sent one of our mechanics out to the junk yard and he removed the air compressor for the brake system from our retired bus. We then flew the part by commercial air down to Clarkesville. True to his word, Harold had his mechanic replace the part and as our bus returned from Texas, they again changed buses in Nashville and retuned home.

Greyhound, or Trailways could not have done it more smoothly. Here we were, neither of us having very much money, both of us on a very tight budget, but God allowing us to be able to pull this off like we were a million dollar corporation. If Dunie had broken down anywhere else in the whole United States, I would have been practically helpless to have assisted him. But the breakdown occurred in the one place I could get help.

Some may call it happenstance, but I call it Providence and I believe God just delights to demonstrate over and over again the need for us to depend on Him and His unlimited grace and reserves for whatever we need. Oh, did I say, there were some real spiritual decisions made on that trip as well and God worked through the Rally, but I believe He worked even more in proving Himself completely sufficient for a most impossible situation. The kids involved may forget what took place at the Rally, but they can never forget how God intervened in their helplessness.

CHAPTER TWENTY ONE

Oh, By The Way Reverend – She's Deaf

In the days of the Teen Encounter Center ministry we worked very closely with various city agencies that were involved in one way or another with the teen population. That included Children's Service agencies and the Juvenile Police Department. In fact, the greatest promoter of our ministry was the head of the Juvenile Department, Captain Charles McCaffery (he had been promoted from Lieutenant).

When he had a teen that was in trouble that he thought we might help, I had told him that he was free to call me anytime day or night and he took me very seriously. So my phone would ring in the wee hours of the morning and when it did, it was usually the police wanting us to respond to some situation that would not wait until morning.

I was not particularly surprised then when my phone rang one morning at about 2 AM. The Sergeant on duty had a young girl who was fourteen years of age and had been molested. He informed me that they had checked her out at the hospital and she was alright, but they had no place to put her at that hour. "I don't want to lock her up," he said, "she's been through enough trauma for one night."

I agreed and offered to take her in to one of our three centers. We choose the one at Franklin Street. I told him I would call our coordinator, Bruce Dick, and let him know she would be coming and I told the police to give our people about thirty minutes to get ready and then take her over there. I was just ready to hang up when the Sergeant said, "Oh, by the way Reverend, she's deaf and dumb."

"Oh, by the way?" I said. "Come on Sergeant, how are we going to communicate with her?" I had only met one other deaf person in my life at that time (the hitchhiker on a Kentucky road), and knew only vaguely that sign language even existed. This was before the days when every evangelistically aggressive church had someone who signed for the deaf. Deaf ministries and understanding of the deaf was pretty slim in those days.

"Well, she can read lips pretty well," he responded, "And you can always write a note – she's really very bright and she can read well, and beside, it's only going to be temporary until we can find placement for her," he assured me. I was always glad to be able to help and I wanted to help this young lady, but I was concerned for the amount of disruption that a new resident always caused to the staff and other resident teens, especially one who arrives in the middle of the night and now one who is deaf as well. But I agreed and called to explain the matter to Bruce. He assured me he would care for it and I breathed a prayer and went back to sleep.

Sunday morning I checked in with Bruce and he indicated that all had gone quite well. Linda was indeed, a very bright, and very attractive little girl and she was very deaf. She could talk, but in the strange monotone of the deaf, and communication was obviously going to be a hurdle.

If you had asked me how many deaf there were in York County, I probably would have hazarded a guess of maybe fifteen to twenty and I would have been very, very wrong. That afternoon fifteen deaf teenagers suddenly just showed up to check on Linda and make sure she was OK. I learned two lessons that day; first, there were many more deaf than I had ever dreamed (about 500 registered in York County), and secondly, that the deaf community have a network of communication within their culture that works very well and very rapidly and they keep track and look after one another.

While Linda's arrival at the Center went smoothly, it was soon evident that "temporary" was a relative term and that placing a girl in a foster home who was Linda's age with her limitations would not be easy for the agencies. I have also guessed that both Police and Children's Services were pretty content to let Linda where she was and so we began to realize that we needed to do something to increase communication skills.

For one thing, we were all about sharing the good news of the gospel with every young person who was given to us and we were not making much headway with Linda. It is one thing to communicate the routine matters of keeping a household schedule, doing your chores, completing your homework, getting to school on time and the like. But to communicate the reality of sin and the need for a Savior is quite another and I sensed we were not at all prepared for that task.

Church was another problem. There was not an evangelical, gospel preaching church in the county that was, at that time, ministering to the deaf. That almost seems strange to many of us who have become familiar with the "signer" who stands at the side of the church and signs out the hymns and the pastor's message to several rows of deaf in many churches in our day. Dr. Falwell was an early promoter of deaf ministry and as far as I know, if he had begun reaching out to deaf at this time, it was not well known – certainly not known to us.

One might argue, as some have in their innocent ignorance, that if the deaf can read, they can read the gospel. True, they can read. But they have never had the connections in conversation and experience that come so naturally to us and teach us the real meaning and nuance of words. They read words – but the words do not communicate to them the same message they do to us.

I also learned something about "lip reading." There is a certain amount of information that can be understood by carefully watching the formation of words on the lips and the deaf are trained at doing that. Experience taught us however, that even when communication seemed to take place, even when Linda would pleasantly indicate that she understood, her resulting action demonstrated clearly that she did not.

We learned about something called, "the Deaf Yes." I refer to that pleasant response often given by a deaf person to convince you that they truly understood what you said – when in reality it means, "I like you very much and would like to please you, but haven't the foggiest idea what you just said." It always reminded me of that old line from the Nixon days, "I know you believe you understand what you think I said, but I'm not sure you realize that what you heard is not what I meant." In other words – we needed other words.

So we began to do some inquiring and I learned that Tennessee Temple University actually taught the sign language. I called and was put into contact with Dr. Clifford Smith, one of the professors, and learned that he conducted week long seminars in the sign language. I was able to establish a date that spring when he would come to York.

My original intent was to simply train myself and my staff in enough sign language to effectively communicate with Linda and some of her friends whom we had come to know. But as I talked about the need of the deaf to pastors, they asked if they could send someone from their church to take the seminar with us.

Then the Police showed an interest. Finally, the word got to the one sign language person who was used by the Police and the other agencies as needed, and she decided to attend as well. I rented one of the lectures halls at York College and opened enrollment to the community. We had over twenty enroll.

As the seminar progressed, I was delighted when I realized how skillfully Dr. Smith would weave the gospel message into the "signs" as he taught them. What that meant was that social agency people, police and the people from churches, not all of which were evangelical, were getting a clear and constant dose of the gospel every day while they were also learning the sign language.

I have never regretted the effort. Several churches began ministries to the deaf and the seminar opened up another opportunity to us as well. We learned from Dr. Smith about the Bill Rice Ranch, a large camping ministry in Murfreesboro, Tennessee, that held two weeks of camp for the deaf every summer.

Dr. Bill Rice and his wife Dr. Kathy had a daughter who became deaf as a result of an early bout with the measles. Instead of simply grieving, they took it as an opportunity to reach thousands of deaf people throughout the world through their camping ministry.

I contacted the ranch and they graciously invited me to bring any deaf children I might gather for a free week that summer. That contact not only opened a new door of ministry but a new relationship as well. Dr. Bill and Kathy Rice became dear friends and would later participate in our own camping ministry.

Since our people had just gone through a sign language seminar, they were anxious to reach out to the deaf community and since I was broadcasting over stations in multiple states, we made known that we would provide transportation and chaperons for any deaf teens who might want to take advantage of the opportunity to attend a week at camp. Ruth Unger, one of our volunteer ladies who had taken the seminar helped organize the trip and went as a counselor every year we sponsored it.

That first year we took about thirty deaf teens from three states. We used one of our school busses that first year, and then later began using the ACF Brill Coaches we had purchased for that trip to Texas. It was a rather expensive venture, but God always provided when the bills were due.

The reports that came back from those trips were encouraging indeed and many of our deaf teens understood the gospel for the first time and accepted Christ as their Savior as a result of those efforts. And yes, Linda came to know Christ as well.

And what about temporary? Linda was with us at Teen Encounter from the time they placed her until she graduated from high school – and entered the work force as a happy glowing Christian whose disability had been used of God to open the door to reaching scores of others with the gospel.

Seven years after we began the deaf trips to the ranch I received a call one day from Dr. Kathy Rice. She told me that Dr. Bill, who had suffered a stroke that past year, wanted Ruby and me to come to Murfreesboro for three days. She assured me they would pay our flight fair and take care of all our needs.

It was the middle of the summer and in the midst of the camping season at our camp and I asked, "Dr. Kathy, what does Dr. Bill want me to do?" She replied, "I can't tell you but if you come you'll be glad you did."

I deferred this one to Ruby and after discussing it we concluded, Dr. Bill has run a camp for years. He knows how important it is for a Director to be on the job during the camping season. So if he is asking me to leave my post, he must have something really important in mind. We agreed we ought to say yes.

We flew to Murfreesboro and were graciously received by the camp staff. They housed us in Dr. Bill III's Airstream trailer – a beautiful unit we thoroughly enjoyed. When we entered we found a large fruit basket with a letter welcoming us and giving us a little of the schedule – a gracious gesture we had never seen before, but one which became a pattern for us whenever we hosted people from that time on. For two days we enjoyed the services the activities and the meals at the Ranch, but I still hadn't found out why I was there. Then came the last evening and the banquet and closing service.

I remember we sat at a supper table across from Billy Renstrom, the very effective soloist on the music team. As we talk, Billy began to tell me his story. He had been at Normandy on "D-Day." While storming the beaches, a shell had exploded a few feet away and Billy lost his sight in both eyes. Later he came to know the Lord and had been singing the gospel for many years.

About a year or two before I met him, Billy told me that he was in meetings and a man approached him and began to ask him about his lost eyesight. The man was an eye surgeon and he asked Billy, "When is the last time anyone has examined your eyes?" Billy thought and said, "It's been years – there is just nothing they can do for me."

The man continued, "Billy, there is so much we have learned about the eyes in the last years and there are new techniques we have that were never available before. I can't promise you anything, but would you let me examine your eyes?" Billy agreed.

After examining him the doctor said, "I can't be sure, but if you will allow me to operate, I may be able to restore your vision." Billy said he and his wife prayed and decided to take the chance.

Billy said, "The day they took off the bandages, my wife was not there and so I asked to call her." When she answered, Billy said, "Woman you are in big trouble." "Why Billy?" she asked. "What is wrong?" Billy replied, "Anyone who would put a man in a pair of pajamas this color is in big trouble." Billy told me his wife squealed with delight and joy, "Oh, Billy," she screamed, "you can see!"

I sat and listened as Billy finished his story. The tears were coming down my cheeks by then and as I wiped them away, the waitress removed my plate and that is when I saw it for the first time – The place mat had a picture of some of the signs used by the deaf along with the Bill Rice Ranch Brand and then all across the top in big letters the words, "HONORING BILL & RUBY SHADE . . .BEST FRIENDS AWARD."

So that was it – Dr. Bill wanted to say "Thank you" for the seven years we had brought deaf children to the Ranch and with his typical flare, this was his way of doing it. Dr. Bill was on the platform in his wheelchair that evening and we had some pictures taken. It was a precious moment we will never forget. It was also the last Best Friends Award Dr. Bill ever gave. A few months later he was ushered into glory to a better reception than even the one he had so graciously given us. The next summer, Dr. Bill's son, Dr. Bill Rice III would speak at Camp of the Nations.

That phone call in the middle of the night that placed Linda with us would add a dimension to our lives and ministry that we would otherwise have never experienced. I still think of the Sergeant's feeble attempt, "Oh, by the way Reverend – she's deaf," and thank God we responded.

CHAPTER TWENTY TWO

"Pitts, Get Born Again"

Our interaction with the Black community had started early in our ministry while we were still in Kentucky. Besides helping with what was known as "Colored Camp" at Camp Nathanael for a number of years, we had done vacation Bible school with the black children and had become friends with many of the adults.

When we moved north and began the inter-city work, the first Pinebrook Retreat was entirely made up of black teens from York, Philadelphia and Washington. About one third of the teens we kept in residence at the centers were black and I had become close friends to a number of black pastors in Baltimore where I was asked to preach meetings in various black churches.

Pastor Joseph Brown was a favorite friend of mine. He was affectionately known as "Preacher Brown" and he had a radio ministry that aired over one of our local stations. I loved his clear presentation of the gospel and when I met him in person at a NRB (National Religious Broadcasters) Convention I also discovered that we shared the same radio agent.

Both Joe and I used the services of the Tom Harvey Agency, which also served Oliver B. Greene's nationwide ministry. Joe had no way to duplicate his radio tapes speedily and economically and so we took on the ministry for him.

I had Joe speak on occasions at the Rally and he invited me to speak at Calvary Baptist in Baltimore. It was a wonderful experience getting to meet and know his people and sense his passion for souls.

On one occasion Joe asked me to do an entire week of meetings. I stayed at a down-town motel about six blocks from the church and used to walk through that all black neighborhood to the meetings praying for the people along the way as I went. I always sensed that the Lord walked with me and so enjoyed the security of just moving in His will.

Sometime during that series of meetings the monthly black pastor's conference took place and Joe invited me to sit in with him as his guest. I looked forward to it hoping to get to meet other black pastors, especially those who were true to the Word of God and wanted to lead their people in a Biblical manner.

It happened that in early 1968 there was much excitement about Dr. Martin Luther King's activities and what might be accomplished for the plight of the disadvantaged. There was a lot of "buzz" going around the room about such things when the Moderator of the meeting walked over to Joe and whispered something in his ear. Joe turned to me and said, "Our speaker did not arrive – looks like you are the order of the day." I was completely surprised and unprepared.

After a few items of business they introduced me and I went to the platform to address this vast room full of black preachers of all stripes and denominations. I took my text from John 6:35, *I am the bread of life, he that cometh to me shall never hunger and he that believeth on me shall never thirst."* It was the same text I had used with gang teens during the Pinebrook retreat, but it was a text that speaks to a universal experience – that of hunger and thirst.

I tried to express my congratulations for the victories that had been won during their struggle for civil rights. I was truly happy for the gains made that removed the stigma of separation and created a more level playing field of opportunities for people of color. But then I cautioned them against thinking that such victories would meet and satisfy the real needs of their people.

I had just had a series of situations over the preceding months that reminded me again that only Jesus Christ could meet the real heart needs of anyone. There had been that retreat to Pinebrook where I used the same passage to talk to gang teens about the gnawing hunger and the burning thirst that they felt inside and were trying to satisfy with sex and drugs and violence, but which only Christ

Himself could fill. Over forty of those kids responded and found that fulfillment in Christ.

Then within the weeks preceding that Pastor's meeting I had been in an apartment of a wealthy couple overlooking the Palisades in New York City and found them so empty and unhappy that it took two police offices to keep them from killing each other. A few days later I was sitting in the palatial mansion of a wealthy banker in another city whose family was falling apart and he confessed that he had nothing worth living for.

As I recited these stories, I reiterated the theme – social and financial advancement are helpful, but they cannot replace what only Christ brings to our lives. These things never satisfied my people, I told them, and they will never satisfy yours. I concluded, "Give them Jesus – because He alone in the true Bread and Water of Life."

Well, I had not reached my seat when a middle aged very sharply dressed man stood up toward the back of the room and shouted, "I've heard this stuff all my life – I want my rights!" I later learned that the vocal gentleman was Dr. Lindsey Pitts, graduate of Yale University and ranking liberal among the preachers.

However, it didn't take long for those who understood what I had been saying to meet the challenge. Suddenly a very large man, whom I would guess to have weighed three hundred pounds or more and was sitting on the front row, got up, climbed precariously onto his chair and turning toward Dr. Pitts shouted, "Pitts, get born again – then you know what he talk'n about." My supporter was Dr. Charlie Leadum, pastor of a Baptist Church in the city and graduate of Moody Bible Institute.

Well, the whole assembly erupted in debate and Joe decided it was time to move me out of there before we had a repetition of the uproar at Ephesus recorded in Acts nineteen. I left however, a happy man. I had watched the development of the civil rights movement and had rejoiced over many of the injustices it had been able to right, but I saw it as being spiritually deficient and I had been given the opportunity to address that concern before a major audience and I went away thankful that God had given me the grace to do it.

I was later asked to preach in a number of the black churches and for some time had a close relationship with several of the pastors that were in that meeting that day. When we began to organize for our March for Christ in York, some of these very pastors brought their entire congregations up by bus to march with us.

CHAPTER TWENTY THREE

Wounded in Action

The following Spring (1969), after we started the deaf ministry, we encountered a problem in the Bible Club work. We had been conducting Bible clubs, in the schools where we could, and out of the schools in nearby locations where we couldn't get into the school. There were three clubs operating when we were asked to take the ministry – that number had now grown to fourteen.

My director at that time for the Bible clubs was Russ Aults, and I remember Russ told me that we had a club going on at West York High and the faculty member who had volunteered to sponsor the club was a member of one of our fundamental churches, but he had just told Russ that he was also involved in automatic writing. Russ had come to me and said, I don't really understand too much about this, but I think we had better talk to him. I said, "Okay, I'll meet with him."

I recognized that so-called "automatic writing" is an occult practice in which a person puts himself (or herself) into an altered state of consciousness and becomes a sort of spirit medium for demonic forces. In other words, I knew we were dealing with something that was on a spiritual level that would require spiritual warfare.

I fasted and prayed the day that I met this particular teacher – it was on Saturday, and he came into my office for the meeting. We talked for a long, long time. When I asked him to describe what was happening and what he did he began by telling me that departed people – people who had died – were communicating with him and telling him what to write. When I showed him from Scripture that such a thing was not possible, he shifted his story and told me that the communicators were angels.

I told him that the likelihood was that they were fallen angels, or demons that were trying to deceive him. Since God forbids all forms of divination, His holy angels do not do what He forbids. We talked and read Scripture for about two hours before he finally, and rather reluctantly, admitted that what he was dealing with was wrong and evil.

It was at that point that he told me that he had involved two very intelligent girls in this practice and that they had been receiving messages and writing even more than he. He said, "I've gotten a couple of these girls deeply involved in this, and you really need to meet with them and talk to their parents as well." I agreed, and we set up for the next day, Sunday afternoon, for me to meet with the girls and their parents.

Sunday afternoon, I went to his house to meet with the girls. I still had not eaten, I was still fasting, for I sensed that a very big spiritual battle was raging and that I should not eat until the battle was resolved and I made up my mind not to do so.

When we met, I was impressed with how keen and sharp these girls were. The teacher had convinced them, and their parents, that they were chosen of God to receive the messages they were writing down. When someone believes they are a chosen vehicle for God's message, it is a deep deception and not easy to break. I read pages of their material and while there was a moral tone to these broken messages, there was no mention of the blood of Christ or of sin or redemption – a tell-tale indication that God was not behind the messages.

As we began to share the Word, it became evident that our teacher friend was entrenched again in his objections and tried to defend what they were doing. The parents of both of these teenage girls were completely ignorant of what they were dealing with and I knew that only God could make it clear to them. After several hours of looking at the Word of God, they finally all agreed that from what I had shown them in the Bible, this must be demonic. Even my teacher once again reluctantly agreed. They asked, "What can we do?"

I began by sharing the gospel with them as simply as I could. The girls and their parents were all members of old-line denominational churches where they had never been confronted with the clear presentation of the gospel. That was not true of our teacher and that deeply concerned me about him.

After sharing the gospel I asked, "Have you ever before heard this message that I have just shared with you?" One of the girls said that she had not, but the other said, "Yes, a few months ago, I was at a Billy Graham meeting, and the preacher said just what you said." I asked whether she had responded to the message and she said, "When the invitation was given, I wanted to go, but my friend said, don't go. And so I didn't." I asked, "How long after that was it that you got involved in this business of automatic writing?" As she thought she told me, "only a few weeks." When the good seed of the Word falls on wayside soil, Satan is quick to snatch away that which was sown.

Finally, both girls and their parents got on their knees and renounced what they were doing, calling upon the Lord and asking Him to save them. The teacher insisted that he was already saved, and that he just hadn't understood these things so he did not pray. After prayer I told them that if they were really renouncing what they had done they should destroy all that they had written.

We all went outside to his back yard fireplace and they burned a lot of tapes and a bunch of stuff that they had. After the bonfire the teacher insisted that we celebrate by eating some food they had fixed. When I declined he argued that the battle had been won, there was no reason not to join them. Finally I agreed and joined them. I believe it was at this point that I opened myself to Satan's attack.

I later learned that he had deceived me and had made duplicates of some of these tapes and writings and had held them back so that what I saw, what appeared to be accomplished, was not fully accomplished at all that day and the deception was now at a deeper level.

At any rate, Tuesday of that week, one of the girls contacted me again. I met with her in the evening. She was beginning to have recurrences of demonic oppression and was hearing voices again urging her to record their messages, and again we claimed deliverance in the name of Christ and by His blood.

Wednesday, I went to pick up our motorcycle. The motorcycle had been inspected, so I went to get it and remember riding it back that evening; it was raining, and several times I was scared that the thing was going to leave the road with me. I had a sense just then that I was under very strong demonic oppression myself, and the demons we had been dealing with in these girls were fighting very, very hard, so I actually felt a sense of being in danger apart from walking completely in the Spirit.

The next day we took a busload of kids up to Caledonia State Park for an outing. We ministered the Word of God on the way up, and had a picnic, went swimming, and really had a great time. I checked the oil in the bus, as I always did, before leaving the Park.

It was a great bus, one that had been given to us by the Kiwanis Club of York for our work with the teens and it was really in nice shape. We started back and we got almost into New Oxford. We were just coming over the hill before you get there, driving at about fifty five miles an hour, when all of a sudden there was a terrific bang in the engine – the oil pressure gage just dropped off completely, and the engine locked up. I was helpless to do anything to bring it back.

I threw the bus out of gear and coasted into a gas station that was about a quarter of a mile ahead, and there the bus came to a halt. The motor had blown for no apparent reason. We later learned one of the bolts apparently from the bearings had somehow worked itself loose, and the splashers had picked it up, thrown it up into one of the cylinders and jammed the cylinder. Basically this was a good engine that had just had a very freak situation occur. I had to start making phone calls, and trying to get these kids home. The staff and some volunteers brought cars out, we got them back to their homes, and I got home late.

It was June 19, our wedding anniversary, and Mother had dinner ready for us at her place when I finally got home. They lived right next door so we ate over there, thanked them for their kindness and our whole family went back over to our house.

The kids were coaxing me to take a ride on the motorcycle that I had just brought home the night before. They hadn't been on the motorcycle all winter and I had just gotten the inspection done so it was legal to ride. I was tired, but I said to Ruby, "well, look, cut the cake, put the coffee on, and I'll take the kids for a ride on the motorcycle and when we get back, we'll celebrate our anniversary."

I took Steve first; Steve was always quickest to get his helmet on and jump on the bike. I took him in a circle going about a mile or so down the road and back. Phil climbed on and we went down again. About halfway through this trip, I suddenly became conscious that there was somebody in a car coming up very close behind me. The car would come up close and then back off, and then they would roar up very close to me again. The whole thing was unsettling.

When we got to the stop sign on the road below Panorama Hills (Dad's housing development), I had to turn left onto East Prospect Road and go west to come back up to my place, and I said to Phil, "Hold on tight because I don't like what this car is doing. I am going to try to lose this guy."

I took off from the stop sign and up the road at a pretty good speed and got ahead of him, but when I went to turn into our lane, there were cars coming the other way, and I could not make the turn, I had to wait. As I waited, I looked in the rear view mirror and I saw car lights coming up on us very, very fast. I cleared the engine, hoping to have enough time to get out of the way as the last car passed, but suddenly, just as the last car was going past me, there was a terrific squeal of wheels and then it all became black. That is all I remembered.

I later learned that he had hit the bike with such force that Phillip and I were thrown about twenty feet up the road. Phillip came off the bike but I was left still straddling it. The driver had hit me so hard that he literally amputated my left leg against the motor casing with the bumper of the car. In spite of that, God was still in control.

In the providence of God that particular night a Christian nurse had decided that it being a warm evening, she wanted to take a walk – something she had never done before. She was walking along the highway and was about one hundred feet away when that accident occurred. She ran to me and put a tourniquet around my leg which stopped the bleeding, really saving my life right there on the spot.

I was unconscious, as was Phil. I'm not sure who stopped the traffic, but someone did. Someone called for an ambulance. We are not clear about what all happened at this point.

When we didn't come back, Ruby began to become concerned. Finally, she walked out on the back porch, looked up toward the road, and saw lights flashing from an ambulance. Then she looked down the road and realized that traffic was backed up all down the hill. Ruby told me the Lord just said to her, "That's Bill and Phil in that accident."

Once the truth of the situation hit her, she immediately started running up the road toward the highway in her bare feet getting about halfway there, when she met Stephen coming back. Steve had gotten there first and saw me in a puddle of blood and his brother laying on the highway, and thought that we were both dead, and he was screaming and hysterical. Ruby tried to calm him and when she couldn't, she finally slapped him and when he stopped crying, she told him to go to the neighbors, and not to bother my dad and mother for fear that Dad would have another heart attack. A dear neighbor woman took him to her house, then Ruby continued up to the accident site.

When she arrived at the accident scene a crowd had gathered and she could not see anything. When she tried to make her way through the crowd some of the people tried to stop her because they knew what she would see. Ruby said, "That's my husband and my son down there and I'm going to them." That is one time that she asserted herself – they were not going to keep her from being with us.

She got down first by me but I was unconscious, and not knowing whether I was dead or alive she went over to where Phil was lying on the highway. Phil was just coming to, so kneeling down beside him, she took him by the hand and she prayed with him right there.

When they loaded us into the ambulance they asked if she wanted to ride along to the hospital, and she immediately climbed in, still in her bare feet. I was unconscious during this entire time, although Ruby says that as she prayed, my lips would move and I would say, "Amen," and "Yes, Lord," but I was not aware of it.

The first thing I remember is waking up on a gurney in the hospital with tremendous pain in my leg and asking her what had happened, knowing my leg was hurting badly. "I asked, is it all right, is it going to be all right?" She said, "No, Honey, the doctor said you are going to lose your leg."

I remember that moment, because just before I woke up, going through my mind were the words, *this is the good and acceptable and perfect will of God*. And so I told her, "Honey, I was just thinking the words, *this is the good and acceptable and perfect will of God*, and she said, "Well then, Honey, we can live with that; we can't get anything better than perfection.

About that time the doctor came, and I said, "Doc, can you save my leg?" And he said, "No, it was injured too badly, there is nothing I can do for your leg." And I said to him, (and this was a remarkable thing because I had never in my life thought about the ramifications of an amputation), but I said to him, "Doctor, are you going to be able to save my knee?" And he said, "I don't think so." And I remember saying, "Doc, you are in charge, and I am going out (they had already given me a pre-op shot), but whatever you do I am going to live with for the rest of my life, and I really would appreciate it if you'd try to save my knee."

He told me later he was very angry about that request, because he had already planned how he was going to do the operation. He went back and tried to re-plan it, leaving me just enough below the knee to get by. He said he had no idea if it would heal. He didn't even sew up the wound, he just put drain tubes in and decided that he would leave it for several days and at least show that he had attempted to save it, and then probably end up operating again, and taking it.

But wonderfully, several days later, it had begun to heal so well that he pulled the tubes and closed it up and my knee was spared, and so I had a below knee amputation instead of loosing my knee. The significance of that in allowing me the freedom of movement I have enjoyed all these years was huge.

The Lord did some other wonderful things. That same nurse who saved my life out on the highway came in and volunteered without pay to become a private duty night nurse for me for an entire week during the really difficult times when I would wake up, and she would be there, and she was like an angel of mercy. I thanked God many, many times in tears, for her mercy to me in those very, very difficult times.

Phillip had a broken femur and a crushed ankle, and he was in traction. He was only eleven years old at that time and very scared. Even though he kept both legs, he really had a longer ordeal than I did and later became diabetic when his pancreas shut down because of the trauma of the experience. Both of us have had life-long effects from the accident, but his were more serious than mine.

I never met the man who hit me, he never came near me in the hospital, we settled through attorneys. He had very minimal insurance, and so we just barely got some immediate expenses covered in the settlement. Later I learned that he was from the Caribbean Islands, and that he had a history of mental illness. I was told he did not even own the car that he had when he hit me.

With that kind of background, we are relatively sure that he was involved in the occult and most likely with the same demonic spirits that I had been opposing in the lives of the girls. So I believe that what took place that night, was a tremendous spiritual attack. I was reminded that when Paul cast out the demon from the girl in Philippi, he shortly found himself in prison with a beaten bleeding back. Satan does strike back when we attack his kingdom, and when he does, we sometimes are wounded in action.

I seemed to have lost that skirmish, but thank God, He wins the war! And I am completely content that what He allowed and purposed was in His will for me, and that He will get glory to Himself from it. Only eternity will reveal how many have already come to Christ from the written testimony of that accident.

Of course everything had to go on in spite of my being in the hospital. The work of the Centers could continue through my staff, but the radio broadcast was a different story. No one had ever engineered the broadcasts but me. We fed in announcements from a cart machine, music from a turntable, other material from two tape decks and then, of course the microphone has to be controlled for the speaker. I manipulated all of this rather automatically when I produced my broadcast and then did the same for Ruby for the children's story. All she had to do was tell, or read, the story.

The week following the accident I had scheduled Dr. Henry Morris to be with me and we planned to make two weeks of Broadcasts together. The night before he was to come, Ruby spent hours working out the sequence to all the knobs, switches, and gauges that were before her on the Master control board. When the time came she introduced Dr. Morris, gave our listeners an update on my condition and cared for everything.

I was largely unconscious for the first week, just drifting in and out, so I knew nothing of the extreme load she was bearing. Caring for the rest of the kids – getting them to where they had to be, caring for the responsibilities at the office, then spending hours with Phillip and me in the hospital – an almost unbearable load. But she never complained and was always cheerful when she came to see us.

Just after Dr. Morris' homegoing, his daughter Ruthie wrote me and said that she had discovered some recordings of broadcasts her dad had done for me. She asked if I would like to have a copy and, of course, I said I would. When they came, they were the broadcasts that Ruby had engineered. No professional could have done it better. Her radio persona was wonderful and she faded the songs and announcements without a single glitch.

Later, Tom Harvey, my radio agent helped until I could get back at the board once again. But Ruby saw that everything continued while caring for both Phillip and me. Thank God for all those who helped us through a very difficult situation, and thank God for a wife who did everything that was needed both for her family and the ministry.

Just two months after the accident, I was scheduled to preach a prophetic conference at Pinebrook, sponsored by WDAC radio station in Lancaster. I had promised Paul Hollinger, the station owner, a year previously that I would do the conference, and now I found the dates coming quickly upon me.

I was still on considerable pain medication and I would not be ready for a prosthesis for another three months, but I felt that I was good enough to be able to preach. So Paul graciously picked me up at the house and took me to Pinebrook where I would share the sessions with Rev. Dick Canfield, well known radio speaker and Christian counselor.

The theme of Prophecy has been a favorite of mine since I came to know the Lord as my Savior. In those early days I read all the booklets of Dr. M. R. DeHaan and studied my Scofield Reference

Bible. Then I studied under Dr. Clarence Mason and Dr. Dwight Pentecost and Prophecy became a part of my DNA.

Each session was about an hour long, and since the various topics were often complex, it took me the entire hour to fully develop my theme. Since I had never preached sitting down and felt uncomfortable doing so, I stood on one leg behind the pulpit for each entire session. Needless to say, by the time I had finished a message, I was ready to head back to my cabin, take another dose of pain pills and try to sleep until I had to prepare for the next session.

It was on one of those trips back to the cabin that it happened. I was coming along on my crutches with my trousers pinned up over my stump when I came upon a mother and her young son walking toward me. The little guy took one look at me and very loudly asked, "Hey Mister, what happened to your leg?"

His mother was, of course, embarrassed and tried to apologize, but I assured her that it was quite alright and that I would like to answer his question. So I simply said, "Well, son, I was on a motorcycle and a car hit me and cut off my leg." That seemed to satisfy him and his mother thanked me and started on when the boy thought of the next obvious question and called back to me, "Hey Mister, where is it now?"

Now his mother was totally mortified and tried to correct him, but I said, "That's alright, I don't mind – let me tell him. Only, I want to tell him the truth and I'm trying to think what the truth is." Finally I said, "Well son, I don't know where it is right now, but when Jesus comes again I'll get it back, because He said, 'Of all the Father hath given me I will lose nothing but will raise it up again at the last day'." "Now that's as good as having one foot in heaven, isn't it?"

His mother thanked me again and hurried him down the sidewalk before he could think of any other questions, and I returned to my cabin to write the little tract, "One Foot In Heaven." God has used that tract all around the world to encourage other amputees and to bring many to a saving knowledge of the Lord Jesus Christ. But it probably never would have happened if a little boy had not wanted to know what happened to my leg and been bold enough to ask.

Off to the Holy Land

The fall before the accident (1968), we had celebrated one of our best years on radio and a very well attended radio banquet. My agent, Tom Harvey, had suggested that I do something to build stronger relationships with those who listened to and supported the broadcast. We talked about an idea I had always wanted to do anyway, take a trip to the Holy Land.

Over a year in advanced I made my plans with a tour agency and began to announce to our radio listeners what we were going to do. It was an elaborate plan to say the least for someone who had never even been out of the country. We planned to fly to Egypt and spend several days seeing the Pyramids and the Valley of the Kings, then fly to Lebanon to visit Beirut and motor across the mountains into Baalbek. From there we would fly into Cyprus, since direct flights from Arab countries into Israel were no longer possible. Once in Israel we would tour the land from north to south for over a week. Finally, we would fly to Greece and visit Athens and the ruins of ancient Corinth, and end our trip in Rome as the Apostle Paul had done long before.

There was an amazing amount of interest and we soon had a fairly sizable group of people who wanted to go. In the end, there were thirty one of us.

There had already been several challenges in the early days of our preparations. The tour company I was with was extremely slow to answer my questions or requests and the closer we got to the event the more uncomfortable I became. Finally, one day, after an extremely frustrating attempt to get information from them without success, I told the operator, "If I can't get answers from you people when I'm here in the same country, how will I ever get them when I'm in the desert of Egypt?"

I cancelled with the company and decided to look elsewhere. Tom put me in touch with the Piranians, a Christian couple from Philadelphia who supplied ships that came into port there and ran the Independence Travel Agency on the side. As soon as I met them I was so glad I had made the move. They were marvelous people.

Al Piranian was a German born Austrian who had served as a translator during the Nuremberg trials following the World War. Magdelena Piranian actually operated the tour part of the business and was a lovely lady that was totally competent and could speak in five languages. Plans for the trip were going along quite nicely when I lost my leg in the accident.

I didn't get into my first prosthesis until October, during an evangelistic meeting in a Methodist Church just south of York. I started the meetings that week on crutches and finished on a cane with a new limb. But there were plenty of challenges.

I actually learned to walk again fairly quickly. But as my stump rapidly began to shrink I began dealing with sores on pressure points that made every step painful. We were due to leave on the Tour in April and I could not walk a complete city block.

I sat on the bed one night and bemoaned my plight to Ruby and suggested, "Look, Honey, we have all these people signed up and paid to go. We just can't disappoint them. But I can't lead this Tour. I can't even walk a full city block and we are going to have miles of walking to do. Ruby, why don't you lead this one for me?"

My wife has been remarkably willing to do most anything I ever asked of her, but that idea was DOA. Ruby let me know immediately that was not going to happen. I decided it was time to pray that God would show us how to handle this. Hardly had I said "Amen," when a thought came.

The problem I was having with my stump was that it had reduced and now loose skin would get folded in the socket of the leg and create a blister or an open sore. If I could just hold that skin together. When I was younger I had torn a cartilage in my right knee and had to have an operation. After that, for a long time I had to wear an elastic knee brace to keep it in place. Finally the knee had strengthened and I had not seen the brace for years – but I knew it was around somewhere.

We found it in a drawer, I slipped it over the now flabby stump and Voila!, it held everything in place and I was able to slip into my socket with a degree of comfort I had not known for months. The problem was solved. I would lead the tour.

Still I realized how very inexperienced I was and I would have all of these dear people to look after. The closer the day came the more concerned I became and then Al called and said he would like for me to do him a favor. He had already done so much for us, I was anxious to do whatever I could. Al said, "Magdelena has been all over the world, but she has never been to the Holy Land. She told me she would like to go with you on your tour. Would you be willing to take her?"

I couldn't believe my ears. God was giving me a professional tour person to travel with me at no charge. I was more than happy to do Al that favor and having Magdalena with us was absolutely a life saver. I could never have given the Tour Group the same wonderful trip they had if she had not gone. When the tour agencies in Egypt and Lebanon heard that the wife of the owner of a tour company in America was coming, they rolled out the red carpet. We got the best rooms, the best guides and all the extra attention we could never have received otherwise.

But beyond all of that it was an experience of a lifetime. To be in Egypt and see the "Pyramids along the Nile" was spectacular. My hotel room had a large balcony that reached out over the river and it was delightful. Lebanon was wonderful and beautiful, who could forget it? I cry when I see it now devastated by war and terrorists. Crossing the Sea of Galilee, I preached on Israel's prophetic future for over an hour only to learn that my Jewish crew were all listening on the inner-com and the captain hugged me and wept as I left.

What an experience it was to be at the Garden Tomb, where we had communion remembering our Lord's shed blood and victorious resurrection. We actually stayed in the Panorama Hotel on the Mount of Olives where I could stand on my balcony and overlook the city of Jerusalem. We traveled where Paul did to Greece and Rome and said our goodbyes there. Some of our people went on to Switzerland, while we returned to the U.S.

In all our travels God allowed me to be able to climb every hill and see every sight in spite of my amputation. I went swimming in the Dead Sea and climbed the smooth granite rocks of Mars Hill while God kept me ambulatory through it all. I used to wonder why Ruby sometimes complained of her shoulder being sore as we retired at night. Then we got the photos developed and there I was, in every picture, leaning my hand on her. Seems I've always done that, at least figuratively, but that time it was for real.

God allowed us to build some life long lasting and deep relationships through that experience, and although we never attempted it again, I was always thankful we had been allowed by a gracious heavenly Father to experience it. He really does do, *"exceedingly, abundantly, above all we could ask or think."*

CHAPTER TWENTY FOUR

Operation Penetration

In 1969, the city of York exploded. In June I lost my leg in the accident. By July there had been a number of racial incidents and mayhem began to break out all over the city. The Governor called for a state of emergency and National Guard troops patrolled the streets of York. During that time there were several people shot and some 27 buildings were fire bombed.

I had just gotten out of the hospital and was on heavy medication for pain. Nevertheless, I was concerned that all of our Centers remain manned. I argued that the people who live in the neighborhood had nowhere to flee. If our staff forsook the neighborhood for a safer location while things were bad, how could we ever return and face or minister to those who had to remain.

My staff understood, but the Coordinator of the Duke Street Center had not been there long and did not have a background of working in the inner-city. He was terrified and called to tell me he was leaving. He blamed his action on concern for the safety of his wife and children, and I suggested that if that was really what he was concerned about, he should take his wife and children to safety, but that we needed to have someone there at the Center no matter what happened. He finally agreed that he would stay but then panicked and left. He called one of our other Directors to let him know what he was doing and that Director in turn called me.

I saw no alternative to manning that Center myself at that very crucial time. I got a neighbor to drive me into the city before the curfew went into place and I let myself into the Center. My leg was still in bandages and I was walking on crutches. I turned on the light and settled in for whatever was going to happen.

As the night progressed there was the sound of rifle fire nearby and the roar of Army half-tracks rolling up and down the street. Then about ten o'clock there came a knock at the door. I grabbed my crutches and hobbled to the door. Looking out I saw Larry Hodgson standing there. Suddenly Larry began to give the orders. "Let me in," he said, "I'm staying with you tonight." I asked about the Franklin Street Center and Larry assured me it was covered. "But if anything happens here you will never get out," He replied. "So I'm staying." We got through that night and eventually covered the Center with staff until God brought Dean and Patty Bult to man it for us.

But I was deeply concerned about the situation in the city. I had stood on a number of occasions on a hill east of York that overlooked the entire city and had cried out to God to let us make a difference. I wanted to see God move in a way that even the city officials could not ignore Him, and so evidently that the entire city would be confronted with His gospel. I believed we had to do something dramatic, but I didn't know just what.

I was still praying a year later. I knew that York was a very difficult place to do any kind of work. We had been to the former Mayor's office and had requested permission to do open air ministry, and they would not allow us to use even a PA system. After the summer of rioting, a new Mayor was put in place and I felt that perhaps, now was the time something could be done.

Just about that time George Wiggs called me and asked if I thought there was any possibility of using a Pocket Testament League van in the city of York to show films and do open air preaching during the coming summer. I paused, knowing the situation in York, but went ahead and told him to schedule me tentatively. I never told him about all the city ordinances against that very thing.

That spring I was on my way to Harriman, Tennessee, for meetings, and I drove down as far as Abington, Virginia, and stayed in a motel. As I was having my devotions and praying the next morning, I was reading from Romans 13, verse 15: ***Now the God of hope fill you with all joy and peace in believing that ye may abound in hope*** *and in the power of the Holy Ghost.* As I read that verse over and over, the Spirit of God began to powerfully speak to my heart and I began to lay hold on God with a great sense of hope and anticipation as to what He wanted to do, not just in our up coming meetings in Harriman, but in the City of York.

There on my knees, the Lord just formulated in my mind the idea of a very aggressive evangelistic effort for the entire City of York. Before I left the motel room that morning, I was envisioning street ministry, door to door work, and even the possibility of a large march across the city and I was so certain in my mind that God was going to do it that I was super pumped up.

I drove to Harriman. While I was there, I contacted Harold Witmer, and Harold came over from Clarkesville with a group of teens, on the last night of the meeting. He also brought a former, Church of Christ preacher, a man by the name of Dr. Bill Corley with him. Corley had just recently been saved and Witmer brought him along to give his testimony. I was so excited to have this man I asked the church to move the meetings to the Municipal Auditorium for our final service.

Bill Corley gave his testimony, telling how Harold had visited his office, but before leaving he had asked, "Dr. Corley, do you mind if I ask you a question?" Corley said, "Not at all Harold, what is it?" Harold said, "Dr. Corley, do you know Jesus?" Corley said, "I gave him the standard Church of Christ response that I had been baptized and joined the church when I was in my teens."

Harold listened and then responded, "I don't believe you understood me, Dr. Corley, I said do you know Jesus?" Corley said, "I was irritated by this time so I decided to put this guy in his place. I gave him all my educational credentials and reminded him that I was president of a college and pastor of the largest Church of Christ in Nashville."

But Harold refused to relent. With tears he reached across the desk and took me by the wrist and said again, "Dr. Corley, do you know Jesus?" Corley said, "It got through to me that time and I jumped up from my desk and ran over and closed the door to my office and returning to the desk I put my head in my hands and began to weep." I said, "No Witmer, No. I've done it all, but I don't really know Jesus."

Bill Corley said he met Christ that day and knew at once for the first time that his sins were forgiven and he was going to heaven. The following Sunday he stood in his pulpit and asked his congregation the same question Harold had asked him. Over one hundred people eventually responded admitting that they had gone through the steps taught by their denomination, but had no real relationship with Jesus Christ.

Witmer and I talked about York and what I wanted to do, and he promised that if we got this thing going, he would bring a group of young people and help us with the whole campaign.

After the meetings in Harriman were finished I returned home. By this time it was already May, and we wanted to pull this off in June, so I knew we were talking about a month to organize and accomplish something that to do in that length of time would require a sheer miracle.

I drew up a proposal to present to City Hall. Just as I had returned from Tennessee, they held a hospital fete in which they had set up booths at Continental Square to raise money for the York Hospital. I took pictures of what the city had permitted the hospital to do to bolster the argument for something similar.

Next, I drew up a notebook which laid out five requests – four of which I knew there were city ordinances against. First, I asked permission, not only to use sound systems in the city, but for the operation of a Pocket Testament League van every night from which we would show films and give testimonies. I gave them a list and a map and told them we would let them know in advance where we were going to be, and then I asked the city to put up barriers at both ends of the block during the time we would be operating – I argued for it on the basis of safety.

Secondly, I asked for the four corners of Continental Square to set up a literature table and a place for our people to share with those who would pass by as well as ministering to the hippy crowd that hung out there most of the time.

Then I told them that we intended to do door-to-door evangelism throughout the city leaving literature in every home. We divided up the city into the areas where we intended to hold meetings that evening. Then during the preceding day we would pass out gospel literature in the neighborhoods around those locations and invite people to the meetings that night.

Next, I laid out a plan for a "March for Christ" on Saturday evening to originate at Penn Common, where most of the racial unrest had originated, and proceed over to Memorial Stadium, a distance of over a mile through the very center of the city.

Finally, I asked for the use of Memorial stadium itself to conduct a rally at which we would bring in a number of outstanding speakers to reach particularly the teen crowd.

I drew all of this up as carefully as I could and put it in a notebook, including clippings and pictures of various things that had happened in the city previously that would have given some precedent to what I was asking for, and prepared to go in to meet the mayor.

Now the City of York had a brand new mayor. Mayor Eli Eichelberger was a former medical doctor and he had just been elected as Mayor. On that day he came over to Captain Charles McCaffery's office to meet me. Why I didn't go into his office, I don't remember, but he came over and we met there in the Juvenile office, and after a brief greeting I took the notebook and laid it down and showed him exactly what I wanted to do. I went through the notebook page by page, picture by picture, proposal by proposal. I'll never forget his reaction, he said, "Reverend, anything we can do to help you, we will do." He placed his stamp of approval on the entire plan.

Once I had his word of commitment I asked for his hand, and as I took hold of his hand I realized that his hand was cold and clammy and he was actually shaking. I said, "I want to pray for you Mr. Mayor." God had obviously touched him, and I bowed my head and prayed that God would bring him to a personal relationship with Himself and do something for the city. I prayed for the entire city, prayed for the police, and I walked out of that office with signed permission to go ahead with the entire plan.

That was only the beginning. We began to contact churches and ask them to participate in something that was less than a month away. I was asking them to join us in the march and in the rally and tried to describe the importance of what we were going to do. I reminded them that we had never been able to do any of this before and that we might not ever have the opportunity of doing it again, but this one time God was giving us a chance to confront a city with the gospel.

As I called, church after church would say, "Well, no, we can't do that because we have this or that planned for that weekend, or we've got something else scheduled." After we would talk for awhile, they would say, "You know, maybe we could shift the date for what we've got, and maybe we could get in on this." There were conferences that they cancelled or shortened and all kinds of adjustments were made – things that churches just don't normally do. It was obviously a work of God. God did this thing. He wanted this to happen, and it was obvious He was doing it. I called George Wiggs of the Pocket Testament League, and gave him the go ahead to bring the PTL van and team to York.

The day to begin finally arrived. Every day we started with prayer. Dean Bult was very much involved in organizing all of this. Dean and Patty led those early morning prayer meetings. Harold set up our booth and a literature distribution place at Continental Square and we had the rallies with the PTL van at night. The police cooperated beautifully and set up the barriers every evening before the meetings.

We averaged somewhere around 100-200 people who stood at the van and watched the films and then listened as the messages were given each night. I think we averaged somewhere around 50 responses each evening to the message. Some evenings were better than others obviously, but the kids gave their testimonies from the top of the van, where we showed the films.

First we would show a sports film. Then as we changed reels, kids give their testimonies up on the van platform. Next, we showed a brief Gospel film, followed by a brief challenge and invitation. We then gave Gospels of John to everyone who would accept one, and follow-up materials were given as well. It was a tremendous opportunity and amazingly we had practically no resistance from the neighborhoods in spite of the fact that just a year previously they had exploded in violence.

At Continental Square there were several of our people on every corner. Those were the days when the Vietnam War was being fought and a lot of kids gathered there, especially the anti-war demonstrators. We put Wynn Van Nang down there to talk with them. Wynn was a Vietnamese member of the Pocket Testament League who had seen the fighting and understood what they were fighting for.

Wynn was later martyred when he went back to Vietnam, but he was a tremendous witness for Christ and certainly more than sufficient to not only answer a lot of the arguments of the anti-war people, but more than that, just witness to Christ and His power and people really began to come to the Lord. Many began to bow their heads and come to Christ asking Him for salvation right there on the street.

Pastor Jack Orr got involved with our team and began spending time at the square witnessing as well. Jack was a veteran soul winner and he was a great encouragement to the younger ones.

In the afternoons as we would go out witnessing, we ran into various groups such as a group of *Hells Angels* that were occupying several houses on Queen street. These were all white guys, but they had the leather jackets and the brass knuckles and they definitely intended to intimidate.

We walked up to them, and I began to aggressively share Christ with one of them, and these guys literally turned pale. They were so shaken that they went numb when a bunch of unarmed youngsters, aggressively shared Christ with them. We didn't have any professions of faith, but we had a great opportunity to sense the awesome power of God in that encounter

Later in the week, we realized that we didn't have any pictures of what was happening. I called a friend at WDAC radio and told him about the problem and he recommended a photographer by the name of Glenn Eshelman. I didn't know Glenn, and I didn't know anything about him, and all I could think of was, "if he is a commercial photographer, it will likely cost us a lot of money which we didn't have."

I finally decided to call him, and I introduced myself on the phone by saying, "Mr. Eshelman, my name is Bill Shade; I operate an organization called Teen Encounter here in York. . ." I got that far, and I heard him say, "Honey, guess who I've got on the phone."

I quickly found out that Glenn and Shirley were radio listeners and loved our radio broadcast. When Glenn heard what was happening and that we needed pictures, he said, "No, I don't think we should take photos, we ought to take film," and so we arranged a time and Glenn arrived in York with Henry Brubaker, his assistant. Both of them were equipped with professional cameras and shot 16mm film of all that was going on.

Henry Brubaker and one group of us went up to City Hall where we filmed Captain McCaffery and his office and some of the events that took place there, and then we went to the mayor's office. Eventually the mayor came out onto the steps of City Hall and we had Wynn Van Nang formally present him with a PTL Gospel of John and had the Mayor welcome George Wiggs and Wynn Van Nang to the city for this event.

While we were at City Hall, we got delayed when the desk sergeant said to me, "Reverend, if you guys don't soon quit, I'm not going to have any officers left." And I said, "What do you mean? I thought we were helping you guys." He said, "I had a cop come in here and asked for a transfer, or he wanted to quit." Of course I was surprised and I said, "Tell me what's happening?" The Sergeant said, "I'll let him tell you." So he waved for Officer Brown to come across to where I was and I said to him, "Officer, what's the problem?"

He said, "I'm stationed down there at the square and those kids of yours (the Teen Encounter kids) won't let me alone. They just keep talking to me about being saved and if I don't get saved I'll go to hell." I said to him, "Officer, is there a reason that you don't want to be saved?" "Well, no," he said. I said, "Give me your hand and let me ask you something." I looked him right in the eye, and I said, "Do you believe that Jesus Christ is the Son of God?" "Well, yes," he replied. I said, "Do you believe He died on the cross for your sins?" "Yes," He said again. I said, "Then I am asking you to receive him right now as your personal Savior. I want you to bow your head with me and I'm going to pray for you and then I want you to pray after me," and he did, right there on the parking lot.

It had taken longer there at City Hall than we had anticipated, and I knew that Glenn was "antsy" about time and I was afraid he would be upset with us because we were later than expected. We got back to the square to pick him up, and I never saw a more excited guy in my life. He kept saying, "People are actually accepting Christ out here. I have never seen anything like this in my whole life. I've been in church all my life; I believed the Gospel; but I've never seen anybody get saved out on the street like this." He was so enthusiastic and excited he had shot all of the film that he had with him. Ultimately he gave me six containers full of film and said, "Here, go edit these." I knew nothing about editing film but that is the story of yet another miracle.

Mr. Brubaker came back on Saturday evening long enough to set up, on the roof of the van, and film the entire March for Christ and all of the things that happened at the Municipal Stadium. With all of the cooperation from churches – even a few from Baltimore – we were able to march 1,000 people across the city carrying placards with gospel verses and challenges.

The March began at Penn Common in the heart of the city. Penn Common was a place where white people could not safely go. In fact, just about a month before that, a friend of ours from another city had wandered over there and come back with blood literally all over him, he had gotten beaten up so badly.

But earlier in the week we went over there, set up the van, and walked around letting them know we were going to have a meeting. Of course, these guys recognized us from having circulated in that neighborhood and given out Gospels before, and while some of them cussed at us they never tried to touch us. We set up and preached. We dealt with a number of them afterward.

I'll never forget one guy who came to the meeting drunk. Witmer dealt with him and the guy made a profession of faith. Witmer brought him over and had him talk to me. He claimed to have received Christ but once he walked away, I turned around and said, "Come on, Witmer, that guy's drunk. He's about as saved as that tree over there."

About 15-20 minutes later, we were getting packed up and ready to leave and Witmer walked over to me and said, "You know, I've been looking at that tree you talked about, and it looks to me like it has a lot of life in it." Well, it turned out that young man went to the police the first of the next week, and turned himself in as one who had rioted and apologized for what he had done and told the police that he had received Christ. Apparently, Witmer was right.

We organized the March from Penn Commons without incident, and marched right across George Street and up Pine Street and finally to Municipal Stadium. Because we arrived a little earlier than we expected, we marched around the stadium once before everyone took their seats. Before the meeting began, there were about 1700 people that came out to the meeting.

A volunteer work team had built the platform the afternoon of the campaign because there was a ball game there that morning. We could not move in and construct that platform until after the ballgame was over – but somehow they did it in record time. We moved an organ and a large sound system into place in time for the meeting.

I had asked Rev. Joe Brown, the black preacher with whom I had held those meetings in Baltimore, to preach. Joe was a radio preacher and a pastor, but he was also an evangelist – and Joe knew the heart of the people in the inner-city.

Beside Joe we had Reggie White, with the Baltimore Redskins, give his testimony. Then the Seal Sisters from Brooklyn sang, with Gerry Boyer at the organ. Then Mayor Eli Eichelberger and his wife joined us on the platform and brought greetings to the crowd.

The cooperation and enthusiasm was fantastic, and as is evident from the pictures that were taken, when the invitation was given, there were quite a number of people, who came to receive Christ. Throughout the week there had been over 300 who had come to profess Christ as Savior. The long-term results of what we did in terms of individual decisions is difficult to assess, but the impact of the entire effort on the City was tremendous.

The very next week I got a letter from the Mayor of the City of York (see pictures), which says that during that one week of Operation Penetration, not a single crime was committed in the City precincts of York, indicating something of the tremendous power of the gospel on the city.

There is a sequel to this story that is worth telling. Glenn Eshelman had placed six cans of 16mm film in my hands and said, "This is a gift – I hope you can use it." Now remember, shooting movie film was Glenn's idea, not mine. We didn't have any plans to put together anything like this and so all we had was a lot a raw footage. Furthermore, apart from threading a 16mm projector I was completely ignorant about movie film.

About a week after the event the Quartermaster from the Police Department stopped by the office and set a large black box in the entry. The Police frequently brought things to us that they had recovered from robberies and then had been around for a long period unclaimed. Rather than destroy it, if they thought we could use it we got it.

I passed that black box about a dozen times that day, but I was too busy to stop and see what was in it. Finally toward the end of the day I paused to examine it. The label on the top read, Bell & Howell. I opened it to find a compete set of 16mm editing equipment. The police knew nothing about the movie footage we had shot or our need for the equipment, but God did and His timing was, as usual, perfect. I was going to Altoona the next week for a conference so I decided to take the film, a projector and the editing equipment with me. However, I still knew nothing about editing.

The first day I had free during those Altoona meetings, I looked in the Yellow Pages for a photography shop and hoped to find one that could help me. I found one on 12th avenue and walked in. The clerk behind the counter looked up when I said, "I'm Bill Shade and. . ." Immediately he stopped me. He said, "I would have known that voice anywhere. My mother listens to your broadcast every morning. How can I help you?"

I explained about the 16mm film and what we had done and he just smiled. "Do you have any idea what I do here?' he asked. "Not really," I replied. "I edit movie film," he said. "Come on back and watch me and I think I can get you started with everything you need" . . . and he did.

During the Conference the church had put me in a home where I had the entire basement room to myself. There were some clothes lines strung up around the room with clothes pins on them. How perfect can this be? I watched the footage over and over again and gradually a sequence began to take shape. I cut the film section by section and hung each section up on the lines using the clothes pins.

Then I put together what I had in sequence and when I got back I asked Glenn to come for one additional shoot – this time to shoot some bridges so that the whole thing would make sense. Finally I wrote a script, narrated it and put some music in the background recording the whole thing in our radio studio.

After the Board looked at what I had done and listened to the sound track we had developed on tape, they authorized me to take the entire package to Pittsburg to have it done professionally. Glenn knew the place and he and I drove there together. It was during those hours together that Glenn became interested in the Bible Correspondence Course I had developed. He took the course and was later licensed to preach. Glenn also began using the multi-media slide shows he was producing to incorporate the gospel in an ever greater way.

One day he told me about a dream he had to build a $100,000 multi-media theatre in Lancaster County where he could freely give the gospel through the programs. I must confess I had some doubts but Glenn went on to build *Living Waters* the *Sights and Sounds Theatre* and within a decade the *Millennial Theatre* which seats 2000 people at a showing and runs three showings a day in peak season. Every program is a Bible story presentation with a strong gospel appeal at the close.

Several year ago, when Glenn heard that Ruby and I had never seen the live production of Noah (one of their productions), he invited us to come and join he and his wife Shirley in the vestibule of the theatre. I was left speechless by the wonder of the entire facility and the production, but Glenn put his arms around me and wept on my shoulder and told me, "You know when this began? It began when you took me out on the streets and I saw real evangelism taking place. It began when you gave a tract to the guy at the turnstile on the turnpike and witnessed to the waitress where we ate. I told God then I wanted to use everything I had to do his work and this is what God has done."

Glenn is also an artist in oils and when Phillip was injured in the accident with me, Glenn took him to his house for a whole week and taught him to paint in oils. If one of the long term effects of Operation Penetration is the ministry that Glenn now has both in Lancaster and Branson, Missouri then the effort was worth all we put into it.

CHAPTER TWENTY FIVE

Honey, Don't Look Now

In the years that followed Operation Penetration the outreach of the ministry grew rapidly. We increased our number of radio stations, opened several bookstores to sell Bibles and Christian books and started a weekly television program. Invitations for evangelistic meetings increased and I traveled to states all along the eastern seaboard from Vermont to Florida. Our staff grew and so did another area of our lives.

I was working in my office that particular morning in 1974, when Dick M. walked by. My door was opened and I could tell by the look on his countenance that he was in the doldrums. Now Dick was the type of person who was either up or down and either way he profoundly affected the people who were around him. About the second time he passed my door that day I knew that I had better intervene.

I called Dick into my office and told him to close the door. "What's wrong," I asked? "What's eating you?" "I can't even talk about it," Dick replied. "Well, we are going to talk about it," I responded. "You affect everyone when you get down like this and I need to know what is troubling you."

"OK," Dick responded, "It's my wife – I think she's pregnant." I could hardly believe my ears. "So what's so bad about that?" I asked. "Children are a heritage from the Lord, and the fruit of the womb is His reward," I quoted. "Not this time," Dick moaned. "My youngest daughter is nine years old and look at the distance there will be between them. Beside that, look at our age (Dick and his wife were nearly forty) – we are too old to be having babies."

I tried for the next two hours to comfort Dick finally getting on my knees and praying with him. I reminded him how he could trust God for the situation – how God never makes a mistake. Finally, I let him go, with the admonition to "Brighten up before you have us all in the doldrums." Dick left my office with a weak smile on his face and a few minutes later Ruby appeared to remind me that it was lunch time. I closed down things and walked to the car with her to get our lunch.

"How was your morning?" Ruby asked. "Terrible," I replied – "I didn't get a thing done of the pile I had on my desk." "What happened," she inquired. "Oh, I spent the entire morning trying to talk Dick out of the doldrums," I said. "What is troubling Dick," she continued. "Anything you can tell me, or can't you talk about it?" "Yea, it's no big deal," I said, "he thinks his wife is pregnant and he's all upset." And that's when the conversation took an unexpected turn – "Well don't look now dear," Ruby responded.

"Ruby, that was not even funny," I retorted. "I didn't mean it to be," she softly replied. "I think that what you have been doing all morning is counseling yourself," she said . . . and she was right.

Well, Dick's wife, as it turned out, was not pregnant, but Ruby was and we needed to tell the kids. Rachel was the youngest – she was fourteen. The boys were flabbergasted, but Rachel was elated. She had persisted for years in praying for a sister and now she was sure she was going to have one. I was not so sure – in fact, I steadfastly declared that the baby would be a boy and we would name him Daniel. Ruby softly tried to get me to discuss a girl's name, but I would not. "The baby will be a boy", I affirmed.

December 23, almost Christmas, and Ruby went into labor. We took her to York Hospital and about eight hours later a very lively and beautiful baby girl was born with eyelashes so black and so long they were the first thing the nurse observed about her. Immediately I was smitten – not because it was a girl, but because I had been such a jerk and now I was afraid Ruby would think I was disappointed. "She is beautiful," I said, "And I am thrilled."

I wasn't pretending either. After Rachel's birth we had been warned that we had a blood conflict and could not have "any more normal children." The doctor in York had even suggested that Ruby might have an abortion when she learned she was pregnant. We never considered it, even if Beth would have been born with disabilities. But she was not. It was at once evident that our baby was completely normal and very healthy.

I asked the obvious question, "What are we going to name her?" "What do you want to name her," Ruby asked graciously. "I don't know I replied. You need to name this one – I don't deserve to name her." Ruby complied. "Alright we will call her Elizabeth – Elizabeth Ann," Ruby said. And so it was.

If there is anything in a name she could not have chosen a better. The more I have learned about the name Elizabeth and the persons who bore it, the more I realized that it was born by queens and royalty – and those Elizabeths were some of the most powerful personalities of history. Time would soon demonstrate that the characteristic was decidedly present in Beth. She was alive and quick witted, and though usually obedient, she could be stubborn and was able to argue and reason you into, or out of, almost anything. She was very quickly the joy of my life and when I would come home at night exhausted by the burdens of the day, she could make me forget all my troubles in a moment.

However, that was not all I forgot. I did not choose her name and I had trouble remembering it – so I nicknamed her Dodie – a name she bore until she entered school. And if someone happened to call her Elizabeth, she would stamp her foot and say, "Name's Dodie!"

God knows what we need at every season of our lives and we needed Elizabeth. She was loved by all the other children, they all doted on her in spite of the fact that they were all either in high school or college. The interaction with older siblings showed too. She was only about four years old and still in her high chair, when after frequent attempts to get her mother's attention, she suddenly surprised everyone in the room by chirping, "My mother is definitely preoccupied." We couldn't believe our ears.

I was still doing television in those days. I did a half hour telecast each week, usually recording several at the time to air later. Having used a lot of rear projection multi-media in my other meetings, it was natural for me to rely on the chroma-key effect to utilize those same graphic effects on TV. It made the program, not only interesting, but technologically ahead of its time.

From her earliest years Beth loved to watch my TV show, and it was during one of those programs that God chose to speak to her young heart about her need for Jesus as her own personal Savior and Lord. What a joy it was for me to know that God had used me in some way to lead my precious daughter to Christ.

Elizabeth is very much like me in many ways so that as she got older I could almost predict how she would react to any situation. She tended to mimic some of my habits as well which made me have to look at myself at times. I used to have a rather consistent habit of emphasizing a point by pounding my fist on the pulpit or whatever was handy.

Once, when we were in the dining room at camp, Beth suddenly began to pound both of her fists on the metal tray of her high chair. Ruby looked at her and said, "Stop that Beth." But she looked back at her mother and in a defiant tone said, "Me do's it! – Daddy do's it! – We do's it all the time!" as she pounded her fists several more times.

Ruby immediately assured her that Daddy's habit did not need to be hers and that if she pounded her fists one more time she would be taken from the dining room and punished. The pounding ceased, for the children all knew that if Mother said she would punish them, she most certainly would do so, and so despite, "Daddy do's it," Beth did not do it again.

Beth was born the year we took the camp property and she quickly became a part of everything we did. She thrived in the atmosphere of the camp and we thrived watching her. In my memory I can still see her as she worked fearlessly with the horses, milked the goats, cleaned the barns and grew in wisdom and stature and in favor with God and us.

Our children are the most precious gifts a loving heavenly Father can give us. Each of them is special – each makes a contribution to our own lives. But there are seasons of life where we need them more than at others. God knew that as the others began to find their way in this world, we would need Beth in a special way. How good and how very wise He is.

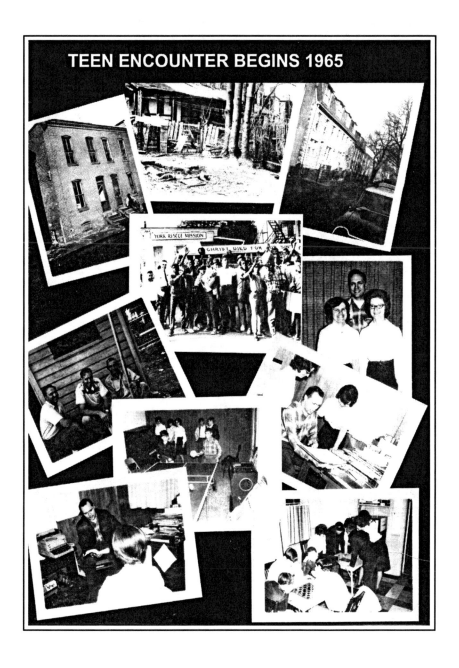

TEEN ENCOUNTER BEGINS 1965

SATURDAY NIGHT TEC RALLY AT DUKE STREET

Picnic with TEC & Lt. McCaffery
at Dick Burd's

TEC GYM
1969

TEEN ENCOUNTER KIDS WITH DEAN AT PIANO

TEEN ENCOUNTER RETREAT FROM FRANKLIN STREET 1968

Deaf Children going to Bill Rice Ranch / Linda front row right

FIRST BILL GOTHARD SEMINAR AWAY FROM CHICAGO AREA
1967 YORK JUNIOR COLLEGE - SPONSORED BY TEEN ENCOUNTER

LIBERTY BELL

Rev. Shade received the Liberty Bell Award from the York County Bar Association on Law Day 1973 in recognition of ENCOUNTER'S local ministries.

AWARD

GOLDEN SPIKE

Mayor William Stauffer watches as Rev. Shade signs his Bible after presenting him with Altoona's GOLDEN SPIKE. Rev. Shade is a native of Altoona, Pa.

**Bob Herrington
with Mayors Eichelberger (York) & Stouffer (Altoona)**

TEEN ENCOUNTER AWARDS NIGHT

GATEA BOARD OF DIRECTORS

DEAN & PATTY BULT
DUKE STREET COORDINATORS

'Teen Encounter' Growing Up

By DOUG DOHNE
Of Our York Bureau

YORK — A former tavern is being transformed by several York firms and individuals into a headquarters for a program aimed at reducing juvenile delinquency in the City of York, it was learned yesterday.

To date at least six businesses and individuals have donated materials and labor worth several thousand dollars for reconstruction of the building on the southwest corner of East King and Pine streets.

It's all part of Teen Encounter, a project of the Grace and Truth Evangelistic Assn., which is headed by Rev. William Shade. The Rev. Mr. Shade was interviewed by the Sunday Patriot-News several hours prior to the Thursday night motorcycle crash which left the young clergyman in serious condition at York Hospital.

Teen Encounter is concerned primarily about the future of inner-city youths, whom the Rev. Mr. Shade has said previously are being bypassed and forgotten by the church, which has moved to the suburbs. The TE staff members have been instrumental in salvaging youths who had been considered as incorrigible by their parents and other people, city police have reported.

York Federal Savings and Loan Assn. made the first move on the King Street property when it turned the deed over to TE several weeks ago. In addition, the bank donated $1,000 to help pay for the needed renovations.

A TE spokesman reported that Leroy Kreidler, a retired electrician, temporarily went back to work and re-wired the 10-room structure.

Other persons who donated labor and materials were Earl Kohler, a plasterer; Kenneth Shade (the TE director's father), a building contractor; Richard Schnetzka, a tile contractor, and Raymond Bertzheimer, a painter.

The new facility, which still is in the reconstruction process, is the third TE center in York.

Most TE benefactors also chipped in with their time and materials when the two existing centers — situated at 37 N. Franklin St. and 401 S. Duke St. — were renovated, the spokesman reported.

Teen Encounter has branched out in another direction, the Rev. Mr. Shade said. The program now includes periodic camping trips on a farm near Glen Rock, thanks to Richard Grim, a York businessman.

"Use of the farm has been a great asset to our program. It's very difficult in large group situations to make any progress with these young people, but the farm offers just the perfect setting," the Rev. Mr. Shade explained.

The change of environment, he continued, "is accompanied by a sense of being alone. The new surroundings make possible a complete removal of that which is basically familiar. It's a big step."

In addition to camping in tents, the city youths fish in a heavily-stocked pond and hike.

The coordinator of the new center is Larry Hodgson, a native of Monongahela, a graduate of the Lancaster School of the Bible. Also in residence at the TE center are Larry Loney, a Philadelphia College of Bible student; Douglas Wenditz, who expects to enroll at the Philadelphia institution this year, and Junie Landis, a junior staff member.

The Franklin St. Center is coordinated by Miss Ruth Hengst, of Manchester, who graduated this spring from the sociology department of the Philadelphia College of Bible. The center also serves as a home for five other females.

Ron Shea is director of the Duke St. Center, which has a boys' program and attracts up to 30 neighborhood youths.

A Teen Encounter project slated to begin in the near future, a spokesman reported, is the visitation of 300 homes in the vicinity of the three centers. The TE workers hope to make six stops at each of the homes — 3,000 visits in all — to distribute literature and promote their pro-

★ ★ ★

STAFF CARRYING ON

TE Work to Continue Despite Shade Injury

YORK — The work of the Teen Encounter (TE) program "will go on" despite the serious injury of the Rev. William Shade, who founded the organization, an aide said last night.

Rev. Ronald Shea, coordinator of the TE center at 401 S. Duke St., said "the staff knows what is expected of it. Bill Shade is very orderly man. The work will go on."

The Rev. Mr. Shade, 34, was injured in a motorcycle accident along the East Prospect Rd. near his home on Thursday night. He underwent a traumatic amputation of the left leg at York Hospital following the mishap.

Teen Encounter was founded by the Rev. Mr. Shade approximately three years ago. The move was inspired by an address by Inspector Charles L. McCaffery, of the York City Police Department.

The Rev. Mr. Shade remained on the serious list at the hospital last night but was removed from the intensive care unit. His son, Phillip, 12, a passenger on the motorcycle remained in satisfactory condition with a fracture of the left leg.

TEEN ENCOUNTER'S ACF BRILL BUSES

ESTHER

PREACHING AFTER THE ACCIDENT

HOLY LAND TOUR 1970

OPERATION PENETRATION

OPERATION
PENETRATION
1970

OPERATION
PENETRATION
1970

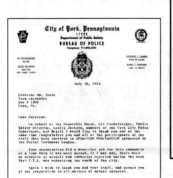

TEC MARCH FOR CHRIST
1970

Chapter Twenty Six

We Go Camping

As we worked with the inter-city kids and with those from the Centers, it became evident that one particular approach worked better than any others – getting the teens out somewhere in a camping environment eliminated a world of problems.

When you have grown up in the city there are patterns that develop just because of the nature of the city itself. You become a part of the environment – a part of the culture – you know the expected response to everything. Everything around you is familiar, including the noise, the tension, the traffic, and the various forms of media blasting the airwaves all around you. You know the smells, the sights, and the sounds.

Now let me transport you to a wooded area outside the city. There are no street lights here. When it is dark, it is very dark. There are noises, but they are strange to your ear. There are crickets chirping, frogs croaking and an occasional owl hooting (not to mention the call of a coyote in the distance). You can't distinguish them. You aren't sure they are safe because you are not sure what they are. Pretty scary, huh?

One night after the Rally, we were walking up the street toward the car. Our family had been in the city many times and it was not unfamiliar – still it was not their natural environment. As we moved up the sidewalk, our foster daughter, Esther got ahead of the rest of us and hid between a couple of cars. When the boys walked past, she jumped out producing a startled war hoop from both boys. She thought it was hilarious that they were frightened. She was in her environment – they were not.

Several nights later I needed to get a small package to Dad's house, a short distance away in our semi-rural subdivision. Esther was with me so I asked her to take it over to "Grandpa's house." Her eyes became wide and she said, "But Daddy, it's dark out there." She was right, there were no streetlights out there at that time, but the safety factor was much higher than it would have been in her well lighted city. She just wasn't comfortable with that because she was out of her environment.

All of that, and much more, plays into the fact that in reaching inter-city youth, getting them into a camping situation has tremendous advantages. Sometimes just getting out of our zone of security gives us a consciousness of our vulnerability and need. So early on we began to find and employ camping situations.

The first opportunity we had was when Richard Grim offered to let us use his farm for a week of camping the next summer. "Anytime after we make the hay you can come down and camp here with the kids," he told me. We could use the fields for games, the wooded area for tenting and the ponds for swimming and fishing. It sounded great and it was. The whole Grim family helped us and the kids joined in with the campers.

Of course there were those practical matters like where we go when necessity calls. We dug potty holes and put up some rough shelters. We cooked on Grim's outside kitchen and used the tool shed for changing after swimming. As primitive and crude as it was, it provided something exciting and different for the kids and the first real genuine spiritual decisions we saw came from those early camping trips.

Once again transportation was a problem and I was approached by the Christian & Missionary Alliance people to see if I wanted to buy an older International school bus they had been using for getting kids to Sunday School. I believe they asked me $75 for it, and I concluded the deal.

I picked up the bus from the driveway of one of the members. He told me they hadn't used it for many months but it started fairly easily. I backed out the driveway, turned to go down the slight grade to the end of the street and as I did I tramped on the brake peddle only to have it travel all the way to the floor. I suddenly realized I had no brakes – I was on a hill drifting toward a stop sign and the street I was on dead ended at that intersection. There was nothing to do but pray and drive and by the grace of God I got it around the corner and drifted up the street to a gas station where it stayed until we had the brake cylinders replaced.

Those were exciting days. We were living on nothing, but God was providing as we had the need. True, we looked pretty shabby sometimes, but we were getting things accomplished and lives were being touched.

Still, no matter how we tried in those early days, it seemed we made little in-depth progress. Most of the kids we were working with were black and I felt like what I needed was a black man who could relate, but who at the same time was Biblically sound and trustworthy. Someone told me about a young black evangelist who was a student at Philadelphia Bible College. His name was Crawford Loritts. They recommended that I ask him to come out to York and minister to the kids and I followed that advice.

The night Crawford came, he brought with him a friend who played the guitar. We had been conducting camp that week at Grim's farm and the meeting would be in the barn. I was not in charge and I simply wanted to check in and see that things were going well, so I arrived late and quietly made my way to the barn.

As I opened the small door and stepped in I will never forget the sight. About twenty inner-city teens were sitting on bales of hay in a circle. Crawford had just spoken to them and they were singing very softly and passionately. I could see immediately that many of them were crying. God did a wonderful work among many of our city kids that night and some of them were our residents at the Centers. I believe it was the first real breakthrough I had seen and the beginning of some eternal work in a number of lives.

The problem with using Grim's farm was that we never knew exactly when we would get it. "Whenever the hay is made." Of course every farmer realizes that depends on weather, and a whole variety of variables that can shift the projected dates one way or the other by weeks. We needed something more predictable in order to plan.

I was introduced to Bob and Vera Kensinger at a youth Rally in Lancaster and brought them to York to minister at our Rally. Bob's uncle had a property north of Lancaster county he had given Bob to use as a camp and they had developed it in an imaginative and rustic manner.

Sleeping quarters were lean-tos open on one side. The dining hall consisted of a circle of benches around a large fire pit and broiling grill which served to cook whatever was cooked. A pond was available for swimming and Bob acted as a lifeguard. He gave hayrides extraordinaire. They consisted of a low wagon with about two foot sides and a little hay thrown in. It was pulled by Bob's jeep and instead of the usual leisurely ride; Bob took that thing at some pretty snappy speeds up and down the little hills and across the fields. It was a really exciting time for the kids.

Finally, Bob and Vera had laid out a "quiet time trail," for the devotional period each morning. They would begin walking from the dining area and Bob would place them at separate locations along the trail. They had a Bible and sometimes a Quiet Time Journal and were instructed to use the time in reading and prayer seeking to find what God wanted to say to them that day. I felt the idea was so effective; I later employed it at Camp of the Nations.

We rented Circle K Camp (the Kensinger camp) for a week each summer for a number of years. As wonderful as it was, I longed for a place where we could extend the time, accommodate more campers and so I found myself looking at property after property over the next several years, but each time, it was evident that God had not opened the door. I began to doubt whether He ever would.

After looking at a number of camps and finding in each case a seemingly closed door, I concluded that a camp was not in the plan of God for Teen Encounter and decided to resist any further impulse to look at camp property. That is why I reacted as I did when I received a call from the Philadelphia area from a realtor named Bill Emmerick. Bill identified himself as a listener to my radio program and a long time friend of Anthony Zeoli, the famous Italian evangelist who had earned the title, *The Walking Bible*.

Bill told me he had a camp property in the Poconos that he wanted me to see. He remembered from earlier broadcasts that I had said we were looking for such a property. My response was, "Thanks Mr. Emmerick, but no thanks. I have looked at a number of properties and concluded that God just doesn't want us to have a camp at this time." Bill continued to urge but I had made up my mind. I was not going to chase around the country looking at camps (or potential camp) properties, only to get our hopes up and then have them dashed. "Thanks, but not this time."

However, Bill was gently persistent. A week later he called me again. "Are you sure you don't want to see this property? I really think it might be ideal and I think we can get a very attractive deal." My answer again was the same. "No thanks Bill, I have a lot of other things to do and can't take time to run on wild goose chases."

A week or two later Bill called again. "I won't call you any more, but I just wanted to see if you might have thought about it and could take the time to at least look at it," he said. "Where did you say it was?" I asked. "In the Poconos," he told me and gave me something of the exact location. "I tell you what Bill," I said, "I'm supposed to speak at Word of Life in the Adirondacks in two weeks. I have to come up through the Poconos to get there. But if I stop to look at a camp on the way, it will turn the trip into a two day trip. Do you want to get a motel for me for the night? If you do, I might take time to look at this."

Bill assured me he would get me a room for overnight and I agreed to look at the camp. I rendezvoused with Paul Davis on the way. Paul worked for Emmerick and was from the Souderton area. We drove to the camp Bill had wanted me to see and looked over the property. If ever I saw a completely developed camp, developed wrong for my purposes it was this one. Everything about it seemed wrong for what I needed, so Paul said, "Well, follow me and I'll take you for supper. Then Mr. Emmerick is giving you his cabin up near Binghamton, NY and you'll be on your way for tomorrow."

I followed Paul and on the way we met Lyle Leonard, another agent of Emmerick. Paul walked back to my car and said, "We have listed another camp property right up the road and I haven't seen it yet. Would it be alright if we took a few minutes and stopped there before we go to supper?" I said that it would and that I would just follow them up the road.

As we approached the property we turned up a very steep hill onto a dirt/gravel road flanked by tall pines on either side. I couldn't miss the fact that it looked a lot like the road into Camp Nathanael where I had worked in Kentucky. As we climbed I thought to myself, it may be beautiful, but I told Paul that I would not consider a location that didn't have a good sized lake and I doubt there will be a lake on the top of this mountain.

As we drove up the road to the property, I could see that it was only moderately developed and that the existing buildings needed a lot of work. Then we crested the top of the hill and Voila! In front of me was a large lake ringed by fir and pine. They had tricked me into seeing this place and they had me very interested.

The lake divided the campground and they had begun to develop a series of RV sites on the lake's lower side. I immediately saw the possibility of operating an adult camp from the RV Park and developing the other side of the lake for a teen camp. The biggest plus seemed to be a brand new swimming pool just below the recreational building.

I learned that the property had 225 acres and that the asking price was a quarter of a million dollars. That was a lot of money back then and especially a lot of money to me. Nevertheless, I determined that this would not be my last visit to this mountain. As I spent the night in the lovely cottage Bill had provided, which overlooked another lake, I prayed earnestly about the property I had seen. It would require an infinite amount of work, but it had tremendous potential and I couldn't stop thinking about it.

When I returned to York after ministering at WOL, I called several of our Board members and told them about the property. We set a date and almost the entire Board made the trip to South Gibson, Pennsylvania to see what I had seen. We ate at the same restaurant in Great Bend where the realtors had taken me and talked about what God might want us to do. I proposed a plan. Make an offer of $1,000 per acre for the raw land and everything on it. In other words, offer nothing for the buildings, RV sites or pool. "If they accept, we will have an indication that God wants us to have the property," I concluded.

The current owners were a conglomerate of individuals who had dreams of developing the place but had fallen out along the way. Trying to get all of them to agree on anything would be difficult. Frankly, we all thought it would take a miracle and that is exactly what I wanted. I did not want to step into something that God was not in and so we agreed, made our offer and waited.

About a month later they finally got agreement and we paid $25,000 down toward the purchase with closing scheduled for the last day of the year 1974. We held several radio marathons and did a lot of praying and talking and as the days wore on we saw about two thirds of the needed money come in.

My friend Bob Neff intervened again and asked how things were going. I told him confidently we were well on the way. "Have you thought about what you will do if you are short of the total you need at settlement?" he asked. "Well, no," I admitted. "And even if you have enough to close, what will you have to begin development?" he continued.

No one knows better than I do how much of a miracle it is that God would do the things He has for me. I am still extremely financially naive and I was much worse back then. I frankly admitted I hadn't thought that far ahead. I was still absorbed with just getting through settlement. Bob suggested I consider getting some financing.

Those were the years of austerity and Banks were not making loans. I started looking for financing and I traveled all over the state of Pennsylvania to major cities talking to bankers, without getting a dime. My dad suggested we try York Federal Savings and Loan since they had already helped us by giving us the King Street Center. I was still skeptical but I determined I would try.

I called to make and appointment and went in. When I walked into the outer office of the President, low and behold, there sat Pricilla, the very lady who had been secretary to Mayor Eichelberger and had been so kind to me on so many occasions. I used to say that if I wanted to see the Mayor, she would get me in unless the President of the United States was with him. When she saw me she welcomed me warmly. I told her what we were doing and what I needed and she assured me she would use all her influence to help me get the money. She must have done so, because in a few days, the money we needed was made available.

The day for settlement came and I was told that we would not need to bring a lawyer since the other side would not have one. The Title Company Attorney would be there and that would be the only Attorney needed. I soon realized that was bad advice. The sellers appeared with an Attorney from up state who immediately asked that we post date the settlement to after the first of the year. He insisted it was for "tax purposes."

I had a big problem with that. The very elaborate contract we had entered into called for settlement on or before December 31. If we did not settle by that date, it indicated that we would be in default and lose our entire down payment. I told them I could not take that kind of chance with money that belonged to God and had been given by many very sacrificially. The attorney refused to budge.

I asked to talk to Bill Emmerick privately. "Bill, I said, "I can't do this. What they are asking is a breach of the contract terms and they could claim we defaulted and we could lose everything. I wish we had a lawyer." Bill thought for a minute and said, "I know a very good lawyer, but the chances of getting him are very slim. He is a high powered guy who is very busy." I responded, "Please call him! We need help or we are going to lose this whole thing."

Bill called and of course got the secretary. She informed us that Mr. Hunn was at a settlement, but that he usually kept in touch with the office and as soon as he would call in she would relay the message. That really didn't sound very hopeful and I was feeling some deep panic, when suddenly the phone rang and Attorney Pat Hunn was on the line. He told Bill he had just completed a settlement and was only about a block away. "I'll be there in about five minutes," he told us.

When he arrived I met briefly with him explaining what was happening. Pat indicated that he understood and thought he could resolve the matter. We returned to the table.

Pat began by announcing that he was representing us in this transaction and asked to see the deed. Once he had the deed in his hands he went over it briefly and told the other attorney, "We have come to settle according to the terms of the contract we have with you. We have the money and I have the deed, so all we need is your signature acknowledging that you received the money and we will quickly resolve this."

The other attorney argued and said that he would not settle unless we changed recorded settlement date to after the first of the year. Pat indicated we would change nothing and offered him our check. Instead of taking it, the attorney reached across the table and attempted to grab the deed back out of Pat Hunn's hands. Pat leaned back in his chair with the deed still in his control and turning to Bill Emerick said, "Call the police, I've been assaulted."

Everyone in the room just sat there looking shocked. Pat repeated his demand, quiet forcefully this time, and Bill went to the phone and called the police. While we waited, Pat looked across the table and said to his opponent, "I don't know how you practice law up where you come from, but before we leave this room today, I'll have your license."

Once the police arrived, Pat said, "If you are willing to do this my way, I won't press charges." The attorney was obviously terrified. He realized Pat meant every word, so a few minutes later, under the watchful eye of a Philadelphia police officer, the attorney meekly settled as the contract required and we had purchased the property that would become Camp of the Nations.

After everyone had left but Bill and Attorney Hunn, I thanked him and asked what we owed him. Pat laughed and said, "I haven't had so much fun in a long time. I should pay you. You don't owe me a thing."

As I returned with the deed and everything settled, I was once again amazed at how God had taken care of me. It was stupid to come without counsel, and I was totally helpless to resolve the matter myself. *"God preserveth the simple"* should be my life verse. He deserves all the glory.

Which brings me to the next part of the story. We hardly got settled at CN when men from the Department of Environmental Resources (DER), paid us a visit. We had to do perk tests. The tests showed the ground did not perk sufficiently to sustain the kind of camper population we were projecting. Their conclusion was that the septic system that was installed and had serviced the campground under former management, would not pass for us – we would have to install a full scale sewage treatment plant.

When the Board learned about it, there was an immediate knee jerk reaction on the part of some to sell what we had just bought and cut our losses. That was not what I thought God had brought us this far to do. I began trying to learn anything I could about alternative systems but it finally came down to the hard fact – we had to do a complete plant. I knew we were looking at an additional $100,000 just for the plant itself, and that was just for starters. Believe me, we prayed.

One day my secretary, Bernice Petticoffer, walked in and laid a Lancaster newspaper on my desk with the question, "Is this what we are looking for?" I read the column, "Sewage plant for sale." It seems a large construction company had wanted to begin a housing development, but there was no hook up to municipal sewage available. However, there was a plan to extend the municipal system within two years. In the meantime building costs were rising and the company decided that it would be cheaper in the long run to install its own sewage plant so that building could commence immediately, and then switch over to the municipal system when it was available. It all happened just as predicted and now the plant, only about two years old, was for sale.

There were several things I knew. I knew we didn't have any money to buy such a plant and secondly, I knew we were mandated to come up with one so I asked my secretary to set up an appointment with the owner of the company.

I drove to Lancaster and met with Abe Mellinger and set forth my case. "We are working with young people," I told him. Then I told him how Christ had changed my life and what we are doing to bring that message to others. "We have purchased a camp property for the ministry and we have been told by DER that unless we install a full treatment facility we cannot open it." Finally, I explained that I didn't have any money for the project so I was asking the company to consider donating the system to me. I made my case, and I simply stopped and waited.

Mr. Mellinger turned around from his desk to the credenza behind him, and I saw him reach for something. He laid a Scofield

Reference Bible on the desk before me. Now it was his turn to tell me what God had done for him. In a very few minutes he had called in his accountant and began the process of donating to us a complete sewage treatment facility that a few minutes before had been for sale for $80,000.

Of course, that only secured the plant. Getting this huge over-sized monster moved from Lancaster to the Endless Mountains and up the winding roads to camp was another matter. I was informed I would need a crane to lift it from its present place, special low-boy flatbeds to carry it and special permits to transport oversized tanks across state highways.

I had just recently met Charlie Zeager and I had little idea of the resources the Zeager Brothers Lumber Company had for the very tools we needed. When they heard of our opportunity they immediately jumped into action. They got another company to donate a crane, moved their trucks into place, obtained the necessary permits and delivered the entire plant onto the camp ground, free of charge.

Still the miracles were not over. Over a year later when a neighbor brought suit against us and tried to stop us from installing the sewage treatment plant, I found myself needing Pat Hunn's help again. I was not sure Pat would remember me or be interested but I called. In a few minutes, his secretary called back and said, "Reverend, Pat says he certainly remembers you and he will look forward to seeing you again."

I went to his office and he listened as I explained our new predicament. After learning our situation he said, "Wait a minute, I have a man who specializes in this type of thing." His associate came into the room; we explained once again our situation and Pat said, "I think we can handle this for you. Mr. Holland will have to travel up to Susquehanna County to represent you, but we can do that."

I thanked him, and as we were about to leave, he turned to his associate and said, "Oh, by the way – I set a precedent with Reverend Shade. We don't charge him anything." I could hardly believe my ears. Once again God had taken us by the hand. When the case went before the judge the suit was thrown out of court and we had no further legal problems.

When I say we serve a God of miracles, I know what I am talking about. I moved forward on this entire venture, with nothing but rather simplistic faith and hardly a clue of the obstacles I would face, and God allowed me to sweat more than once wondering how He could ever get us over the next hurdle. But in His own perfect timing He removed each obstacle one by one in ways I could never have guessed.

The destination was important, but it was the journey where the lessons were learned, and God showed His faithfulness and His strength to us time and time again. I am ever amazed by Grace.

CHAPTER TWENTY SEVEN

More Miracles

S hortly after we secured the Camp property I wanted to hold our first event and begin with a youth meeting bringing the teens we had been working with in the York area to see this camp property. After all, the new venture was only fifteen miles from the New York border and York was near the southern border of the state. I needed to get those teens used to the idea that there was something that far north worth traveling to.

The plan was to begin with a banquet the night before and have a first overnight. But we had no dining room as yet. I had just purchased an entire commercial kitchen from Philadelphia Bible College. They had purchased the old Robert Morris Hotel in Philadelphia and were not going to use the kitchen facilities. I bought the entire equipment package for $1,000 and the cost of moving it (which we did ourselves).

Now we had the next challenge. The old building we wanted to use for a dinning hall had a rotten floor that had fallen through in several places. Not only did it need a new floor, it needed leveled up and some structural repairs. I had a work team on hand for the work, but they had spent several days on just getting the structure repaired. When the day came for the banquet, I still did not have a floor and I had not been able to get LP gas delivered for our ovens and stoves.

The local LP dealer would not deliver the size tank I needed without immediate cash. I didn't have it. Sometime that morning someone gave me the name of a man in Liberty New York, a couple of hours away, and told me he was a Christian who might consider helping us. I called Med Benton and explained our situation. Without a moment's hesitation Med told me he was on the way. When he arrived he and his dear wife set a couple of huge LP tanks in place and hooked them up. He adjusted every stove, every burner, every oven – everything that uses gas and got us going. Med and I became life-long friends that day and I bought LP from him as long as he sold it.

The men finished the floor while we set the tables that had just been brought in and the banquet came off on-time and just as planned. The entire retreat turned out great even though we had to sleep the kids wherever we could. Some even spent the night sleeping on the picnic tables we had moved into the dining room, but there was such a spirit of expectation and enthusiasm that no one seemed to mind those small inconveniences.

I decided I really needed to try to get to know the terrain and features and begin to plan ahead for developing it. I made a trip up to the property with my sons Phillip and Stephen. I'm not sure just why I was on a cane at the time. Apparently it was one of those times when I had walked a sore on my stump, but in any case I was walking with a cane.

Two hundred and twenty five acres is a large property and especially when it is wooded, and broken by steep hills and cliffs, so although I had "seen" the property, I was quite aware that I had not really seen it.

The boys and I parked the car on the dirt road in front of a spot where I envisioned the main auditorium would be placed and began to slowly make our way back into the woods, working our way along an old logging road that ran next to a stone wall. As we moved deeper into the woods suddenly I realized the truth. The former owners had harvested the trees from this whole area starting about one hundred feet in from the edge of the woods so that the situation was not detectable from the road. It was one of those "don't ask— don't tell" situations. We hadn't thought to ask and they didn't tell us. We would have to live with the consequences.

The loggers had dropped the tops and limbs and left them where they fell in a tangled mess that was so thick it took me well over an hour to get to the boundary of the property less than a thousand feet from where I had begun. I was able in spite of it all to envision the likely location of the first cabins but by the time we returned to the car several hours later I was exhausted. I handed Steve the clip board on which I had all my measurements and sketches and on which I had drawn a rough map and climbed wearily into the car and headed for York, three and a half hours away.

I knew I would have to translate all my data immediately before I forgot what I had done so as soon as we drove into the garage in York I asked Steve for the clipboard. There was a long and ominous silence. The last thing he could remember was laying it on the roof of the car when we were getting in. I was less than charitable. "Get back in the car," I ordered. "We are going back." I can't afford to lose all of that work we did today." So back in the car we got and up the road we went.

On arrival (at about 11pm) it was completely dark and after searching with lights for about an hour we decided it was not going to be found. We reluctantly headed back down the road toward York. But it was the days of the gas shortages, the stations were closed and I was about out of gas. About midway down the mountain we had no alternative but to coast into a closed gas station, near Tamaqua, put down our seats and try to get some sleep while we waited for morning.

Next morning after gas and a bite of breakfast I decided to make one final attempt to recover our lost work, thinking that perhaps we might find, in the daylight, what we had been unable to find in the dark. We turned north again and returned to the camp. On arrival I met Howard Clinger, the man who would be our cook for many years, and who had already moved into an old cabin we rather euphemistically named Camelot. Howard walked out with the missing clipboard in his hand. He had found it on the ground the evening before, but was in bed by the time we had returned. We got our clipboard, checked some measurements and headed home. Three trips in one day were a little much.

When I got home I was also very concerned about the problem of the fallen trees and the terrible tangle in the woods. I remember saying to Ruby, "I've made a terrible mistake. We will never get that woods cleaned out in time to get cabins built." Ruby tried to encourage me as she always does, but I was not to be encouraged. She just hadn't seen it and didn't know how bad it was.

Finally, in a last attempt to help her understand the extreme impossibility of the situation I exploded, "Ruby, it would take a hundred men with as many chain saws to clean that place up in time to get our cabins built." It was hardly out of my mouth when I heard the Lord rebuke me – "So, it would take a hundred men with as many chain saws . . . what's wrong with that?"

Almost at once I thought of Paul Bunyan, the legendary woodsman who could cut down a forest in a day. I sent out a bulletin to all the churches and individuals I could think of proclaiming the first *Paul Bunyan Day* at Camp of the Nations, and God brought the men. We didn't have one hundred, but we did have eighty and they came ready for work.

As the men began to arrive in the evening, Howard fired up the ovens and stove and served a wonderful dinner. I met with the men after the meal and went over the task ahead of us. We divided the property into sections and then appointed lead men over each group. I pointed out the area each group was responsible to get clean. After a very early breakfast the next morning the teams dispersed and the sound of chainsaws filled the air. It was a deafening roar, but it was music to my ears.

We specified the length logs would be cut to fit the fireplaces and the stoves. We got a chipper circulating from group to group. I realized with the cold weather and the hard work, if the men came in for noon meal we would lose hours and maybe never get back into the woods. So I told Howard to fix something hot we could carry out to the crews as they worked.

We loaded everything on an old jeep and drove right into the woods. We would arrive, call everything to a stop, sing a verse of a hymn, thank God for our safety and for the food and after serving steaming hot bowls of Aunt Kitty's chicken corn soup and coffee we would go to the next crew.

By the end of the day, every section was completely cleaned. Cords and cords of firewood had been hauled and stacked and the men had enjoyed the time so much we decided to make it an annual event. As long as I directed the camp, we had *Paul Bunyan Day* every year and most of the firewood for the season would be brought in on that day.

Once we had the property, there was the matter of providing some kind of accommodations for campers. We had borrowed an extra $100,000 from the bank for settlement and raised $130,000 with two radio marathons, but there were multiple challenges ahead of us. I wanted to open in June and there was no place for campers to stay.

I had envisioned a Swiss chalet style cabin and had sketched out what I had in mind. Then, grappling with the problem of heating (we wanted to be year-round from the beginning), I had taken my original plan, pushed two chalet's together (on paper), provided a double wall with an air channel between the two sides and designed them to be heated by one furnace, dumping hot air in from above and pulling cold air in from the floor through the channel between the two walls.

This design accomplished a number of things. It eliminated one outside wall for each of the doubled units. It meant we could use one furnace instead of two. Each of the units featured sixteen built-in bunks (we didn't have to buy beds). That meant that a counselor and a junior counselor on each side would allow for fourteen kids, a perfect seven to one counselor/camper ratio.

Because of the evident difficulties of providing plumbing, we simply elected to leave these units without plumbing and arrange them around the central auditorium where toilets and showers were available.

Glenn Eshelman painted an artist's impression of the chalet setting in the woods and we used that to begin advertising. But I had no money to begin building cabins of any kind. Ruby and I talked and prayed about that problem and began to come to a common conclusion.

When we moved to Dad's development, Panorama Hills, we had built a very compact little house – attractive, but small. We had built it however for a little over $13,000. In the course of things, Dad had built a very large Cape Cod style home just across the street from us and sold it on a sales agreement. The purchasers had failed to meet the mortgage payments, and after a failed attempt to set the place on fire and make it look like an accident, they just disappeared one night and were never heard from again.

The house was an absolutely beautiful structure with more room than I had ever imagined, but when the purchaser left it, they left it abused. While it looked good on the outside and was full of new furniture on the inside, the oak floors had been stained, the paint chipped, light fixtures broken and absolutely looking like no one had ever run a mop or a sweeper over the floors for the two years they had lived there.

I wanted to help Dad get it back on the market so I took a few spare days and got some of the kids from the Center to help and we went in and thoroughly cleaned the house from top to bottom eventually removing all the furniture and refinishing the floors.

There is a little side story to that furniture. The former occupants had furnished every room with the latest and the best including a lovely piano. They had, for some strange reason suddenly paid off all of the furniture, and then, almost as suddenly refinanced it.

The finance company called Dad when they learned that the people had gone and got very caustic about how Dad would have to pay for the furniture. The whole situation was bad enough and now this was the last straw. Dad decided that before he handed over money for furniture he didn't want (and couldn't afford), he would make sure the finance company had re-recorded the debt at the court house. Dad asked his attorney to check the records.

A few hours later with more threatening calls from the finance company the attorney called to tell Dad they had failed to record the second loan and that the furniture all belonged to him. What a twist. The next time the finance people called and demanded Dad "Pay for the furniture," he asked, "Why should I pay for furniture I already own?" They never tried that ruse again and Dad had a house fully furnished.

In the midst of all of this, Dad had come to Ruby and me with a proposal. "Your house is small and you have already outgrown it. I am holding the mortgage on this place. Why don't you consider selling your present home and moving in here. If you want to do that, I will let you pick up the present mortgage where the other people dropped it." His offer meant about a twenty percent reduction on the market price of the Cape Cod and we were elated.

So, this family of missionaries, who never made more that a monthly support check and lived by faith, suddenly found themselves in an expensive Cape Cod home with a double garage, a huge sun deck, overlooking miles of country and situated on an oversized lot. Our first house sold immediately for nearly double what we had invested in it. Is God good or what? I remember Dr. Ralph Stoll once telling me that I was just one of the Lord's *spoiled children*, and I believe it.

Owning that home allowed us to do many things. We initially placed the radio studio in the basement. We were able to take into our home a number of the kids from the Center either for a weekend or a short term stay. It was there we lived when Esther came with us. She and Rachel shared a large bedroom upstairs that had four beds in it each with their own dressers and accessories. The boy's bedrooms were downstairs with ours. They each had their own room. It was the nicest home we have ever had and much more than we had ever imagined having.

But there was the matter of those cabins. We had a camp, we needed to get it developed quickly, and we had no resources to do it. Ruby and I looked at the situation and both came to the same conclusion. God had given us the house, it was a huge resource. We enjoyed it and it held wonderful memories, but now it was time to part with it.

We decided to sell the house. But we couldn't stand the capitol gains of an outright sale, and we intended the money to go to the organization anyway, so we actually deeded the house to the Grace and Truth Evangelistic Association and drew up an agreement whereby they would use the funds for the building of those needed cabins. The sale provided the monies for the first four Chalet units capable of housing 128 campers.

As I tell this story, if you are getting the idea that I jump into things without the benefit of thinking them completely through you are absolutely correct. I do not recommend it. I am not proud of it. I think it is a weakness and a fault – but *"The Lord perserveth the simple"*. He well knows the faulty instrument that I am and He chooses to use me anyway – to God be all the glory. When I sense that God is leading, I simply move and leave the consequences to Him.

As soon as we had the Chalets underway I had another dream. It was building a combination gym and auditorium where large meetings could be held. I knew exactly where it should be placed, but the ground was soft and marshy there. In fact, if I pushed a stick into the ground at certain spots and drew it out, water would bubble up to the surface for a few minutes at that spot. I knew we had to begin by creating a solid base and that would likely be expensive.

Just at that time Lyle Leonard, one of the Realtors who had worked with us on getting the camp, told me that he had a gravel pit on his property. If we would supply the trucks to move the material, he would donate the gravel we needed. I immediately bought our first dump truck for $500 and hired several others. They hauled more than a hundred loads of stone into the area and created a solid base that not only would hold the building, but serve as a large parking lot for many years to come.

Next we designed the auditorium. I met Charlie Zeager who was one of the owners of Zeager Lumber Company in Middletown, just below Harrisburg. Some months before Roger Schultz had flown Charlie up to the campsite to see what we were doing. Charlie had promised us all the lumber we needed for our buildings free of charge. He had also shown me a simulated log siding that they had developed and I choose to use that exclusively for everything we would build. So we knew what the building would look like and we had the lumber for the walls. But we needed a concrete floor, bathrooms, showers, trusses, roof, ceiling, just a host of things.

I announced I would have the building up by June, but we barely had the footers in. I announced we would have it by July 4, but on that date I was standing in the place where the platform was going to be, ankle deep in mud. It just wasn't coming together. It was the biggest single building I had ever tried to build and the most expensive.

September came and I was in my office in York preparing to leave for a retreat at a camp in New York where I would be speaking. I got a call from the secretary to Ben Lingle, one of the largest coal mining operators in the state. I had met Ben nearly a year before while having meetings in Dubois. His nephew attended church there and set up an appointment for me to see him and tell him of the camp and our needs. I remember well the day.

I arrived a few minutes early and Ben's secretary, a girl named Shirley met me. She said something like, "Mr. Shade, I don't know what it is you want to see Mr. Lingle about, but you had better get to the point very quickly. Mr Lingle is a very busy man and he has a very short interest span. If you're lucky he may give you fifteen minutes, so tell your story as quickly as you can." I always obey the advice of the boss's secretary (and I always remember her name).

I told my story and Ben asked some questions. I answered him and he asked some more. I realized my fifteen minutes was long gone and we had been talking for nearly forty five minutes. Then suddenly he said, "I want to hear more about this but I have to look at a job. Can you just sit here and wait for a few minutes? I shouldn't be over fifteen to twenty minutes." I assured him I could and he walked out of the office to a helicopter pad, boarded the machine that was already fired for action and flew off to see one of his job sites. True to his word he returned in a little while and we talked some more. We cordially said goodbye and I went my way. Over a year went by and I had heard nothing from Ben Lingle.

Now came the telephone call and Shirley was telling me, "Ben wants to see you today." "Shirley," I said, "I am scheduled to speak at a retreat that is being held in a camp in New York State this evening, and I was just about to leave for there. I don't see how I can make it today." Her reply was very simple, "If I were you," she said, "I would see Mr. Lingle today." I got the point. "I'll call you back," I said.

I knew I was in a fix so I called the man who had booked me for the retreat and asked, "What time were you planning for me to speak? I've got something that has come up and I could be getting in very late." He laughed and said, "Hey, these kids are going to be up all night. It doesn't matter when you speak, so get here when you can." I thanked him, called Shirley to let her know I was on my way, and hit the road.

Clearfield is in north-central Pennsylvania. It took me until mid afternoon to get there. When I walked into Ben's office he greeted me with, "Do you still want to build that auditorium at the camp?" I assured him I did. "Well how would it work to dedicate that building to my son?" he asked. Then he told me how his son had been killed in an automobile accident since I had seen him last and he wanted to do something in his memory. I assured him it could be done. Ben's next question was, "What do you need to finish that building?" I told him that we needed $78,000. Ben never flinched. He pushed the intercom button on his desk and asked his accountant to come in. He gave him the amount we needed and told him to prepare a check. It was almost like a dream.

The full force of what had happened didn't hit me until I got out in the car. I bowed my head to thank God for what He had done, and God seemed to speak to me very clearly. He said, "You remember when you were in school at PBI and Addison Raws spoke at chapel? You remember how he told of a time when Keswick Colony needed four thousand dollars or they would lose the place?"

Oh, yes, I remembered well, though I hadn't thought about that for years. I remembered how they had prayed and how on the very day the amount was needed Dr. Raws had opened a letter from an attorney. The letter told of the death of a friend of the Keswick ministry and how he had determined that a certain percentage of his estate would go to Keswick at his death. The letter concluded by saying, "the enclosed check in the amount of four thousand dollars represents that amount."

I remembered clearly that day, and I remembered that I had never heard anything like that before in my life. I was a young Christian and such things were totally strange to me. But I remember what I did. I bowed my head as that chapel ended and said to God, "Lord, if he is telling the truth, and you do things like that – do something like that for me."

It wasn't the money I wanted, it was the miracle. I wanted to see God do the unexpected and the miraculous and that is what I was asking for. That day as I prayed outside Ben's office, God said, "See that check in your hand – I heard your prayer and that is my answer." The thing that really thrilled me was not the size of the check (though it was many times the amount Addison Raws had talked about), but the fact that God had heard a young Bible student's prayer and had not forgotten even though I had. That is grace.

In November we dedicated the Great Commission Auditorium in honor of Ben's son. Dr. Bill and Kathy Rice came to that occasion. Bill spoke and Ben was there in the service to help unveil the plaque with his son's name on it. The building when completed seated about seven hundred at full capacity and doubled as a gym and recreation area. Charlie Weaver built a beautiful fireplace at the back of the building and we installed hot water heaters and heated the entire building with a wood fired boiler located in a boiler room in the back.

Hundreds and hundreds of young people and adults found Christ as Savior in that place and scores dedicated their lives to Him for service. The building served us for about eighteen years, until the year of the continuous snow storms – but that is another story.

CHAPTER TWENTY EIGHT

But Seek Ye First the Kingdom of God. . .

When my longtime secretary, Bernice Petticoffer got her first license plate from the State of Pennsylvania, after leaving her lucrative job with Sperry-New Holland, she ordered a special plate which read; **MATT-633** (Matthew 6:33). The reference was of course to the words of Jesus, *But seek ye first the kingdom of God and His righteousness, and all these things shall be added unto you.* It was exciting to see how God fulfilled that in Bernice's life, providing for her the very things she needed, and some things that were simply her desires. God always keeps His word and it has been one of my passions to try to communicate to a new generation that Jim Elliot was absolutely right when he wrote; "He is no fool, who gives what he cannot keep, to gain what he cannot lose."

Ruby and I saw that played out again and again. We would give something away and God would provide for us again more than we could have imagined. In Chapter 27, I told the story of our Cape Cod house – the one we deeded over to GATEA to sell, so that we could have the monies needed to build those first cabins at Camp of the Nations. After that transaction, we lived for the next three years in an apartment complex on the north side of York. What a let down, from a beautiful Cape Cod house in a suburban development – but God had other challenges for us.

To begin with we had four teenagers at that time; our oldest son Phillip, then Stephen, and Rachel plus our foster daughter Esther. In addition we had a new born – Elizabeth, or "Dodie", as I called

290

her. Our situation was somewhat relieved in September when both Phillip and Esther went off to Philadelphia College of the Bible.

Rachel was still with us and could continue at Christian School of York, but for Stephen it was a different story. Christian School of York only went to the eighth grade at that time. Stephen would have to attend public school. Now all three of the older ones had already been in a public High School since the eighth grade, but because of our former location they were in Red Lion High School, a school where Teen Encounter was able to conduct a Bible Club, establish a Christian presence, and a school with a good academic standing. Moving to the north of the city put us in a completely different district and we were immediately faced with a dilemma.

Working as closely as we did with the city and conducting clubs in many of the schools gave me a pretty good feel for what each school offered and the school where we would have had to place Stephen had a reputation for drugs, and violence. We agonized over the situation. I began to wonder if I had done the right thing.

After much prayer I determined that I could not risk my son's future on that kind of situation, especially now that his siblings were no longer around him. We made a decision to attempt to place Stephen in Ben Lippen Academy in Asheville, North Carolina.

Actually we faced a number of hurdles. First the school was expensive. It had a reputation of being the premier boarding school for Christian youth at the time and many of the students were from families that had considerable means – we did not.

Then the school had a rule that they would not take anyone in the final year of their education. A student had to enroll no later than their junior year to be accepted – Stephen would be a senior. We prayed about the matter. We now had two children in college, one in Christian School and were considering sending a third to an expensive boarding school. What were we thinking?

Well, first of all, while we gave Phillip some help with his expenses, Ruby was able to find grants to greatly reduce the burden and Phillip worked to help pay expenses. Ironically, she learned that if we had owned a home, Phillip would not have been eligible for those grants, but because we now owned nothing, he was. We never realized that when we gave up the house, but God did.

Esther, we learned, was eligible for government grants as a foster child who had neither a father nor a mother. We had wanted to adopt Esther and we had discussed it with her and would have done so, but I realized how little I could help her with college and if we did not adopt her, her way was fully paid. We agreed God had made that provision and we would not derail it. Still there was the challenge of keeping Rachel in Christian School and sending Stephen to Ben Lippen, if indeed we could even get a placement.

God is always previous and we decided He would provide for Stephen's tuition if he was accepted. After several tries, the Head Master made an exception and Stephen was given a place at what was easily the best private Christian boarding school in the country. So here we were – we had given up all we had and God was caring for us and our children as if we were kings.

Of course there were some minor trials. We were in an apartment complex where we had no basement, no shop space, no where to do anything. I have always loved to work with my hands. Growing up in a home where we built houses, we learned to do most everything for ourselves. I loved it. I never could get interested in chasing a little white ball all over a large green lawn, or any other form of recreation that produced nothing as an outcome, but I loved to create and build and it was, for me, a form of release. The apartment situation frustrated me.

Then there was the "music." Rock was just coming into fashion and big booming sound systems were all the rage. I had neighbors on both sides of the apartment who loved that stuff and we were caught in the dissonant center where the two sound waves met and the bass woofers caused the walls on either side of our room to vibrate. Our infant managed somehow to sleep through it all, but there were times when even her crib vibrated.

Our salvation in those days was the fact that we had just purchased the camp property and I was making one or two trips every week over the one hundred and eighty mile stretch, spending most weekends at the camp to help with retreats. The music and the atmosphere there, were definitely an improvement.

After three years in that situation, the Lord opened an old farmhouse for us in South York, on Dave Markey's property and we moved there until we moved permanently to the camp. The farmhouse provided a basement where I set up shop once again, allowing me to do such projects as restoring a boat which we later used extensively.

We also had room for the kids to come home and several rooms where we lodged Bernice and our staff artist, Lucy Adkinson. In addition there was a large kitchen where Elizabeth, now three years old, would ride her plastic tricycle in circles around the table at such speeds that she spent most of the time on two wheels rather than three. The house was old, but I was in my element again and happy.

One very quick memory of that place was the winter it snowed a wonderful wet snow which laid beautifully on the pine branches and the ground. I went out with Elizabeth (Dodie), and we built a snowman – quite a production – and she was thrilled.

The next day as we drove her to nursery school we passed many snowmen on the way, but the sun was out and I remarked that snowmen might not make it through the day. Dodie immediately informed me, rather dogmatically, that her snowman would survive. She had prayed about it she told me, and God would protect him.

I had my misgivings as we returned home that afternoon. Every snowman we had seen that morning was either reduced to a shapeless heap or completely melted away. I tried to prepare Dodie for the reality that snowmen are very temporary, but I met with total resistance, "My snowman will still be there" she affirmed. I gave up and resigned myself to her inevitable disappointment. But when I turned into our drive, low and behold, there was Dodie's snowman standing straight and tall and Dodie was ready to let me know that God had answered her prayer.

I realized, as I looked at the situation that I had inadvertently built the snowman in direct line with several large pine trees that had shaded it from the afternoon sun and sure enough, Dodie's snowman had been spared. But not only was it spared that day, but the next day and the next day and when there was no signs of snow anywhere else in town, finally on Friday, the snowman, which had begun to lean, toppled over.

I have since often thanked my heavenly Father, that He cared enough to answer a little girl's prayer about something as insignificant as a snowman. As I have watched Beth as a grown woman with a houseful of her own children, exercise her faith again and again in difficult matters, I have wondered what affect that stubborn snowman, that stood when everything else was gone, might have had on the mature faith I can see today.

In 1980, we finally moved our entire operation to the Camp. The frequent trips were taking a toll and the work we had begun in York had changed with the changing complex of the city. Now God moved us where we could give full attention to the project.

A camp property, the size of Camp of the Nations, is like a large elephant. He knows how to eat and has a voracious appetite. He can consume all your resources in a very short time if he is not put to work to earn his keep – and that was the challenge now before us.

God had been amazing, and in spite of my limited financial abilities, we had survived the first five years, paying our mortgage payments on time and improving the facility tremendously. We built a total of seven wonderful chalets all equipped for winter, the Great Commission Auditorium, that could seat seven hundred people and double as a gymnasium, and we had made numerous improvements and expansion in Family Camp on the north side of the lake.

I had refinanced the mortgage once to provide funds for continued development and we had built a large maintenance barn and created additional housing sites for mobile homes. About that time came the Atlanta Project (see chapter thirty one), and the subsequent fall off in camp registrations which we suffered over the next couple years. For the first time in our lives we missed a mortgage payment.

I was not too concerned because after all, we were in friendly hands. I knew Stan Glatfelter, the Bank President, and was sure he trusted me sufficiently to cut me some slack, so I did nothing that month. Then the second month came and again we could not make the payment.

When the third month loomed with the same problem I decided it was time to contact Stan and talk about how we planned to handle the situation. I called the Bank. When I asked for my friend, I was told that he had recently retired and I would be given the new President – and a woman's voice greeted me.

I explained who I was and that I was calling about the Camp of the Nations mortgage, and she immediately interrupted me by saying, "Mr. Shade, I'm glad you called, we will have our meeting this week and we are ready to foreclose on your property unless you can perform." I assured her she would have the money in full before that meeting, and hung up.

I went to Ruby and asked, "What do we have? Where can I find the money to pay this thing?" Ruby assured me there was nothing available in the camp funds that would meet that large a demand and the only thing we personally had that large was our life insurance policy. We made an immediate decision – "Cash it in!" I took the funds from the insurance and brought the mortgage up to date, saving the Camp from foreclosure.

Well, we had gotten through the crisis, but it had left Ruby and me without any savings at all. I had opted out of Social Security early in my ministry, and now I had no life insurance. No home, no Social Security, no insurance – all of our assets were gone.

I reminisced about that moment recently as I was talking to our financial consultant. "What did you do?" he asked. "We began to look for ways to invest small amounts of money as we got it" I said. "We slowly began to recover. Then one day we realized that what we had done was the best decision we had ever made. It forced us out of the security zone to think about serious saving. Slowly the amounts grew. Once in a while a significant amount would come from a relative's will, or a special gift from a friend and we tried to carefully invest as much as we could. Our financial situation today is a result of that." He shook his head in amazement.

Ruby and I have both reached the age now where we have to take our IRAs. But we have never had to use those funds. To date we have been able to roll everything over into further investment and although we are far from rich by any human standard, we are working on a plan to establish a Trust to care for things after out death.

Imagine! You give it all away, and somehow it all comes back. But isn't that exactly what He promised? *And every one of you that hath forsaken houses, or . . . lands, for my name's sake, shall receive an hundredfold, and shall inherit everlasting life* (Matthew 19:29). Everlasting life is our inheritance, because we are His children by

Divine new birth, but "a hundred fold" is the interest He pays on what we invest, and that is equivalent to 10,000% interest on our investment. If any Bank in the world offered that on investments, you would get trampled in the rush trying to invest there, but God promises us that on the investments we make with Him, and we doubt Him and grasp our possessions ever more tightly.

Beloved, God pays big dividends. We have never regretted anything we have ever given up for His name's sake and I am convinced neither will you.

CHAPTER TWENTY NINE

The Relocatable Building

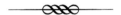

It is perhaps ironic that as I sit down to record this particular story, I am staying in the guest room here at Grace Bible Baptist Church in Baltimore. The guest room is part of a one hundred and sixty foot church complex that was constructed from another building some years ago and as I sit here and contemplate that story, I am actually in a part of the very building this story is about.

We now had a fairly well developed camp ground at Camp of the Nations for the adults with sufficient amperage to the sites for most camping situations. The Shower house had been refurbished, several single-wide house units had been donated and set up and we could accommodate about 50 family units.

The Children's Chapel was a favorite spot for the kids and we tried to keep our staff on duty as much as possible to keep the children active and happy. Old Pine Lodge had been just a screened in pavilion and we installed windows and made it a great spot for the adult Bible hours.

We had a total of seven Chalets on the teen side of the lake, each having two sides capable of holding 16 individuals with several having additional space in the basement or loft for a capacity of 252 campers. However, when we hosted conventions we sometimes expanded that by setting up three tiered bunks down the center of each Chalet. When that happened we maxed out at 450 campers.

The original dining room was more than crowded when we had large groups and we were still renting space at the adjacent farm for our offices. I dreamed of being able to build office quarters and actually designed a complex and requested a grant for funds to build it from a Foundation, but was unsuccessful. About the time my faith was wavering badly about ever getting additional quarters I received a call from my dear friend Dr. Earl Johnson in Baltimore, Maryland.

Earl told me that there was a relocatable metal school building about four miles from his church and the city was planning to destroy it. It had only been used for about a decade and was in excellent condition and Earl had approached the city about donating it to his church on the condition that the church remove the building within a set period of time.

Surprisingly the city had given rather tentative approval to the plan but Earl now realized that he did not have enough space on his present church property to accommodate such a large structure, and that secondly, he did not have the manpower to complete the operation. He asked if I was interested.

I was, but I had just fallen and injured the stump of my amputated leg and was at that time on crutches. Feeling helpless to go look at the project myself I asked Roger Schultz who was only a few miles away in Hampstead, Maryland to look at it and give me his opinion.

Roger did, and his opinion was, as usual, very explicit. "It is a fabulous building and just what Camp of the Nations needs to completely change its image. It is structurally sound and was engineered to be de-constructed and re-located. And having said that – don't even think about it. It is far too big a job and you could never get that building moved up to where you are. It would require cranes and heavy equipment and a lot of manpower and know how and you do not have it – so forget it."

Well, I thought about that and the more I did the more I decided I could not just walk away from it without a closer look. So I contacted a number of men who were in various areas of the construction trade; Paul Liskey and Charles Weaver were masons, Bob Martin built silos, Phil Fahs was a plumber and an electrician and Dad was a general contractor. I got all of them to meet me and I drove them to the site of the school in the inner-city of Baltimore.

Roger had described it well. It was 360 feet long and 60 feet wide with 10 foot high ceilings. It consisted of a frame work of steel columns and beams. The web of the beams was five feet high at the center and tapered to about 2 ½ feet where it rested on the column. The roof was supported by steel purlins and the walls were made of a composite of hard cement-like material layered on both sides with sheets of steel. The whole building was set up in four foot increments like a huge erector set.

Everything was in working condition – in fact they had held school there until within a few days before I saw it. The plumbing was still in the bathrooms and in very good condition. The A/C Heater units were all in place and working. There were lockers and desks and equipment of all kind. It was a dream – but it was big – and none of us had ever tackled anything like this before.

We spent several hours looking it over then headed back to Pennsylvania. As we drove I asked each man to give me his opinion. Each one said pretty much what Roger had said. It would be great and the Camp needs it and it would make a great church building for Earl and there is plenty of material there to do both, but it is just too big an undertaking – we could never do it.

After a rather extended silence, someone realized that my father had not said anything. Dad was the oldest man in the group and the others respected his wisdom. "What do you think Shade?" they asked. I will never forget his reply. "I think we have the grasshopper complex like those spies that Moses sent out. God has given it to us, so why don't we just take it? If God is in it, we can certainly do it."

No one spoke for several minutes. Then finally someone said, "Well Bill, I'll put it this way, I hope you don't. But if you do, I will help." And they each said about the same thing. I decided that was God's indication to move ahead and I let Earl know we were in.

When Earl went down to sign the papers we hit another hurdle. He called and told me, "Now they are saying that we have to remove, not only the school, but the slab that it sets on. That slab is two and a half feet thick and covers 21,000 square feet." I agreed with Earl that this would be too much and if we couldn't get relieved of that we probably would have to pass on the whole project. Suddenly I had a thought. "Look," I said, "Go back and tell them they don't want to destroy that slab. They have a wonderful ready-made area for tennis courts, basket ball courts, and all kinds of things. Don't destroy it – use it."

Earl decided it was worth the try and presented our response. I think we were both amazed when they bought into that and agreed we should leave the slab in place. Two years later they had to remove it to build a new building, but it was no longer our responsibility.

How do you eat an elephant? The answer is, "one bite at a time." And that is how we began. But before we even moved the first thing, I suggested that we lay some ground rules for ourselves and all those who would work with us. They were simple, and went something like this; "Earl and I have been friends for a long, long time. We intend to be friends long after this project is finished. So there is nothing in this project that is worth loosing our friendship over. We began with nothing and anything we end up with is pure profit, so we will divide and yield what ever the other group feels they have need of."

It worked wonderfully. There was never a single incident of arguing over who should get something. Those who participated said that there was a greater sense of unity amongst this very mixed group of people than they had ever experienced.

The shear logistics of putting this together were staggering. It would take the labor of fifty to sixty men continuously to get the job accomplished. Many of those men would have to travel from northern or central Pennsylvania to the site in Baltimore. That would be expensive. Moreover it would be time consuming and it would shortly wear out the patience and the determination of most. Earl proposed the solution.

The church would abandon their family activity center. Cots would be set up in the main hall for as many men as would be staying. Meals would be served morning and evening and lunches would be prepared for the men before they left for the site in the mornings.

Imagine the situation. Fifty to sixty men coming in each evening. They are tired, they are dirty and they are hungry. The ladies of Grace Baptist did themselves proud with cooking meals that were tasty and nourishing.

Now comes clean-up time. How do fifty to sixty men get showers in a facility planned for perhaps ten to twelve? I really don't know, but somehow they did. If you can't stand someone snoring when you are trying to sleep, you didn't want to be laying on one of those cots.

But it worked. It worked because the men determined that it would. It worked because God had given them a mind to prove to the city that God could do what they had said couldn't be done in six months. Their demolition crew wanted six months to just knock it down and haul it away. They had given us eight weeks to carefully take it apart and preserve and move every piece. I'm sure they were laughing up their sleeves at this bunch of dumb preachers who thought they could get it done.

But we had undertaken it and we were on the way and through organized prayer and God's provision, we were not only accomplishing the task, but drawing these men who were participating closer to one another and closer to God as they saw Him at work daily.

One of the biggest problems was transportation of the material. I had a seventeen foot van truck and a twenty foot stake bed but they looked like toys next to the task ahead. I found a retired Brockway Tractor in fairly good condition and bought it for $2,500. After a few repairs and a new tire she was good to go. Zeager Lumber company offered us the use of a flatbed so I now had a complete rig. The first few trips convinced us we were still woefully under equipped.

As soon as we were given access to begin, we started by removing all of the furniture, lockers, and other equipment that had been left behind. The city later quarreled about our taking this, but they had told us to begin and the implication was that we were to remove everything. We did. These first moves we made using our own trucks and equipment.

I immediately realized I had no place to store so much material and began looking for storage boxes. I purchased three retired trailer units before it was over and filled them. Then I bought an old army mess tent and set it up on wooden platforms to keep the stuff up off the ground and stored until we could begin to put it back together.

The first teams on the job were made up of volunteers from Grace Baptist Church (Earl Johnson's church), and our Camp of the Nations Staff. Dad volunteered and stayed on the job the entire time until it was finished. Soon some of our electrician, plumber, and other construction people began to volunteer.

They emptied the inside of the school and then began taking down the internal walls. They removed everything internal in order to leave the protective outer walls in place as long as possible against vandalism. Since the internal partitions were free standing and were not part of the structure, they could do that without affecting or weakening the building.

But now whole sections were coming down with wall panels that were ten feet tall, four feet wide and weighed over 100 pounds each. All the frames for those panels began to come down, then the doors and the hardware had to be moved.

It became evident that my three trucks and the couple Earl had rented were not going to be able to move the material fast enough to keep it out of the way of the workers. And nothing could be left piled on the outside of the building because it would have been stolen immediately. While the men were working one day a police chase ended when two drug dealers ran from their car into the construction site and shots were exchanged. We had two wall panels with 38 cal. slugs imbedded in them.

I was getting concerned about the transportation issue when I received a call from Jack Winters. I had never met Jack, but Paul Liskey had contacted him at church and explained our predicament. Jack owned and drove a large rig with a flatbed and could make the two hundred and forty five mile run from Baltimore to Camp of the Nations in about half the time my little rig could. Jack offered to run as many loads as he could for $500 a run. I immediately hired him.

Once everything was out of the building, the next hurdle was the roof. Emerson Brandon was my lead man on the job and he called me one morning with, "We've got a real problem." I asked what else we had had since we started, but told him to go ahead and tell me what it was. "We have 73,000 self threading sheet metal screws holding down the roof. Many of them have been in place now just long enough to be rusted. It takes a power wrench to remove them and I'm timing it at about three minutes per screw. If that holds, given our present manpower, it will take us past the deadline they have given us to just get the roof sheeting off." I agreed – we had a problem and I did not have any solutions.

Early on in the project I had contacted everyone I knew to try to enlist help, among them the Mennonite Central Committee that sends work teams all over the world. They had been very courteous and seemed interested in what we were doing, but told me frankly, "Actually, Bill, it just isn't a Mennonite project." I told them I understood and asked them for their prayers.

About a day after Emerson's call, a man from the Mennonite team called me back. "It still isn't a Mennonite project," he said, "but I've got some men who are free right now. Could you use about thirty men for four days?" What timing! They took our roof sheeting off, stacked it, strapped it, loaded it on the trucks and had the job done in three days. Do I need to observe that God was superintending this project?

The next challenge came with the structural steel. Engineers from High Steel, a large Christian company in Lancaster came by and told me we could never get those beams down without a crane. That's when I called Don Frick, a brother I knew from Easton, Pennsylvania. I knew his company majored in moving equipment that was considered impossible to move, so I asked him to look at our situation. I had described it to him so Don actually arrived with the piece of equipment he said we needed – a simple three stage fork lift.

Positioning the forks in the exact center of the beam he then had the men unbolt the ends of the beam from the columns. Once done he very gently moved the lift with its very overweight load at a slight angle to the columns and slowly let it down to the floor. From there, they unbolted the center bolts which held the two pieces of the beam together giving us two beams, each about thirty feet long. These he lifted one at a time onto the flat bed. When he was finished he turned to Emerson and said, "Now that's how it's done. Here are the keys, call me when you are finished," and he climbed into his truck and drove away. We de-constructed all the remaining beams in exactly the same manner without incident and there was never any charge for the lift or its delivery.

I remember that day it dawned on me that the eight weeks they had given us to accomplish this were not only almost up, but that we in fact did not have eight weeks. We did not, because the seventh week was the week of Thanksgiving and the last week was the beginning of deer season in Pennsylvania. Now it wasn't that these men weren't dedicated to the task, but if you live in Pennsylvania, you most likely hunt. As I said to Emerson, "These guys will miss the Rapture if it happens over deer season." I told Em – "I don't know how you are going to do it but you have to finish before Thanksgiving."

Tuesday morning of Thanksgiving week Emerson called me and said, "If you want to see that last beam come down you will need to be down here this afternoon – we are going to finish." I drove down to see it with my own eyes.

The weather had been unbelievably cooperative. It had rained a few times while we were still working inside the building, but from the time we opened the roof and began the outside work every day was dry and perfect.

As I drove on the site it was almost unbelievable. Several trucks were loaded ready to leave. They were indeed getting in position to take the final beam down. The entire slab and the yard around it were clean. There was not a thing setting around anywhere.

The fork lift made its final move. Then bolts were loosened from the column and Emerson did his slight turn. Then they eased the huge beam down to the pavement. After that men removed the bolts from the center flanges that held the two thirty foot sections together and now we had two separate thirty foot beams to load onto the waiting truck. As the beams were being loaded the men removed the columns and loaded them as well. It was almost five o'clock in the afternoon.

As I stood watching, I noticed that the sky had clouded over and it was becoming much colder. As they struggled to load the columns a soft midst began to fall. It was the first rain in all the weeks we had worked since we began taking down the main structure.

I followed the trucks out of a completely empty school yard. Nothing was left but the bare slab the building had been setting on. We drove the short distance over to Grace Bible Baptist Church to join all of the other men. The parking lot was full of loaded trucks ready to make the final run up the mountain.

The ladies of Grace had prepared a Thanksgiving meal that was beyond belief. We sang, we prayed, we praised God and we wept, because only God could have accomplished such a feat. Everyone was hugging each other. They had built life long relationships in those weeks together.

Finally it was time for goodbyes – and then someone said, "I don't think we are going anywhere." The rain had been freezing and there was over a half inch of ice on everything. It was several days before the trucks could move their cargo, but the work was done.

A week later, a permit officer came over to Earl's office and dropped off a permit he said we would need before we could finish the work. Earl thanked him and politely asked if he had been by the building recently. When he said he had not, Earl suggested he swing by and see how things were going.

Grace Church was able to keep up their momentum and I had the joy of speaking at the dedication of their new relocated building – the building in which I am now sitting as I write this. At the Camp it was a different matter and it took five years before we were able to reconstruct our part. A camp does not enjoy a congregation that can get behind a project like this, and there were other problems we had to face.

The building in Baltimore was on basically level ground and the church simply poured a slab and rebuilt it. There is no such level place at camp and our part of the building was 200 feet while the Baltimore section was only 160 feet. When we established where we wanted the building to go we chose a location that looked to the eye fairly level. When we set up a transit and shot the grade we found that the ground actually fell away from one corner to the other by thirteen feet. The Board decided that it made sense to build a basement under our building. It made sense, but the original building was not engineered for that.

Well, I struggled with the early concepts and decided all we needed to do was tie the vertical columns that were on twenty foot centers together across the sixty foot span by a steel beam. We could build the walls of the basement out of twelve inch block to give it maximum stability and strength, then build into that wall special block piers every twenty feet to support the beams. The columns would then be bolted to the beams and the rafter beams bolted back in place as before and we would have constructed a solid box.

Bud Brown, an architect from York, laid out the foundation and we did the necessary excavation ourselves. By this time we were well equipped with heavy machinery and had our own crawler loader. We poured the footers and got ready to lay block.

Does anyone realize how big a project a twelve thousand square foot building is? Several teams of masons volunteered for periods but in the end it was our dear friend Paul Lisky who just stayed with the project until it was completed. We were able to get our steel beams from a company at cost so now we were ready for the floor.

There were several conventional systems we might have chosen to create a floor but we couldn't afford any of them. No one seemed to be able to come up with an answer. I knew we needed a concrete floor but the only material I could get at no cost was lumber.

I remember going to bed one night with the problem heavy on my mind and waking up about four in the morning with an idea. I got up and went to the kitchen table and began to draw out what I had envisioned.

The plan was to use twenty foot long two by twelve oak beams at sixteen inch centers to provide support for a floor. Then I suggested using one inch thick oak boards to actually create the floor. Over the boards we would place a membrane of roll roofing and plastic. That would keep the concrete from binding to the wood and allow the two materials to expand and contract without one affecting the other. Finally, we would pour up to four inches of concrete over the membrane, heavily reinforced by rebar and steel mesh.

I had no idea whether I could get State approval for such a plan, but I decided it was worth a try. I contacted Zeager Brothers and took the drawings down for them to see. One of the men immediately responded that he thought it would pass. "We just built a bridge using a very similar design for Three-Mile Island. If the State would approve that, I think they will approve this."

They gave the drawings to their structural engineers and they modified them slightly using three by twelve beams on twelve inch centers. Other than that they submitted the plans just as I had drawn them.

Within a couple of weeks word came back that they were approved. I notified Zeager that they could go ahead and cut the lumber for the job. They told me they planned to start on it the following Monday. Saturday night the entire Zeager mill burned to the ground. We were shocked and grieved for our dear friends, and we were also wondering what we would do now.

Zeager informed us that they were going to rebuild and that if we could wait, they would still do our job. Reconstruction took an entire year, but it was rebuilt with more modern equipment much of which was now computerized. The first job they cut after getting back into business was ours, even though they were not charging us for it. I am still moved to this day when I think of their commitment.

Nearly five years after we took the building down in Baltimore we dedicated the new Administration Building. In the lobby I was able to get a large eighteen foot oil mural that depicted the major Biblical events from Creation to the final Judgment. The mural was built into a half round shadow box that went from floor to ceiling by our dear friend Elvin Martin. The upper end of the building was offices, the other end, dining room and kitchen.

It featured a modern kitchen and a four hundred and fifty seat dining room decorated with an Olympic theme at one end and a panoply of Swiss shields at the other. The southeast wall of the dining room was all windows and looked out over the Endless Mountains in the distance. There was also a cantilevered balcony that ran the entire length of the building and had stairs at both ends.

The basement level opened out onto a road which ran down behind the building. It sported a dormitory that increased our camper population capacity by thirty some campers. There was also a large shower and bathroom area. There was a large meeting and recreation room in the center and then we reserved another large area under the dining room for our printing operation, which I still hoped to revitalize. Finally, under the kitchen, we had a large pantry with a walk-in cooler and freezer.

Much of the masonry work on the building would have been done by Weaver Masonry, but Charlie Weaver, the owner of the company and a Board member had died in a tragic automobile accident. We wanted to remember him and got family permission to dedicate the dining room, *The Weaver Memorial Dining Room*. The other end of the building was dedicated to the one man who had helped us more than any other single person, my father, and it was called the *Kenneth L. Shade Memorial Wing*.

Dedication is always a triumphant event, and it was attended by hundreds of campers and friends. It brought closure to the saga that had started with a telephone call from Earl Johnson five years before. The Baltimore building was now a part of Camp of the Nations.

CHAPTER THIRTY

Murder in Atlanta

It became national news as day after day one child, then another went missing in Atlanta and turned up dead. The evening news talked about it, LIFE magazine published a cover story showing the faces of over twenty kids who had disappeared and then been found murdered that summer. Ruby and I were at the camp but we had not escaped hearing about what was happening.

But Atlanta was a long way off and I was extremely busy. If I thought about it at all, I probably didn't think about it long until that particular night. It was all very simple, very usual – we were getting ready for evening service with the teen camp and our little daughter Beth, who was six years old at the time, came to me with a common request. "May I go to Children's Chapel Daddy?" Simple enough – Beth (and all the children in Family Camp), loved Children's Chapel.

We held Chapel for the children every evening at the time of the adult Bible study. We accomplished two things – we actually got to minister to the children in a setting they enjoyed. Every evening there were Bible stories, verses to memorize, and a clear presentation of the gospel to little folks. Secondly, by having the chapel each evening the adults could concentrate on their Bible study without distraction.

Children's Chapel was a miniature tabernacle built out of logs with open sides and a tin roof. Everything was miniaturized. The benches were made to fit children under twelve. There was sawdust for a floor and a stone pulpit stood at the front. All around the chapel was a fenced-in play yard full of exciting things to do.

It was the brain child of an autistic man named Glenn Martin who spent his summers with us and built all manner of delightful things – windmills for the front yard of the cottages, arching bridges to go across streams, and ever so much more. In this yard, among other things, was a very large wooden locomotive that the children could climb onto and into. They could pretend they were engineers steaming across the plains or through some mountain pass. So it was no wonder Beth (and all others eligible) wanted to go to Children's Chapel.

I answered her with the same instructions I had often given before, "Sure honey, just be sure you come back and meet me at the snack shop as soon as the Chapel time is over." She thanked me and went bouncing out the door, and that is when it happened.

My serious minded wife looked at me and said, "Honey, wouldn't it be awful if we were living in Atlanta and you wouldn't know if you would ever see her again?" I felt like someone had just gut punched me. Actually, I had to take a deep breath. "Ruby!" I said, "You don't say that kind of thing to a father." But I got the point and the point would not leave me.

The next day I made a phone call. We had Advisory Council people who lived all over the country and one of them lived in Atlanta. I called and talked to Nadine about the situation. The killings were still happening at the rate of one every several weeks. I said, "Nadine, I know this doesn't make any sense. You are in the heart of Dixie and I am in the northern mountains of Pennsylvania. But if there is anything you can think of that I can do please let me know."

She replied, "Do you think you could take some of these children to your camp if we could arrange to get them there?" "Certainly," I said. "I still have some sponsorship money and if you get them to me I will keep them as long as we have camp if necessary." We both promised to pray about it and I felt relieved that I had made an offer, but I must admit, I rather assumed it would end there. It did not.

Several days later I received a call from Atlanta. The voice on the other end said, "Dr. Shade, my name is Camille Bell. I'm the chairman of the *Mothers to Stop Murders in Atlanta Committee*, and I was told that perhaps you could do something for our children."

"What would you like me to do?" I asked. She said that she had heard I had a camp and could possibly take some of the children and keep them there for the rest of the summer or until the crisis was over. "Well, yes," I said, "I have some sponsorship monies, but I would have no way to get the children here." Camille said she thought she could arrange for that and then asked how long I would be willing to keep them. "There are five more weeks to camp Mrs. Bell – I suppose, if it were necessary, I could keep them until camp ends." "Wonderful Dr. Shade," she said. "How many children can you accommodate?" "How many do you want me to accommodate?" I asked. "Could you take one hundred?" she ventured.

She was pressing my faith and my commitment. I have to admit I had not considered the possibility of that many. I certainly did not have one hundred sponsorships even for one week, much less five. But there seemed to be an opportunity here. Could I really say no? If I attempted it, I could not only protect that many children from a murderer on the loose, but in five weeks, I was certain we could introduce many of these children to Jesus Christ. And what if I said no – could I even live with that?

I heard myself respond something like, "Mrs. Bell, if you can get one hundred children to me we will care for them for up to five weeks." We talked about the details of age (no one under eight and no one over fourteen). After some time she told me she would get back if she could work out transportation.

I remember walking excitedly into the next office where Ruby was and announcing – "Guess what! We are going to get one hundred kids off the streets of Atlanta for the next five weeks to give the gospel to." That was all I could think about. What an opportunity! I remember Ruby's reply.

"OK George Mueller," she said, "you have them, now how are you going to pay for them?" "I don't know," I said. "After all, what is it going to cost me?" She did a few key strokes on the adding machine and looking up said, "Just a tidy little $42,000." I came back down to earth. I suddenly began to hope that Camille would not be able to get transportation. That was an awfully lot of money.

A few days later I got a call that buses had been donated to transport the kids all the way from Atlanta to Camp of the Nations. They arrived early Sunday morning, but what I hadn't expected and what I never dreamed of arrived with them – camera crews from several major news networks. They wanted to see this camp that would take one hundred children from the streets of Atlanta and keep them for five weeks free of charge. I think they thought we were a little crazy, and frankly, we were.

We had worked with inner-city youth from our northern cities for over a decade and a half and I supposed this would not be any different, but I was in for a number of surprises. First, those who put the group together had not followed the guidelines regarding age limitations. I quickly realized that there were children on those busses who were younger than eight years old. About a dozen of them fell into that category. Then there were some older teens easily sixteen or older. All of that complicated the task we had ahead of us.

The second thing we discovered was that many of them did not bring their own bed covers or sleeping bags. It gets very cool at night in the mountains and we went scurrying to try to find enough blankets to keep everyone warm. And it was not only blankets they lacked – many had only the most meager clothing, no jackets, not much more than the clothes on their backs.

Finally, and most challenging was a spirit of belligerence that seemed to control many of the kids, especially the older ones. They complained about nearly everything. There was no television to watch, no radios to listen to – they were in a strange environment and they were not sure how to respond to it.

Thankfully, Beth made friends immediately with the younger crowd and started to show them around the camp. She looked like a sort of *Pied Piper*, leading a pack of about a dozen children. She not only took over initially, she continued throughout the entire stay to get these children to where they needed to be, to comfort them when they had difficulty and to assure them when they were confronted with new activities such as riding the horses.

Dealing with the older set was another matter. They had one very predictable response to any one or any thing that displeased them. They were ready to fight. They fought with each other and they did verbal battle with their counselors or anyone in authority. When they fought each other they would pick up sticks or whatever was handy and do serious warfare.

I remember one day when I saw Reggie heading for the dining room with a stick in his hand about five feet long and an inch in diameter. A very formidable weapon in the wrong hands, and his were definitely the wrong hands. I had learned by now that direct confrontation, or simply ordering him to put it down would accomplish little. There had to be another way.

I called to him, "Hey Reggie, come over here – you look like Moses." "What do you mean I look like Moses?" he asked. "Well, you've got that rod just like Moses had – you know about Moses' rod don't you?" I knew the answer before I asked. I had finally realized that these kids knew nothing about the Bible or Bible stories. They were the most biblically deprived group I have ever worked with in my entire life.

"No, I don't know about Moses," Reggie responded. I said, "Let me show you Reggie – give my your stick for a minute." Reggie complied and I went into detail about Moses' rod becoming a snake, about how he used it to turn water into blood, and how he opened the Red Sea by just holding it up. Then I suddenly said, "Reggie, you'd better hurry or you are going to be late for dinner." Reggie headed for the dinning room leaving me standing there holding Moses' rod in my hands and figuring I had averted a major catastrophe.

There were other challenges as well I hadn't thought through when I said yes to Camille. Camp ends each week on Saturday morning and we let the staff take the vans into the city to do their laundry and shop or do whatever they wish. They have to be back by supper time and dressed up for the evening concert. If we have a few kids staying over, we just assign them to one of the groups of staff people and they do their laundry just as the staff does. But how do you handle one hundred at one time?

I had to contract a special laundry service to handle the load for those five weeks. I also had to figure out how to get clothing for the children to wear while their laundry was being done, and to keep them warm on cool days and evenings. Thankfully, that is where the press coverage we received helped me.

313

Because we had been carried by the news services, people were aware of what we were doing. I began to get calls asking if we needed anything. People wanted to help, especially around the Scranton area. Within a week we had been donated enough clothing and bedding to care for all the kids and provide them with several outfits and warm jackets.

The lack of a value system became evident when camp was over, because much of what had been given was left scattered in the cabins. They just couldn't be bothered being responsible for taking it with them.

The biggest challenge came when we tried to minister. I had worked with inner-city kids before, but these kids had no knowledge at all of the Bible or of Jesus, except as a curse word. We tried just about everything. I brought in speakers that could hold an audience spell bound, but they couldn't interest these kids.

Finally, I called my good friend Mel Floyd from Philadelphia. Mel had been named, Philadelphia's Man of the Year, by the city because of his work with the inner-city community. I had brought Mel to York and found his message effective there. I asked him if he would come and give it a try. He did and we struck gold.

Mel came on stage doing the turkey walk and he had their attention immediately. He shared his own story of growing up with the gangs in the city and some of the tragedies he experienced. Then he told them how Jesus Christ had come into his life and changed him from within. He told how, as a city cop, he had begun to work with the gangs and how Christ had changed many of them as well. Mel communicated and scores of kids made commitments to Christ that evening. By the end of the five weeks, ninety seven of those who came had professed faith in Jesus Christ.

By the end of those five weeks my staff was exhausted. They had not had a single day off since the Atlanta kids arrived. They were ready for this to end, but at the last, as the busses drove away out of the parking lot, one big counselor fell to his knees and began to sob uncontrollably. God had given them a love for those children in spite all of the obstacles.

And the cost? KYW News Radio out of Philadelphia sent a camera crew up to film the kids and see what the camp was doing.

At the close of the five weeks they asked me to come down to the city and be interviewed on their TV channel about the project. Both situations proved tremendous opportunities to share the gospel in a very clear fashion, but they also brought attention to our need and people began to give. Before it was over we had made an actual cash outlay of $37,500 and the Lord had sent in gifts totaling $38,000.

By the time the busses rolled home, Wayne Williams was in prison under arrest for the murders. While some doubted that the police had gotten the right man, the fact is that as soon as he was arrested the murders stopped and never recurred again.

There was another price I paid for my venture. Our regular campers, many of them white and most of them "church kids," had been cheated of the good times they usually had by all the attention we had to give to the Atlanta kids. In addition, they were often intimidated, threatened and even struck when one of the Atlanta group got angry. Although we tried to deal with each occurrence as it happened, I lost as much as twenty percent of my regular campers the next year and it took me several years to recover.

Costly as it was, we gave the gospel to those children and saw God do some remarkable things, and I can never be sorry for that investment. Good things inevitably come out of doing the right thing, even when the right thing is not rational or at least not practical. One huge benefit is seeing God come to your rescue and supply every need and get glory to Himself.

CHAPTER THIRTY ONE

Camp is All About Missions

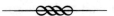

C amp of the Nations was all about missions. The name of the
camp suggests as much. The camp verse was Matthew 28:19,
20 *Go ye therefore, and teach all nations, baptizing them in
the name of the Father, and of the Son, and of the Holy Ghost:
Teaching them to observe all things whatsoever I have commanded
you: and, lo, I am with you always, even unto the end of the world.*
The auditorium/gymnasium was named *The Great Commission
Auditorium*. All of the camper chalets were named for countries of
the world. Below the auditorium stood the beautiful *Fountain of the
Fields* with its ten foot diameter globe of the world, shimmering in
the colored lights as the water poured over it from the fountain jets.
Camp of the Nations was all about missions.

When Chet Bitterman was martyred in Columbia, we built the
Chet Bitterman Memorial Soccer Field with its lovely memorial and
its quarter mile track. JAARS, the air arm of Wycliffe Translators
flew their STOL aircraft in for the dedication and the county of
Columbia sent a representative from the embassy.

Every Friday evening we did a missionary drama. One year we
dramatized the Chet Bitterman story. Another year we did the story
of the five missionary martyrs in Equator. That particular year on
our summer music team were two sisters and a brother whose last
name was "Saint". I only learned after we began doing the drama
that they were nieces and a nephew of missionary Nate Saint, who
was one of the martyrs whose story we were dramatizing.

Each week as we emphasized the call to missions, young people would dedicate their lives to become missionaries. We used name badges at the camp to identify our paid campers. Among other things the badge was their ticket into the dining room for meals.

When a camper wanted to dedicate themselves for missions, they would throw their name badge into the Fountain of the Fields. In order to get into the dining room they then had to go to the office and ask for a replacement badge which cost them one dollar. We averaged about eighty badges per summer in the fountain. How many actually got to the mission field I have no way of knowing, but we counted eight fields where former campers served after I stepped down from the camp.

We not only preached and taught missions, but tried to interact with missionaries and mission groups. One year we hosted the African Children's Choir while they were on tour in the States. We had them perform for a Saturday night concert and then discovered that they had only a couple of local bookings for the next two weeks and no certain promise of lodging. We immediately made the decision to invite them to stay at the camp and cared for their housing and meals as long as they were there. By doing this sort of thing we sought to set an example to others that we were committed to missions even when it meant a substantial investment.

Along with the emphasis on missions was a parallel emphasis on leadership. The very first year the camp opened we ran an LIT (*Leaders in Training*) program. It was a three week experience that was designed to stretch the participants to the limit.

The first week was basically classes in the morning (training in counseling and soul winning), and work in the afternoons. When I say work, I mean work. I told the kids up front that if I did not put blisters on their hands by the end of the first week I would consider myself a failure. I didn't fail very often.

We broke the kids up into groups of about four or five. Then we would assign one team some strenuous task like grooming the quarter mile track. They had the next four afternoons to accomplish the task. Each day they would choose a leader among themselves. The leader's job would be to see that everything they needed to do the task was on the job. He or she would set the goals for the day, give directions and participate in the work. Finally, the leader would see that all tools and equipment were put away properly when the work was done.

At the end of each day the team would evaluate the performance of the leader and the leader, in turn, would evaluate the performance of each member of the team. Each morning I would review the previous day's activities and accomplishments. We would talk about what went right and what went wrong.

In the second week, the Leadership Group would act as junior counselors assisting in oversight of campers and using the skills learned in their classes during the first week, attempt to lead someone to Christ. During this week they were evaluated by the senior counselor under whom they served.

The third week, we tried to prepare the entire group for the wilderness experience that was ahead of them. On Wednesday after classes, we would bus the entire leadership group down to an entrance to the Appalachian Trail. There we would unload the kids and two adult chaperons where they would begin their first stage of the thirty five mile hike. We knew exactly how far they had to get each day, so no matter how hard it got, they had to reach the distance for that night's camp.

When they camped, their selected leaders took charge. They determined where they would stretch their tarps to create shelters and where each pair of campers would be. They assigned various ones to duties like gathering firewood and others to begin preparing for the evening meal. If they made good time that day they would have some daylight left to get settled in. If they were late starting or had difficulties along the way they had to get set up in the dark.

The next morning they rose early, prepared breakfast, conducted group devotions and started on the longest leg of the journey. The second day was always the most trying. The small discomforts of the first day were magnified on day two. If they had blisters, they had to be treated, but the hike had to continue. Whatever the weather was like, they had to endure. If it rained or was cold it was really miserable. Or if it was very hot the bugs and the mosquitoes made the trip more difficult.

At the end of the second day they were very ready for a stop. They set up camp cooked a good meal and went to bed, knowing that it was the last food they would have for almost twenty four hours. Next morning they rose early and were dispersed along a ridge overlooking miles of woodlands. It was truly an inspiring view. Each camper was allowed their Bible, a songbook or devotional book and a notebook. They would spend the next five hours alone with God. What they did was up to them, but they were fasting and communing with God and many had experiences they would remember for life.

At about noon the chaperons would come by each site and pick up each individual. They would then begin the final and shortest leg of the hike arriving down at a loading area about an hour later where we would have the bus parked for their return to camp.

When they arrived back at camp it was mid to late afternoon. They still had not eaten, but they unpacked their gear, hung out what needed to dry, got a hot shower and rested for several hours.

That evening was Banquet night. Everyone would dress in their finest and we would serve a meal fit for a king with all the extra trimmings. After supper we went to the GCA for the evening service. There I had several of the kids give their testimony of what God had done in their lives during the Leadership experience. Often they would testify about the time spent with God that morning. Then we did a mission's drama and gave an invitation. God used the entire program to call many into serious relationship with Himself and others into full time commitment for service.

One of the highlights of each year was the Accelerated Christian Education (ACE), Convention. I had been asked to speak at a convention the year we opened the camp. While speaking to the youth assembled, I also talked to the leadership about holding the convention at Camp of the Nations the coming year. Before the end of the week, a decision was made and the following year CN hosted its first ACE convention.

The Convention brought together youngsters from all of Pennsylvania. There were always between four and five hundred in attendance. There were non-stop competition events going on continually during the entire four days of the convention. These included competition in academic subjects like math, science, history, spelling, etc. etc., but also athletic competition such as track and field events. It was a busy, busy time.

At mealtimes we set up the dining room so that there would be two to four lines passing the food bars at all times. The path was set from the food bars to the tables and from the tables to the rear door of the dining room so that they would be no confusion with kids trying to come in and go out the same doorways. Kids were responsible for bringing plates and tableware to the tables and then bussing tables on their way out so that they cleaned them for the next occupants. Once the procedure was perfected we found that we could feed over four hundred kids in forty five minutes.

The highlight of those conventions was getting to know the kids themselves. Our staff acted as judges for much of the competition. I particularly loved to judge the "Preacher Boy" competition. In fact it was at one such event I heard young, sixteen year old Tom Palmer bring a message and determined that the hand of God was on that lad. I invited him to be the preacher for the junior camp the next summer that helped launch him on a career in evangelism.

One of the delights of my life has been observing God at work in the lives of certain young people and trying to give them the opportunity to try their wings at serving God. I did something similar one evening as I sat in the audience and watched my youngest son Steve perform with the Lancaster Bible College (LBC) Choral. I saw a baritone who watched the conductor so intently and put himself into the music so enthusiastically that I purposed to meet him after the concert.

When I did, I invited Jim MacArthur to join our summer staff. Jim later distinguished himself in missions with *Christar* eventually becoming their National Director. So many young people have done exploits for God who got their start at CN that it has made every trial and testing along the way worth it to see God's hand at work.

Missions became a very personal thing about this time. I was sitting at my desk at the camp one day in 1984, when a letter came to me from India. Ruby and I were always interested in India and I opened it with some excitement and curiosity to see who would be writing us from this land we had prayed for so long. I had no idea what I would find.

The letter was from an Anglican Bishop named Mani and it thanked me for consenting to be their speaker at the All-Church Conference to be held in Kottayam, South India. I wondered what in the world I was reading. I had never heard of Bishop Mani and I was not sure how he could have heard of me. Furthermore I knew nothing about a conference and I certainly hadn't agreed to speak at one. Then I emptied the envelope to find a flier with my picture on it and a bio all printed up announcing that I was to speak. I was completely dumbfounded.

I decided to call my friend Chief Bob Atwood because I knew Bob went back and forth to India every year. I wanted to see if he knew anything about this. Bob was an evangelist who was also an honorary American Indian Chief and I used to have him every summer at camp to minister to the teens.

I told Bob about the letter and wondered further about an Anglican asking me to preach. "It's even got the imprimatur of the Archbishop of Canterbury on it," I said. "What is a bishop in the Anglican church wanting with a Bible thumping preacher like me?" I asked.

Bob immediately assured me that he knew Bishop Mani and told me that he had been in America and had been saved in the Asbury revival some years before. "I thought Dr. Stewart Lease was going to be preaching the conference," Bob told me, "Mani won't have anyone but a Dallas grad preach at the conference." "Well I'm not a Dallas grad," I replied, but I think I'm beginning to figure this out."

I got on the phone and called Stuart Lease. Dr. Lease was president of Lancaster Bible College. "What do you know about this?" I asked. "Oh, my doctor told me that I should not make the trip," he replied, "so I just recommended you. I had to send them some information so they would know who you are." "Well they took it as a done deal," I replied. "I guess I'm going to India."

By the time the plans were complete we were to fly into Bombay and then on to Bangalore. I would teach at the Asian Christian Academy for the first week, then I was to fly to Cochin where they would drive me up to Kottayam. There I would do the conference and then go back to Bangalore and do a week of evangelistic meetings in a large city church. Finally I would fly to Puna in Maharashtra where I would meet our dear brother Martin Rajnoor (whom Ruby and I had hosted in our home and helped support for a number of years).

There is much about the journey I would love to tell. Suffice to say that as we finished our week at the Academy we got to see the hopelessness of a Hindu funeral. I wandered uninvited into the grave yard where the cremation was to take place, but before I left, I had given my tract One Foot in Heaven to many of the mourners.

Then we traveled down to Cochin and I preached each night of the conference. I had never preached through an interpreter before and it was an interesting experience. During the mornings I was asked to do a Bible study with the priests. I found myself in a room with about thirty white-robed priests and a Roman Catholic lawyer. I choose to teach the book of Romans.

The first day they argued as we moved into the book and through the first three chapters. The second day the reception was better. The third day they showed real interest. By the forth day they were asking real questions and excited about the study. The final day they wept as I walked them through Romans eight – "No condemnation, the Holy Spirit to enable us for righteousness and for prayer, the assurance of eternal life and ultimate resurrection, a renewed earth and a glorious heaven." I learned they had never gone through even those first eight chapters of Romans before.

On the final night Dr. Ramesh Richards arrived and was asked to preach the final message. At the end he gave an invitation asking all those who had received Christ during the week to stand. About fifteen of the priests joined many others to indicate that God had visited us and done a miracle in many lives.

During the last several days, Dr. Richards spent some time with us and asked me to come to Delhi after I finished my stay in Maharashtra. I realized it would take some changing in my travel plans but I decided it would be worth it and it certainly was.

The next week we held meetings in the church in Bangalore. It was a very western setting and I could preach without an interpreter. The highlight of the week came on the last night when a dear Muslim lady came forward to profess her faith in Jesus Christ. I little realized at the time what her step of faith would likely cost her, but it was clear that she had firmly believed in Christ.

We went on to Rahuri and stayed with our friends the Rajnoors. As I traveled about some of the villages I remember walking through what looked like some very old gates and brother Rajnoor saying, these village gates are over four hundred years old. It struck me that my country, America, was half that age. India is indeed an ancient civilization.

One evening we ordained a deacon in one of the churches. I remember the man to this day. He was a farmer and wore, I'm sure, the best that he had, but his shirt was torn and worn.

After the meeting a young couple urged us to come see what the church had given them for their wedding. They had just been married and were so thankful for what God had done for them. They were permitted to stay in the room just off the meeting room of the small stone building that housed the church.

As we entered, at their insistence, to see their treasures I was shocked to find myself in a totally empty room. There was absolutely nothing in the room but a small fire place formed by two stones between which lay some coals. I looked up to see a hole in the roof to let the smoke go out.

"They gave us this room to stay in," they told us excitedly. "We can bring the mats from the meeting room in and it makes a bed for us. And look what they gave us," they continued. I raised my eyes to a stone shelf about half way up the wall. There on the shelf was a copper tea pot, two copper plates and two copper cups.

I tried to act as excited as they were but inside my heart was smitten. They could be so happy and thankful for so little, while how many times I have been thankless for so much.

That evening Ruby spoke to the ladies. The meeting could not be held until about ten o'clock, because that is when their husbands would allow them to come – after they had prepared the usual late Indian supper. Ruby spoke to the dear ladies under the light of a gasoline lantern. Three nights later she would be speaking to the ladies gathered at the Canadian Embassy in Delhi under a chandelier that was easily fifteen feet high. Such is the contrast in Indian society.

We finished our trip by going to Delhi and I spoke at several places on Sunday. Ramesh's church was scattered all over the city and had no building of its own so it met in hotels and function houses or where ever it could in small groups. Sunday night, Ramesh told me that an Indian professor from America by the name of Ravi Zachariah was coming to hold meetings and would bring with him our astronaut Dr. James Irwin. There was to be a governmental reception for the astronaut at the Sheraton Hotel that evening. I had the privilege of being there – an experience I will never forget.

We entered the auditorium filled with government officials – both Hindu and Muslim. On the platform was a huge screen. In a moment the room was darkened and they showed the moon landing with Dr. Irwin stepping down from the space capsule. As the brief showing ended they introduced Dr. James Irvin.

Dr. Irvin came to the microphone and thanked everyone for inviting him to India and for receiving him so graciously. Then he spoke some words I will never forget. He said, "I know it is very important to everyone that man has walked upon the moon. But I came to India to talk about something far more important, and that is, that God has walked upon the earth in the person of His Son, Jesus Christ." I could not have been more thrilled. Imagine that as an opening line before that audience. I was not only glad I was a Christian, but I was glad at that moment to be an American.

After six weeks of travel and ministry we returned to America. At long last we had been permitted to minister in India and I sincerely hoped it would not be the last time. Back at the camp all we had experienced in India had strengthened our resolve to keep missions in the spotlight.

*****

In 1989 the eastern European country of Romania exploded in a bloody Revolution. One of the features of the repressive regime of Nicolae Ceausescu had been the systematic persecution of evangelical believers by the Securitate – the secret police of the Dictator.

Over and over again they had spirited away anyone who had the courage to raise a voice against the brutal tactics of the regime. They were especially violent enemies of Christianity, even forbidding the people to observe such holidays as Christmas.

On December 16, a protest broke out in Timisoara when the police tried to arrest Hungarian Reformed Church Pastor Laszlo Tokes. Tokes' congregation somehow learned of the attempt and formed a circle around the church and manse standing three deep and daring the police to enter. When the police attempted to disband the parishoners by force a riot ensued and soon others joined the discent. As word quickly spread of what was happening riots broke out spontaneously in other major cities.

The dictator attempted to resolve the unrest as he had done many times before by gathering a huge crowd before the palace in Bucharest and before national TV cameras denouncing what was taking place in Timisoara. But to his shock and surprise instead of the reaction of support he expected, the crowds began to chant *Timisoara, Timisoara, Timisoara.* The shocked dictator realized that a full fledged rebellion was underway and that he was in danger and he attempted to flee.

His private pilot flew him from immediate danger, but claimed to have engine trouble and put the helicopter down in a field on the road to Pitesti. Ceausescu along with his wife Elena were taken by car to a plant in Targoviste and there placed under arrest. Two days later, ironically on Christmas day, Nicolae and Elena Ceausescu were condemned by a military court and summarily executed by firing squad.

Now nearly a year had passed and Don Kyer was ministering at Camp of the Nations and invited me to go with him to Romania and assess what had happening since the revolution. Don had traveled to Romania before and had attempted a trip just preceding the Revolution, but was denied entrance. After prayer, I decided to join him on this trip.

There were four of us (all Baptist Preachers) that made the journey. We flew into Belgrade and rented a van. One of the major purposes of the trip was to deliver about twelve cases of Romanian Bibles to the churches. During the days of the Dictator, it had been almost impossible to get a Bible and the only way Romanian believers could have the Word of God was if those in the West would smuggle it in. Don had done some of that as well. Now we would test the new regime that was promising religious liberty. We loaded our Bibles and began the journey north to the Romanian boarder.

It was a very dark night and a wet snow had begun to fall. The ground was too warm for it to lay in any depth, but the situation created a light fog and the further we drove toward the Romanian Border the deeper the fog became.

About midnight, just before reaching the Border crossing, Don related how a year previously he had approached this very same boarder crossing. The guards had ordered him out of his vehicle and made him stand for seventeen hours while they asked him the same questions over and over again.

Finally, they had thrown his passport on the floor and when he bent over to pick it up they kicked him. When he was finally able to get himself back on his feet they refused him entrance and sent him back to Belgrade. That story was certainly comforting on this dark night as we approached the same crossing.

We stopped at the guard post and one of the guards asked for our passports and visas. As that guard took our papers into the guard house, another guard commanded us to open the van and let him see what we were carrying. We complied and when the door was opened there were our twelve cases of Bibles. They were unmarked so he asked what was in the boxes. I decided the best thing we could do would be to tell them the truth and accept the consequences. I told him there were Romanian Bibles in the boxes.

He demanded to see them so I opened a box and pulled one out and handed it to him. He looked it over and then asked, "May I have this?" I assured him he was welcome to take the Bible. He walked a way and a few minutes later a second guard approached us. "May I have a Bible?" he asked. I was delighted to oblige.

We had probably waited there about twenty minutes when the chief officer approached us with our passports and papers. Extending them to us he said, "I wish you every success in Romania." We thanked him and as we did, he said, "I have a guard who must board a train, fifteen kilometers up the road. You have a large van. Could you take him with you?" We told him we would be happy to do so and the young officer climbed into the van sitting right next to me.

As we started up the road on the dark foggy night I began to ask him what he thought of the Revolution. Gently, I asked, "Do you think that God had anything to do with what happened in your country?" As we approached his destination he answered, "I'm not sure about it, but I know the time is coming when, *God shall wipe away all tears from their eyes; and there shall be no more death, neither sorrow, nor crying, neither shall there be any more pain:*

for the former things are passed away. And he that sat upon the throne said, Behold, I make all things new. And with that he stepped out of the van and disappeared into the night, leaving four Baptist preachers rather speechless, for there was not a one of us that could have so perfectly quoted that text.

I later tried to tell this story during one of my messages but my translator at first refused to translate it. He insisted that it couldn't be true, that all those guards are Communists and atheists. Only with great difficulty did I convince him that I was telling the sober truth.

There were unforgettable experiences during the next days, such as the night I was preaching in a little house church and an old man suddenly got up, and with much emotion said something directly to me in Romanian. I turned to my translator for an explanation and he replied, "That man said, 'When I was in prison you visited me, when I was hungry you fed me. Blessed are you who come in the name of the Lord.'" Then he continued, "That old man spent nine years in prison for his faith." Those were the kind of experiences I encountered again and again.

It was during this first trip that I took a side trip to Austria, a story I will relate in another place. Within a year I returned to Romania and taught a course on the Pentateuch in a church in Arad. On several subsequent trips I taught Eschatology. It was Eschatology that I was asked to return and re-teach to former graduates.

On one of those trips I visited our Source of Light Branches – one in Brasov and one in Otelu-Rosu. Donna Beltechi traveled with us as my translator and interpreter. It was on that trip she related to me how, as a seventeen year old girl, she remembers one night when she was at church and the Securitate had burst into the evening church service and publically beaten two of the church leaders before the eyes of the congregation. After beating them bloody, they dragged them off to the prison.

Donna recalls how the church began a season of intense prayer and about midnight decided to confront the police. About three hundred of them quietly trudged through the snow to the prison and asked for an audience. The police insisted they could not talk to three hundred people so they said, "Just choose someone to represent you and let him come in to us and we will talk with him." One of the leaders who had been absent earlier stepped forward and they opened the gate and allowed him to enter. But the moment they had closed the gate they began to beat him as well.

Then Donna told me, "Suddenly we heard the trucks coming in the distance and we knew they had called for the army. We had no choice but to run as fast as we could. I remember running for hours through the woods so as not to be caught by the soldiers who were chasing us." And then, as if to add a postscript she said, "They told us we were persecuted, but I thought that was just the way it was – that's just what it meant to be a Christian." Her story had a very humbling affect on me as I cried out to God to grant me the faith of these dear believers.

All told I returned to Romania six times. I still have many dear friends there and would love to return again if God ever allows. It was experiences like these that constantly brought Missions into the life and program of Camp of the Nations.

CHAPTER THIRTY TWO

I Have A Hobby?

I have often been asked if I had a hobby. I'm never sure just how to answer that, but there are some things I really enjoy doing. Some of them are just fun pursuits like scuba diving or snorkel swimming. I've had the privilege of doing both only once or twice. Nevertheless I've always been thankful for the experience.

I like to hunt and during the days at CN, and later over at Thompson, Ruby and I relied on venison for most of our meat. I never claimed great skill, but like Jacob, I would have to say, I got it "because the Lord God brought it to me."

Of course I really enjoy flying, but like some of those other pursuits, I have learned that for every thing there is a season, and when that season passes, so does the opportunity to enjoy certain pleasures. The believer simply accepts that and thanks God for allowing us the pleasure we were able to enjoy for a time.

But one of the more unusual things I enjoy is painting – no not painting pictures, although I have done that in both chalks and oils, but just painting anything that needs painting – houses, furniture, equipment, tractors, cars, just about anything.

I'm not sure whether it is the task I enjoy or the result. I love to see a piece of furniture that looks like it needs to go to the dump, completely restored, shining like new and treasured by someone. I love to see a car that is shabby and looking bad, look like it just drove out of the showroom – or at least like it was something someone had cherished and cared for.

I have such a passion to make things look good that it had never bothered me to drive an older vehicle, but I can't stand to drive one that has been damaged and looks bad. Something down deep inside drives me to want to repair the damage and make that old car look good again.

Furthermore, I early came to the conclusion, that the only satisfactory way to paint anything was with a spray gun. I vividly remember my first experience. I was a teen working for Blatchford Furniture Company at the time and Dad had assigned me to paint a couple of lawn chairs. I went to the man that did the window display work for the Furniture Store and talked him into letting me take the spray outfit home that they used for that work.

I had absolutely no idea that the little outfit was made only for water-based paints and I was using a rather thick green enamel. How I ever got the job done I really don't know but it took me hours, much to the distain of my dad, who showed me how quickly he could do it with a brush. It was true he got finished far faster than I did and for a brush job, he did well – but in my mind there was nothing like a spray job – after all, isn't that how the car companies did it?

While Dad was not at all sympathetic to my passion, we had a neighbor who was. He had purchased a small compressor and gun to paint his house. It was marginal at best, but he got it done and then sold the outfit to me. I can't remember what I paid for it, but I would end up using it for years to paint everything imaginable and when the compressor gave up the ghost, I got a cast off refrigeration compressor, mounted it on a tank and went back to my passion for painting.

Actually, the thing worked pretty well and I used it extensively in Kentucky when we tore down a house that fire had damaged and used the material to rebuild ours. The house had a furnace, a stoker and a ton of other stuff that had been only smoked damaged. I salvaged it all and painted it all and make it look like new. I even ended up painting the old International truck I had bought for $75 and sold it for $125.

When I got to York, the car I was driving was a Rambler that had rambled up creek beds and hollows and had about eighty thousand very hard miles on it. I decided I wanted it two-tone and ended up painting it in Dad's garage. He was getting tired of me having it in there so I tried to hurry it up a bit. When I backed my shinny white and green car out of the very narrow garage, my front tire caught the corner of the chrome bumper that I had removed and laid beside the car. When it did, the bumper flew up in the air and came through my windshield. Well, not everything works out right on these jobs. I drove that car for some time after that (with a new windshield) and finally gave it to Larry Hodgson who was on my staff and who drove it for several more years.

We were given a small Ford for the ministry sometime early on and I decided to paint it. It was a blue metallic and I wanted to stay with the same color, but every time I did a job I learned something. Metallics are hard to handle and require a continual mixing motion to keep the material uniform. It turned out alright, but I wasn't ready to enter it in any restoration contests.

That was my last car job for a couple of years. Next it was a school bus. I painted that the traditional bright yellow, and since I didn't have a garage it would fit in, I painted it outside on a rather windy day. The bus looked good, but I didn't. You couldn't be quite sure which yellow object was the bus.

I remember that job especially because that is the evening Rachel decided to get her daddy's attention. She was about six years old and had been riding her bike with helper wheels on it when she turned into the driveway where I (still covered with my yellow paint), was standing. As she stopped, the helper wheel failed and the bike began to tip over. I could have caught her but I never realized she would not simply stretch out her leg and stop her fall. Instead she fell right at my feet and the moment she did it was all too evident she had broken her arm. I was devastated.

Ruby and I put her in the car and headed for the hospital (yellow paint and all). The examining physician had all the bedside manners of a drill sergeant. He looked at the break and mumbled something about, "It's right at the growth center, this will never grow again." The mental picture I got was of a grown woman with the arm of a six year old.

I kept my composure while I was with Rachel, but when I got out in the car, I prayed the loudest and most fervent prayer I ever prayed for a miracle for my little girl. Actually, the miracle was already done. What the doctor meant was, that the arm would be retarded at one small point. If it ever was, it certainly is not evident now, but there I was in all my glorious yellow, crying out to God. I wonder if He smiled.

Shortly after we got the former Teamsters Union office building, I learned about a new version of spay equipment. The main office complex had acoustical plaster which is a soft, sound absorbing type of plaster. It's wonderful for what it was developed for, but you can press your finger into it without even trying and painting it with a brush or a roller would be a disaster.

I asked help from Ray and Bob Berkheimer and they had the solution. They had purchased one of the first Graco Airless Paint machines and they offered to do the job for me. Not only did it turn out great, but I never saw paint go on so fast in my life. It absolutely ruined me for any other kind of painting.

Once we were up at the camp I saw a new opportunity for my passion. We had been given several old Ford tractors. They ran well but looked old and rusty. By this time the Berkheimer brothers had gone from general painting to selling automotive paint. They opened a company called BAPS (Berkheimer Automotive Paint Store). I went to them for my supplies.

What I learned was that every now and then they would do a custom mix for a body shop and then the job would fall through. Custom mixes are, well, custom – so the chances of getting that particular paint ordered again are almost nill. As a result, BAPS had a growing stack of high quality paints setting in their warehouse and they offered them to the camp. Since we were a non-profit corporation they could donate the paint to us and at least realize a tax write off.

Each time I would get a load of paint (which was about one or two times a year), I would bring home between $500 to $1,000 worth of auto paint. Before long I had shelves of different color paint. When I needed a color, all I had to do was find a near mix and then play with adding whatever was needed to reach the desired shade. I think when God gives you an interest and a passion for something, He also gives you a certain amount of natural ability. I seemed always to have just the right colors on the shelf to allow me to get a mix close enough to match almost anything. And that is how I transformed two old rusty tractors into the identifiable blue and white of the contemporary Fords.

Along with painting there is, of course, the preparation and that meant learning to handle straitening bends and filling dings with Bondo. It meant learning to use fiberglass and filler and all the tricks of the trade. When I prepared a paint mix, it would be a measured portion of paint, then a reducer, then a hardener, and depending on the job possibly a small amount of "fish-eye eliminator." Auto painters also have to be chemists.

I enjoyed not only the work, but the results. I remember a young lady who came to camp to work in the kitchen one summer. She was driving a rather well worn sport car that had once been somebody's pride and joy. One of the staff took a special interest in her and offered to do the prep work on the car if I would paint it. I was happy to oblige.

By this time I had accumulated so many gallon cans of paint that I could find almost any color and the only thing I had to buy was the chemicals to activate it. Our kitchen girl drove home with a shinny silver sports car that looked great. Too bad it didn't run as good as it looked.

During the years I painted heavy equipment such as our front-end loader, and a full sized road scrapper we used to keep the four miles of roads we had on the camp property. But it wasn't just equipment I got to paint.

Once the new Headquarters Building was completed it was obvious we were going to need a lot of office furniture. And the second thing that was obvious was we didn't have the money to buy it. I learned that my friend Tom Maharis over in New York had gotten a load of free office furniture out of City Bank. They upgrade their banks on a regular basis and then donate the used furniture to non-profits for a write-off. I applied.

Their response was, that while we were a worthy organization, we were more than fifty miles from New York City and they did not make donations outside that fifty mile radius. I tried again.

This time I pointed out to them that while we were geographically separated from the city, we were regularly taking scores of inner-city teens from NYC free of charge and giving them a week at camp. In fact, I had just taken about thirty teens from a group Tom had sent me several weeks before. I asked City Bank to reconsider.

They did and let me know we could pickup one load. I took our seventeen foot Chevy box truck down into the city and appeared bright and early at the City Bank warehouse. I quickly learned they had four floors of furniture and we could pick out almost anything we wanted.

As we interacted with the warehouse people they became more and more friendly and began encouraging us to take more. When the truck was filled to capacity they asked when we were going to get our next load. I questioned whether we could get a second load and they assured me they liked us and we could get as many loads as we could use. Before it was all over we hauled four truck loads of furniture to the camp.

The greater part of the office furniture we got was steel and was all in relatively good condition, but I wanted it to look brand new to go into our new offices. We were going to place at least a desk and a credenza, plus some files in each office and I wanted everything to match.

So I had the men off-load everything to the rear of the new building and set up a paint shop there. I painted every desk and every credenza and file cabinet and every table or stand or anything that went in any office. It all matched in each office and it all looked great. I even refinished some of the wooden desks and tables and a very large credenza that ended up in my office.

While that paint shop was still in place we acquired about thirty metal tri-bunks. These were units that slept kids three high and could be used to increase our capacity during large events like the ACE conventions which we hosted every spring. I had every piece of metal sanded, primed and painted before they were placed in the cabins. I tried to see that even if something was old, it never looked old.

Then there was that ten foot diameter globe of the world we placed in the center of the fountain we called, *The Fountain of the Fields* (representing the mission fields of the world). We had formed the globe from rebar and then Nevin Moyer had welded the continents in place using sheet steel. It looked great but was subject to rust so I had it transported out to the maintenance barn where we suspended it from the roof trusses by chains. There I climbed in and out of the thing, making sure that I had covered every inch with epoxy primer. Then I finished it with a gold/bronze metallic. It looked great and it never developed any visible rust so long as it was in the fountain.

When Beth needed a car to go to college I went down to Allentown to visit my old friend Andy Merrick. Andy took in donated cars and usually let us buy them at a very reasonable price or gave them to us. I went looking for the ideal car for Beth.

I had always had an aversion to foreign cars so when Andy tried to point me to a Subaru they had just taken in, I said, "Thanks, but I think I'll pass." After all, it was covered with moss (it must have been parked for some time under a tree), and the left front quarter-panel was damaged as was the grill.

A short time later however, I found I had to move the Subaru to get to another car I was looking at and I climbed in. I was immediately surprised and impressed at the like-new condition of the interior. When I started it, it ran rough but the mileage was unusually low on the speedometer and I figured it probably just needed a tune up – which turned out to be a correct analysis.

I came back to Andy a second time. "What did you want for that Subaru?" I asked. "Actually, it just arrived and I haven't even looked at it." He replied. "If you think you want it, you can have it," he continued. "And by the way, there is another one up in the junk yard with a good quarter-panel if you don't mind pulling it." I certainly didn't and I made arrangements to get both cars up where I could work on them. The tune-up, using one of Andy's mechanics, cost me fifty bucks, so I was pretty excited when I got everything together.

I didn't let Beth know anything about what I was doing and found a garage in Thompson, about nine miles away, where I could do the work. I replaced the quarter-panel and grill and prepped the car for paint. It was one of the nicest jobs I ever got and it looked and ran great.

It was almost Christmas so I waited until Christmas Eve. Then as we exchanged gifts in the living room I handed Beth a package.

Inside she found a set of car keys. I suggested she look in the carport. There sat her Subaru in all its glory, with a large red ribbon and bow tied around it.

There is a little sequel to that story. A year later Beth came home from college for Thanksgiving on a very icy day. She had made it all the way home but as she tried to turn into the driveway the car went into a skid and hit one of the stone pillars center on. We were all rather devastated and when I looked under the hood, it was evident that the motor itself had been displaced. The car was simply totaled. We pulled it to the grassy area across from the house and left it till I could tow it to the dump.

The morning I decided to move it was sunny but very cold. The ground was frozen and I crawled under the little car to tie a tow chain to it. As I laid there looking up at the damage, I thought, "If I could just pull that straight then . . ." and that was the beginning of over one hundred hours of restoration. On Christmas Eve Beth got the same set of keys as a year before and found the same car wrapped with the same red ribbon and I believe she was happier than even the first time she got it. I love to make things new.

I guess the classic tale was the restoration of a grand piano which someone had donated to the York Rescue Mission. My former business manager, Bob Bracilano was then in charge of the Mission store and gave the camp most anything we wanted. I wanted the piano. It had been in a bar room and it really looked and sounded pretty bad. However, while I knew I couldn't restore the mechanism, I wanted to see what I could do with the cabinet.

There were structural challenges like split legs and cigarette burns on the surface, but I believed I could work through them to what I could see in my mind's eye. I had always wanted a white grand piano and knew I would probably never have one, so here was my chance. After all, if I failed no one would be the poorer. Some of the staff already wanted to just junk it. I had it moved to my carport and started work on it there.

I worked through the structural problems with epoxy and lots of sanding. The harp had once been gold but was badly faded. I opted to carefully mask everything so that I would not get any paint on the strings and yet restore that golden look to the harp. I used a small detail gun to accomplish the task.

White is seldom ever really white (unless you are painting a refrigerator), so I choose a soft off-white and used a flattening agent so that the finish would appear satin rather than a high gloss. I removed all of the brass hinges and fittings and polished them back to high gloss. I used a heavy epoxy primer over all of the wood to give me the hard surface I needed to get a professional finish. Every piece of the instrument was done separately and then I began to reassemble it.

Just as I began to get it together again, a man I had never seen before stopped outside my car port and walked into where I was working. I learned that he traveled to missions and volunteered his services. When I asked what he did, he told me that he repaired pianos – I could hardly believe my ears. When he saw what I had done with the case of the piano, he was inspired to do whatever it would take to bring the instrument back to full service again. He worked tirelessly on it for several weeks replacing what ever needed replacing and fixing whatever needed fixing.

Sometimes in telling a story like this, it becomes hard for some to believe, but while I can't remember that dear man's name, that is exactly how he appeared. Someone had told him about the camp. He was in the area and had actually stopped at some other camps to see if they needed help before coming to us. But I cannot escape the fact that he came just when he did. I believe God wanted to bless me by bringing someone who could make an old piano sing again.

In the end it was a remarkable restoration. It was a beautiful instrument and it sounded great once again. I had even mounted a mirror behind the keyboard. When the lid was opened the golden inner case reflected against the white and it truly looked like a million dollars. The feature strips around the case were all trimmed with gold.

Just about that time a concert pianist was taking part in the ACE competition and offered to do a concert on the piano one evening. Sitting on a raised platform in the new dining hall he made it sound as good as it looked. The next day, just before leaving he brought a porcelain image of a flying eagle into my office. He told me anyone who loved an old instrument enough to do what I had done with that piano deserved it. It is one of my favorite things – I still cherish it to this day, especially because I remember why it was given.

Painting has given me a lot of pleasure because it has allowed me to restore old things that would have been cast away and make them beautiful again. That's what I did for a J-5 jeep that had been given us. I don't know what it had been through, but the fenders were both out of shape, and the frame needed welding. The top was no good, but the motor ran well. It had been donated with the idea of using it in the woods to pull trees we had cut. But then we had tractors that could do that.

I looked it over and asked our maintenance crew to move it to my carport when they were done welding. They did and a month or so later I had transformed it into a later model by not only painting it a metallic bronze, and clear coating it, but putting Wrangler decals on both sides of the hood. Frankly it looked and drove like a new machine.

I later bought a new top and doors for it and drove it constantly for years even after I left the camp. I finally sold it when we decided to come to Florida much to the displeasure of a number of my grandchildren that loved to pile into it and ride with the top and doors off. I still had great pictures of the machine and wonderful memories of many a pleasant ride that Ruby and I enjoyed in our jeep.

I still keep painting when I have the opportunity. Ruby and I painted the Florida property with my Graco Airless and I painted an International dump truck we sent to Ethiopia for SLM.

When a straight-wind storm collapsed Dee Dee's Volvo roof, I got Haile to straighten it and I bondoed it and painted it, restoring it back to original. As I write this, I have just finished using the airless to put over twenty gallons of paint on the second floor of the headquarters Building here at Source of Light in Madison to help move the job along.

As Dad grew older, and I got a little more proficient, he no longer looked down on my passion for a spray gun. Like any boy, I'm glad when I can please my dad and I was finally able to do that. He looked with pride on some of the things I restored. But I believe I have pleased the Lord as well, and I have had a lot of pleasure doing it.

OUR HOME AT PANORAMA HILLS

FOUNTAIN OF THE FIELDS ~ A PLACE FOR DEDICATION

GATEA BOARD OF DIRECTORS 1977

CN SUMMER STAFF 1975

CN PERMANENT STAFF 1990

CN SUMMER STAFF 1990

The Director with Penny the Pony

The Director with a young colt

4th of July at Camp of the Nations

Dr. Shade, Dr. Dale Linebaugh. Dr. Glenn Dix

Beth on Red Bar Lace

Horse Barn at CN ~ Built by Elvin Martin & Volunteers

NEW INTERNATIONAL HEADQUARTERS ~ BUILDING FROM BALTIMORE

Charles Weaver Memorial Dining Room

Dedicating Charles Weaver Memorial Dining Room

ENTRANCE MURAL AT CN

Atlanta Children

CN ENCOUNTER LIFE SINGERS 1990

Dr. Alfred B. Smith

Dr. Bill Rice III

Dedication of Chet Bitterman Memorial Field
The Director with Chet Bitterman's father
and representatives from Wycliffe / JAARs / Columbia, S.A.

CHIEF EAGLE FEATHER & ANNA

Mother & Dad Shade
Always Faithful Helpers

Dr. Andrew Telford

Dr. Dave Virkler

Collapse of the GCA

THOMPSON HOUSE

THE NEW ALL-STEEL GREAT COMMISSION AUDITORIUM 1994

MINISTRY IN INDIA

BHARAT BIBLE COLLEGE STUDENTS & FACULTY
2001

Ruby with Class

Dr. Bill with Class

KOTTAYAM CONFERENCE / 5,000 ATTENDED

RAJAHMUNDRY INDIA

INDIAN BANJARA CHILDREN

RAJNOOR BIBLE INSTITUTE

COMING TO CHRIST

STUDENTS SAVED DURING MEETINGS IN PEDDAPALLI

WITH RAMESH RICHARDS AND CSI PRIEST

CHAPTER THIRTY THREE

We Get Away

In 1995 at 61, I stepped down from Administration. The Organization had a new Director and I thought that perhaps just getting away from the Camp and letting the new Director operate without having me in the mix might help resolve some of the problems we were sensing. Ruby and I had only once taken an extended vacation during our camping years. That was when Dan and Rachel finished language school and Beth had finished her junior year in high school. I had promised Beth that someday we would do something really special.

Before the days of having the Camp, our family had gotten away one to two weeks each summer (usually in August). We had some great adventures in places like Raystown River, where we stayed in Vince Porte's cottage. Then there was Michigan's Upper Peninsula, where we stayed in the Hurlbert cottage on Spirit Lake and enjoyed times at camp Hiawatha. Those were wonderful times together.

Of course the kids remember not just the fun times, but the fact that I would have them write down their goals for the coming school year during our evenings together. Then I would ask them on a second night to define how they intended to meet those goals. Finally, I would talk to each of them separately and ask what changes they were going to make in their lives in order to attain the goals they had set. These were rather intense and thoughtful times, but they set the course for their coming school year.

However, Beth had missed all of that. She had been born the very year we took the camp so we never had gone away with her while she was growing up. During her junior year at Baptist High School, I went to Romania to minister. It was just after the revolution and things were in turmoil.

During several days when I wasn't preaching (I had gone with Don Kyer and wasn't assigned every day as I was on later trips), I decided I wanted to try to see Dan and Rachel in Vienna, Austria. I had not seen them in some years and it was only about a day and a half journey from Arad to Vienna. I started by trying to get the necessary information to cross the border into Hungary.

Everyone thought I would need a visa to enter either Hungary or Austria and I could not get one. The Romanian brothers were so concerned that I get to see my daughter that they drove me from border crossing to border crossing, but to no avail. Finally, more to relieve them than anything else, I announced that if no way was found by lunch time on that day I would accept it from God that I was not to go. I was confident that I had ended the matter.

However, as we sat eating our lunch the phone rang. Pastor Zacharia answered and immediately began to talk in an excited tone of voice. As soon as he got off the phone he informed me that some American Missionaries, who used to smuggle Bibles into Romania in their small Renault Motorhome, were stopping by on their way to Baden. Baden, it seemed, was only forty five minutes south of Vienna. He had asked them if they could take me with them and they said they could. It turned out they knew that as Americans we didn't need visas to enter either Hungary or Austria.

Now what made this trip so interesting was that we had no way of contacting Dan or Rachel to find out if they were even home and to let them know that I was coming. I just decided to go by faith and let God do the rest.

I arrived in Baden where my friends gave me several schillings so I could make a telephone call. Thankfully, I heard Dan's voice answer the phone. He told me to just get on a trolley and get off at the Vienna Opera House. He would meet me there.

I boarded the trolley and noticed at once that there were no visible conductors and no place to drop money for the fare. I later learned that riding the trolley in Austria is a prepaid affair. I don't read German very well, but I was intelligent enough to discern that the sign I saw on the train was saying that if you got caught riding without paying your fare, you would be fined 250 schillings.

I would have asked someone for advice, but quickly learned that while many Romanians had learned to speak English, none of the Austrians I met had, or if they did, they were not about to communicate that to me. As I rode I wondered how I would find the Opera House. I tried again and again asking one or another.

Finally, a man listened to me and after several tries at saying Opera House (with my distinctively American accent), he suddenly understood and said, Oh, Ya! Oopra, Oopra, Ya! Ya! He graciously directed me to get off at the appropriate place. However, as I looked up and down the trolley island I saw no Dan in sight or anyone else I recognized.

I thought perhaps I was at the wrong corner so I decided to cross the street. Suddenly I realized no one was crossing the street. Then I saw some steps leading downward and concluded that they must lead to a concourse. I made my way through the concourse to the next corner – still no Dan.

Back I went into the concourse to the next corner. Again the same result. By the time I got to the third corner I was thoroughly frustrated with the fact that I could not find anyone who spoke English enough to even ask for help.

Suddenly I saw an airline office. Concluding that surely they had to be bi-lingual to do their work I walked into the long room with many desks on both sides and standing in the middle of the aisle I cried in my best outdoor preaching voice, "Does anyone in here speak English?" They all began to laugh and assured me they could help. They sent me back to where I had begun saying that was certainly where I would meet my party.

Sure enough when I got back, Dan and Charissa were waiting. It seems they had gotten cold and had gone for a hot chocolate, which was the very time I arrived. I hadn't known how much I missed my granddaughter, but immediately broke into tears as I hugged her. I enjoyed an evening and another day with the Zuchs in Vienna and then Dan put me on the Oriental Express to return to Arad.

One thing about that ride – we were in a typical European compartment set up for six people three and three, facing each other. It was full and Dan had remarked, "Well, a lot of people go to Budapest, but most of them will debark there and after that stop the compartment will probably be empty." I later told him he was "half right."

Indeed, all of my compartment companions got off at Budapest, but what Dan had not counted on was that this was after the Revolution and Romanians were able to leave Romania for the first time. Romanians flooded the entire car, the hallway outside the compartments and our compartment. I learned quickly that Romanians apparently have no idea how many people are supposed to be in a single compartment. I think we had eight or nine in ours.

After some time I pulled out of my bag some Romanian language gospel tracts and offered them to those in our compartment. They all enthusiastically received them and when those standing in the aisle outside our compartment saw through the window what was happening, they motioned that they too wanted a tract. In less than a couple of minutes I had given away over eighty gospel tracts to some very spiritually hungry people.

The other thing I remember about that journey was that a very large woman had taken her seat immediately across from me. She could sit on only the front edge of her seat because someone else was sitting in the back portion. I had made the mistake of crossing my legs and she straddled my legs with hers. I simply could not find the room to get them uncrossed.

When we got to the border, the police checked all of our passports and then let the train set there on the border for five hours. All that time my legs were crossed and when we finally got to Arad, I had developed a blood clot and had to go on an aspirin regime and keep my leg elevated for a day or two.

Just before I left Vienna however, I had told Rachel that on my way from Baden I had seen multiple advertisements for the show, *Phantom of the Opera*. I asked how long it would continue to play. Rachel said it would still be playing during the summer when they would be finished with language school.

I knew our Beth had become a fan of the music score by Weber and Rice. Ruby and I had traveled to Florida with Beth that fall and had to listen to Phantom music the entire way. I wanted Beth to see Europe, and I wanted her to see the opera so I planned to bring Ruby and Beth to Austria the next summer.

That summer, in August, Dan and Rachel had finished their language training and had a three week break before beginning actual assignment. Ruby, Beth and I flew to Austria to spend the time with them and their two children, Charissa and Richard (Michael had not been born yet). We had a wonderful time traveling all over Germany and Austria and perhaps the highlight (or at least one of the highlights) was going to actually see the opera. Of course it was in German and Rachel had to translate for us, but it was a wonderful experience and one I hoped none of the family would ever forget.

I also took the opportunity of taking Beth and Ruby down to meet my friends in Romania. I wanted Beth to see something of a country from behind the iron curtain and to catch the enthusiasm of the youth, who for the first time since the revolution, were able to travel freely and exercise their faith by singing and testifying for Christ.

We had planned to drive to the border and be picked up by my dear friend and brother, John Pantea, whom I had gotten to know and love from my previous journeys. However, while we were in Budapest we learned that there was an eleven hour wait at the border and I decided to take a train instead. As we boarded the train I told Dan, "You have to get a phone call through to John and Maria. They will be coming to the border to get me and I will be arriving by train. You have to let them know."

Little did I realize what I was asking. There had been flooding in Romania and phone service was completely out. Dan tried again and again from the rail station in Budapest, but with no result. Finally a man near by, hearing what he was trying to do said, "It is no use to even try – the phones have been down in Romania for weeks." Thankfully, Dan did not take his advice. Praying earnestly, he told God he had to get through and tried one more time.

We of course knew nothing of this. We simply enjoyed the trip across Hungary in our ignorance and pulled into the station at Arad in record time. I was concerned when I saw hundreds of people on the station platform. How would I ever find John? The train came to a stop and I looked out the window at the people immediately in front of me and found myself staring into John's smiling face. The train had stopped so that we were just where he was standing.

We out-loaded our luggage through the window and debarked from the train. Lovenia, John's teenage daughter, was there and immediately took Beth with her. The two girls disappeared in the crowd while John loaded us and our luggage into his Dacia, and we made our way to their home.

When I entered the house Maria's first words to me were, "God must love you very much." I assured her He did, but asked why she thought so. Maria said, "I work for the phone company. There has been no phone service in Romania for over two weeks. There is no phone service now. Yet several hours ago our phone rang and that man (meaning Dan), told us you were coming on the train. Then the phones quit again." It is difficult to deny God's hand at times like this. Indeed, He loves us very much.

Lovenia and Beth had made it back to the house before we did and they were completely involved with playing the small organ in the hallway. Lovenia was an organist and was delighted to learn that Beth played too. Before long a group of young people had gathered and then asked if they could take Beth with them to meet others from the church. I agreed, and Beth spent most of the next days traveling with this group of Christian youth who seemed to radiate their love for God. We enjoyed a tremendous time during those days, even getting to see a Romanian wedding.

Returning from our adventure, we had stayed around the camp that final winter, while Beth finished her last year in Baptist High. The next summer, Ruby and I felt that we needed to be away from the camp. I began looking for a van that we could use as a camper, one we could sleep in, so we could travel more economically. The Lord provided a Volkswagen van with a full bed and a table already installed.

I popped out the two rear facing seats and built in a closet that had a portable chemical potty hidden under it and a shelf for a small TV over top. Then I was given an A/C D/C refrigerator which I built a cabinet for and built in a stove top above it. We had everything we needed and more.

We made our first trip down the Skyline Drive through Virginia and North Carolina. We camped along the way and enjoyed each other and the freedom we had never had. We even spent several days in Cherokee North Carolina and tried to understand something of Ruby's Cherokee heritage.

When we returned, we did not want to go back to the camp so Tom Weber invited us to stay in his dad's place for the summer. His dad was in the hospital (from which he never came out), and we again enjoyed our new environment.

During that time we decided to take two of our grandsons on a camping trip with us. We chose to take David and Jonathan, Steve's sons. We wanted to spend time with all our grandchildren, but felt like these two needed the most attention just then.

We spent the first day or two at the home Tom had provided for us. It was a farm and away from other houses and I took the boys out to shoot a single shot 22 caliber rifle I had. It was already an antique, but deadly accurate, and each boy took a turn shooting until David suddenly said, "Grandpa, I can't get it open to load." I took the gun in my hands and examined it. A small lever that pulled the breach open had come unscrewed and was lost. We looked and looked for it, but it was no bigger around than a straw, and no longer than a half inch, besides, it was black. Finding it in the grass was not likely and without it the rifle was useless, so we had to cut short our shoot. David was so disappointed that he nearly threw a fit, throwing water all over the bathroom, which his grandmother commanded him to clean up. He complied, but learned a lesson – you don't throw fits with Grandma.

Next we went to Gettysburg to visit the battlefield. I had been there so many times I had memorized the movements of the armies so I could pretty well lead the boys around the battlefield in the order in which it all happened. When we came to the Pennsylvania monument they found a name inscribed, "William K. Shade." Recognizing both my name and my initial, David asked, "Grandpa is this you?" I assured him it was not.

At home that evening we watched the film Gettysburg, which is an excellent documentary of the four day battle. I had insisted we view only the first two-hour segment that night and see the rest later, but the boys begged me to continue so I placed the second film in and we watched it. That is, three of us watched it – David went to sleep about a third of the way in.

When I asked him the next morning what he thought of the second part of the film, he said that it was sort of boring after the first half. The entire major battle of the engagement was filmed on the second film – Pickett's famous charge across the meadow after a long bombardment. David remembered nothing – he had slept through bombardment and all.

Then we packed up and headed for Reidsville on the Chesapeake Bay. We camped at a KOA right on the water and spent the next day crabbing – something neither I nor the boys had ever done. We caught so many crabs just fishing from the dock that I could hardly get one off the line before they had another. In all we caught something just short of twenty and decided to choose only the three biggest ones to cook. The rest we returned to the water.

The next morning we left about five thirty in the morning and drove to the dock in Reidsville. The fishing boat was just docking with the night's catch. We not only enjoyed talking to the fishermen and seeing the catch, but bought a couple fish right off the boat and brought them back to cook over a fire of coals. The entire experience was delightful.

One of the highlights of that trip was when we took the cruise out to *Smith's Island*. Neither boy had ever been on a ship before, and the trip itself was exciting. The sun blazed down on a crystal clear surface as the boat plowed smoothly through the water. If you were going to take a maiden cruise, this certainly was as good as it gets. Once we arrived we were lead through a maze of little shops displaying models of fishing boats and crab traps. We bought lunch at the local restaurant and had, what else, soft-shelled crabs.

Then we learned how the Island had been known originally as *Rogues Island* and was occupied by pirates and murderers until a Methodist preacher named Smith evangelized the Island and nearly the entire population was converted. So complete was the transformation, that it became, instead of an Island of rogues, a Bible conference, where hundreds resorted each summer to hear the teaching of the Word of God. What a surprise! We had chosen to take the trip to give the boys something special to remember and God used it to preach to us again the power of the gospel of Jesus Christ.

Some of our evenings were special too. One evening we began to talk about answers to prayer. David wanted to know if God would give us anything we asked for. Ruby explained that God gives us what we need, not what we just want. Then Ruby asked the boys if God had ever answered their prayers.

Jonathan immediately said God had certainly answered his prayer when his mother had run off with a Mormon and taken the boys with her to Utah. Jonathan said he had prayed every night that God would get him back home and at last his mother had enough and fled with the boys. The car gave trouble, but Jonathan told how God had gotten them back home at last. We had a time of rejoicing together and praising God for all He had done for each of us.

We returned to Tom's place after a week. Since we had talked about answers to prayer, I decided to pray. I asked God to let me find that tiny piece to the rifle we had lost a week before. I walked out to where we had been shooting, looked down at the ground and there it lay. I have to admit I was surprised to find it so quickly.

When I showed it to the boys and declared that God had let me find it in answer to prayer, David immediately asked, "Grandpa, was that something you really needed or something you just wanted?" Well, leave it to boys to put you on the spot. However we were again reminded of the promise, *"Delight thyself also in the LORD and He will give you the desires of your heart"* (Psalm 37:4).

CHAPTER THIRTY FOUR

A Gathering Storm

As the seventies waned and the eighties loomed, I found our ministry had reached a critical stage. We were operating three resident treatment centers, (called Teen Encounter Centers), we still had the Saturday night youth rallies, the high school clubs, the daily radio broadcast, a weekly television program and now the Camp of the Nations. In addition we were working with about sixteen churches using the WWBI program and operating Bible Institutes in their respective churches. We had opened a bookstore in the front of our King Street Center and another in Red Lion in a rented store front. We were seemingly prospering everywhere, but I was feeling overwhelmed and spiritually drained.

Then, very suddenly, our television ministry collapsed with the death of Bill Menge. I had met Bill at NRB and he claimed that it was through my broadcast and several others, that he had come to trust Christ. Bill was a millionaire and had provided Jerry Fawell with his first airplane. He wanted to do something for me and so promised to underwrite the cost of my television ministry.

Bill had done that for several years, but he always was about a year late paying the bill. That disturbed me, but the station manager would say, "Don't worry about it. Bill's good for it—he's just always behind. He'll take care of it." And I'm sure he would have, but Bill went out one morning to mow the high grass around his pond and the tractor flipped and Bill Menge was suddenly and unexpectedly in glory. Furthermore, there was nothing in the estate that promised to cover my bill – so I was suddenly a year in debt for television time and I found myself having to sell off various things in order to try to pay that debt.

Then came a crisis in radio. I had two rather large companies that sponsored my program on the two most expensive and most productive stations we were on. At that time I had a total of 23 stations scattered up and down the eastern seaboard and across the Caribbean, with one way out in California. The income from the two strongest stations helped carry the cost of the others that were less responsive.

Then in a single year both of those companies were sold and I lost the underwriting for both of those stations. Without that I had to use the funds that came in from those stations to pay the bill for that particular station itself and was left with nothing to help carry those other, less responsive stations. One by one I tried to solve the problem by cutting stations.

Then the WWBI project began to falter. We had about sixteen Institutes started in churches, but the students were matriculating more slowly than we had anticipated and that meant we were not selling materials quickly enough to keep up with production costs. I still believed very much in the validity of the program.

When Dad offered to give me the remaining ground in his development if I could sell it, I accepted it and by God's grace sold it for five times what he had been previously offered. But even that could not sustain the program forever.

One of the last things I did before I left York was to try to raise money for WWBI and when that fell short of what was needed I tried to borrow money, but I was not successful, and so our whole WWBI operation gradually reduced. I had to lay off staff and finally suspend production.

Then the year after we purchased the camp one whole section of the city of York in which we were working went down in urban renewal. When it was rebuilt, the entire complex of the neighborhood had changed and the work we were doing that had been successful before was not working with the new changes.

We began with the sale of the last Center we had opened, the one at King Street. We had been operating a Christian bookstore on the first floor and I was having difficulty staffing it. Then there came the sale of Franklin Street property. It seemed that after twelve years that area no longer was responding to the type of ministry that we had there.

Glenn Keenan was our Duke Street coordinator and he wanted to organize that center into a local church. Glenn felt that he could have a greater impact on the immediate community that way. After some time we agreed and the Saturday night rally was discontinued and we set Duke Street Center free, donating the entire complex to the new church.

I was still living in York but had to make one to three trips a week up to Camp of the Nations. That was a one hundred and eighty mile trip that took at least three and a half hours to make. It became evident that we needed to be at the camp more and more so we made the decision to move the remainder of the operation up to that location.

The plan was to set up our print shop in a block milk house, but it never happened. One of the presses was damaged in the move and after putting them in storage in an unheated milk house over the winter, it became obvious that we could not, under our existing circumstances, restart that part of the ministry again.

With the sale of the York office we lost the sound-proof air conditioned radio studio we were used to for so many years and I found myself trying to produce a broadcast out of a farmhouse at the camp. In six months it was obvious that after twenty two years of continuous broadcasting we could no longer continue, and I left the radio ministry finding it impossible to produce quality broadcasts under the circumstances and with the multitude of other demands upon me.

As each part of the work fell away, I would be haunted by remembering a dream that I had some years before. I think it was in the early 70's, possibly '71 or '72.

Jack Wyrtzen came to Lancaster for a rally and I took two busloads of inner city teens over to the meeting. Several of our kids went forward that night along with many others, and I went into the inquiry room and counseled with several kids who were there. I prayed with them to receive Christ and counseled with them, then I went back out into the auditorium and tried to gather up the gang, to get everyone together to start home. As I did, Jack was on the platform talking to several people, and he spotted me and called to me, and I came over to the edge of the stage where he was.

Jack said, "Bill, you know about the tragic death of Rock Royer?" Rock was a great coach from Lynchburg, VA. He was a solid Christian, a great speaker, and he had been killed just about a month before in an airplane crash. I said, "Yes, I know, Jack," and he said, "Bill, Rock was scheduled to be our speaker at snow camp, and I need to find a replacement. I want you to replace him."

Well, I think I said something to Jack like, "Jack, I can NEVER replace Rock Royer, but I can give what God has given me and if you want me to do that, I will come." And so the time came that January that I went to Word of Life to preach at the Snow-Camp.

I remember the first night, Harry Bollback was speaking. Harry spoke on the Four Soils, and brought a great message. I was to begin speaking the next day. Jack had me placed down in one of the speakers' cabins right along the lake at the Bible Institute complex. It was a very lovely little cabin, that had one of these self-standing fireplaces, and there was a nice warm fire in it – it was really very beautiful and very cozy.

I was very, very tired – very tired emotionally, but keyed up, and just physically tired when I went to bed that night. I shall never forget what followed. In the middle of the night I had the most disturbing dream I had ever had. I have hesitated to speak of it and the exact details are a bit vague, except that I remember walking down a rather wide street brilliantly lit on every side. There were on every hand evidences of the work I had been involved with – there were the Bible clubs and the rallies and the Teen Centers and radio and television and all of the things that had been built through the ministry.

Then suddenly it seemed as though I saw some of these buildings (and they stood as buildings in my mind), but I saw some of them begin to crumble. And one after another, they crumbled and disappeared, and as I kept going, the road became narrower and darker, down to a narrow alley – a very, very dark narrow alley. Suddenly, as the last thing crumbled, a very dark figure whom I recognized to be Satan himself stepped out of the darkness and took hold on me and tried to pull me back into that dark alley.

I cried out, and as I did I woke up, and suddenly I was sitting up in bed with a cold sweat streaming down my face, shouting out loud, "I claim the blood of Jesus Christ for my protection." Well, it was one of those experiences that was traumatic enough it is impossible to forget. I didn't understand it; I put it aside, and eventually went back to sleep. I was thankful I didn't have any more experiences like that.

God gave us a good time there at snow camp and obviously must have used the ministry because Jack invited me back for the next three years to summer camp, and it was during those wonderful years that I had an opportunity to minister at the Island, as well as at the Inn.

We founded Camp of the Nations in 1975, and that was the last year that I ministered at Word of Life. Jack had invited me to come again that year, but I told him I felt that I didn't dare be away from Camp of the Nations that first year, and once you turn Jack down, he goes in some other direction, and sets up his pattern, so I was never back to Word of Life as a speaker again.

Somewhere in the deep recesses of my mind I could not forget that dream. There seemed to me to be an ominous warning that I would lose the ministries that I had and that thought sometimes haunted me. So as the ministries slowly melted away, I felt like it was a fulfillment of something I had seen years before it happened.

The final years with GATEA were the most difficult years of all. In addition to the disappointments we faced through the loss of various parts of the ministry, there were internal pressures as well. I had inherited a defunct rescue mission in Wilkesboro through the death of one of my Board members who directed it. He had asked me to step in and help and I worked them through the transition after his death.

When the Board of the Mission asked me to be their director, I told them I could not direct two organizations at the same time. I suggested they either find someone else to direct the work, or merge with Grace and Truth and I would accept the challenge. When they unanimously agreed to the merger I proposed that they consider converting the entire ministry complex to a home for unwed mothers. The Board listened and agreed asking me to do that.

The Rescue Mission facility was a formerly beautiful hospital complex that was so badly deteriorated that the roof was leaking, the stucco was cracking, the building desperately needed repaired and painted, and the entire plumbing and electrical systems were faulty and needed replaced.

It looked as if I had really walked into an impossible venture this time. The former director had gotten old and had shut down their outlet store where they sold things that were donated to the mission. The problem was, that although they no longer had an outlet for donated things, they continued to take them in, and the entire building, except for a couple of rooms where the men stayed, was literally full to the ceiling with donated stuff.

One day I was walking in the basement along a narrow path between heaps of boxes and paraphernalia stacked almost to the ceiling. I dropped my keys and as I bent over to pick them up I realized that I was standing next to a counter. The counter had three stainless steel rods running parallel along its edge – obviously a serving bar but piled so high with things that I had never before realized it was there.

"This is a serving counter," I reasoned, "and if so, then I must be standing in a kitchen." When I finally was able to dig through the piles of rubble, I discovered I was correct. There was a full kitchen with stoves, refrigerators and a serving counter, all hidden under the endless heaps of clutter.

Our first job was to rid ourselves of what we could. We started with an extreme yard sale and sold everything we could, then we began giving things away. When I could no longer give it away we moved it in one of our camp dump trucks and hauled it to a dump.

In the course of doing this, every day became an adventure. One day, after removing clothing of various sorts that almost filled a room, I found three color TV sets, buried under the clothing. Each set was brand new and still in its cartoon. I learned they had been given as premiums for opening bank accounts in local banks.

That discovery made us ask if perhaps the mission actually had money stashed away in some bank account somewhere. I discovered that although it looked like the ministry had absolutely nothing, the former director had stashed away large sums of money in a half dozen different banks.

On another day we were cleaning the stacks of books that were waist high all over the office when we suddenly realized, that what we had thought was a table on which an addressograph machine was setting, was actually a very old safe. I tried to find out from the former secretary what she might know about it, and she claimed she knew nothing – in fact she hadn't even known it was there.

I realized that to find out whether there was anything in the safe I would have to get a professional to drill it which would cost money. I wrestled with putting out money and then perhaps finding it was just an empty safe, but decided we could not afford to get rid of it without knowing, so I hired a man to open it.

After several hours of very hard work and a bill of $100, I drew from its hold a very old portfolio. I turned it over to my assistant Jim Camacho and paid the worker. Just as I did I heard Jim say, "Bill, you had better come in the office." I walked into the office and he showed me what was in the portfolio – Bonds totaling over $32,000 in value, belonging to the mission, and another set totaling $14,000 belonging to the widow of the former Director. She never knew they were there, nor did anyone else. What a joy we had in turning those bonds over to a very needy widow and what a thrill to find funds to do the work that needed to be done on the mission property.

By the time we had tracked down all the money that was in bank accounts we actually had enough to move forward and we completely renovated the building and the attached apartment with all new electric, plumbing, roof, surface repair and paint. It became a really beautiful facility once again and we named it *Wayside Maternity Home*. I rented a local theatre and brought *Life Action* in to do the *America, You're too Young to Die* program as a benefit and through that raised sufficient funds to open.

Our oldest son Phillip came to direct the home and things were moving alone very well. We had several girls, one who had already refused abortion and delivered her baby and another who was about due. The first year was tremendously difficult with drug dealers trying to use our location as a transfer point for their wares and children's services harassing one of our young mothers (and eventually even Phillip's family), because she had spanked her child (who decidedly needed to be spanked).

Phillip had simply defended the young mother's right to corporally discipline her child and the entire agency turned on him. We managed to weather the storm of harassment until one day the agency moved in on the school where Phillip's son was attending and had him brought into the office and stripped. Then they proceeded to the Home and demanded to see the naked bodies of the twins. While they found nothing and no charges were ever brought, the psychological pressure was creating problems for the family.

Just about that time I was approached by the Director of VOA (Volunteers of America), an organization that ministers to families in the Wilkesboro area. They had wanted to open a ministry for unwed mothers but had not been able to do so. Now they offered to buy our facility and carry on the work we had begun.

They too had been harassed by Children's Services in the early days but had finally made peace with the agency and thought they could probably operate with less restraint than we could. We discussed and prayed about the proposal and finally I made a decision.

I was incensed that Phillip had been maligned and attacked by this agency with its humanistic and anti-biblical bias and I was determined to try to vindicate him as well as our own reputation. I agreed to sell the ministry to VOA on the condition that they would operate it following our biblical principles as set forth in our operational manual, and retain Phillip on their payroll to operate it for at least one year. They agreed to the terms and we turned over that ministry to VOA.

I was approaching sixty years of age. I would soon complete thirty years with Grace & Truth Evangelistic Association – twenty of those years at the Camp. I had seen it grow from a small beginning to its position of a camp known throughout the country and I longed for more but seemed to have reached a plateau in my ability to move it forward. I began to think that younger leadership might be able to accomplish what I had not been able to accomplish and talked to the Board about stepping down from Administration when I reached sixty.

The Board worked together with me and we drew up a transitional plan that would allow me to remain as a member of the Board, and be active in the WWBI development program but be relieved of the major responsibilities of promotion, fund raising, and the day to day operation of the camp.

The last year at the camp was probably the most difficult year of all. I had never been able to replace the swimming pool and no matter what precautions we took to protect it every spring it took major time and money to restore what ice and snow had damaged over the winter.

To address the problem and to increase our ability to handle family groups, I had designed a two story split-level lodge that would encompass an indoor pool in that same location where the present pool was. I felt that if we had that one building we could attract a larger adult and family clientele and turn around the financial situation which was always close.

We had paid off our mortgage on the Camp in 1991, so I had gone to the bank with the proposal for the new building and it had gone all the way to the final approval, when the bank merged and the entire process started all over. The second time around the same thing happened – a second merger, but as the process neared the decision stage I had verbal assurances that it would succeed. Then came sudden disaster.

It had been an unusually cold winter. Snow had fallen in October and the ground remained covered until April. Hundreds of deer died of starvation or loss of blood from cutting their legs while trying to paw the icy ground to find food.

Of course such weather makes for a good retreat season since it is ideal for winter sports. We were expecting one of our largest retreats the coming weekend, but the weather became even more severe. It snowed a heavy snow, then partially melted, and snowed again four days in a row. Then the temperature dropped to twenty below zero and the winds began to howl. I had seen that kind of wind before and it usually meant we would lose several trees before it was over.

The night the retreat group was supposed to arrive, the snow fell again. The retreat leader called to tell us that the weather was so bad they were afraid to try to make the trip. I understood, but I also knew it would drastically affect our bottom line. Nevertheless, I let our people know we would have the weekend off and went to bed while the wind and the snow continued.

The next morning I was up, the sun was shining and I thought maybe we would get a break in the weather, when Ray Mitchell, my camp director called. "Dr. Shade," he said, "I think you'd better come up the hill – it looks like there may be something wrong at the Great Commission Auditorium." Little did I realize that he was grossly understating the situation so as not to alarm me too badly.

I jumped in the jeep, put it in four wheel drive and began plowing through the unplowed road up to the GCA. As I got to where I could see the GCA, my first thought was, "well it doesn't look too bad, it's all there." Then I rounded the corner to the parking lot. The entire front of the building was in tact, but from the front of the stage to the back fireplace the remainder of the building was collapsed and lay in a tangled mass on the ground. The GCA was a complete loss.

By God's grace, somehow the front around the stage had survived and the wooden facades that acted like stage curtains had held the falling beams off the stage area so that both our organ and our Kawai Grande Piano had been spared. There was not a scratch on either of them.

More important still, those who lived closest to the GCA told me they heard a load noise at about eleven o'clock the night before, but hadn't checked because the weather was so bad. That was no doubt the time it happened and from all reports it happened so suddenly that no one had any warning.

Imagine if that large retreat group had been in the building (which at that hour they would most certainly have been) with over a hundred kids. We could have had a horrendous loss of life, but God spared us. As the staff gathered to thank the Lord for what He had spared us from, we formed an emergency crew to begin assessing and reporting the damage.

Camp of the Nations was well known to the Scranton TV stations after having such events as the Atlanta project, the African Children's Choir and Bob Holmes "one man volley ball exhibitions," all of which attracted the camera crews and were carried on TV news reports. Once we notified them of what had happened, we immediately had a crew on the grounds reporting the damage. From that report we were able to get out a short *Winter Storm Emergency* video which we sent to many of our friends. As we did funds began to come in to replace the building.

When I meet with the insurance adjuster, I learned that they had lost over four hundred buildings that same night due to the extreme cold, the high winds and the heavy snow. We had replacement value on our building and so we applied for the funds to rebuild.

Of course we had lost a wooden structure, but when I considered what could have happened in the collapse of that building, I determined to replace it with steel. I realized that would cost much more than wood, but God graciously provided the additional funds and by Labor day that year we had completed a new GCA that was twenty feet broader, ten feet longer, and had a full basketball court with goals that would raise and lower. We had bleachers on both sides so that the building would seat over a thousand. The best part of it all was that all bills were paid and, although it was an extremely stressful project with many difficulties, the results were well worth the work.

When I had asked the Board to replace me, I wanted to be relieved from the responsibilities of Administration and be free to travel and preach as the Lord would open the doors. We had already made several trips into Romania after the Revolution to help the struggling church there, and I had also been to India and I wanted to go back and minister again. I intended to continue working on the WWBI curriculum and representing GATEA as I had opportunity. At least that is what I and the Board had agreed on.

But when the time came for the transition, it soon became evident that what I had in mind was not in the mind of the new Director. It took only a few months until we realized that this was not a transition, this was a takeover, and things were being done that hurt us deeply.

The emphasis on Missions was just no longer there. The Beautiful Fountain of the Fields, erected with monies left from my mother's estate and set with a plaque in her memory, was dismantled and the ten foot steel globe of the world rolled into the dump. Money was freely spent on projects that had no hope of a return and an entire philosophy became apparent that I could neither control nor condone.

After agreeing to a transition period and promising to meet with me to learn the history and background that had made Camp of the Nations what it was, the new Director met with the staff in his very first meeting and declared, "I don't want to know anything that has happened here in the past. Today this is a new camp and we start over from this point."

Then there came accusations, and wedges of rejection were driven between us and a staff whom we loved and had worked with for years. Now, suddenly, they had to choose a new loyalty or risk their jobs.

When Ruby, who was still serving as accountant, tried to mildly counsel the new leadership to avoid financial ruin, she was not only shunned but accusations were made against her impugning both her motives and her honesty.

All the while this was happening I had the strange sense that I could reverse it at any time. I had been in Administration for thirty years and I had weathered opposition before. I knew that as the Founding Director, I could take drastic action and take over control again, and I knew in my heart I could succeed, but this time God said "No." God gave me the distinct sense that His will for me at this time was to submit to what was happening and I followed that instinct, as painful as it was. I resigned and left the organization I had founded.

All of my savings were invested in the Camp, as were much of Dad's and Bernice's (my secretary). I was able to get a release on Bernice's but Dad and I could get nothing. When I left I did not have the money to even pay rent or get a house. Phillip, who had left the camp staff earlier and returned to the Souderton area, still owned the house he had purchased in Thompson, which was just nine miles from the camp. Phillip offered to let us move in, rent free, until we could get some funds. Those early days after leaving the camp were days of darkness and deep hurt.

In the darkness of the days that followed that whole situation, Satan tried to drag me into that alley I saw in my dream, but just as the blood of Christ had protected me on the night that I had the dream, so His Word and His blood sustained me and His Spirit strengthened me through that period of time. Always He was there reminding me that He had not changed, that no matter what was gone, no matter what we had lost, we still had Jesus. He was still faithful; He still loved us; He still had good intentions for us, and a purpose and a plan for our lives.

I remember that wonderful day when He spoke to me, as I was reading the Psalms from Psalm 71, verse 17, *O, Lord, Thou hast taught me from my youth and hitherto have I declared Thy wondrous works. And now, O Lord, when I am old and gray headed, forsake me not, until I have shown Thy strength to this generation and Thy power to everyone that is to come.* That became my desire and the definition of my ministry from that time forward. It is the reason that I am trying now to relate these stories – that I might share the wonderful works of God with this generation and with every generation that is to come.

CHAPTER THIRTY FIVE

We Come to Source of Light

When we decided in 1995, to leave GATEA and Camp of the Nations, we had to decide where God would have us go. For a while we worked as B&R (Bill & Ruby) Ministries, but God had something else for us. Around the time we were leaving GATEA, Roy Anderson had indicated that his organization, the Pocket Testament League, would like to have the WWBI program. WWBI had grown out of the original Through the Bible Correspondence Course and had metamorphosed into a three-year, six-semester curriculum.

My successor at the Camp was not interested in the program and so arrangements were made with the new leadership at GATEA and the entire stock including shelving was moved to PTL headquarters in Lititz, Pennsylvania.

I thought this somewhat ironic, since back in the mid seventies I had been approached by the man who was at that time Director of PTL and asked if I would consider coming to succeed him. I had not sensed any indication from the Lord at that time that I should do so, and the matter was dropped and eventually Dr. Roy Anderson had become the very capable and qualified Director.

Once WWBI was secured by PTL, Ruby and I decided we would apply for membership as well. That way we could continue working with the program in which only about half the curriculum had been developed. We applied assured by Roy that our membership would be a routine matter – it was not.

PTL was also in transition and Roy was stepping down as General Director. The man who was to replace him had been carefully groomed and had worked under Roy for over two years. All the preparation we had tried to build into our transition at the Camp of the Nations had been built into theirs. It should have worked beautifully.

But hardly had Roy stepped down, before his successor told him that he must move his office out of the headquarters building. He was not to be around the office at all. Then he informed me that he was Reformed in theology and would not use our Dispensational courses with WWBI. Furthermore, since Ruby and I had been close friends with Roy Anderson (Roy had been a former classmate at Wheaton and had served on the Board of GATEA), he didn't want us either. Our applications were turned down. We were distressed and perplexed. I was given the ultimatum to move the WWBI materials from PTL and had nowhere to move them.

I called my friend, Dr. Glenn Dix, and told him what had happened. Glenn, who had served for many years as General Director of Source of Light, had approached me on a number of occasions to see if Source of Light could work with us, or at least use the WWBI material. It had never worked, because the structure of our operation was so different from SLM. However, now they could actually own the material. Glenn immediately agreed and we sent the entire stock down to Madison Georgia. All copyrights were assigned to SLM and they now had the entire program.

I came along and helped for the second time to get the shelves up and the materials organized. In addition I talked to Glenn about joining SLM. The mission welcomed us and Ruby and I became members in 1996. However, we were not living at headquarters and Glenn put someone else in charge of the WWBI material. Once again it languished on the shelves without any further development.

In the meantime, SLM asked me to represent them as I traveled in meetings. So Ruby and I equipped ourselves with a display and materials and began representing the mission where ever we went. As far as schedule was concerned we had none and we were free to travel and minister where ever we wanted.

It was during this time, in 1996, that we went to India to teach at Bharat Bible College. We were there for three months that year and certainly enjoyed a very fruitful ministry. In fact, it was at Bharat Bible College that God revealed to me the reason behind all of the disappointments and losses we had experienced during the last several years.

Ruby and I had tried to make sense of it all, but it really didn't seem to come together. We had tried to apply our understanding of Romans 8:28 to the situation, but that didn't seem to fit either. I had been taught that the key to understanding that verse was in the words "all things work together." H. A. Ironsides had likened it to baking a cake. He said, "Not all things that happen to us are good – some are decidedly bad. This is like the ingredients of a cake. Flour by itself is not good, neither is lard. But when they are worked together they produce something that is distinctly good and delicious."

Frankly, I understood him to mean that eventually all these things would come together and the result would be that everything would turn out right in the end. Well, perhaps – but that didn't seem to be the case with us. It seemed I couldn't get my cake to bake.

At last we had just decided that although we did not understand why God had allowed all of this to take place, we would simply go on serving Him as best we could and leave the final answer to come when we got to glory. God had something better for us.

One morning I came to chapel at the college and an Indian evangelist had been invited to speak. He began by apologizing that he had not had the formal training the students there were receiving, but God had called him and he had answered the call. He announced his text that morning as Romans 8:28 and 29. I immediately sensed that perhaps I would learn something that day I had not learned through all my training, and indeed I did.

After reading the verse he asked, what I at first, thought to be a very strange question. He asked, "What is the *good* that God has promised us in this verse?"

I had never thought of such a question before. I had interpreted the word *good* to mean simply a general condition of good such as "everything will turn out right in the end" or to put it in Disney terms, "they lived happily ever after."

This man insisted that the word was specific, and that it was defined by the context. Then he read verse twenty nine. ***For whom***

He did foreknow He also did predestinate to be conformed to the image of His Son, that He might be the Firstborn among many brethren (many just like Him). In other words, God has determined to make us like Jesus. He then asked, "Is that good?"

I saw it in a flash. What God had promised us in verse twenty eight, was not that everything in life would turn out pleasantly, or that we would be vindicated. What He had promised was that He would use everything that happens in our lives, the good as well as the bad, to conform us to the image of His beloved Son.

Suddenly it all made sense. God had taken me through the fire to make me like His Son, and I thought my heart would burst. I cried out from the depths of my soul, "Lord, if all that I have gone through was purposed to make me like Jesus, then Lord, let it be. I will embrace it, and rejoice in it, and thank you for loving me so much."

Now it didn't matter to me how things turned out, it only mattered that I be conformed to his Son. At last I knew I had learned the real meaning of Romans 8:28. We returned to America, more ready than ever to serve Him.

We returned from India to our home in Thompson. About that time our pastor, Jerry Safstrom decided it was time for him to retire. Much to the dismay of the church he did and I was asked to assume the position of interim pastor. I accepted that assignment because SLM had not defined my role and apart from representing them in various venues, I was free to pretty well determine what ministry I would have. Ruby and I jumped back into the role, teaching and preaching and visiting. I knew the term would be temporary but we still relished the opportunity to minister to these dear people.

We had the additional benefit of having Dr. Carl Elgena and his wife Susan serving with us. What a blessing they were, and we became good friends. Susan offered to continue to lead the VBS for us and threw herself into it unreservedly. That year she asked Ruby to do the missionary story and Ruby puzzled over what to do. I suggested she tell the story of Christopher Boda, the Banjara boy from India who had been actually born in the mud. Ruby said she didn't know it that well so I offered to write it down. That was the beginning of actually producing the visualized story known as, *Born In The Mud*.

Ruby told the children Christopher's story, and they loved it. There were about 87 kids in the VBS. Each year they would do a project for missions. This year we suggested they give money toward getting a Banjara New Testament printed. The usual goal each year had been $100. Sometimes they made it, sometimes they did not.

This year, however, as the story progressed the enthusiasm for it became greater and greater. They decided to go and wash cars, mow lawns and do whatever they could to raise money for the project. In the end they raised over $600 and several of the children received Christ, as the gospel was unfolded in the story. I decided if it could have that kind of effect on one group, perhaps God could use it among many more.

On my next trip to India I asked Christopher for permission to write his story. I went over a number of details and decided to do it as a children's story using large pictures. I pretty well determined what pictures I thought we needed to illustrate the events. Now I had to find an artist to illustrate it.

I learned that my friend Diane Brask was going to India and would be with Christopher. I further learned she would be taking a photographer with her. I wrote, giving her a list of 20 pictures I needed in authentic settings. In the course of our correspondence, Diane's secretary told me that she was an artist, and that, while she did not know anything of the Indian, or Banjara culture, if she could see the pictures, she could paint them. The result was months of doing one picture at a time and approving it, then doing the next, but at last a very realistic and authentic set of pictures was produced.

As I talked about the project I learned that our new SLM Director, Tom Weber wanted SLM to print and publish the book. The problem with that was that I wanted the book to not only produce spiritual fruit, but I wanted it to produce funds for Christopher's ministry and Christopher got his American funding through Christian Aid Mission. In order for us to help him, I would have to appeal for funds for Christian Aid and their mission address would appear, not SLM's. I discussed the matter with Tom and he decided to go ahead anyway. Thus SLM printed and published the book, *Born in the Mud*.

As an outgrowth of the book, I wondered about the radio program Unshackled, featuring Christopher's story. Unshackled has a world-wide audience. They had done two dramatizations of my story through the years and I thought they might be interested. I sent my manuscript to Flossie McNeal who vets the stories used on the broadcast.

After some time Flossie called me. "You know Bill, it is my job to read these stories and determine what we can use. I read a lot of stories and I want you to know I don't cry over them. As emotional as some of them are, I guess I have gotten used to it. I bawled my head off over this one."

By the grace of God, Christopher's story was produced and broadcast over Unshackled and through the book and the broadcast God has provided funding for four large orphanage programs under Banjara Tribal Ministries. One of the joys of ministry has been those times when something I could do, was used of God to bless and help another ministry.

Eventually Thompson Church got a pastor and Dr. Elgina and I found ourselves being asked to serve as deacons. We each consented and for the next year or so we grappled with some fairly intense situations. There is nothing like a small church in an equally small community to create a large conflict in which, before it is over, most of the community gets involved. Carl and I stayed the course until the storm blew over, but it took a toll on us both, and I think particularly on Carl who was older. Not long after he and Sue moved to a retirement community and Carl's next move was straight up to glory. We had some moving to do as well.

In 1999, Ruby and I again accepted a teaching assignment in India. In addition, our new position with Source of Light was opening many other doors of ministry in far off places. We wanted to see the work Aloni was doing in Uganda. In addition, we had been requested to come to the country of Ghana. So in 1999 we left for what was the longest overseas trip of our ministry. It began in July and lasted until mid November taking us to India, Kenya, Uganda, Ghana and England. Where ever we traveled we found it true that the gospel is still, *"the power of God unto salvation to everyone that believeth, to the Jew first and also to the Greek"* (Romans

1:16). What an honor it is to be an Ambassador of the Gospel of Jesus Christ.

As summer of 2000 approached I knew we needed to be on the road for SLM but we weren't just exactly sure where we needed to be. I had many contacts in the east that I could visit, but I had never been further west than the Mississippi River except to fly to Los Angeles on one occasion for the Bill Gothard Advanced Seminar. I virtually knew nothing about the west.

Strangely enough, I received two invitations for that summer. The first was from an IFCA church near Wichita Kansas. The other was a general invitation to IFCA men to provide a chaplain for the Carpinteria Campground on the California coast. I applied and was accepted. It did seem that God might be directing us westward.

We decided that since this was the case we would take this one opportunity to make the most of it. I wrote a letter to Med Benton (the man who had provided LP Gas for me while I was at the Camp). He and his wife had moved to Cody Wyoming after retirement and they were only a few miles from Yellowstone Park, a place we had always wanted to visit. They called and warmly invited us to come and stay with them as long as we wished.

Then we decided we would like to visit Wheaton College again. We had not been on the campus together since we left in 1956. Just north of Wheaton, Annie Rathburn, one of the Scripture Memory Mountain Missionary ladies we had worked with in Kentucky, was now retired and in a nursing home. We decided to visit her on the way.

We also wanted to see some other folks we hadn't seen in years. Caroline (DeBusk) Riggs and husband Mike had supported us for years. Caroline had served as a secretary during the early days at Teen Encounter. Dr. and Mrs. Henry Morris and John lived just south of Los Angeles and we contacted them and received a warm welcome.

Finally, Ruby had not seen her former pastor Marshall Swoverland since that day we had visited them in Indiana and blown an engine on the way back to Wheaton. They now lived in Desert Palm Springs and we wanted to visit them as well.

We decided we could afford the trip using the Volkswagon Van. We could sleep in it along the way, make our meals on the stove, transport our food in the refrigerator, watch TV if we had a cable hook-up and generally travel very economically and comfortably. Thus we started our trip – a trip that would be both enjoyable and fruitful and prepare us for the next big step in our lives.

CHAPTER THIRTY SIX

The Completion of WWBI

About three years into our work with SLM, I received a call from my dear friend Elwood Pfaunmiller. Elwood was serving as pastor in the Altoona area and was also Director of *Way of Truth Ministries* that was organized in Altoona, out of Faith Baptist Church. The Mission and the church wanted to begin a Bible Institute program. Elwood wanted to use the WWBI curriculum and he wanted me to come and train them in the use of the material. I told him I would let him know.

I called Glenn Dix and explained the request. At that time I had no jurisdiction over the WWBI material or authority to set up a school, so I had to inquire if Glenn would allow me to do that. He did and Ruby processed the material to prepare for the training. I went to Altoona and did the training program over a period of several days. Toward the end of the training, Elwood called SLM to reinforce his enthusiasm for the program. He was apparently excited about the training and the material, because I got a call from Glenn that evening in my motel room.

Glenn said, "Bill, I think I've made a mistake. I should have put you in charge of WWBI. From now on, WWBI is your project." That was the permission I needed and it opened a whole new door of endeavor.

Immediately, we began to try to accomplish three things: First, bring the courses that had been already written up to par. Secondly, we tried to discover what was written but not published (some were only partially complete), and finally, we decided what we needed to write or get writers for. With a new excitement we jumped into the task of finishing the project God had given us so many years before. But we soon realized this was a monumental task.

All written material was transitioning to computer. Nothing we had produced was in computer. We struggled to change that. Once we got it into computer, we realized that in word processing programs, the formatting tended to migrate. We would get it exactly as we wanted and the next time we opened the program, part of the material was on another page. We struggled for several years just working out the technical details of production.

In the meantime, I was making progress on writing new course material. I still had permission to use Dr. Ironside's material for some of our studies. Now I approached Dr. Renold Showers, with whom I had gone to Bible School, and asked him to let us use his course in Daniel. Dr. Showers was more than willing, but the copyrights belonged to *Friends of Israel Gospel Ministry*. I traveled to the mission and met with Bill Sutter the Director. Before I left, I had rights to Showers book on Daniel. This was first rate course material and I was elated.

Finally, we tried to evaluate what was yet to be done. Getting it all down on paper and estimating from known times for production, I reckoned that if I had four people, we could finish the entire task in one year. I put out an APB to everyone I knew in an emailed Prayer Bulletin and prayed. Not long after I receive a reply from a lady who I did not know. She was from Wisconsin and had just retired as a school teacher. She said she was willing to come for a year and help with the project.

Susan Scott arrived and we soon realized that God could not have found anyone more ideal for the task. Susan was careful, accurate, detail oriented, unbelievably patient and willing to work long hours to complete the task. We had to put everything that had been written into a publishing program, make all the necessary corrections and formatting changes and then put the finished product in pdf format.

As the months passed by two things became evident: For the first time we were making permanent progress. We were getting as close to perfection as a humanly produced document could be. And better still, we had it in a program that held everything in place. No more migration from one page to another, or even one line to another. Furthermore, as we completed each course with a final proofing, it could be transferred to a pdf format so that it remained unchanged and unchangeable. No one could do a re-write on the finished product. Finally, we had all the work on file in the publishing program, so that if, any time in the future we wanted to change, or improve a course, we could. I was ecstatic. Susan was doing a terrific job.

But the second thing that became evident was – we were running out of time. One day I stopped by Susan's desk and jokingly remarked, "Well, Susan, when I advertised for volunteers on the project, I asked for four people for one year. You are the only one who came, so I guess its one person for four years." She laughed, but I could tell I had not made the case. However, I think I did make the point that we really needed additional hands on the work and Susan contacted one of her friends from Wisconsin, a widow by the name of Sonja Weidman. Sonja had gone to Word of Life Bible Institute after her husband's death and was anxious to serve the Lord in a meaningful way. She was also an excellent proof reader and so Sonja joined the team at SLM.

The two women were making so much progress, that I knew I had to provide them with the remaining courses so they would not run out of work. I dug out a course that had been written but never published on Religions and Cults. The work that had been done was excellent, but it was now several decades old. I determined to bring it up to date. Furthermore, it lacked real depth on the eastern religions and especially Islam. Before long, I had added a ninth STEP to the course, and brought our facts up to date as current as the latest news.

We had Dr. Showers course on Daniel, now I went back to Friends of Israel and asked for Dr. Levy's course on Revelation. They consented, and we began making a course out of a book. I redid our previous work on the prison epistles, taken from Ironsides books and wrote the courses for the Pastoral Epistles and 1, 2 Peter.

Finally, I wrestled with the weighty subject of Ethics, in a course called, An Introduction to Christian Ethics. The course discusses the contrast between a philosophy of relativism and a biblical philosophy when it comes to ethical issues. The last several STEPS of the course deal with contemporary ethical issues like Abortion, Euthanasia, Capitol Punishment, Homosexuality and War.

Now WWBI was complete with a full three year, six semester curriculum. Almost at once, it seemed our foreign Discipleship Training Branches wanted to start Schools. Before we even got the word out that we had completed the project, requests were coming in for training seminars and material.

Some years before, and before WWBI was even complete, we had started Institutes in Maharashtra, Andhra Pradesh, Bengal, and Karnataka, India. Now we were being asked to come to the Philippines to train people there. Eventually we did. In 2010 we held four training seminars in the Philippines, certifying 21 pastors and leaders to use the WWBI material.

Today, the courses are all completed and available in printed form, as well as on CDs. One of our men has begun producing the entire curriculum in Braille, and we have developed a number of Power Point lectures to supplement the courses. In the future, we hope to have all of them available in audio as well.

As I write, a new Bible College is opening in Uganda using the WWBI curriculum, and six other countries have made requests for us to come and set up schools. It has been a long way from that day in 1959, when God first gave me the vision for the original studies, but God has been faithful and today we rejoice in the material He has put in our hands to help His Church learn and teach the Word of God.

CHAPTER THIRTY SEVEN

Adventures With A Buffalo

In 2003 we made several life changing decisions. The first was when we decided to sell our home in Thompson and move to the home Dad had left us in Sebring, Florida. I remember the day. We had talked about it over a period of time, finally we agreed we would act on it and we made the commitment in prayer. We were sitting in the living room of our Thompson house having devotions.

We said "Amen," and as we did I looked out into our front yard to see two men standing there. One with a measuring tape in his hand, and the other with a surveyor's rod – right there in my front yard. I walked out and greeted them and inquired, "What's up guys? What are you doing?" "We are surveying for a new sewer line," they told me. "Come on," I said, "You guys have been going to put in a sewer line here for the last fifty years." One of them replied, "Yea, well this time it's going to happen. We are starting in about two weeks."

Great, I thought, just what I needed. I decide to sell my house and they decide to make it impossible. You can't sell a house in a village that is all torn up with sewer lines being installed, and no one wants to pay the installation fee, so any sale will have to wait till this job is done.

As we drove to Florida I raised the question of getting a mobile home, using Florida and Madison, Georgia as our base, and working out from there in meetings. As we talked, I decided to talk to Roger Schultz about the 4905 GMC Bus Conversion that he owned.

Roger and Art Colburn had completely converted the old "Buffalo", as the 4905 was called, into a combination living quarters and office space. Roger and Ruth had used the bus to travel for several years, recruiting on behalf of African Evangelical Fellowship, a mission Roger had flown for, during a year-long term in Africa. In the last couple of years, Ruth had come down with Alzheimer's and as her condition worsened, Roger had to give up traveling. I suggested we stop and see him on the way through Orlando, and see if he would be willing to sell the bus to me.

The bus had not been driven in several years and was obviously worse for the inactivity, but when I asked, Roger suggested he simply donate the bus to us for a tax write off. I talked to the CFO at Source of Light and the deal was made.

Since I wanted to park the bus at our place in Sebring, I now had to go to the city and get a permit. I quickly learned the biggest hurdle would be to construct a concrete pad that would go between the paved road and my graveled drive where the bus was to set. I completed that, and built it strong enough to run a Patton Tank over, and then with the help of Art Colburn, we ran electric, telephone and water to a hook up for the bus. I had everything I needed, except a dumping station.

Of course, I had never driven a coach of this size before and needed some serious instructions. I had my commercial license for airbrakes, but the 4905 Buffalo was built with only one rear axle, so that the span from the front to the rear axle made it the longest in the industry – a factor that translated into a challenge when trying to negotiate tight places, especially right hand turns. The dashboard and side panels had so many switches, they looked like a commercial airliner. I needed some concentrated help.

Roger offered to drive the bus down to Sebring, with me riding beside him, and ostensibly I would learn what I needed to know. We started from his home in Orange City and traveled without incident along route 4 through Orlando, until we reached the western end of the city. That is when Roger, suddenly decided that he had to use the bathroom.

He pulled the bus to the burm and jumped up from the driver's seat, instructing me to put on the flashers. I searched in vain for anything that looked like a switch that would activate flashers. There were two red switches marked "emergency" so I figured one of them had to be it. I flipped it, and the engine began to sputter. I switched it back, but it was too late. I looked into the mirror, to see a huge cloud of smoke coming from the engine compartment. Obviously, I had hit the wrong switch.

When Roger returned, he told me I had hit the override switch to stop the engine and now we would have to manually reset it before we could start it again. We went to the rear of the bus and opened the engine door, (which I immediately determined had to be repaired since I was not sure it was going to stay up). As we worked, a state patrol car pulled up behind us. We assured him we had simply had an accidental engine failure. Roger reset the engine switch and started the engine from the rear. We returned and I drove the rest of the way to Sebring. With that kind of beginning, I sensed this was going to be a challenge.

For the next couple of weeks, we cleaned and arranged our living space, and spent some nights in the bus, to become accustomed to it. My maiden voyage was scheduled for Easter Sunday morning. I was scheduled to preach that morning in Valdosta, at Grace Bible Church, for Pastor Rick Hoffmeister.

I had checked all the vitals including the tires. The four rear tires needed to be replaced, but I knew that I was headed to Pennsylvania in a few weeks, and decided that if I could limp along until then, I could probably get tires at a very good price, or perhaps even have them donated. I decided to try.

We left Sebring before daylight and hit every green light along the way. I don't think I ever got through Sebring so quickly. Everything went smoothly and I could not have asked for a better trip, until just after getting on Route 75 off the Florida Turnpike.

There is a rest stop about five miles up the road and I was just coming around the final curve before arriving there, when I heard my tire blow. Thankfully, it was the right rear tire (and the outside one at that), and I was already in the right lane, so no one was affected. I simply coasted into the rest stop and viewed the situation. That's when I realized my problem was a little more serious than I thought. I had a spare, but no way in the world could I have turned the nuts off that tire. I had to call for help. Six hours later it came, and I was back on the road, but I obviously was not going to preach.

It was dusk when I pulled into Pastor Rick's driveway. I determined not to play any more games with these tires. I asked Rick to get me to someone who would be honest and could replace all four of the aberrant tires. He did, at a modest $400 each. Then the tire store mechanic cautioned me that the front two tires really needed replaced too. They looked fine, had lots of tread, and did not look severely checkered. But the dealer looked up the numbers and told me they were more than five years old. "Better let me replace them too," he told me.

Well, Roger had told me I would have to replace the four rear tires, but he had insisted that the front ones were fine. I decided to believe Roger. We got back on the road and enjoyed an uneventful trip to Madison, where we worked at the Mission several weeks, before our trip to Altoona, Pennsylvania, where I was key-note speaker at the Missions Conference, at Faith Baptist Church.

We left a day early for Altoona and everything went smoothly. I cruised across Route 20 to Columbia, jockeyed my way through the traffic and headed north on route 77. We breezed through Charlotte and north toward Virginia.

I was crossing Lake Norman just north of Charlotte and I was cruising. I had the peddle to the metal and was doing seventy miles per hour in the passing lane on the causeway. As we crossed the lake, I was exclaiming how beautiful this lake area was, when it happened – there was a loud retort as if from a cannon, and I saw fragments of tire fly through the air as the left front tire literally exploded.

There was nothing I could do but try to keep the bus going straight ahead and keep it from flipping into the lake. I wrestled with the steering and gently, oh so gently tried to apply the brakes. At last I came to a stop – still in the passing lane – and as I did I heard the ominous sound of air escaping. Whatever the tire had hit, it had apparently broken open, and air was escaping much too fast.

Now, you have to understand that these buses are totally dependent on air pressure. They ride on air and when the bags are deflated the bus is almost on the ground. The brakes are inner connected with the other systems so that everything locks up (safety feature), and you cannot move a bus until you have at least 80 pounds of air pressure. Everything depends on air. I was setting in the middle of the passing lane of a major highway without air – and I was not going to be moving.

I immediately called an emergency road service for motor homes. He came, but took one look at the size of this converted bus and said he had no way of helping. Motor homes are one thing – buses are another. A State Trooper pulled up behind us and began flagging traffic. It was 3:45 in the afternoon, and the evening traffic was beginning to build from Charlotte. I tried another road service – same result.

It was obvious that our Trooper was not happy and for good reason. We were beginning to back up traffic. I told him I had tried everything I knew, if he could get someone that could move the bus, I had no choice but to let him do it. He called two state trucks with cable winches and they arrived and hooked onto the front towing loops of the bus.

Both trucks set their brakes and turned on the winches at the same time. Both trucks began moving backward while the bus remained immobile. With air pressure gone, the brakes were automatically locked up and with the tire flat and the air out of the airbags, the bus was literally sitting like a large hen on her chicks, with not even enough room to get a jack under to lift it up.

By now it was after six o'clock and we had backed up traffic clear into Charlotte. The evening news had their helicopter overhead talking about this bus that was blocking everything and the Trooper's patience was definitely beginning to wear thin. "I'm going to cut this thing in pieces and haul it away," he declared.

Ruby and I had prayed from the time this had happened, but now we really got serious. I literally cried out to God for help. I had no idea what to do. As I said "Amen" the thought came, I have a generator on board. Why not start the generator, and then start the on-board compressor. Maybe I can build enough air to at least raise the bus high enough to get a jack under it.

The diesel generator started and in a few minutes I started the compressor. The best I could get was about thirty pounds of air – not enough to raise the bus. Just then a tow truck pulled up in front of the bus and a friendly looking man got out. It was great to see a friendly face, because the angry drivers who were whizzing past me were frequently cursing and some even threw things at us, as if I wanted to be there.

This fellow approached and said, "I see you have a problem." I responded in the affirmative and walked him to the left side of the bus, where we were just on the edge of the road. "I think we have burst an airbag," I said. "You see the grass moving where the air is escaping – but the bag is behind the tire and until we can remove the tire, we can't get to the bag." He said nothing but reached up under the bus at about the location where the air was coming from. A second later, the air stopped. He grinned and said, "You didn't blow a bag. The tire knocked open a petcock that releases air and I just shut it." It was that simple.

Now it was possible to move the bus. The tire was still flat, but with air, everything unlocked and I could move again. The Trooper stopped all traffic while I wrestled the bus over to a wide spot on the right burm and parked it. Now to change the tire.

The Trooper had called for a tire truck but the man had never changed a tire on a bus (only on trucks). Buses do not have frames. They are constructed like boxes and their strength comes from that. Thankfully, the man who had stopped the air was still with us. He had a jack that would work. He knew where to place the jack to raise the bus. He helped remove the tire and mount the spare, (while I held my breath as scores of frustrated drivers who had been tied up for several hours went past at speeds that were unbelievable). In the final analysis, whoever that tow truck man was, he was the only one who knew how to get this done and he stayed with us until everything was finished.

As soon as we were road worthy the Trooper came to us and said, "You guys settle up somewhere off this highway. There is an exit about three miles up the way. Pull off there. I don't want you on the highway any longer." We gladly complied.

The tow truck was in the lead and pulled out first, next the tire truck, and finally, Ruby and me in the bus. By now it was nine o'clock and dark, but we were in tandem and I had my eye on the truck ahead. As I pulled up the off ramp I could see the tow truck stopped up ahead, the tire truck stopped next and I stopped in the rear – exactly the order we had been in before, three miles back on the highway.

The tire man came back and I paid him, then I waited for the tow truck operator to present his bill. After waiting about five minutes I asked Ruby to approach him – "I'm afraid to even leave the driver seat after all this," I said. Ruby complied and soon returned. "Bill, you're not going to believe this," she said, "but that was not the same man. He says he is just parked waiting for someone and doesn't know anything about this." The Tow Truck Operator who knew all the answers and had helped us so much had simply disappeared. I couldn't escape being reminded of that verse from Hebrews, *"you have entertained angels unawares* (without knowing it)."

I drove to the nearest shopping center and asked permission to park for the night. I called my son Steve and asked if he had any suggestions for where I might get a tire, since he is a trucker. A few minutes later he called me back and gave me a number. "Call this guy at 7am sharp and he says he can help you." I thanked him and Ruby and I cooked a light supper and went to bed, very much aware that God had heard our cries and had answered.

Next morning I called at 7:00. When I told the man who answered where I was, he said he had a man that lived up that way and he would send him directly over to get the job started and send another truck up with two new tires.

In a short time the first man arrived. As we talked, I realized he had some deep spiritual needs and seemed to be trying to find God. I shared the gospel with him, going over it several times, and had prayer with him. By then the tires arrived, they were mounted and by 9am we were on our way north. We enjoyed a wonderful trip with no further problems and stopped just short of Everett, Pennsylvania. We stayed in a Wal-Mart lot for the night, got a good night's sleep, and the next day we arrived in Altoona.

I had met Pastor Gary Dull, but I did not know him well. When we arrived he directed us to a nearby campground and sent someone over with a car for us to use while we were there. When he learned the bus was a 4905 GMC Buffalo, he was excited. He used to drive that model bus and, in fact, continued to drive tour busses on his day off for Fullington Bus Company. I related my tale and mentioned wanting to get someone to service the bus. Gary felt he could get Fullington to do the service job.

One afternoon during the meetings we drove to their garage in Clearfield. The mechanic on duty was a guy named Oscar, who took one look at the bus and said, "I have serviced so many Buffalos I could do it with my eyes blindfolded." I hoped out loud that he wouldn't, and he obliged, but it was obvious he did know the machine. I was missing several parts and had a broken wiper arm. Oscar thought for a minute, and said, "I think we still have some left-over parts for Buffalos – let me look." In a few minutes he returned with not one but two new wiper arms. Before I left everything was working.

While the bus drove well, several of the windows were leaking, it needed a new paint job and it was difficult to cool in summer and impossible to heat in winter. Nothing was insulated. While I was at Fullington, I learned of a man in Clearfield who could replace the old bus windows by first removing them, then installing insulation in the sides and ceiling, and then covering the entire side of the bus with a sheet of fiberglass, allowing the use of replacement, motor home type thermal windows, in select locations. I decided if we were going to make the 4905 Buffalo our home, I needed to have that done and so in the spring of 2004, I took the bus to Clearfield.

In September, Ruby and I went to India for several weeks and, when I returned we flew into Atlanta to report to the mission and care for some things there. Tom Weber had become the new Director at SLM, and he and Karen picked us up on our return flight. I remember asking, "Have I become some kind of celebrity or something, that the Executive Director now picks me up at the airport?" Tom avoided my question.

As we traveled toward Madison, Tom asked if we were hungry. "Well," I said, "we haven't eaten for about eleven hours, so yes, I guess you could say we are hungry." I don't remember where we stopped, but it was a lovely restaurant and Tom even insisted on buying our dinner. Finally, he said, "I guess we've enjoyed all the niceties we can, so I need to tell you something." "OK" I responded, "What do you have to tell me?" "It's about your house," Tom began. "While you were gone it was ruined."

I said something like, "Yes, well we have heard over the news of the hurricanes in Florida (four had hit that year), and I thought we might have gotten hit." "No, no," said Tom. "Not your Florida home, your one in Thompson, Pennsylvania." "What happened," I asked, "did it burn down or something." "No," Tom said, "It was flooded." "Impossible!" I responded. "That house has a creek below it, but its twenty five feet higher than the creek and it could never have reached a level high enough to flood that house." "I don't think it was the creek," said Tom. I think it was something to do with the boiler." It didn't take me long to figure out what had happened.

I had called our heating company about a week before we left for India, to tell them that I could hardly get any water out of our hot water lines. We heated our water using a domestic coil that ran through the oil fired boiler. So, when we were heating the house, we got the added benefit of hot water. The down side was that, during the summer, the boiler had to turn on to heat water, which seemed to cancel any economy the arrangement might otherwise have had.

The heating company had sent a man to examine the problem and he solved it by putting an acid solution through the heating coil, which cleaned out all the calcium residue and restored a free flow of water. What he did not do, was check the coil to be sure the acid had not compromised it and created any leaks. It had, and so as I left for India, unbeknown to me, there was a constant flow of water leaking into the boiler. Of course, the boiler responded by trying to heat the water. Soon the steam lines were filled with boiling water. When the water reached the old iron radiators, it filled them until it reached the air-valves. Then the pressure of the heated water, blew the air-valves out of their sockets, and began spraying hot boiling water into the rooms.

I had asked a farm family nearby to look in on the house while I was gone and they had said they would. But it was summer, and they were busy, and anyway, what could possibly go wrong? A few days before we were due home from India, they decided to make a casual stop, just so they could report that they had done so, and found a three week disaster. Most everything was ruined. Plaster was down, floors were warped, the basement was flooded, all my tools were under water – it was a major disaster.

The farm couple had called my son Phillip and he had already activated the insurance company to action. Ruby and I headed for Pennsylvania. For the next two months we did little more than move the project along. We lived in motels, (courtesy of our insurance company), and ate out, and tried to see that things got done.

We had sold the house just before we left for India and were supposed to have settlement on it when we returned. Now, I had to notify the buyers that the house they had agreed to buy no longer existed. I told them that of course, they could simply back out of the contract, or, if they wanted to stay with it, they could choose all the replacement cupboards, paints, carpet, everything and have a "like new" house. They decided to opt for that and got a great bargain. On top of everything else, they got a new boiler and $36,000 worth of renovation, for the price they had originally offered.

Settlement came just after Christmas. Ruby and I got to spend one final night in our home before settlement. We had not only sold the house but everything in it, so we virtually left it all. After settlement, we drove to Clearfield to pick up the bus. Again we spent a night or two in a motel until it was ready. The last day of December, we drove our completely redone bus to Florida, pulling a small trailer in which we had everything we had saved from fifty years of life and ministry together. Ruby drove the little Chevy car I had bought to tow behind the bus. New Years day, we arrive to our next challenge.

Four hurricanes had indeed hit Florida, and all four had managed to clobber Sebring. When we arrived, our fruit trees were laying on their sides, the boat house was in the canal behind the house, the sea wall was partially collapsed (and would eventually give way to total collapse), and the roof shingles were scattered all over the yard. It was the next phase of a seemingly endless stream of testings we were destined to go through.

CHAPTER THIRTY EIGHT

Coming Back Into Administration

W e arrived in Florida the last day of December and I found what looked like a disaster area. I parked the bus on the pad we had prepared for it and hooked it up. Just behind the pad, both of my fruit trees were down. The boat house was in the canal.

The boat itself had been chained to a concrete block buried in the sand. It remanded in place, but had tipped up, with the bow in the air as far as the chain would reach. The boat cover and tarp had been torn, and the boat was filled with rain water, which meant that the inboard engine was completely submerged and had been that way for several months. I was not at all sure we would ever get it going again.

I began by making arrangements for the boat at a Marina I used. They had recovered a number of boats from similar situations, and the mechanic told me they would give it their best shot.

I returned and began working on the trees. It was obvious I would lose both of them. They had been wonderful fruit trees, that had blessed us with fruit of exceptional quality, but now all I could do was cut them in pieces, and stack them to be hauled away.

Next, we had to get the remains of the boat house out of the canal. I decided the bus was ideal for the job. I tied onto some of the boat house frame that was sticking up out of the water with a logging chain and tied the chain to the bus. Very gently, I moved forward.

When something as big as a 4905 Buffalo moves, whatever is attached to it is going to move with it. As the main sections of the boat house showed above the water, I placed a couple of 2x4s down as runners to drag the house up over what was left of the sea wall.

I had noticed that the hurricanes had taken a toll on the roof as well. I had known for several years that I was due for a roof, but hadn't the money to replace it. I had coated it with white roof coating, but the wind of the hurricanes was more than it could stand. There were shingles all over the yard.

I called a local roofer and got an estimate. With that in hand, I contacted our home insurance agent. He told me he had seen our roof and had decided it was not bad enough to warrant an entire new roof, but that since I had already gotten the estimate, he would authorize it. We got a new roof with new skylights, and architectural shingles – much more than I could ever have done without the storm.

I had been in Florida exactly one month. January 31, was the date I knew the Board of Source of Light was going to meet to choose a Director to replace Tom who had resigned. Ruby and I had prayed for the situation that morning. I have to confess there was a very quiet whisper in my heart that somehow I was destined to play a part in all of this, but I tried to silence it and not allow myself to think about it, except to pray that God would do something special for the Board.

About eleven o'clock that morning my phone rang. I heard Dr. Paul Bufford's voice greeting me. Paul said, "Bill, we are here at the Mission, and we've been praying all morning for God's direction in the choice of an Interim Director for Source of Light." I answered that I was aware of the meeting and that we had been praying for them. Paul continued, "Well, I believe God has answered. I believe we know the man God wants for the job."

I said, "Wonderful, Paul. Is it a secret or can you share with me who you are looking at." "I can tell you Bill," he replied, "It's you – and you can't say no. We have prayed for hours and we had five other names we considered – you weren't even among them. But we had no peace about any of them so we went back to prayer and immediately afterward someone wrote your name on the board and there was and immediate and unanimous reaction that you are the man. Will you do it?"

I said, "Paul, administration is not new to me and I suppose I could, but I will need to talk to Ruby and to the Lord before I give you an answer." Paul agreed, but asked, "Do you think you can give us an answer in the next two hours – that's as long as some of us can be here and we don't want to walk away from this meeting without someone in place." I told him I would try.

I went into the house and found Ruby and told her what was happening. We immediately went to prayer. She reminded me that I knew only too well the pressures of administration, and the price to be paid for being there, and I agreed. But we also agreed that if, by paying that price SLM could be saved and strengthened it would be worth it all. Neither of us wanted to go through something like we had gone through before. On the other hand, I felt strongly that SLM needed direction and I wanted to at least help them over this hurtle.

After praying together, I called two close friends who had served with me in days past and knew me well, and asked what they thought. Each of them affirmed that I should accept the assignment and believed I would be able to help the organization. Within my two hour time limit I called back to SLM. "Ruby and I are ready to come. We have some loose ends here that will have to be tied up first, but I will plan to be at my desk by February 15." We arrived a day early.

We were permitted to live in the guest house. It was a wonderful assignment, because I could not afford to pay to run two houses, and we were not ready to sell the house in Florida. By being willing to provide hospitality to traveling guests, we could live rent free with all utilities paid. In addition, the guest house had been built and furnished by a retired business woman who had served as the Mission Hostess for a number of years and since had moved to a retirement village. She had donated the house and the furnishings to SLM, so all we needed were some clothes and we were ready to begin work.

I well remember the first day I sat in the Director's office and asked myself what I was doing there. I had been with SLM for eight years but really did not understand the size and complexity of the organization. What did God want to accomplish and why was I in this place. One thing I knew, I had done absolutely nothing to influence my getting here. It had been completely a work of God and that gave me a deep sense of assurance that God had something good ahead for me and for the mission.

When I walked into my office that first morning, I found a cartoon drawing on my desk. It showed large rockets going off in many directions, but a crumbling platform from which they were being launched. The accompanying notes made it clear, that while SLM was expansive in its outreach, it was weak and unstable at the base and desperately needed attention. I got the message.

Before I came to the Director's office, SLM had contracted with Dr. Roger Parrott to spend a day with us as a consultant. My experience with "consultants" had not been very good and I considered them a waste of money. I tried twice to get the Board to cancel in order to save a chunk of money I felt we could ill afford to part with, considering the condition in which we found ourselves just then. The Board assured me they wanted to go forward with the arrangement, so I complied.

Dr. Parrott was with us for only one day. He spent nearly the entire time asking questions, especially about what SLM was all about. How did Source of Light begin? Why did we exist? What had those who began the mission wanted to accomplish? What was our vision then – and what was our vision now?

He took us through an exercise of defining ourselves as a Mission, not as some entity we thought we might be, but who we really were. We resolved it in these words, *"Source of Light Ministries International reaches the people of the world through Christ centered and time tested materials that result in evangelism, discipleship and church planting."*

Knowing who we were, would guide us in knowing what we should do. I have never experienced a more profitable day. It provided for me the very ingredients I needed to begin to see where the Mission came from and where it needed to go.

I came to the Directorship the middle of February and the annual Board meeting was the first week in March. I was ready. I had drawn up a seven year projected plan of what I believed needed to happen and where I believed the Mission needed to go. I walked the Board through the plan and found that I had seemingly hit the heart of what each of them knew intuitively. They affirmed the entire plan and encouraged me to move forward to implement it.

One of the first challenges I faced was the question of our mission publication. For years – as long as I could remember – Source of Light had put out a publication called The REAPER. It was the primary organ of communication and kept the SLM constituency aware of what God was doing through the mission in many places.

During Tom's tenure its publication had been erratic, then eventually dropped altogether. Instead they experimented with a tabloid size sheet they first called The *GLEENER*, named after a publication that SLM had done in the past as a supplement to the REAPER, only now they did it in four colors and on glossy paper. It was attractive, but while the articles were interesting stories, they did little to promote the mission or convey what it was doing. It certainly didn't motivate toward service or funding.

Next they renamed the publication *REFLECTIONS* which seemed to me to be ominously descriptive – it is a long way from reaping to reflecting.

Now, as all of this was happening under Tom's tenure, I was not at the Mission Headquarters but out on the road. As such, I was becoming increasingly concerned. I was a Mission member who really tried to keep up with things, and I was confused. What about all the folks out there that weren't as close to the Mission as I was? If I sensed the Mission might be loosing its focus, what were they thinking?

What donors were thinking was not difficult to discern. When your giving constituency gets confused, and is no longer sure you know where you are going as a ministry, they have one predictable reaction – they stop giving, and SLM's income was reflecting that response. We desperately needed to communicate to our giving public that we knew who we were, where we were going, and how we planned to get there.

The next challenge I faced, was when I was informed that the print shop had dug its heels in and said they would not print another REAPER. I realized very quickly that this was not GATEA where the Director's word had been final. Apparently, at SLM, Directors simply made suggestions. I felt like I needed to make some very soon.

I called for a meeting of the entire publications and printing department. I announced that I wanted to determine what, if anything, we were going to do about an organizational publication. I reminded everyone that publications are far too time consuming and far too expensive to have one, just for the sake of having one. So I suggested we do a little brain storming.

What should a mission publication accomplish? We wrote down a whole host of things – Keep people informed, publish our needs as a mission, introduce our missionaries, tell about needs overseas, carry a recognizable identification that at one glance says, "this is Source of Light," and not the least, inspire readers to a greater love for Christ and a greater desire to do something meaningful.

After about a half hour or more I asked, "OK, we know what we want a publication to do, what form of publication can best accomplish everything we have listed here?" Someone said, "Well, the only one we've had that can do all that would be the REAPER." That was the answer I was hoping for – but it was no sooner said than immediately our printer said, "Well, I'm never going to print another two-color REAPER." He had obviously drawn a line in the sand and was daring me to cross it.

I responded, "OK, if you want me to drive a Cadillac, I'll drive a Cadillac. Give me a four-color REAPER." "It can't be done," he replied, "we don't have anyway to collate, fold and cut a REAPER off the sheet press." Gil spoke up, "Yes we do, we have . . ." and at that point the conversation got too technical for me to follow as they bantered about pieces of equipment and how this could happen. Finally, after some time they agreed – "OK, it can be done." Now it was decision time and the decision that came next was – "We will print a four-color REAPER."

Saying it is one thing – doing it is another. We got all the content together for that first full-color REAPER and sent it to press. Suddenly the printer was in my office and he was obviously angry. "You have no idea the difficulty you have given us," he stormed, "this thing is going to take longer to get out and we will be late . . ."

I tried to be understanding, but I asked, "Tell me, how is it that we can print upwards of eight million lesson booklets a year, that are all the same size and configuration as the REAPER, but we can't print the REAPER?" "That's easy," he said, "they are all two color and the REAPER is four-color." "It wasn't me who demanded a four-color REAPER," I reminded him. "That was your idea, so my friend, it's your problem." He said no more.

They got that REAPER out, and they were justly proud of it. After that we fell into a routine and have managed by the grace of God to be pretty much on schedule with our REAPER ever since.

The result was almost immediate. No sooner did the REAPER begin to show up in the mailboxes of our interested friends, than new gifts began to show up in our mailbox. We began to see a clear turn around in giving and we were all encouraged.

By the September meeting, the Board had come to another decision as well. I was informed that I would be stripped of my title, Interim Director, and be named General Director and Chief Executive Officer of SLM. It was a humbling moment but it was an indication that God was blessing and had better things in store for us and for the Mission.

The next challenge we faced was interdepartmental tension. I realize all organizations have that sort of thing but we seemed to be blessed with an extra abundance of it. The center of most of the problems seemed to be the Madison Discipleship School.

MDS was how we did ministry with the lessons we produced. We attracted correspondence students and serviced (graded) their lessons, thus discipling them. Around the world there were about 2,500 schools doing exactly what we were doing, and many of them doing it very effectively.

The Department was housed in a fairly sizable area toward the back of the building and was divided up into separate offices by a system of office dividers. Within each office it appeared there had grown a separate kingdom and as with all things, when there is no unity and central leadership, everything suffers, so the number of students was gradually decreasing. My predecessor, Tom Weber, had seriously considered dropping the school altogether.

My feeling was, that if this was the way SLM did ministry, then the MDS should be showing the way for all the other schools in our global outreach. I wasn't ready to give up on it, but I knew it desperately needed fixing. I asked the only man I knew who could give it any attention to do so, and he made some valiant efforts. In spite of all he tried to do, I kept getting reports of about two explosive situations a day. I knew we needed some drastic shifts in personnel, but I had no choice but to wait.

Our next challenge was the antiquated way we were producing our printing plates. We literally cut and pasted, then we took the finished product to the camera room and photographed it. Then we developed the film, checked it carefully, taped it up on a sheet and placed it on a metal plate under an arc lamp. Then we developed the plate and prepared it for printing.

Sure, that's the way printing had been done since the beginning of the offset method, but none of the commercial companies operated that way anymore. They produced everything in a graphics computer, sent it to a plate maker and Voila! – out came a plate ready for the press. Cost of computer to plate technology – about $100,000.

Our printing department said they needed it, so I told them, "if you need this, research it, tell me exactly what you need and what it will cost and I will make the need known. We will see what God will do." Well, they gave me what they thought we would need and I made the project known. That is when they came back and said, we need this to be in closer proximity to the print shop. What we need is a room right off the print shop, to house the entire graphics department and the plate maker.

There are some details I'm sure I don't remember, but this much I do remember clearly. Within two weeks of making our need known, the entire amount was in to purchase the equipment, and we were able to find some funds to expand the printing office and build that room.

I was just rejoicing in all that God had done, when the print shop called another meeting. This time they told me, "You know, none of this equipment is going to do us any good unless we have someone who has experience in both graphics and printing, and who knows how to transfer from the old technology to the new." Frankly I was a bit flabbergasted. "Guys," I said, "why didn't you tell me this before we moved ahead? Where do you think I am going to come up with the person you have described? You don't just pull someone like that out of the air you know."

Little did I realize that was exactly what the Lord intended to do. Our Board Chairman called me from his home in Greenville, SC. the next day without knowing anything of what had transpired at that meeting. "Bill," he said, "I have a fellow in my church that has just come home from the mission field. He has been in graphics and printing all his life, even while he was overseas, but his wife became ill and he had to return. Right now he is volunteering at BJU helping them convert to Computer-to-Plate technology. He is really looking for an open door of ministry – do you think you could use him?"

I couldn't pull him out of the air, but God could. When I met Mike, I asked him what would be reasonable as regards timing to start work at SLM. He responded that he was not employed, he was living in someone else's home, he had no obligations so, "why not Monday?"

Now that we were moving to the new technology we suddenly had a new problem. About a forth of the floor space of our one story office complex was taken up with large drafting tables used for layout, dark rooms, developing tanks, plate burners, and a huge file of negatives. Now, we suddenly were doing it all in less than 600 square feet. It was time to recover some space.

It had long bothered me that SLM had a large building easily capable of two floors and no second floor. The way that had come about was simple enough. The Mission had been donated the approximate twenty acres on which it rested and had built a double unit of offices forty feet by eighty feet. When combined as one building it created an eighty by eighty office – plenty of space to begin with. Then came expansion. A north wing was added with a flat built-up roof. Then a second addition on the east with another flat built-up roof.

That kind of roof construction is notorious for leaking and the valley between the two forty by eighties leaked as well. Furthermore Source of Light needed a larger Chapel and an all purpose meeting room. So, in the final days of Dr. Glenn Dix's term as Director, plans had been drawn to put one large building over everything. The new building would be large enough to give the mission a chapel and high enough to accommodate a second floor. The building was approved and built before Glenn stepped down and that was SLM's physical plant when I arrived.

The problem was, that those who built the building, always envisioned putting a second floor on it, however, when engineers examined the steel structure that made up the original building, they found it too light to sustain a second floor. That fact led my predecessor to conclude that the present building could not possibly serve SLM's needs and therefore he proposed to move the entire Mission to another location.

Research and planning for that move had consumed much of SLM's energies in the two years before I came as interim Director. When I arrived, the first thing I was told was that the present building was inefficient and impossible to correct and we needed to rebuild starting from scratch.

Now I had a problem with that, and it was this. I earnestly believed that the men who preceded me were praying men and gifted men. I could not see how they could have made such a colossal mistake as to build a building that had the space for everything we could need, but no way to make it happen. In fact, I spent time walking the roofs that were now covered, looking at the cavernous space, under that beautiful and modern superstructure, and asking God how this could have happened. At last, I had to find out if it really was an impossible dilemma, or just a perceived one.

I was introduced to Tom Gregory, Architect and Engineer and founder of TMC (The Master Architect), and asked him to look at what we had and give me his opinion. Tom came one afternoon and spent hours, climbing, crawling, measuring, recording, and photographing everything. At the next Board meeting Tom had a conclusion to present to us. He told us that, while reconstructive renovation would be difficult and expensive, there was no reason we could not accomplish it if we decided to do so, and that it would certainly be less expensive than comparable space if we were to start new.

The Board agreed and gave the go ahead to begin. I decided to try to finance a large portion of the project through Foundation grants and made application to about ten likely sources. While I am familiar enough with Foundational patterns to know that it is extremely unusual for a Foundation to accept a new client on the first appeal, I expected to do well with several who had known of Source of Light and contributed in the past.

My grant appeals went out the very month everything fell out from under the financial markets and were met with silence except for one Foundation who was concerned enough to actually send one of their people to see the work. In the end, I had asked for $300,000 from that Foundation and got $1,000, although considering the shape of things I was thankful for that.

In the meantime, we had proceeded to begin moving and dismantling the eighty by eighty center of the building. Church groups of volunteers carried the steel beams out and tore out the old wood floor. By the time we found out we were not going to get help from the Foundations, we were too far along to turn back. I cried out to God and He spoke to me from that remarkable story of Elijah and the widow of Zarephath found in 1 Kings, chapter seventeen.

The word of the Lord to the helpless widow was, *"the barrel of meal shall not waste nor the cruise of oil fail until the day that the Lord sends rain upon the earth."* That was enough. I told the staff and the Board I had a promise from God and as I write these words, we are about to complete the entire project and we have never had to wait for funds or stop the work. We have seldom had abundance, but always had enough for the next step.

In September of 2010 we dedicated the renovated first floor and by the end of 2012, we are ready to dedicate the entire second floor of nearly 12,000 additional square feet. Great is God's Faithfulness.

In the meantime there was still the challenge of providing leadership for MDS. I had heard that CEF in Warrenton, Missouri was using the same Mailbox Club lessons we used for children and, in fact, we were actually printing their lessons for them. We sold them at cost to TMC who then resold them to CEF. The correspondence ministry there was servicing nearly 15,000 students every week and was run by Bob Hearing and his wife Wanda.

I knew Bob. He had at one time been associated with Scripture Memory Mountain Mission and Camp Nathanael where we had begun our ministry. I decided that nothing succeeds like success and if I wanted to find out how to run a successful school I needed to learn from someone who was doing it – so I called Bob and asked if I could visit and pick his brain. He graciously consented and I asked Tom Gregory to go along to see how they housed their volunteers.

Tom and I arrived at Warrenton and could not have been received more graciously. Bob answered every question I asked and showed me their entire operation, including the way they prayed for every student and then prayed three times for every student's prayer requests. I was tremendously blessed by what I saw, and brought a pile of ideas home with me, but I knew the strength of any ministry is in leadership and we were lacking that.

About a month after I had been to Warrenton, someone told me that after decades of service with CEF, Bob had resigned over changes that were being forced on him by new management. I called him again, and this time I said, "Bob, we need to talk."

I wish I could say that I convinced Bob he should be with SLM, but that was not the case. We talked, but Bob continued to seek the Lord's will elsewhere, until God shut the doors and he concluded that SLM was where God wanted him.

When Bob arrived we were just about to begin that renovation project. One of the first things we did was to move MDS out of the old eighty by eighty section of the building and into temporary quarters in the Chapel. The maintenance men set up temporary dividers and installed the necessary computer and telephone connections, and Bob and his department had to begin under a handicap.

But leadership is everything, and instead of complaints the staff of MDS rallied to support the move and the ultimate promise of new offices with more than double the space they had before. Bob took firm but gentle control, set up some operational parameters and inspired the staff to believe God could expand their outreach and their effectiveness.

As I write, MDS is now in their new offices, they have the strongest cohesion of any department in the mission and they have gone from a low of 4,500 students to 36,000 and still growing. Every time the bell rings over the intercom, it signals a soul that has come to Christ through the lessons, and we average between 35 – 55 per month. Thank God we didn't scuttle the department.

God has been extremely faithful to all our departments. The Printing Department listed seven pieces of equipment they wanted to replace and they have just added six of them.

SLM Overseas

But that's on the home front, what about overseas? Source of Light had twenty eight foreign Discipleship Training Branches (DTBs – it now has thirty five). Many of them were truly amazing in what they had accomplished and continued to accomplish.

I soon learned that, like most of the rest of SLM's operation, it was all accomplished with very little guidance or input from head-quarters. That is wonderful, so long as everything is working well, but in some places, it was not.

One major trouble spot seemed to be in India, where Source of Light's India Branch was known as AJI (Amar Jyoti India). The name roughly translated means "Source of Light India" and, as I learned later, it was also the name of a major Indian company pro-ducing light fixtures. I had a contact with AJI's Director many years before when, on one occasion, he had visited Camp of the Nations and stayed there with us for a week. I had also met another part of the team at the 2000 International Conference in Madison. These men had been responsible for putting together a team of evangelists that had won literally thousands to Christ and planted over seven hundred churches throughout India.

While Tom was Director, he had asked Ruby and me to go with him to visit the India Branch to celebrate their twenty fifth Anniversary and we had done that, so we were not strangers to the AJI staff. We had even met many of the Indian Board members at a conference in Cuttack. AJI had six zones in which they were working which covered much of India.

Not long after I assumed the Directorship I began to get emails and even phone calls from some of the AJI evangelists. They complained about everything from lack of funds (a not uncommon complaint among folks in ministry) to being abused verbally by the AJI office. I tried to listen with a discerning ear to what they told me, but I have been in administration most of my life and I know all too well how those who work under our leadership can easily find fault with anyone who is in authority. The person who has to be liked by everyone had better stay far way from an administrative post. So I listened, I took notes, I prayed with some of them when they called, but I tended to find myself sympathetic to those who had to lead. But the emails and calls kept coming and they were consistent in their stories.

About that time I was introduced to Tim Dodson. Tim was pastor of Calvary Church in Menomonee, Wisconsin but was active in mission efforts in a variety of places and had financed the building of a church for one of our AJI men. This particular brother was in a tribal area where I had held meetings on the tail end of one of my trips. Tim knew about the discontent and was forthright and direct and wondered about a mission that would tolerate one of its Branches behaving like this. Frankly, I had to agree with him and promised to look into it more deeply.

The India situation reached a crisis when I was informed by an American Service Mission, that normally focused on building projects for nationals and other mission agencies, that they had taken over our North Zone operation in India. AJI's North Zone Director, had been badly affected by the relationship with the home office at Cuttack and was hardly receiving enough funds to live on, much less try to carry on the work. The American Mission had just come into a large sum of money and it's Director simply offered funds, equipment, a car and other benefits as enticements, if the entire North Zone would join their organization. So without ever resigning from AJI, they agreed, and I was notified they now belonged to the other Mission.

I met with the Director of that Mission here in the States, and it was obvious he felt he held all the cards. While being conciliatory on the surface, he dictated the terms of any further involvement we at SLM might have in the work in North India.

Ironically, the North Zone, as with our other Indian Zones, used our lessons as their chief means of contact and evangelism. They wanted to continue that – but the temptation of substantial funding and an apparently sympathetic ear to their woes, had put them in, not only an untenable, but an unethical position.

I listened for several hours to the Mission Director's explanations and agreed that AJI had not treated the North Zone people properly or fairly, but in the end I pointed out to this brother, that accepting a group of workers into his Mission, before they had resigned from their present Mission, was akin to marrying a woman before she was divorced. It was simply unethical, regardless of the reasons behind it. Therefore, I said, SLM could not have any part in working with them as long as the situation remained in its unresolved state.

I further told our North Zone Indian director that until and unless he tended his resignation from AJI, he was not in any position to join with another organization. Although I had taken a firm position on what our relationship would be, the discussion ended indecisively and I felt I had little leverage to change things until Tim Dotson again contacted me.

Tim and his church had invested in helping the North Zone leadership to build several church buildings. They had sent teams to minister to the North Zone people. When Tim heard what that American mission had done he immediately contacted our North Zone Director and informed him that he would work with him only if he belonged to SLM/AJI and not to another mission. He scolded him severely for yielding to the temptation, and I believe, helped him realize that he had gotten himself and the entire North Zone into an untenable position. Now, Tim was calling me to assure me of their support. It was the action that we needed to bring the North Zone back under SLM.

While getting the North Zone, back under our wing was paramount, we were agreed that something had to change in AJI. I contacted the AJI leadership and asked for a meeting to take place in February 2006, just one year after I had assumed Directorship of the Mission. I further asked that all of the Zonal Directors be present and let them know we would finance their travel to see that it happened. AJI agreed and I asked Pat Dye from our Field Department, who has some great management skills, to draw up a game plan for the meeting.

As we prepared for the meeting, I learned of another issue. Rather than focusing on the use of the lessons for discipleship, AJI actually used them primarily to initiate interest and draw a group of people to what was called a "Seekers Conference" where the gospel was clearly presented over a period of several days and then they were given an opportunity to receive Christ, and often even to be baptized. It was a great plan for evangelism and church planting, but little was done to translate and make available the lessons so desperately needed for discipleship and growth in grace. Some Zones were working with only one course translated and printed in that language.

I was also aware that all our printing for India, no matter what language we were printing, was done right in the Cuttack office. While the quality had sufficed for many years, Indian printing was improving and some of what we produced was not.

I was burdened about this state of affairs and had been praying about it when I had the opportunity to meet with a donor who had done so much for our East African Branch, particularly in financing the production of lessons. Shortly after we met, I approached him with an appeal for funds to print lessons in China. This would be a completely new venture for us and because of the need for secrecy, much of what we would be doing would not even be known to those who financed it. Nevertheless, the donor accepted the challenge and provided the funds for the printing of 2.5 million lessons for the underground church in China. Now we needed to do something similar in India and I decided I would approach him about making an investment in India as well.

We put together a package of four of our major courses, each one building upon the other. Then we asked our Indian evangelists what language groups they were working in for which they needed lessons. I was amazed and a little shocked, when I found out how little they had to work with. We chose nine major languages and determined on a printing of 5000 copies of each course in each of these languages.

Since each course has as many as twelve to eighteen lessons, the goal was formidable to say the least. Before we had finished putting it together, we had a project that would cost $120,000. I prayed and submitted my request. By God's grace our donor's Foundation responded and provided the money. Now, I had the job of seeing that we used it to the best advantage.

In January, I flew to India with a number of friends who were interested in seeing what we were doing. Ruby was to have gone with me to help manage the group, but at the last possible moment, the Visa Service reported that they had lost her passport, and with three days left before we were to leave, it was obvious she was not going.

We made our first visit to the North Zone, holding a conference in Delhi where I had the opportunity to discuss frankly with our Director there, the position he had placed himself and us in by his actions. I truly believe he was a victim of the ambitions of a very convincing American Mission leader and he truly wanted to work out the situation. At the same time, he told me more than I wanted to hear about what was going on at AJI.

The group and I made our way from Delhi to Hyderabad where we ministered with Christopher Boda, staying at the Banjara Tribal Ministries orphanage compound. Then we moved on to join Christudas Earla, who set up some very large meetings in Peddapalli. We spent three day ministering to workers and then Christudas asked me if I would stay over one more day to speak to some students. I imagined in my mind fifteen to twenty in the group but agreed to stay.

To our surprise, over three hundred came, many who were unsaved from both Muslim and Hindu backgrounds, and the meetings resulted in over seventy decisions for salvation. Finally, we spent the weekend with Dodla Wilson, who had planted the first AJI work in Hyderabad. After two weeks of ministry I returned with the team to Delhi, sent them on their way to America, and flew to Cuttack for my meeting with AJI. Pat had flown in from the States for the meeting as well.

I had learned that this was not the first time a SLM Director had tried to address problems in the AJI organization. Both of my predecessors had attempted, although on less serious matters, and had been rebuffed. AJI seemed to think that since they were the largest operation SLM had overseas, and one of the most fruitful, they were pretty free to do as they pleased. In their view, SLM's part was to pay the bill.

I presented our position and asked each of the Zonal Leaders to air their grievances. Considering the culture, I was amazed at how forthcoming they were. They were obviously stressed by AJI's handling of things and expressed themselves, knowing the danger of retaliation which they might face later.

I laid out four corrective steps I asked AJI to take to resolve the situation. Almost immediately several prominent members of the AJI Board confronted me that they were offended by our intervention in what they considered their domain. "We are autonomous," they informed me, "and you should not be interfering in our matters."

That was the same message they had given to my two predecessors. However, I had an answer I felt they needed to hear. "I respect your autonomy," I told them. "I cannot dictate to you about these things. But you must also respect my autonomy, and my right to determine who I can partner with. If you do not want to accept the steps I am urging, then I have no choice but to determine that we can no longer support you as our partners in India." Somehow I think they believed me, and from that point on in the meeting, we got cooperation.

The final matter I brought to them was the Literature Project we had put together. At long last they were going to get the lessons they needed to do the job. However, once again, I laid down certain guidelines. While the funds would have to flow through AJI office, whatever was designated for a particular Zone, must go in its entirety to that Zone. The Zonal Leader who was working in the languages to be translated, would arrange for and oversee the translations, and all printing would be done by commercial printers in the area where the translation was done and where the lessons would be used.

I had several reasons for insisting on those guidelines. First, I knew that if I allowed AJI to manage the translations and the production we would very soon get a bottle neck, and this project needed to keep moving. Secondly, unless I demanded we use outside printers, much more money would go into the AJI office and they would continue to retain their absolute control over everything done in the Zonal Areas. Furthermore, the quality of the printing would be poorer, the translators further removed from the language area where they were spoken, and so for a whole host of reasons I insisted they keep the guidelines I had laid down.

In the end, everyone agreed and each member of the AJI headquarters staff and Board signed an agreement with us. It looked like we were on the way to better relations, more decentralized leadership and a greatly expanded outreach. We all went home happy and rejoicing in what God had done.

God blesses when hearts are right and the year 2007 was one of the best and most fruitful in the history of the work in India. The Zonal Leaders were happy about getting the lessons printed and Pat had pulled them together for a planning session to help them set their own goals for the future.

Sometime late in the summer however, I learned that the former Board Chairman of AJI had resigned. The new chairman, a former military man, had decided that he would not follow our guidelines and that all printing would be done in Cuttack, thus keeping the funds in their hands. He further refused to send designated funds to the Zonal Leaders.

New reports also began to surface about mistreatment of personnel, mismanagement of funds, and the most disquieting of all, was a rumor that moral infidelity at the highest level had been covered up, but now had become public. I tried to get all the information I could. When I began to get letters from American donors telling me that AJI Leadership was trying to get them to send funds directly to them in India and not through SLM, I knew we had to take action.

I made phone calls to key contributors and others that were actively engaged in one way or another with the work in India and asked them to gather in Madison on December 20. Every person I called responded and came, forming an ad-hoc committee to consider the situation.

We fasted the entire day and spent the first hours in prayer. Then we examined the facts as we had been able to gather them. Some at the meeting had additional information of which I was unaware. For about seven hours we prayed and discussed what God would have us do. About four in the afternoon, I told those gathered that I wanted to go around the table and have each man tell me what he believed needed to be done.

As each one spoke there were many tears. Some at the table had discipled the AJI leadership in their early years. All had been in India and seen the work. Most were substantial supporters. As each one spoke they would conclude by saying, "As much as it hurts me

to say this, I think we have no alternative but to separate from AJI."
The decision was unanimous.

After the meeting, I called together our Field Council, and ask them to confirm the recommendation of the ad-hoc committee. They did and passed the recommendation to our Administrative Council. The Council agreed and confirmed the decision by a unanimous vote. All that remained was for me to take action.

On January 4, 2008, I notified AJI by letter of the action we were taking. I told them we would continue to receive and process donations for them for ninety days. After that we would have no further relationship to them as an organization.

My major concern was for the Zonal Leaders and workers. It was they who had first brought the problem of AJI to my attention. Now, if we simply pulled out, we were forsaking them and leaving them in an even worse condition than before. I had no desire to influence them to leave AJI, but I strongly suspected that many of them wanted to leave and had no place to go.

I made a call to Christudas Earla, who had been my student in Bharat Bible College. Christudas had at one time wanted to join AJI, but the Director at that time would not have anyone he had not hand picked. So Christudas and I met on a rooftop one night and prayed for God's direction and he decided that God would have him form his own evangelistic organization in India which he named GAP (Gospel for All People). He had done so and had now achieved Government recognition. I told Christudas I wanted to see him but could not discuss over the phone what I wanted. On January 10th, I flew to India.

There I related to him what had happened. Then I asked the question, "If any of these good men want to leave AJI, could you take them under the GAP umbrella at least for the time being and could I send their funds to them through you?" Christudas arranged a meeting with his Board and I posed the same question to them. They agreed to cooperate.

Before I could even get out of India however several of our AJI men heard that I was there. I immediately began to get requests from the Zonal Leaders to meet with me. I told them I was in Hyderabad and if they wanted to meet with me I would be happy to meet them.

What had happened was obviously traumatic and they were quite upset. They did not want to stay with AJI but the only way we could help them would be if they would work as agents of GAP. They finally agreed, but I told them we would not accept any of them until they had personally resigned from AJI. I further told them I thought they should go to AJI and first try to work out the problems, resigning only as a last resort. They agreed.

On February 8th, we held a day of fasting and prayer for them. They went as one body to AJI Headquarters. Far from being willing to make any concessions, the AJI leadership harangued and threatened them, but in the end they all stood firm and handed in their resignations. Late that afternoon an email came from one of the Leaders. All it said was "Victory in Jesus – We all stood firm."

All but two of the men came with us, and since that time one of them has come. The work in India is free and strong and expanding like never before. We were able to translate and print one and a half million lessons in Indian languages and as I write, the distribution has been so great that we are once again in need of lessons. Thousands have come to Christ. Churches have been planted. To God be all the glory.

Administration is a challenging task. But God has promised wisdom and grace. I thank Him daily for the Victory there is in Jesus!

CHAPTER THIRTY NINE

Putting Faith into Practice in Ethiopia

In 2005, just after accepting the position of Director at SLM, I met Haileselassie Tefera. Haile ran the local Shell station just above Route 20, in Madison. My predecessor, Dr. Glenn Dix had met Haile and discovered that he was a born again Christian from Ethiopia. Haile and his wife Tsedale had been in America for seventeen years and were American citizens. They had three girls, Dee Dee, who was a teenager, Abigail (about ten) and Amen (about eight). The entire family were delightful and had a strong testimony for Jesus Christ.

When you walked into Haile's station you would find no lottery and a variety of Christian books and tracts displayed on the counters. Gospel music played from the radio and Haile was unashamedly a follower of Jesus Christ. Glenn invited Haile to visit Source of Light and see what we do, and he accepted. While at the Mission he was given a number of samples of our lessons.

A few days later Haile called Glenn, "Mr. Glenn, you know there is nothing like your lessons in Ethiopia. If you will open an office in Ethiopia," he continued, "I will pay the bill." SLM operated in many countries, but I don't think we had ever gotten an offer like that before.

Glenn took it seriously and talked to Jack Stiles, our East African Director. They decided to make a trip to Ethiopia, along with Haile and survey the possibilities. Before returning they had indeed opened an office, registered Source of Light Ethiopia, and hired a very capable secretary. Now they had to get Government permission for the lessons.

The process of getting permission dragged on and Glenn and Jack had to return, but Haile refused to come until permission was secured. However, Haile had forgotten how slowly things happen in Africa. Weeks went by and soon a month had passed and still no permission.

In the meantime, Tsedale was trying to run the gas station in Madison, along with a second station in Covington and keep her girls in school. It was a gargantuan undertaking.

Finally, Haile called for a meeting of pastors and interested parties, and about 200 people gathered. They decided to hold an all-night prayer meeting about the matter. The next day, Haile walked into the Government office again and demanded an answer. He was told, "Look, we haven't even looked at your material yet – but we will do so today. You come tomorrow and we will give you an answer."

The next day Haile returned. They greeted him with, "Mr. Tefera, you are correct – these are wonderful lessons. We will give you the permit. And Mr. Tefera, would your organization consider building a school. If you will, the Government will give you the land." Haile called me greatly excited but I had to remind him that building a school is beyond the scope of Source of Light's mandate or capabilities. Nevertheless, he insisted, "My home church has a school and would love to do this." We agreed to consider it, if a partnership could be arranged and Haile returned.

After returning, we met with the pastors and people at Crosspoint Baptist Church in Oxford (not far from Covington), and found that they were indeed keen about the idea of building a school in Ethiopia. We held several meetings and formed a preliminary partnership.

Now it was my turn to go to Ethiopia. The Government had three parcels of land they wanted us to look at and we could choose which would best suit our purposes. This assignment was right up my alley. I had spent my life, it seemed, developing property.

Ruby traveled with me to Ethiopia. We were just about to go through the line at Customs, when I saw an officer waving us to the front and around the line. We were ushered through the door to meet Ambassador Kassa Hiywat, who whisked us away in his car to the Gihon Hotel in Addis Ababa, just behind the former palace of Emperor Haile Selassie. I recognized the name as coming from the Scripture. God had said, *The name of the second river is Gihon: the same is it that compasseth the whole land of Ethiopia* (Genesis 2:13). The river is gone, but the name survives.

We had a number of surprises awaiting us. First we had several students who had somehow learned about Source of Light lessons and had been discipled by correspondence through our people in Madison. Sylvia Pollard, who had served in East Africa with AIM for many years but now works in MDS, had been their Discipler. She gave me their contact information before I left and I wrote to them letting them know I would be in Addis and inviting them to come and meet with me. Both of them did. One had been a former Muslin and the other a former Orthodox. Both were now rejoicing in the freedom and forgiveness that is in Christ.

The second surprise was when the Chief Minister, who serves just under the President, called me from the hotel lobby and asked me to meet him for tea. At tea, he invited me to come to his office which, as it turned out, overlooked all of the city of Addis.

While there he told me some of the things he hoped we as a ministry could accomplish, and I answered him, "Mr. Tedessa, we would love to do many things for Ethiopia. Americans are very generous people and they will give. But we can't afford to pay twice for everything we bring here and you will kill us with tariff."

He looked at me for a few moments and responded, "I will sign a document that will free you from any tariff on anything you bring in for this project." It was that action that allowed us to bring containers with everything from building materials to a dump truck and a large back hoe.

Finally, we went to see the various locations proposed by the government. The third site was located on a plain in the city (small village) of Dukem. It was about ten acres in size, relatively flat, and had the beginnings of a foundation. I asked about that, but was told that the former people had failed to keep their commitments and had failed to pay taxes, so the land had been repossessed by the government. Choosing this site was a no-brainer and we began making plans to develop it immediately.

Just before I left I had the opportunity to see the effect our lessons were having on the young people. Haile had convinced Compassion International to use our lessons among the 54,000 young people they were trying to help in make-shift schools. I visited a number of them.

I will never forget talking to a group of teenage girls who were taking the course, *Understanding True Love*. I asked one of the girls what she had learned. Immediately she responded, "I learned that God's love is Agape love. It is a pure love and that is the kind of love I want." Wow! We flew home satisfied that God wanted to do great things in the country of Ethiopia – but no one ever said it would be easy.

Hardly had I gotten settled back in my office when I received a phone call from the Director of a religious organization based in Washington, D. C. informing me that the property we had just accepted from the Government belonged to them, and if I were a good Christian, I would just give it back. I quickly assured him that I had not known that any other church related group had been involved, but since it was the Government's action and not ours that disenfranchised them, it seemed to me that it would need to be the Government that made the final decision. "If you go to the Government and ask them to review this, and they decide in your favor, I will quietly back out of this without any objection. But, I am not going to the Government and tell them they made a mistake. That is for you to do," I replied.

Well, that answer did not set well and our opponents obviously thought that I was an easier target than the Government, so they began to pressure me. For the next three months I got anywhere from one to three threatening emails every day and a telephone call every few days. I stuck by my position, even when we had paid a ninety-nine year lease agreement on the property for a sum of $30,000. "Take it to the Government who made the decision, and if they find in your favor, I will graciously back out," I continued to say.

Finally they told me they were going to take the matter to court in Ethiopia and that two U.S. Senators had written on their behalf. They also informed me that they had four hundred thousand dollars and were ready to show the Ethiopian Government they were now prepared to finish their original project. They hired a top Ethiopian Attorney and the trial date was set.

We, on the other hand, did not hire an attorney. We did not have any money in hand, and we certainly did not have any Senators working for us. We simply sent Haile to represent us before the court and tell our story. And we prayed earnestly – not that we would win, but that the will of God would be done.

In the end, ironically, we won. I later learned that one of the things that sunk their cause was the involvement of the two Senators. Foreign Governments do not like the interference of powerful Americans in their internal affairs. If for no other reason than to demonstrate that, they ruled on our behalf.

But it still wasn't over. Now my adversary called me and informed me that although we had won the court case, he would still ruin us. He informed me that he had connections within all of the major American news media networks and that he would tell them that, "People will die in Ethiopia, because Source of Light took our land when we would have built a clinic there."

I called our staff together and told them what he was threatening. We wrote up a press release and I appointed a former newspaper reporter that was on our staff at the time, to be the only one who would deal with the press should they come. They never did, and after that final explosion the outside adversaries seemed to fade away.

But that was not to be the end of the crisis. In the ensuing months enthusiasm for what we were doing had grown and had attracted a major donor. He was ready to commit a very large sum of money toward the project when suddenly the report of extreme inflation across the globe, and specifically in Ethiopia, concerned him, and I was told that he was about to back out.

I was further told that I should get out now and cut my losses. I was even given the Biblical admonition to count the cost from our Lord's words in Luke 14:28 – 30, and that admonition got my attention.

So I decided to dig into that passage and see if I could discern exactly what our Lord was saying, and if I sensed the message was to get out, I would do that, in spite of all the battles we had already gone through. I took what I called, a hard look at an impossible situation.

I realized that if our major players stepped out of the game and I kept SLM in, I would be making my Mission responsible for a $130,000 project for which we had no money at all. After a long night of prayer and agonizing over the Scripture, I wrote the following to the principle players in this endeavor:

I received J.S.'s letter about the inflation that is sweeping the world. Our Ethiopian project is in jeopardy. What we estimated to cost $130,000 just a month back could now cost over $200,000 and perhaps even more. The suggestion was made that we back out and simply admit that the challenge is too big for us. I confess that would seem to be the easy and expedient action. But there is something here I fear more than failure.

Years ago, Ruby and I did a daily broadcast. Her program was on Saturdays and it was a children's story. At Christmas we did a dramatized version of a story called, Christmas on the Frontier, the true story of a young pastor's wife and her family facing a very bleak Christmas. It has always been a story I am reminded of in the darker moments of life, especially because it was not just a story – it was a real experience of real people. It went like this . . .

The winter was severe, the cabin could not be heated well, the food was meager, their clothing was worn and Christmas was upon them.

The three children all said their prayers and persisted in praying as they went to bed for impossible things like a doll baby, and a pair of skates for each of the boys. The young pastor was called out in the snowy night to visit a parishioner and his wife, full of despair, sat down and gave way to bitter tears. When her husband finally returned he was as low in spirits as his wife and they both sat and wept over their situation.

Then suddenly there was a knock at the door and a deacon appeared with a package that had come by post – it was his last to be delivered that day. After thanking him, the two opened the box, sent from a church back home, and found a treasure of warm blankets, clothing, and the exact toys the children had been praying for.

Each of the parents had the same reaction. They knew that in their despair and unbelief they had failed God. His faithfulness and love came as a solemn rebuke to them both. They felt completely unworthy of what God had so graciously provided.

After tears of repentance and confession they resolved that whatever they would face in the future, the thing most to be feared was not the specter of hunger, or privation, but the pain of failing God in the time of testing. That's the story.

It is that very thing I fear most about our present situation. If I walk away from this simply because my resources are infinitely out of proportion to the task before me, will God ever again trust me with an impossible task? When have we ever done anything that was not too great for our poor strength and paltry resources? I do not have $130,000 and I do not know where $130,000 can possibly come from, so I must reason that if God could have provided $130,000, He can just as easily provide $200,000 or more, if that is what is needed.

It has been suggested that we need to follow the advice of our Lord, found in Luke 14:28–32. It reads; **For which of you, intending to build a tower, sitteth not down first, and counteth the cost, whether he have sufficient to finish it? Lest haply, after he hath laid the foundation, and is not able to finish it, all that behold it begin to mock him, Saying, This man began to build, and was not able to finish. Or what king, going to make war against another king, sitteth not down first, and consulteth whether he be able with ten thousand to meet him that cometh against him with twenty thousand? Or else, while the other is yet a great way off, he sendeth an ambassage, and desireth conditions of peace.**

There is no question that our Lord is telling us plainly that before any enterprise, we should consider carefully the cost. And after we have taken a hard look at the greatness – no, rather the impossibility of the task – we need to draw the intended conclusion.

And that brings me to ask, what was the intended conclusion? What did our Lord mean to tell us by this text? If I am to act in conformity to the Scripture, and in harmony with my Lord's intension, then I must be sure that I understand the Scripture, and do not make the mistake of lifting it out of its context to make it teach something it was not meant to teach. So what do I honestly believe it teaches?

Did our Lord mean that I should avoid doing anything that might result in failure? That might incur the risk of others mocking me? That might bring scorn or ridicule?

Mocking is hard to take, but both Noah, and Nehemiah, faced it along the way in the formidable tasks they undertook. Eventually they finished, but the task was much harder than they expected.

Or, in the second instance, did our Lord mean that when faced with a foe that is obviously our superior, we should quit the fight and sue for terms of surrender? If so, it would seem strangely inconsistent with the total tenor of Scripture.

What would we do with such passages as Leviticus 26:7, 8 **And ye shall chase your enemies, and they shall fall before you by the sword. And five of you shall chase an hundred, and an hundred of you shall put ten thousand to flight: and your enemies shall fall before you.**

Or what are we to do with the words of Jonathan when facing an entire garrison of the enemy, **And Jonathan said to the young man that bare his armor, Come, and let us go over unto the garrison of these uncircumcised: it may be that the LORD will work for us: for there is no restraint to the LORD to save by many or by few** (1 Samuel 14:6).

You see, the problem with the interpretation that this passage is teaching us to stay away from impossible tasks is that it makes no sense in light of the closing summary statement found in verse 33, **So likewise, whosoever he be of you that forsaketh not all that he hath, he cannot be my disciple.**

That is the summary of a whole section in which Jesus is setting forth the conditions of discipleship. It seems clear to me that what Jesus is saying is this; count the cost of what I am asking of you, and if you haven't the stomach for rejection or ridicule, or if facing an enemy frightens you, and if the sight of blood makes you sick, don't apply.

But if you do apply, if you do want to be my disciple, then know that there will be towers too tall for you to build and armies too powerful for you to face, but I will go with you and make the difference, and however the world may view the outcome, in my sight you will be victorious.

True discipleship requires, not a tentative effort to serve God when conditions are favorable and challenges are possible. True discipleship means total commitment to absolute impossibilities, and if you aren't ready for that, you are not ready for discipleship.

I don't think I have misrepresented the message of this passage, so if I am to follow that advice as has been suggested, I must, **speak unto the children of Israel that they go forward,** *and then lead the way.*

I do not know how my answer affected the outcome, or even if it did – I only know that in a short time I received word that our donor was behind us, and we were both back on the same team, determined to see the task through to the end, whatever the end would be.

CHAPTER FORTY

Looking Over The Faithfulness Of God

I would like to recite, for the glory of God alone, what He has done for Source of Light over the past nearly eight years that I have been privileged to serve as Director. No one person is responsible for these things. God has brought together, often at very crucial moments, people and resources that have made each of these things possible.

While the resources were absolutely essential, it was the people God brought who made the difference. It is they who deserve all the human credit for the advances that have been made. As I recite what God has done I will refer to a number of them by name, but there are always the unnamed "others" who have been the ones who have truly done the work and will be wonderfully rewarded in eternity.

All the praise and the glory belong to God for all that has been accomplished. It has been my joy to be here and watch as He has moved SLM into a position where I believe it is ready to compete in a twenty-first century environment.

One of the first challenges we faced upon coming was the loss of our former publication, the REAPER. God moved our editorial staff along with our graphic and printing department to produce a full-color REAPER of quality both in design and content, which is now well received by over 34,000 readers, and appreciated around the world. It now can compare well with current publications from much larger Mission organizations. To God be the glory.

Part of the challenge of producing a REAPER or any other material was the fact that in 2005 we were using an antiquated system of layout tables, cameras, dark-rooms etc., to prepare our plates for printing. By the Grace of God and His provision, SLM moved in 2008 to computer-to-plate technology which allowed all production and revision to be done electronically and plates are produced ready for press by a single machine.

The result of what God did for us in changing our technology, led to turning one-third of our central office area into obsolescence. Rather than simply renovating that section we explored the feasibility of adding a second floor. Through the architectural assistance of several individuals we were guided to the conclusion that it would be practical to gut the entire center portion of our building, install the necessary structural steel to support a second floor and then totally renovate the first floor area in what became known as Phase One of the Expansion Project. The first phase was opened and dedicated in 2010.

In 2005 we had a three page presence on the web. Since that time, through the efforts of highly skilled helpers, SLM now has a very active web presence and continually changes to keep viewers coming back. We are experiencing a growing number of inquiries from all over the world about our lessons and other materials through our web-presence.

In 2005 I authorized the formation of the Alternative Media Department. God has enabled our men in that area, despite many human limitations, to make our courses available in Braille, in Audio, and on-line. The new Papyrus project promises to take the lessons to non-readers in ten areas of the world over the next year, and the on-line courses continue to be expanded and developed.

In 2005 MDS had been reduced to 4,500 active students and there was consideration that we should actually close the school. I never felt that was what God wanted. In fact, I have always felt that MDS should be our "Flagship" school, showing the way to others. By the goodness of God, Bob and Wanda Hearing provided the leadership that has completely transformed the school, and today it has a far more effective and in-depth ministry to over 36,000 individuals, and continues to grow by more that 100 new students every month.

Just before my arrival here David Newell, our Field Director, had requested to be seconded to Neighborhood Gospel Ministries. That left us without anyone to lead this crucial part of the work. Ben Watson stepped in and led us through the crisis until Greg Miller was sent by God to assume that task.

I can't say enough about the way our present Field Department has strengthened our work throughout the world. It has drastically improved both the regularity and accuracy of reports from the Fields, provided training and training materials for the national co-workers in our present Fields and expanded our outreach into many strategic areas in both Asia and Africa. Again I can only say, to God be the glory – Great things He hath done.

Our Printing Department is the heart of our operation and we have prayed long and hard to have leadership and organization there. The men and women in our present team have transformed the shop into a much more efficient operation and have further re-organized the entire shipping department so that materials can be much more easily found and accurately inventoried. In addition, in the last two years, we have added six new pieces of major equipment to the shop greatly empowering us to produce a better product in less time. The greatest need in the shop now is additional personnel.

When I came I went over with the Board a map of our present property and indicated my desire to upgrade the present housing and acquire additional housing as God provided. God has allowed that to take place and I now look back on the fact that we have added several new houses and there have been major improvements made on all existing units.

In addition we have, just recently, acquired the final block of property (about 1.5 acres) that has closed our north-west corner of this main property along with the house. Obviously this is an on-going project, but while we are not where I would like us to be, we are not where we once were.

When the Board asked me to take on Administration, I was working in the Advanced Studies Department, specifically attempting to complete the curriculum for WWBI, our three-year Bible Institute program. When I accepted the responsibility of Director, I feared that I would not be able to accomplish that goal. Because God sent the key people at the right time, and gave me a wife that could pick up many of my duties, the entire curriculum is complete and produced. I was able to update our course on Religions and Cults and in addition write five of the needed additional courses. There is much on-going attention needed in this project and as God allows, I hope to devote myself to that in coming days.

Phase Two of the expansion program is now complete and we have moved into a second floor area of nearly 12,000 square feet, providing room for expansion for the foreseeable future. God has provided miraculously. The *"Barrel of meal has not wasted nor the cruise of oil failed."* I am indebted to Phil Winder who led the project and to the hundreds of volunteers who made it a reality, and to God, who provided the funding though His people, so that everything we have, is completely paid for.

Finally, one of the most difficult and perplexing problems we faced seven years ago was the lack of integration within our accounting system. Our primary departments were each using different accounting software to keep records leading to the necessity of transferring data manually with the attendant tendency to error.

When we moved to integrate everything into the Peachtree software it became evident that the problems were far deeper than we had realized. God brought Diane Bowers who helped analyze our situation and develop a step by step procedure to correct it. I asked Ruby, to oversee those changes and she did a most effective job, bringing us to a basically clean position in all our records.

Now God has brought Jessica Bush to us. Jessica is a trained accountant and is effectively bringing the entire process to a new level. I want to say to the glory of God alone, that SLM is in a stronger position accounting wise than we have ever been during my time here and I suspect long before.

There are several other things which God has blessed that have helped to strengthen the work. In our first year the Lord led me to establish *Paper Partners*. To date that program has brought in over $300,000 to help finance our printing operation.

In addition, I coined the phrase, *Providing the Tools to Finish the Task.* God has been pleased to use this motto in a most unprecedented way to define us and to inspire our people both here and abroad. I thank Him for the way He has used both of the above initiatives.

As I looked forward to my final year as Director, I realized that SLM would celebrate its 60th Anniversary as a Mission at that time. I wanted it to be a memorable occasion so I planned with our Departmental Directors what would become the Vision 2012 Conference.

The Conference actually took place September 8 – 16, but I believe its impact will reach far into the future. As I took one of our National Directors to the airport, he told me, "The man you are sending back is not the man that came here a week ago. I am a completely changed man. God has done something in me that I have never known before. I have a renewed vision and I can never be the same." *To God be the glory!*

Forty four delegates from twenty one countries joined with our International Headquarters staff and a host of guests, observers, and presenters to engage in one of the most intense and productive weeks of training, sharing, and planning we have ever experienced. The Field Department staff under the direction of Greg Miller took the lead in scheduling each morning and afternoon event.

During the afternoons, we received Field reports from our National Directors and learned what God was doing through the SLM ministry around the world. Among the exciting reports of many thousands coming to Christ, there were the disturbing images of intense persecution that is rising around the world.

Each evening, God provided for us some of the most powerful and life-changing messages we ever heard. Several of them seemed to focus on challenges I am sure the speakers did not even know we were wrestling with, but were led to address. As someone said, "God showed up and showed us His glory." Hearts were touched and lives were changed.

On Thursday and Friday the governing Board of SLM met and made history. A year ago I reminded the Board that I had passed the age limit to be in the Director's chair. I asked them to have someone in place by the end of 2012. God took over and began a series of events that only He could have orchestrated. As things began to unfold we realized that God had ordained what was happening and had begun the process years before.

The man we approached dedicated his life to full-time service for Christ at *Camp of the Nations* in 1988. He served for a year on our camp staff in our outreach team and as head counselor before going to Bible College. After college and seminary he worked in church planting until joining ABWE and serving as a missionary in both Hungary and the Czech Republic. He was then advanced to an administrative position at their International Headquarters.

But as if all that were not enough, Ron Barnes is a grandson of our former SLM Director, Dr. Glenn Dix and grew up right here at the Mission. SLM is in his DNA and I am delighted that God brought him to succeed me. Ron became the new General Director on January 1, 2013.

Ruby and I are continuing here at SLM directing the Advanced Studies Program. There are now Bible Schools in many countries and we hope to provide the help and assistance they deserve. Prayer and dependence upon God are still the keys to spiritual success. It is in these convictions that we move ahead to experience everything God has for us in the future. As Paul expressed it, *I press toward the mark for the prize of the high calling of God in Christ Jesus.* Ruby and I have only one thing to say, in all He has done, throughout these many years, we are still, and will forever be, *Amazed by Grace.*

Source of Light Ministries Int.
Headquarters
Madison, GA
USA

Source of Light Ministries International

Dr. Bernie Didden, Dr. Earl Johnson, Bob Bracilano,
and Dr. Bill
in the air for WWBI

60th Anniversary Award to Hap Struthers

Board Member, Dr. George Palmer

Director Emeritus, Dr. Glenn Dix

Ruby with Advanced Studies Presentation

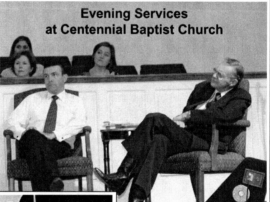

Evening Services
at Centennial Baptist Church

Ron & Brenda Barnes
New Leadership for SLM

APPENDIX

The Shade Family Today

As we close we thought perhaps our readers would like to know where the Shade family is today.

Phillip is in Souderton, Pennsylvania, where he serves as a Choir director and Organist in the Anglican renewal movement (CANA). He is also a representative for Home Technologies Inc., a company that provides emergency alert devices and services to the elderly and home bound. Phillip and his wife Heather have three children, Douglas, who operates his own lawn service business, shown with his wife and first daughter, and the twins, Matthew (right front), who has his degree in Law Enforcement and works with local police and Gregory (left front), who is a Chef in NYC.

Stephen and his wife Lani live in Philadelphia, PA, where they operate the Charis House for International Students, a ministry that seeks to introduce Internationals to a personal relationship with Jesus Christ. Steve also works as dispatcher and office manager for GE Betz. They have two children. Steve also has two grown sons from a former marriage, David and his wife Leslie, and Jonathan.

Rachel and husband Dan are missionaries with TEAM Mission in Vienna, Austria where they have served for over twenty years. In addition to founding a large and thriving Baptist Church, Rachel has helped found an organization called "Heart Works," that ministers to the thousands of women caught in the sex trade who work throughout the city. Rachel and Dan have three children, Charissa and her husband in Columbia, S.C., (they have two children),

Richard and his wife (they have one son), and Michael is a student at Vanderbilt University studying music.

Beth and her husband Dale live in Spartansburg, PA where Dale runs his own saw mill and works in the lumber industry. Beth has eight children, all of whom she home schools and, as can be noted in their picture, they all compete in running and working at Miracle Mountain Ranch, a nearby Christian Camp where Beth and Dale originally met.

Esther lives in Philadelphia and had one son, Jonathan Lee. Jonathan is married to Jamie and is a medical student at Morehouse School of Medicine in Atlanta, GA. They are expecting their first child.

Lo, Children are an heritage of the Lord and the fruit of the womb is His reward. As arrows are in the hand of a mightly man; so are children of the youth, Happy is the man that hath his quiver full of them (Psalms 127:3-5).

At this writing, Ruby and I have four children plus our foster daughter Esther, nineteen grandchildren and five great grandchildren with four on the way.

Always Amazed by Grace,
Dr. Bill Shade

PHIL'S FAMILY

FAMILY

STEVE'S FAMILY

RACHEL'S FAMILY

BETH'S FAMILY

Jonathan (Steve's Son)

Steve's son
David & Leslie

Ruby with Esther

Jonathan & wife Jamie
(Esther's Son)

About the Author

B orn in Altoona, Pennsylvania, Dr. Shade completed studies at Philadelphia Bible Institute and Wheaton College. He began serving in faith missionary work in 1956 with *Scripture Memory Mountain Mission* in Southeastern Kentucky, where he regularly ministered to 10,000 teenagers in seven counties through the high school ministry. During the same time, he became pastor of McRoberts Missionary Baptist Church where he served for eight years.

In 1964, Dr. Shade moved to York, Pennsylvania, where he founded and directed the *Grace and Truth Evangelistic Association* which was active in radio and television ministry, evangelistic campaigns, and conference / camp ministries. He was the founder and director of *Teen Encounter, Camp of the Nations* and *Wayside Maternity Home* for unwed mothers. He also directed the project of preparing curriculum for *World-Wide Bible Institutes*, which organizes Bible institutes in local churches and mission stations around the world.

Dr Shade has served for sixteen years with *Source of Light Ministries International*, eight years as General Director and eight years as Director of Advanced Studies Department which administers both the **WWBI** program and **WW-Lit**. Ruby has served along with her husband in every place and project. The Shades continue actively serving **with SLM** in Bible teaching, evangelism and conference ministry both in this country and abroad.